CONTEMPORARY ISSUES IN SOCIAL MEDIA MARKETING

Within a short period of time, social media has transformed communication, as well as the way consumers buy, live and utilize products and services. Understanding the perspectives of both consumers and marketers can help organizations to design, develop and implement better social media marketing strategies. However, academic research on social media marketing has not kept pace with the practical applications and this has led to a critical void in social media literature. This new text expertly bridges that void.

Contemporary Issues in Social Media Marketing provides the most cutting edge findings in social media marketing, through original writing from a range of the world's leading specialists in the area.

Topics include:

- the consumer journey in a social media world
- social media and customer relationship management (CRM)
- social media marketing goals and objectives
- social media and recruitment
- microblogging strategy,

and many more.

The book is ideal for students of social media marketing, social media marketing professionals, researchers and academics who are interested in knowing more about social media marketing. The book will also become a reference resource for those organizations that want to use social media marketing for their brands.

Bikramjit Rishi is Associate Professor of Marketing at the Institute of Management Technology, Ghaziabad, India.

Subir Bandyopadhyay is Professor of Marketing at the School of Business & Economics, Indiana University Northwest, USA.

CONTEMPORARY ISSUES IN SOCIAL MEDIA MARKETING

Edited by Bikramjit Rishi and Subir Bandyopadhyay

Routledge
Taylor & Francis Group

LONDON AND NEW YORK

First published 2018
by Routledge
2 Park Square, Milton Park, Abingdon, Oxon OX14 4RN

and by Routledge
711 Third Avenue, New York, NY 10017

Routledge is an imprint of the Taylor & Francis Group, an informa business

British Library Cataloguing in Publication Data
A catalogue record for this book is available from the British Library

Library of Congress Cataloging in Publication Data
Names: Rishi, Bikramjit, 1978- author. | Bandyopadhyay,
Subir, 1958- author.
Title: Contemporary issues in social media marketing/Bikramjit Rishi,
Subir Bandyopadhyay.
Description: 1 Edition. | New York: Routledge, 2017. |
Includes bibliographical references and index.
Identifiers: LCCN 2017001492 (print) | LCCN 2017015181 (ebook) | ISBN
9781315563312 (eBook) | ISBN 9781138679177 (hardback: alk. paper) |
ISBN 9781138679184 (pbk.: alk. paper)
Subjects: LCSH: Internet marketing. | Social media–Marketing. |
Social marketing. | Customer relations.
Classification: LCC HF5415.1265 (ebook) |
LCC HF5415.1265 .R57 2017 (print) | DDC 658.8/72–dc23
LC record available at https://lccn.loc.gov/2017001492

ISBN: 978-1-138-67917-7 (hbk)
ISBN: 978-1-138-67918-4 (pbk)
ISBN: 978-1-315-56331-2 (ebk)

Typeset in Times New Roman
by Deanta Global Publishing Services, Chennai, India

Printed and bound by CPI Group (UK) Ltd, Croydon, CR0 4YY

There is in every child at every stage a new miracle of vigorous unfolding, which constitutes a new hope and a new responsibility for all (Erik Erikson).

We hope this book will be the child of us all.

CONTENTS

List of figures   *x*
List of tables   *xii*
Acknowledgements   *xiv*
Preface   *xv*

1   Citizen relationship management by the Government of India
     through social media channels   1
     Rajan Gupta, Saibal Pal and Sunil K. Muttoo

2   Academia goes social media, MOOC, SPOC, SMOC and
     SSOC: The digital transformation of higher education
     institutions and universities   20
     Andreas Kaplan

3   Integrating community and relationship building into
     universities' social media marketing: Implications from a
     case study   31
     Jenny Hou

4   Social media marketing for B2B: From information to
     decision to retention   46
     Roisin Vize and Monique Sherrett

5   Social media stakeholder co-creation of celebrities
     as human brands   60
     Dave Centeno

6 Social recruitment: Investing in social currency 75
Arti Sharma and Arunava Ghosh

7 The struggle of the secrecy, safety and security of social
media and smartphones 90
Ronald M. Zochalski, Jr

8 Creating, contributing and consuming behaviour:
How rational and affective appeals in social media
facilitate engagement 102
Rebecca Dolan, Jodie Conduit and John Fahy

9 Social media engagement and return on engagement 117
Ritu Srivastava

10 The consumer engagement/return on social media
engagement interface: Development of a conceptual model 132
Birgit A. A. Solem and Linda D. Hellebeek

11 An unexpected journey: The influence of social media on
consumer decision-making 149
Wolgang Weitzl and Clemens Hutzinger

12 Network based choice formation: A review in the context of
online communities 162
Shameek Sinha and Sreyaa Guha

13 Creepy and intrusive: A consumer's perspective of online
personalized communications 172
Arlonda Stevens and Casey Newmeyer

14 Social media measurement and monitoring 184
Mudra Mukesh and Anand Rao

15 Attitudes towards brands and advertisements: Qualitative and
thematic analysis of social media data 206
Emmanuel Mogaji and Temitope Farinloye

16 Strategizing social media presence 217
Francesca Pucciarelli

17 Salient role and centrality of trust in social media marketing 227
Anil Bhat and Nirankush Datta

18 Trust relationships in social networks: A typology of
strategies for communication between companies and their
consumers   246
Zandra Balbinot and Sandrine Prom Tep

19 Like-influencer framework: A study of factors influencing
click of 'Like' option by users on Facebook   258
Rashmi Sharma

20 Mechanisms for incentivizing and encouraging online
social interactions – an experiment analysing the role of
recommendations and rewards on advertisement sharing
behaviour   271
William Feitosa

21 The rise of social media: Implications for emerging markets   282
Ogechi Adeola

22 Profiling youth on the basis of their motivations for social
media political participation: Implications for
political marketers   293
Devinder Pal Singh

23 Privacy and information trading on social media applications   308
Sandhya Narayanan and Richa Agrawal

Index   321

FIGURES

1.1   Framework of the study   5
1.2   Distribution of total tweets into various categories of social media messaging   9
1.3   Categorization of tweets according to (a) Ministries and (b) Ministers   10
1.4   (a) Indian national on foreign land confirming procedure from External Affairs Ministry (b) Sushma Swaraj responding to the Indian national and tagging appropriate person (c) Indian national enquiring about the expenses (d) Sushma Swaraj responding and clarifying thus making a point to maintain CRM through social media   11
1.5   (a) Tweet by a passenger complaining about service on the train (b) Response to the tweet by government official (c) Update on the problem faced by passenger (d) Acknowledgment by the passenger thus proving that social media is playing a positive role in CRM   12
1.6   (a) Positive utilization of Twitter by Sushma Swaraj for rejecting inappropriate help (b) Positive intent shown by Sushma Swaraj for child rescue (c) Positive intent shown by Sushma Swaraj for girl's rescue   13
1.7   (a) Examples of a tweet by Suresh Prabhu that incurred a negative response (b) Negative response to Suresh Prabhu's tweet   14
1.8   Twitter and Facebook analysis of major Ministers in India   16
1.9   Framework to manage CRM through social media for various organizations and individuals   17

4.1   Social media marketing: strategy development, tactics and
      performance measurement   49
4.2   S.M.A.R.T framework   51
4.3   The buyer journey: from information, to decision, to retention   52
4.4   Social media metrics dashboard   56
5.1   Stakeholder-actor co-creation of human brand identity   66
6.1   Social media network trends in India   83
7.1   2015 Smartphone ownership by country   93
7.2   Social networking use by Age Group   94
7.3   How Social Media has either improved or lowered
      opinions of their colleagues by Age Group   96
7.4   Example of a fake gmail alert   98
7.5   Example of a fake American Express email alert   99
7.6   Leading social networks worldwide as of April 2016,
      ranked by number of active user (in millions)   100
9.1   The communication cycle   120
9.2   Response hierarchy models   121
9.3   Diffusion of innovations   122
9.4   The communications funnel adapted to social media   124
9.5   Customer decision stages and promotional tools   125
9.6   Social media metrics   126
10.1 Conceptual model   138
12.1 Types of network   166
13.1 Target knows when a woman is pregnant   173
13.2 Facebook is watching what you're watching   176
13.3 The Creepy Quadrant   177
14.1 The social measurement and monitoring process (SMM process)   187
14.2 Influence a brand can capitalize on   192
14.3 Example – developing social KPIs from metrics to tactics   195
14.4 Tweet sentiment visualization for key word 'PokémonGo'
      showing a high confidence/pleasant and alert/active tweet   203
14.5 Bar chart – number of fans/followers for different brands
      against competitor for a given period   203
16.1 Social media road map   219
17.1 Perspectives of study of trust   229
17.2 Network centrality   233
17.3 Network density (left: low density, right: high density)   234
17.4 Proposed model of trust in social media marketing   238
19.1 Like-influencer framework   266
20.1 Share intentions   277
20.2 Usefulness   277
21.1 Social network users   284
23.1 Information sharing continuum   313
23.2 Customer's mental model of data organisation   313

TABLES

1.1	Data points for the analysis of social media accounts	7
1.2	Basic statistics and numbers for the various social media accounts of various ministries and ministers	8
2.1	Social media as a means of overcoming higher education's three core challenges	24
3.1	Extant studies addressing social media in higher education institutions	33
3.2	Content themes on three social media platforms between 29 Feb and 3 Jun 2016	39
6.1	Differences between traditional recruitment methods and social recruitment methods	82
8.1	Facebook Insights metrics for creating, contributing and consuming	108
8.2	Rational vs. affective message appeals coded	108
8.3	Binary logistic regression results for social media content types and engagement behaviours	110
10.1	Expected effects of consumer engagement behaviours (CEBs) on ROSME	140
14.1	Social media audit template	188
14.2	Social media objectives and drivers	190
14.3	Organizing the performance metric, purpose and KPIs	193
14.4	Exercise template – defining a KPI using the following template, build a KPI to measure an objective	194
14.5	Various computations to determine fan/follower growth	196
14.6	Comparative analysis of fan growth for January	197
14.7	Fan growth rate	198

14.8	Share of conversations vs. competitors	199
14.9	Applause rate average	200
14.10	Social media return on investment (ROI)	201
14.11	Sales from social media leads	202
16.1	Social media DOs and DON'Ts	224
18.1	Typology of strategies for communication between companies and their consumers	252
20.1	Some consumer incentive practices to increase sharing propensity	273
20.2	Share intentions	278
20.3	Share intentions, part two	278
22.1	Factor analysis of social media motivations	298
22.2	Cluster analysis	300
22.3	Demographic characteristics	302
23.1	Constructs influencing the permeability of information exchange/trade boundary	314

ACKNOWLEDGEMENTS

We wish to thank many people who helped in preparing this book. First, we thank all the researchers who contributed chapters to this book. We would like to acknowledge the help we received from Routledge Publications at various stages of preparation of this manuscript. In particular, Amy Laurence, Nicola Cupit and Laura Hussey provided critical support as we developed the outline and unique position of the book. We are also grateful to the reviewers of this book for their many insights and helpful suggestions.

Many people encouraged us to write this book. The first author thanks Dr Atish Chattopadhyay, Director, Institute of Management Technology (IMT), Dr Ravikesh Srivastava, Dean Academics, IMT and Dr Somyajullu Garimella, Dean Executive Education and External Relations, IMT for their constant support and guidance. He also appreciates the encouragement, cooperation and support of his wife Amrita and daughter Sharanya for completing this project.

The second author thanks Chancellor William Lowe, Vice Chancellor Anna Rominger and Dean Cynthia Roberts at the Indiana University Northwest for their support and encouragement. He also deeply appreciates the encouragement he received from his wife, Soumita, his children Aishariya and Anusuya, and his brothers, Sumit and Sudip, throughout the process.

Bikramjit Rishi	Subir Bandyopadhyay
Associate Professor – Marketing	Professor of Marketing
Institute of Management Technology	Indiana University Northwest
Ghaziabad	Indiana
India	USA

PREFACE

We are delighted to announce the publication of the book, titled *Contemporary Issues in Social Media Marketing*. 'Social media' is a broad term used to describe websites that connect individuals based on one or more similarities or interests. In the few short years that social media has been in existence, it has revolutionized communication between individuals, between organizations, and between individuals and organizations. In a sense, it has empowered businesses – large as well as small – by providing them with a platform to be heard by the masses. It has also opened up new vistas of social networks that enable people to easily communicate with friends and family members. This book contains twenty-three chapters that offer a smorgasbord of research findings on social media marketing. These chapters encompass research undertaken in more than nine countries, thereby providing the reader with a global perspective on how social media marketing is practiced across the world.

While researching social media marketing, we found a number of books by practitioners. However, we did not find a single book that compiles the extant academic research on social media marketing. This academic research is disseminated through a number of academic journals in the marketing field such as *Journal of Marketing*, *Journal of Interactive Marketing* and *Journal of Digital and Social Media Marketing*. As a result, the extant knowledge on social media marketing is not available through one medium.

In light of this lack of any academic text books on social media marketing that disseminate the extant theories and empirical research findings, our book is expected to fill a critical void in the academic literature on social media marketing.

The chapters in this book cover the applications of social media in a myriad of domains. The book contains twenty-two chapters spread across thirteen research domains, including Government, Higher Education, Business, Branding, Recruitment, Technology, Customer Engagement, Privacy, Measurement &

Monitoring, Strategy, Consumer Trust and e-WOM. The book contains chapters contributed by researchers from more than nine countries. For this reason, the book does not have any country-specific or region-specific orientation, which reflects the universal nature of social media.

The first chapter by Gupta, Pal and Muttoo, titled **'Citizen relationship management by the Government of India through social media channels'**, outlines how Citizen Relationship Management (CRM), a concept derived from the more commonly known Customer Relationship Management, can enable a government to create awareness among citizens about the myriad of services provided by the public sector. The system also helps in attracting and recording responses from the citizens, thereby enabling government employees in responding to citizens' concerns via social media.

The next two chapters are related to higher education. In the first of these chapters, titled **'Academia goes social media, MOOC, SPOC, SMOC and SSOC: the digital transformation of higher education institutions and universities'**, Andreas Kaplan describes the critical challenges faced by higher education today, and outlines how social media can address these challenges. In the second chapter, titled **'Integrating community and relationship building into universities' social media marketing: Implications from a case study'**, Jenny Hou conducts in-depth interviews and content analysis of major social media platforms and demonstrates how social media can be leveraged to augment universities' relationship marketing.

Social media have numerous applications in business, especially in the B2C environment. In the B2B environment, the application of social media is comparatively limited. This is because of the perception that social media sites cannot support B2B marketing goals and objectives. In the next chapter, titled **'Social media marketing for B2B: from information to decision to retention'**, Roisin Vize and Monique Sherret propose a conceptual model of how social media can be effectively implemented in a B2B context.

The utility of social media marketing in branding is well-known. What is less well-known is how it can influence celebrity or human branding. In his chapter titled **'Social media stakeholder co-creation of celebrities as human brands'**, Dave Centeno develops a conceptual model to identify stakeholders in co-creating human brand identity.

In recent years, savvy recruiters have frequently used social and professional networks to recruit suitable candidates. In their chapter titled **'Social recruitment: investing in social currency'**, authors Arti Sharma and Arunava Ghosh survey the extant theories of social recruitment, and outline the advantages and challenges of social recruitment.

Technology, especially related to cyber-security, is of critical importance to the future growth of social media. If proper data security cannot be ensured, people will be very apprehensive of using social media. Ron Zochalski addresses this issue in his chapter titled **'The struggle of the secrecy, safety and security of social media and smartphones'**. He clearly explains how social media data is encrypted and how it is used.

Perhaps the most potent application of social media is in customer engagement. We have included five chapters on this broad topic. The first two chapters in this genre focus on the return on engagement. In their chapter titled **'Creating, contributing and consuming behaviour: how rational and affective appeals in social media facilitate engagement'**, Rebecca Dolan, Judie Conduit and John Fahy demonstrate how to measure the level of engagement due to rational and affective appeals. The second chapter on ROE is contributed by Ritu Srivastava, based on her study in India. She discusses different models of ROE and outlines different metrics to measure each type of ROE.

The next chapter on customer engagement, titled **'The consumer engagement/return on social media engagement interface: development of a conceptual model'**, is contributed by Linda Hollebeek and Birgit Solem. They identify the antecedents and consequences of customer engagement and develop a conceptual model that delineates cognitive, emotional and behavioural consumer engagement. The fourth chapter on customer engagement highlights the new normal in consumer decision-making in the social media environment. Authors Wofgang Weitzl and Clemens Hutzinger argue in their chapter, titled **'An unexpected journey: the influence of social media on consumer decision-making'**, that traditional decision-making models, which are mostly sequential in nature, should give way to more circular engagement models.

The last chapter on customer engagement, contributed by Shameek Sinha and Sreyaa Guha, proposes a utility model to explain how consumer choice is influenced by online communities. The authors distinguish between private utility and social utility. While private utility is mostly driven by an individual's personal preferences, social utility, on the other hand, is influenced by the social interactions that the individual engages in with other community members.

Privacy on social media has become a controversial issue in recent years. While social media users would like to safeguard their privacy as much as possible, companies collecting their data would like to learn more about the users to target them with marketing information. The chapter authored by Arlonda Stevens and Casey Newmeyer delves into this controversy. In this chapter, titled **'Creepy and intrusive: a consumer's perspective of online personalized communications'**, Stevens and Newmeyer outline the trade-off between control of data by the consumer and the transparency of the firm. They focus on the situation when consumer control of data and firm transparency are both low. Terming this the 'creepy quadrant', they suggest strategies to minimize the perceived creepiness.

From a firm's perspective, it is important to have the ability to measure and monitor the effectiveness of its social media strategy. The chapter titled **'Social media measurement and monitoring'** contributed by Mudra Mukesh and Anand Rao, demonstrates how to build, standardize and recalibrate a number of key performance indicators (KPIs).

The next chapter in the volume highlights the relationship between brands and consumers. Social media enable consumers to co-create values and meanings with brands. In their chapter titled **'Attitudes towards brands and advertisements:**

qualitative and thematic analysis of social media data', Emmanuel Mogaji and Temitope Farinloye demonstrate how to use qualitative methods to analyze user-generated data on consumer attitudes towards advertisements and brands.

For a successful social media presence, a firm must have a well-informed strategy. Without a comprehensive social media strategy, a company is unlikely to meet the objectives of its social media plan. In her chapter titled **'Strategizing social media presence'**, Francesca Pucciarelli proposes a five-step road map to develop a social media marketing strategy.

Trust plays a critical role in the success of social media as a marketing tool to influence both individual as well as organizational buyers. Hence, it is important to understand what factors influence consumer trust. It is also vital for businesses to a take a strategic approach in building trust with customers. The next two chapters shed light on this important concept. The first of these chapters, titled **'Salient role and centrality of trust in social media marketing'**, and authored by Anil Bhatt and Nirankush Datta, identifies a number of characteristics including store, personal, social media structure and social media design that have a significant influence on consumer trust.

The second chapter on trust, titled **'Trust relationships in social networks: a typology of strategies for communication between companies and their consumers'**, contributed by Zandra Balbinot and Sandrine Prom Tep, proposes a set of strategies of communication that are expected to build trust between a company and its consumers. They recommend that a bi-directional strategy based on information sharing between the company and consumers is better than a unidirectional strategy involving communication originating only from the company.

One of the major strengths of social media is its ability to spread electronic word-of-mouth (eWOM) communication. Considering the importance of this research stream, we have included three chapters on this topic. In the first chapter, titled **'Like-influencer framework: a study of factors influencing click of "Like" option by users on Facebook'**, Rashmi Sharma studies sentiment analysis. Specifically, she investigates the reasons behind clicking the 'Like' option on Facebook for a post related to a certain product or a service or a brand. In the next chapter titled, **'Mechanisms for incentivizing and encouraging online social interactions – an experiment analysing the role of recommendations and rewards on advertisement sharing behaviour'**, William Feitosa performs a controlled experiment to find out what type of stimulus elicits greater propensity among consumers to share information. For example, he reported that online ads that generate greater arousal and valence tend to make respondents share more information than those ads with less arousal or less valence.

The last chapter on eWOM is titled **'The rise of social media: implications for emerging markets'**. Here, Ogechi Adeola shares the experience of Nigerians in social media, in particular, in eWOM. He suggests that marketers in emerging markets such as Nigeria should not ignore the traditional media of communication with consumers. Marketers should not be swayed by social media to lose site of the important financial aspects of revenue and profit generation.

Chapter 22 on this area, contributed by Devinder Pal Singh, focusses on the influence of social media on youth to participate in the political process. The chapter titled, **'Profiling youth on the basis of their motivations for social media political participation: implications for political marketers'** identifies four types of youngsters: activist, hedonist, utilitarian and versatile. The author suggests that political marketers will be in a better position to motivate young people if they are able to fashion a marketing campaign targeted towards some of their specific characteristics.

The final chapter, **'Privacy and information trading on social media applications'**, by Sandhya Narayanan and Richa Agrawal explores social media apps and information sharing over such apps from the consumer's/user's perspective. The authors conclude that consumers may display an indifferent attitude towards data sharing as they see others around them sharing personal information on apps without much concern.

1

CITIZEN RELATIONSHIP MANAGEMENT BY THE GOVERNMENT OF INDIA THROUGH SOCIAL MEDIA CHANNELS

Rajan Gupta, Saibal Pal and Sunil K. Muttoo

Introduction

In today's world, the Internet, data and security have become important parts of people's lives. The Internet is a significant medium for individuals to communicate with each other, interact and even collaborate in certain instances. Recent development in the field of social media, such as the inception of multiple websites and platforms and the advent of blogs, is also a big change. This widespread connectivity of individuals to the Internet and their significant presence on social networking sites encourages governments to also adopt this medium as its connecting channel to citizens.

Government plays a crucial role in the lives of its citizens. The citizen is the customer of the government, i.e. the consumer of public goods and services. The main objective of government is to provide long-term benefits to citizens, increase their standard of living, and provide solutions to their problems. Citizens are, however, becoming dissatisfied with the usual physical process of getting information from government (through personal visits to office), since the available information is not transparent and many times, the information is not even accessible to the general public (Dudley *et al.* 2015). As a result, in recent years many governments have started using digital mediums especially the social media platforms to provide information to citizens on matters like taxes, schemes and services, public utility, vehicle registration, voting registration, legal assistance services and so on, thereby enhancing their capabilities with regard to Citizen Relationship Management (CRM). Governments are able to deliver services more efficiently with the advent of information and communication technology.

In the Indian government system, recent changes have been noticed in the field of the government's social media interaction, namely the introduction of Twitter accounts for many ministries and ministers. These accounts are highly active and help in solving the problems of Indian citizens, at home and abroad. Instant help is provided in medical cases and embassies are put to work in the case of international issues. These activities help the government in building a positive reputation amongst its citizens. In this way, the help provided also leads to a satisfied citizen base (i.e. customers of the government). This in turn is all part of the activity of citizen relationship management (Rajan 2016; Srivastava 2013). In the following sub-section, CRM will be discussed in detail followed by a discussion of the relevance of this study.

CRM and social media

The term 'citizen relationship management,' or CRM, refers to the use of various management practices, information and communication technology, and channels that enable the public sector to provide customer services to its citizens. CRM has been understood and implemented in various ways and generally applied by government to improve citizen orientation, customer services and public services, and to improve government-citizen relationships. Apart from these objectives of CRM, understanding the needs of the citizen and providing a corresponding solution is one of the main focus areas of CRM. Governments are increasing efforts at all levels for better citizen services as they respond quickly to citizen requests and inquiries to provide general information on processes and procedures to facilitate citizens to receive government services. Information and communication technology (e.g. web portals and social media) is helping government in understanding and meeting the needs of citizens in a cost-effective manner (Latha *et al.* 2013; Shaikh and Khan 2014).

The advancement of social media is redefining the process of citizen relationship management worldwide. Almost all the departments of the government sector have moved forward by introducing accounts on social media to interact with citizens and provide information and solutions to citizens' problems. This has been beneficial to government and citizens in different ways (Andrade *et al.* 2014; Schellong 2006). 'Social media' refers to the applications and websites that enable people worldwide to share content in an inexpensive way. They include social networking websites and applications like Facebook, Twitter, YouTube, Google Plus, Flicker, Pinterest and more. Social media gives users a platform to share their views on anything happening around the world. It offers a cost-effective and powerful medium to provide information to a large audience. By observing the current scenario, it can be said that social media play an important part in people's lives worldwide (Magro 2012).

Relevance of the study

In the recent past, social media have become powerful platforms which allows users to access information from anywhere through an Internet connection. The Indian government has moved forward with this changing environment and has developed its presence on social media. CRM enables governments to attract citizens and create awareness about various services provided by the public sector. Use of social media by government helps them to reach a global audience in an inexpensive way. For government representatives, this study will highlight the participation and engagement of the Government of India with citizens on online media, particularly on Facebook and Twitter. In addition, CRM over social media will provide better tools to improve the government-citizen relationship in this digital age (Sinderman 2011). The study will analyse information provided by the government and citizen responses to this that would be helpful to government employees in analysing their citizen services. The current chapter will help the Indian government to realize how quickly they respond to citizen problems on social media platforms. The study will contribute to improving citizen relationship management in India. The objectives of the study are as follows:

1. To study various CRM initiatives undertaken by the Government of India using social media
2. To study the impact of social media on the improvement of CRM for the Government of India
3. To identify and analyse the positive and negative cases of CRM on various social media platforms

Review of the literature

Citizen relationship management is an important activity for governments to initiate and maintain. The government has a duty to cater to its citizens to the best of its abilities. Particularly in the case of a country like India, citizens form a key component of the whole democratic structure and hence are vital for its functioning. If the citizens are not satisfied then they can prove harmful to the welfare of the country and can even rebel against the government.

India is a developing country and hence is on the verge of enormous growth in a number of fields. India has been slowly and steadily adapting to the digital environment that is increasingly prevalent in the world today and has been making great leaps towards a completely digitized system of government. Digital India is a campaign run by the Indian government to bring all of India onto a digital platform. This offers new opportunities as well as exposes the country to the related risks. Digital India is a topic that is of interest to people and hence they want to invest in it. Researchers are interested in knowing more about it and how it can impact governance as well as citizens' quality of life (Sharma *et al.* 2016; Thomas 2012).

Studies have been conducted nationally as well as internationally that confirm the importance of social media on citizen relationship management (Khasawneh *et al.* 2013; Bonsón *et al.* 2012). With the help of Facebook posts and other channels like Twitter and LinkedIn, analysis is conducted to learn about the importance of social media as a platform of interaction for government officials and departments. In some studies it has also been seen that the government is lacking in the area of social media interaction compared to its citizens (Bonsón *et al.* 2012). Studies also found that government portals do not perform as well when compared to average performance metrics (Shaikh and Khan 2014). There is a general need to harness the power of social media to improve interaction and management practices of the government to strengthen their relationship with the citizens.

Studies have also been conducted that show the support that social media can provide to the fulfilment of the objective of citizen relationship management. Social media has the capacity to provide marketing support to all kinds of organizations and firms, which is equally true of the government for their various policies and campaigns. Social media are an excellent platform for the government to market the policies that it introduces. The government can maintain its customer base and also expand it further with the help of social media (Falco 2011; Karakiza 2015; Khan *et al.* 2014).

Social media also make it easier for the government to develop new programmes and policies. With the help of social media channels, the government can get a general measure of the views that are held by the public relating to happenings in the economic and political spheres. The expectations and perceptions of the populace can be gauged and a real time analysis can be done of the gaps between the two. Moreover, before forming actual policies, citizens can be encouraged to engage in polls through which a proper two-way conversation or multi-level discussions can be instigated (Falco 2011; Karakiza 2015; Khan *et al.* 2014).

Another major benefit provided by social media is that of gaining access to feedback from 'clients'. The importance of feedback has been long recognized in a democratic structure like that of India. Feedback provides the government with the views of its citizens regarding the services that they provide and the policies that they formulate. This in turn helps when making alterations and improvements. Feedback is also optimized given the multiple channels that can be monitored simultaneously and the analytics that can be created for the collected data (Falco 2011; Karakiza 2015; Khan *et al.* 2014).

Moreover, citizens' demand for faster access to services provided by the government and social media is likewise a step towards improvement. Citizens now have access to online services that make it faster to get their work done. However, it is grievance redressal where social media come into play. Citizens can directly contact authorities or even ministers in order to discuss their problems and find a solution.

Time and again, social media have been researched for their effect on consumer behaviour (Fischer and Reuber 2011; Mukhaini *et al.* 2014; Ioanăs and Stoica 2014). Twitter in particular has a large impact on what consumers think when they buy a product or avail of a service, or even before they choose to do so (Chow 2013; Fischer and Reuber 2011). Social media is, hence, extremely useful for the government in order to build and maintain relationships with its customers, i.e. the citizens. The government on a social media platform is described in different ways by different people, namely: Do-it-yourself Government (Dunleavy and Margetts 2010), Government as a Platform (O'Reilly 2010), Social Government

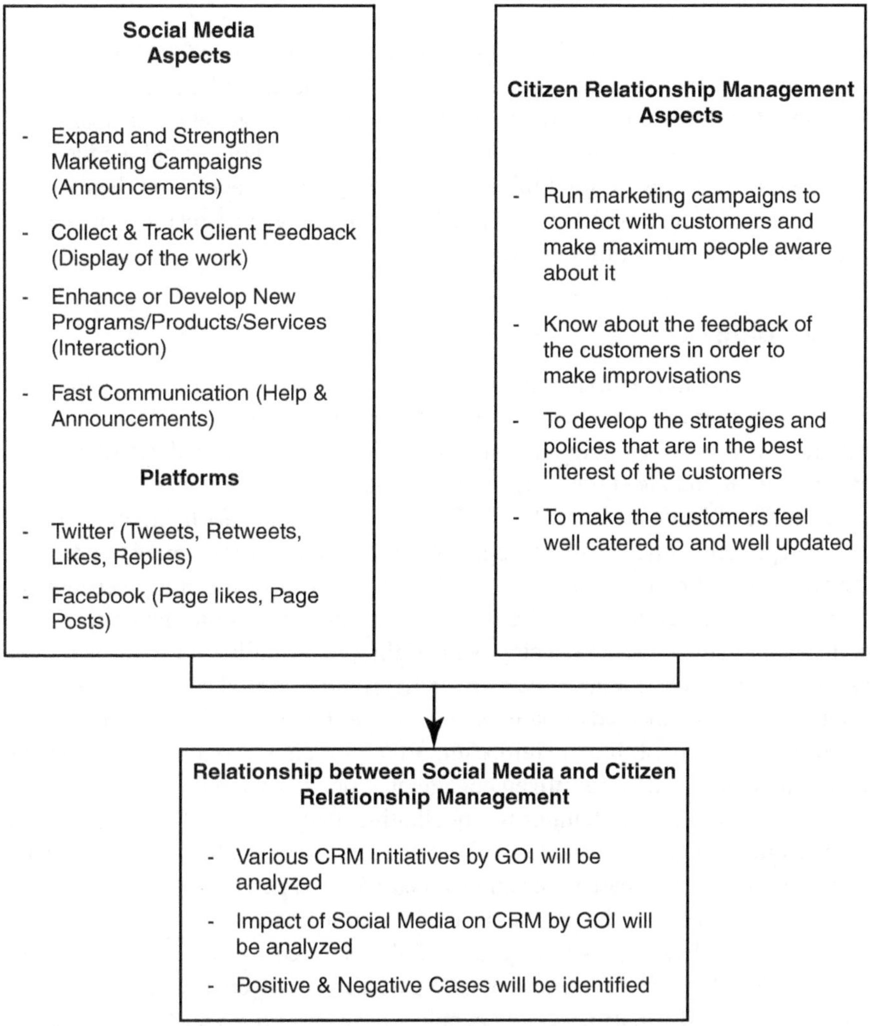

FIGURE 1.1 Framework of the study.

(Khan *et al.* 2012), We-Government (Linders 2012) and the like. There are certain researchers that have proposed social-media-based government models like the E-Government maturity models in theory (Khan 2013; Khan and Swar 2013; Lee and Kwak 2012; Mergel and Bretschneider 2013).

Social media have various risks, as identified by Khan *et al.* (2014), including being social risk, time, psychological risks and privacy concerns. Webber, Li, and Szymanski (2012, p. 3) have defined social media risk as "*the likelihood that a negative social media event will happen (multiplied by) the impact that negative event will have if it does happen*". Psychological risk is the risk associated with the selection or performance of the producer that can have a negative effect on the consumer's peace of mind or self-perception (Featherman and Pavlou, 2003,

p. 455). And, privacy concerns are related to the potential loss of control over personal information of people. Although benefits have also been identified, the risks make it mandatory to carefully assess the role that social media can actually play in helping the government with citizen relationship management. Particularly in a country like India, it is of utmost importance to know about social media usage in the public sector, the digital initiatives taken by governments and their impact on governance levels, whether it is positive or negative. Figure 1.1 provides the proposed framework for this study.

Methodology

The current research is exploratory in nature and has used primary data from social media sites to explore the role of CRM through social media. This study will include a qualitative content analysis and basic quantitative analysis of relevant information on the Facebook and Twitter accounts of various departments of the Government of India and their heads. Twitter was selected as the main source of data interpretation after posts had been observed on both social media platforms. The Government of India has been used as the subject of the study because the country is at the beginning of digital development. The central government and its increasing stress on the development of the digital Indian diaspora is a boon for the economy. The Indian citizens residing in India as well as those outside the country are now connected to each other as well as being updated about the activities of the government. It is therefore important for a huge country like India that studies are conducted on its citizen engagement practices and their actual effects.

In the process of performing the qualitative analysis, 1,100 tweets, with 50 tweets from each government department account, were read and analysed. They were then divided into categories and pie charts of the percentage of each type of tweet were created. For the content analysis portion of the study, the tweets were read through and examples were extracted that showed the speed of replies and the positive and negative instances of CRM. Screenshots were used to depict these examples. A list of departments and people whose Facebook and Twitter accounts were analysed is shown in Table 1.1.

Analysis

An analysis of the Twitter accounts and Facebook pages of Indian government ministries, and of the ministers heading them, was undertaken in order to learn about the social media activities of governments. The Facebook pages of these ministries and people were found to be less interactive than their Twitter counterparts. The posts on the Facebook pages were mostly for the purpose of imparting information and details about government activities. Twitter, on the other hand, saw interactions between these ministries, ministers and common people (IANS 2014). However, on both media it was seen that the number of people following the accounts was enormous and reached a significant figure in the hundreds of

TABLE 1.1 Data points for the analysis of social media accounts

Departments & Ministries	Ministry of Women and Child Development
	Ministry of Petroleum and Natural Gas
	Ministry of Food Processing Industries
	Ministry of Micro, Small and Medium Enterprises
	Ministry of Information and Broadcasting
	Ministry of Human Resource Development
	Ministry of Health and Family Welfare
	Ministry of Textiles
	Ministry of Home Affairs
	MyGovIndia
	NITI Ayog
	Ministry of Finance
	Ministry of External Affairs (Vikas Swarup)
	Ministry of Railways
Ministers	Arun Jaitley
	Rajyavardhan Rathore
	Jagat Prakash Nadda
	Dharmendra Pradhan
	Santosh Gangwar
	Rajnath Singh
	Sushma Swaraj
	Suresh Prabhu

thousands, as shown in Table 1.2. The data analysis was conducted as per the three objectives of the study and results are shown in the following sub-sections.

Analysis for objective 1

It has been seen for all the ministers and their ministries that their tweets reflect a variety of reasons for posting. These reasons were divided into five categories i.e. for the purpose of *Announcements, Interaction, Help, Work Display* and *Recognition*. **Announcement** tweets include new policies, schemes or centres that the government or the specific ministry announces. **Interaction** tweets includes all kind of interactions that the ministers or the individuals execute in order to connect with others. They do so not only with common people but also with their own colleagues and international counterparts. Interactions can range from offering condolences to conveying birthday greetings and festival wishes. **Help** tweets are the ones in which the ministers or the ministries help in addressing the problems of the common people. This is more prominently seen on the accounts of individual ministers or people. The fourth type of tweet, **Work Display**, assists the ministers and ministries in showing the work that has been done by them in their respective areas. **Recognition** tweets are the ones in which the ministers or the ministries recognize the potential of, for example, the participants in a competition or the

TABLE 1.2 Basic statistics and numbers for the various social media accounts of various ministries and ministers

S No	Ministry/Minister	Twitter Handle	Tweets	Followers	Likes	Joined when	FB Likes	Facebook Handle
1	Ministry of Women and Child Development	@MinistryWCD	2,075	33.6K	769	June 2014	215,274	@ministryWCD
2	Ministry of Petroleum and Natural Gas	@PetroleumMin	1,184	28.2K	3	June 2014	7,738	@PetroleumMinIndia
3	Ministry of Food Processing Industries	@MOFPI_GOI	536	23K	9	July 2014	18,423	@MOFPIIndia
4	Ministry of Micro, Small and Medium Enterprises	@minmsme	3,059	37.9K	449	June 2014	27,476	@minmsme
5	Ministry of Information and Broadcasting	@MIB_India	36.8K	614K	186	November 2012	1,223,928	@inbministry
6	Ministry of Human Resource Development	@HRDMinistry	1,515	444K	22	June 2014	83,574	@HRDMinistry
7	Ministry of Health and Family Welfare	@MoHFW_INDIA	6,622	247K	42	June 2014	1,320	
8	Ministry of Textiles	@TexMinIndia	1,320	73.1K	293	June 2014	13,901	@TexMinIndia
9	Ministry of Home Affairs	@HMOIndia	2,384	1.04M	190	June 2014	109,335	@HMOfficeIndia
10	MyGovIndia	@mygovindia	2,245	372K	67	July 2014	218,367	@MyGovIndia
11	NITI Ayog	@NITIAayog	2,086	806K	50	March 2013	1,427,928	@NITIAayog
12	Ministry of Finance	@FinMinIndia	3,724	220K	14	July 2014	992,179	@finmin.goi
13	Ministry of External Affairs	@MEAIndia	12.6K	840K	4	December 2011	1,309,457	@MEAINDIA
14	Ministry of Railways	@RailMinIndia	69.5K	1.16M	322	July 2014	1,004,751	
15	Arun Jaitley	@arunjaitley	1,363	4.7M	24	November 2013	2,585,465	@ArunJaitley
16	Rajyavardhan Rathore	@Ra_THORe	7,737	267K	78	July 2009	81,607	@Rathore
17	Jagat Prakash Nadda	@JPNadda	668	43.1K	59	January 2015	114,050	@JagatPrakashNadda
18	Dharmendra Pradhan	@dpradhanbjp	5,314	168K	640	September 2013	457,860	@DharmendraPradhanOdisha
19	Santosh Gangwar	@santoshgangwar	2,250	7,936	29	February 2010	25,853	@santosh.gangwar
20	Rajnath Singh	@rajnathsingh	2016	2.97M	53	April, 2013	4,677,422	@RajnathSinghBJP
21	Sushma Swaraj	@SushmaSwaraj	4,010	5.3M	4	November 2010	2,521,486	@SushmaSwarajBJP
22	Suresh Prabhu	@sureshpprabhu	14.2K	1.05M	18	May 2010	200,778	@Railministersureshprabhu

people who have put in effort and worked for the implementation of policies and schemes.

Figure 1.2 shows that out of a set of 1,100 tweets analysed from the social media account of ministers and ministries, 592 i.e. 53.82 per cent of the tweets, focused on interacting with the general public or their followers. The interactions included telling followers about the values that the account owners believed in, the achievements of the government in general, the meetings that are held for fruitful purposes, the interactions that ministers are having with people and their own counterparts in other nations. The tweets sharing information about such interactions are expected to inform the general public about the activities of the government and convince them of their good intentions.

The second type of tweet that is most commonly used is for showing the work of the ministers and the ministries. Social media are considered an appropriate platform for telling the general public about the work that has been done and the achievements that have been made. Moreover, social media are known to have a far greater reach than other types of information dispersing media. Another important motive for using social media, as has been recognized through the analysis, is to make announcements. The extensive reach of these media is the prime reason for these types of tweets.

The two types of accounts (i.e. ministries and ministers) showed different levels of the five types of tweets, as shown in Figure 1.3. Both types of accounts primarily used the platform for interaction and showing work. The difference as seen in the frequency of using the accounts for other purposes is that the ministries were interested in

Categorization of Social Media Messages

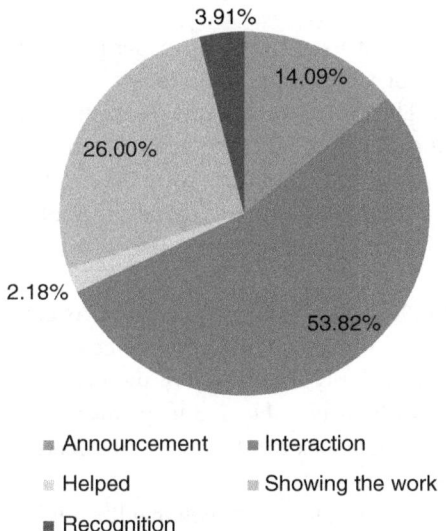

FIGURE 1.2 Distribution of total tweets into various categories of social media messaging.

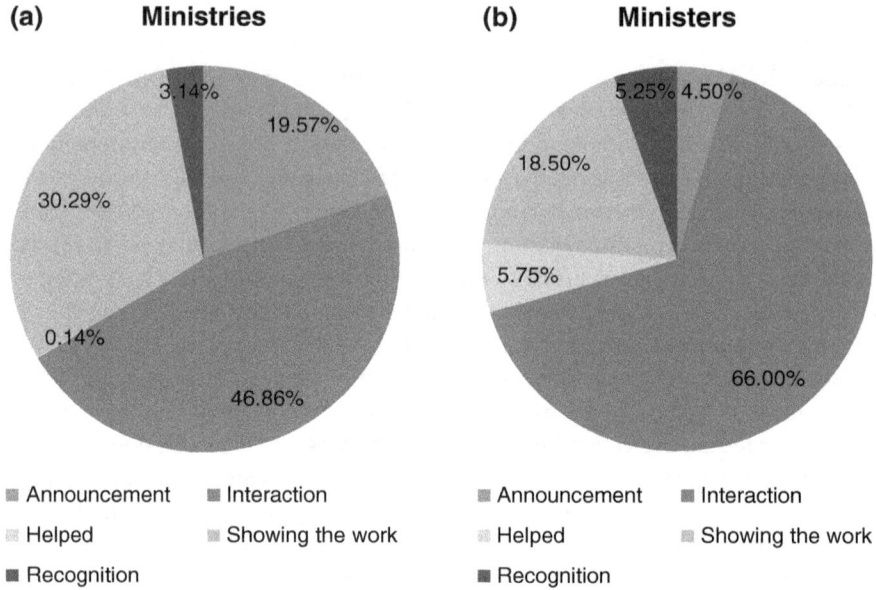

FIGURE 1.3 Categorization of tweets according to (a) Ministries and (b) Ministers.

making announcements through tweets, whereas heads of ministries weren't particularly interested in this. On the contrary, tweets reporting help provided by the account owners were more prominently seen in those owned by the heads of the ministries.

Analysis of objective 2

The grievance redressal systems for government usually run on paper-pen and manual registration. With the advancement of technology, the redressal system has also moved to the electronic platforms. This has made the process faster and more efficient. However, in the case of critical and urgent complaints, complainers cannot afford to wait long periods for their pleas to be heard. Moreover, in the case of complaints that are related to a particular duration of a journey, the solutions, even if provided, would not be useful for the complainer as his/her journey would be completed by then.

In such cases, social media has proved to be a very efficient platform. As can be seen in the screenshots of Twitter accounts in Figure 1.4, the important element of a social media CRM is the promptness of the reply. The minsters and the ministries make it a point to reply to people as early as possible and help solve their problem with the utmost priority. This helps people to solve their problems sooner and they also get to witness immediate action being taken.

In the tweets shown in various parts of Figure 1.4, it can be seen that the minister in question replied within fifteen minutes of when the query was posted. This shows the improved time of reply to the grievances in comparison to the offline or

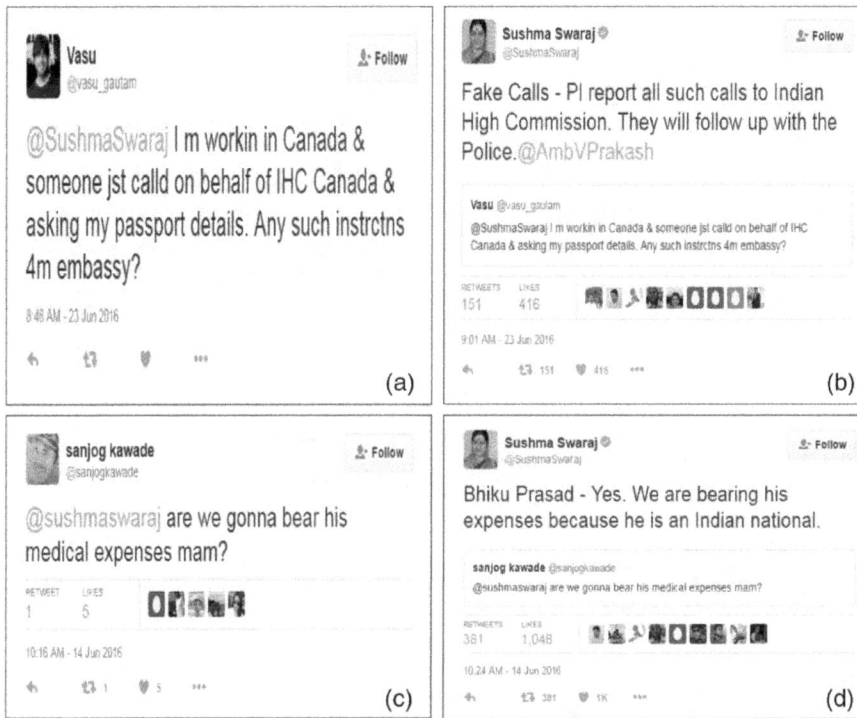

FIGURE 1.4 (a) Indian national on foreign land confirming procedure from External Affairs Ministry (b) Sushma Swaraj responding to the Indian national and tagging appropriate person (c) Indian national enquiring about the expenses (d) Sushma Swaraj responding and clarifying thus making a point to maintain CRM through social media.

online grievance redressal system. In some examples, like the case that has been depicted in the various tweets in Figure 1.5, citizens even get to see the actions that have been taken by the ministers and the ministries and also the promptness of those actions. Within just half an hour, the ministers and ministries forwarded the complaint to the concerned officials and the problem was solved.

The impact of social media for citizen relationship management activities is thus far-reaching and the greater number of people reaching out to the ministers and ministries indicates that their trust level is also rising in the usage of social media.

Analysis of objective 3

The impact of social media usage on the general public has been mostly found to be positive, as shown in Figure 1.6, with few negative cases, as shown in Figure 1.7.

People have been seen interacting with the ministers and the ministries. Tweets have been seen in which members of the general public have shared their problems and tagged wealthier individuals in order to receive help on the matter. It has

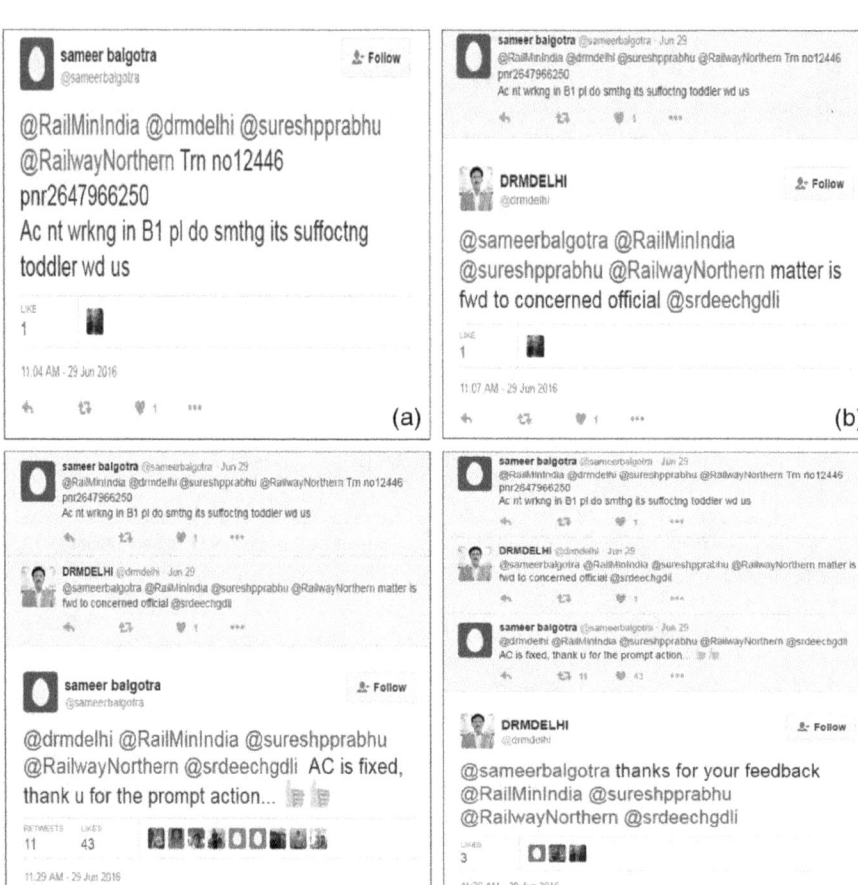

FIGURE 1.5 (a) Tweet by a passenger complaining about service on the train (b) Response to the tweet by government official (c) Update on the problem faced by passenger (d) Acknowledgment by the passenger thus proving that social media is playing a positive role in CRM.

been seen that ministers and ministries have come forward to help these people and address their issues to the best of their abilities. The general public have also praised these ministers and ministries for the help that they provided. On the other hand, cases have also been seen in which the ministers and the ministries have failed to reply to the tweets posted by the general public. This is not a negative case but might turn into one if the issue posted is anything urgent or serious. On the other hand, sometimes the ministers reply to each and every tweet of the public, whether they help them with the issue or not.

The CRM activities followed by ministers and ministries over social media can also turn out to be negative and might not always secure them praises. For example, as in the tweet screenshots shown in Figures 1.6 and 1.7, the minister shared

FIGURE 1.6 (a) Positive utilization of Twitter by Sushma Swaraj for rejecting inappropriate help (b) Positive intent shown by Sushma Swaraj for child rescue (c) Positive intent shown by Sushma Swaraj for girl's rescue.

the good work done by his ministry and their efforts to get things cleared off the railway tracks to avoid any delay in the train services. The activity, however, triggered the suffering travellers' emotions and they complained about their plight, which they had to face due to delayed train services.

Therefore, CRM activities on social media are no guarantee of positive responses or results. Social media is an active platform and is accessible to a lot of

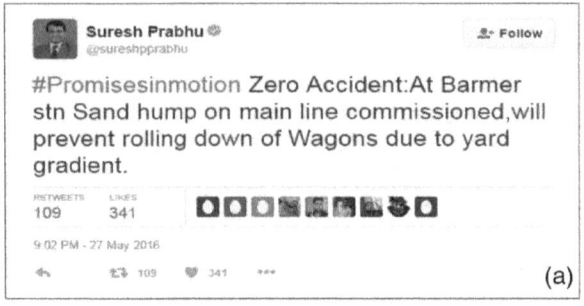

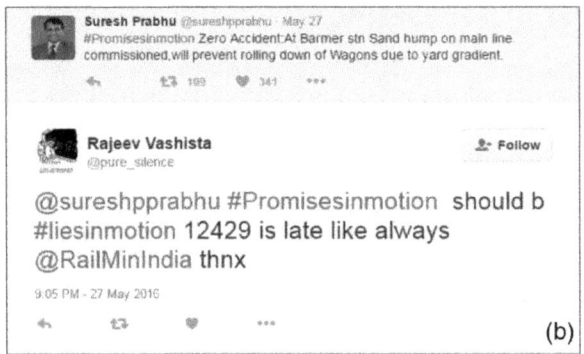

FIGURE 1.7 (a) Examples of a tweet by Suresh Prabhu that incurred a negative response (b) Negative response to Suresh Prabhu's tweet.

people at the same time. Whatever CRM activities are carried out are immediately seen by hundreds and thousands of people. The ministers and the ministries need to be cautious about what they post and how they interact with the general public.

Discussion and implications

Social media are important and the most sensational media for contact between two people, especially if the contact is not personal. Social media as a platform facilitate not only contact but interaction between any two people. The interaction is open and can also be viewed by people other than the sender and receiver. The implication of this can be seen in the form of interactions between governments and the general public. On one hand, the general public can convey their grievances to the concerned ministers and ministries, while on the other hand, the government can make announcements and interact with the public, handling their grievances and addressing their queries.

This study was conducted in order to throw light upon the social media activities of government departments and concerned officials (ministers). Tweets were analysed in order to learn about the citizenship relationship management activities that are carried out by the Government of India through social media.

The tweets that were analysed were categorized into five types: announcement tweets, interaction tweets, help tweets, tweets that show the work and recognition tweets. These five types of tweets showed the types of initiatives taken by the government for CRM using social media.

The government paid maximum attention to the interaction activity. They made it a point to regularly mingle with the general public, exchanging their views and ideas. They tried to relate to the people by conveying their wishes for various festivals belonging to all castes, cultures and religions. They also marked their presence and conveyed their wishes for various global relevance days like Yoga Day, Earth Day etc. This made the public feel more connected to the government and its causes. Hence, interaction was the most important part of the CRM activities.

The second most important type of CRM initiative carried out by the government is informing the general public about the work that has been done by them. Conveying the work done helps the public to see the effort that has been invested by the government and inclines them towards retaining the government. This thus helps the government in not only performing CRM activities but also gaining benefits otherwise. As has been identified in studies by Mukhaini *et al.* (2014), Ioanăs and Stoica (2014), Chow (2013), and Fischer and Reuber (2011), social media have a significant impact in altering the behaviour of customers, citizens in this case; social media can help the government in attaining the best communication and after-effects. Announcement tweets are also frequently used by government departments and ministers, but less so by the latter. Making announcements is easier with the use of social media because of its reach and proliferation levels.

Another important fact that was noticed is the impact of social media on improvement in the levels of CRM activities. It was seen that the reply time for the grievances that were reported by the public has dropped significantly. In the days before social media, people used to complain manually, either in the form of written complaints or otherwise in an electronic format; nowadays complaints are made directly to the concerned ministry, official or minister. Hence, replies now have become faster and more effective as it is now easier to reply and follow up with the consequent events and details. Studies like Falco (2011), Karakiza (2015) and Khan *et al.* (2014) have all talked about the various features of social media, including fast communication and great interaction.

However, one important point that has been noted is the probability of negative CRM. The government departments and the ministers, however, try to connect with the public and maintain a positive relationship. There is still the possibility of the conversation turning out to be negative and the public mistaking the intention. Specific attention, therefore, should be paid to the detail of the conversations that are started or the knowledge that is imparted.

Through the above discussions it can be concluded that social media are an effective, faster and much more convenient medium for the government for the purpose of transferring information to, and building bonds with, their citizens and thereby performing social media activities (Khasawneh *et al.* 2013; Shaikh and Khan 2014; Bonsón *et al.* 2012; Falco 2011; Karakiza 2015; Khan *et al.* 2014).

WHAT THEIR TWEETS TELL US ABOUT OUR NETAS

THE 'SOCIAL' LIFE OF INDIA'S TOP POLITICIANS FROM JAN 1 TO JUNE 30, 2016

Narendra Modi

Twitter handle: @narendramodi

21.1m followers | **11.9 k** tweets | **5.4** tweets per day

Last six months: Prolific and savvy as always. Continued with multi-lingual tweets on his recent visits to Uzbekistan, Mozambique, Kenya, and other countries. A marked number of mentions of Dr B R Ambedkar

Do you remember? Modi tweeted a birthday wish to Afghanistan President Ashraf Ghani in February. Ghani politely pointed out it wasn't his birthday. Modi made amends on May 19, tweeting: 'Happy Birthday President @ashrafghani... got the date right this time. :)'

Facebook: 34.8m likes, average 98.9k likes per post

Anupriya Patel

Twitter handle: @AnupriyaSPatel

452 followers | **2** tweets | **38** following

Last six months: Cyber cipher. Period.

Do you remember? An allegedly communal tweet from the handle @Anupriya_Patel was picked up after her induction as Union minister. She later claimed the account wasn't hers, and that she uses @AnupriyaSPatel — an account created this month. The older account is now suspended

Mamata Banerjee

Twitter handle: @MamataOfficial

396k followers | **1,567** tweets | **2** tweets per day | **Facebook: 1.89m likes**

Rahul Gandhi

Twitter handle: @OfficeOfRG

757k followers | **1,861** tweets | **0.1** tweets per day

Last six months: Though already distanced by not associating directly with the handle (chooses to call it 'Office of RG') the younger Gandhi has been **quick to aggressively attack the ruling party** online on every political issue — be it drugs in Punjab or the Bihar elections. Took special interest in the Rohith Vemula and Kanhaiya Kumar cases

Do you remember? On the JNU issue, Gandhi tweeted on Mar 2: 'The Prime Minister cannot run the country on only his opinion. The country is not the Prime minister. The Prime Minister is not the country.' The tweet was slammed as some recalled the Emergency proclamation by Congress leader Devakanta Barua: 'Indira is India and India is Indira'

Sushma Swaraj

Twitter handle: @SushmaSwaraj

5.36m followers | **4,066** tweets | **2** tweets per day

Last six months: All work and no-nonsense. Has created a reputation for responding to SOS calls on social media. In February, responded to a video of one Gurpreet who said she was stuck in a German refugee camp with her eight-year-old daughter. The woman was rescued and brought back to New Delhi

Facebook: 2.5 million likes

Do you remember? Swaraj's online alacrity led one Twitter user to seek her help in fixing his fridge. She politely declined with: 'Brother I cannot help you in matters of a refrigerator. I am very busy with human beings in distress'

Smriti Irani

Twitter handle: @smritiirani

4.13m followers | **10.1K** tweets | **4.1** tweets per day

Last six months: Aggressive, forthright & feisty. Shared her Rajya Sabha speech discussing Rohith Vemula & Kanhaiya Kumar

Do you remember? Got into a spat with Bihar minister Ashok Chaudhary when he wrote: 'Dear @smritiirani ji, when will we get New Education policy..?'

Facebook: 4.6m likes

Arvind Kejriwal

Twitter handle: @ArvindKejriwal

8.36m followers | **12.8k** tweets | **8.2** tweets per day

Last six months: Quick to respond, pugnacious, given to hyperbole. Also retweets jokes on himself. And others. Current favourite: @RealHistoryPic. Recent Twitter habit of sharing others' claims with the caption 'Is this true?' not received well. Punjab flavour of the season

Do you remember? During the 'Udta Punjab' controversy, co-producer Anurag Kashyap snubbed Kejriwal for his comment of support. 'I request Congress, AAP & other political parties to stay out of my battle. It's my Rights vs the Censorship. I speak only on my behalf,' Kashyap said, without naming anyone

Facebook: 6.8m likes

Last six months: Moderate user, formal in tone and tenor. Posted precious little on the JNU controversy that had most of her peers talking

Do you remember? Banerjee held a public Facebook Q&A in April this year

Maneka Gandhi

Twitter handle: @manekagandhibjp

15k followers | **1,172** tweets | **1.4** tweets per day

Last six months: Recently verified on Twitter. Has been retweeting other Cabinet ministers more than she tweets herself. Has been posting her own quotes with the tag #ManekaSays. **Recent spurt in tweets**

Do you remember? Gandhi's recent move to contain misogynist trolls on social media irked several political commentators online

Facebook: 39.1k likes

Shashi Tharoor

Twitter handle: @ShashiTharoor

4.3m followers | **32.1k** tweets | **12** tweets per day

Last six months: Chatty. Funny. Generous with retweets. The original political pied piper of social media took special interest in the recent 'Brexit' with memes, articles, and opinion

Do you remember? In January, Tharoor responded to actor Anupam Kher's comment that he was afraid to say he was Hindu. 'Come on Anupam. I say it all the time. I am a proud Hindu. Just not the Sangh's kind of Hindu,' he wrote

Facebook: 5.85 lakh likes

Source: Twitter, Facebook & Klear.com. Text: Kim Arora

FIGURE 1.8 Twitter and Facebook analysis of major Ministers in India.

Source: Times of India, E-paper 19 July 2016.

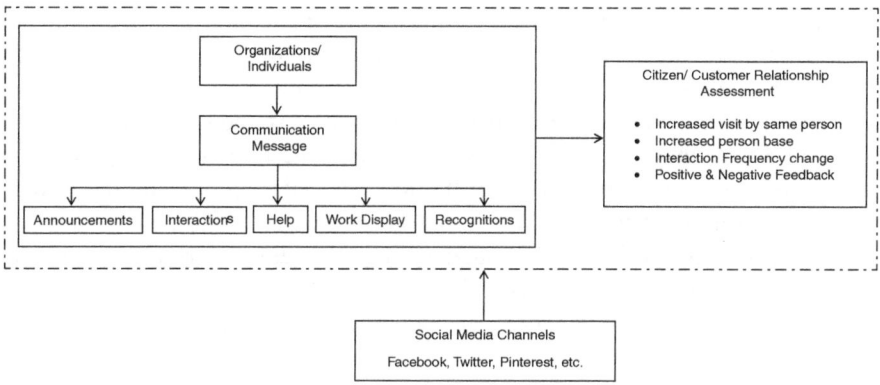

FIGURE 1.9 Framework to manage CRM through social media for various organizations and individuals.

The results are in sync with previous empirical results as well as current trends in the media industry seen through analysing Twitter trends for ministers, as shown in Figure 1.8.

From the point of view of implications for management, the analysis and discussion of social media activities can be summarised into a generic framework which can be followed by different organizations, whether public or private, and individuals in order to engage with their customers through various social media channels.

By looking at Figure 1.9, it can be deduced that since most of the communication messages can be categorized into definite groups, so people involved on social media channels should formulate their messages as per these categories to deal with various citizens and customers. The frequency of messages for each category on social media can vary as per the needs of the organizations and individuals; however from analysis it was found that 'Interactions' and 'Work Showcase' are the most frequently used categories for message communications. The various entities can analyze the performance of their communication campaigns through customer behaviour on social media channels through metrics like positive/negative comments, increased customer/citizen base and increase in communication from the various customers.

Conclusion

The study described the various aspects of enhancing CRM activities with the help of social media. One needs to be extra cautious while using this medium. Its speed can also turn out to be a bane for the government or any user in general. Once a post is dispatched it takes only a few seconds for millions of people to read it and start reacting. Once posted, word spreads like wildfire and can cause a lot of harm to the government's image. Moreover, the harm could be even greater than the benefit it could ever have accrued. The usage of social media as a communication and CRM tool cannot be ignored but it demands proper attention and care before it can be used. Social media managers need to be aware of both the pros and cons of the platform and use it effectively. Social media provides faster communication, high levels of interaction and great insights about citizens' thought processes.

The scope of future research involves validating the framework (Figure 1.9) for various other private and public institutions and refining it according to the needs. Moreover, apart from Facebook and Twitter, other social media channels should also be used for data analysis and adding other dimensions to the derived framework. A comparative analysis of various institutions and individuals can be performed on the basis of their social media based CRM campaigns.

References

Andrade, V. and P. Camacho. (2014). 'Citizen relationship management: what are the determinants that influence the implementation of citizen relationship management in governments?'. In *eDemocracy & eGovernment (ICEDEG), 2014 First International Conference on* (p. 97–102). IEEE.

Bonsón, E., L. Torres, L., S. Royo and F. Flores. 2012. 'Local e-government 2.0: social media and corporate transparency in municipalities'. *Government Information Quarterly*, 29(2), p. 123–132.

Dudley, E., D. Lin, M. Mancini and J. Ng. 2015. 'Implementing a citizen-centric approach to delivering government services'. McKinsey. Available at http://www.mckinsey.com/industries/public-sector/our-insights/implementing-a-citizen-centric-approach-to-delivering-government-services. Accessed 4 July 2016.

Falco, T. 2011. 'Taking social media public: social media for successful citizen relationship management'. *IBM Global Business Services*.

Fischer, E. and A. R. Reuber. 2011. 'Social interaction via new social media: (How) can interactions on Twitter affect effectual thinking and behavior?' *Journal of Business Venturing*, 26(1), p. 1–18.

IANS. 2014. 'How Indian Government is using Twitter'. The Times of India. Available at http://timesofindia.indiatimes.com/tech/social/How-Indian-government-is-using-Twitter/articleshow/36645890.cms. Accessed 4 July 2016.

Ioanăs, E. and I. Stoica. 2014. 'Social media and its impact on consumers' behavior'. *International Journal of Economic Practices and Theories*, 4(2), p. 295–303.

Karakiza, M. 2015. 'The impact of social media in the public sector'. *Procedia-Social and Behavioral Sciences*, 175, 384–392.

Khan, G. F. (2015). The Government 2.0 utilization model and implementation scenarios. Information Development, 31(2), 135–149.

Khan, G. F. and B. Swar. 2013. 'Government 2.0: utilization model, implementation scenarios, and relationships'. In *Pre-ECIS (21st European Conference on Information Systems) workshop: E-Government* (Vol. 2).

Khan, G. F., B. Swar and S. K. Lee. 2014. 'Social media risks and benefits: a public sector perspective'. *Social Science Computer Review*, 32(5), p. 606–627.

Khan, G. F., H. Y. Yoon and H. W. Park. 2012. 'Social media use in public sector: a comparative study of the Korean & US government'. In *ATHS panel during the 8th International Conference on Webometrics, Informatics and Scientometrics & 13th COLLNET Meeting* (p. 23–26).

Khasawneh, F and E. A. Abu-Shanab. 2013. 'E-Government and social media sites: the role and impact'. *World Journal of Computer Application and Technology*, 1(1), p. 10–17.

Latha, P. P., R. Madhuri, K. P. Rao and M. V. Bharathi. 2013. 'Effectual citizen relationship management with data mining techniques'. *International Journal of Research in Engineering and Technology*, 2.

Lee, G. and Y. H. Kwak. 2012. 'An open government maturity model for social media-based public engagement'. *Government Information Quarterly*, 29(4), p. 492–503.

Linders, D. 2012. 'From e-government to we-government: defining a typology for citizen coproduction in the age of social media'. *Government Information Quarterly*, 29(4), p. 446–454.

Magro, M. J. 2012. 'A review of social media use in e-government'. *Administrative Sciences*, 2(2), p. 148–161.

Mergel, I. and S. I. Bretschneider. 2013. 'A three-stage adoption process for social media use in government'. *Public Administration Review*, 73(3), p. 390–400.

Mukhaini, E. A., S. Ismael and I. Al-Dhuhli. 2014. 'The impact of social media on consumer buying behaviour'. Sultan Qaboos University. Available at https://www.researchgate.net/profile/Israa_Al-Dhuhli/publication/275347329_The_Impact_of_Social_Media_on_Consumer_Buying_Behaviour/links/5539e3950cf247b858814ad3.pdf.   Accessed 25 October 2016.

O'Reilly, T. 2010. 'Government as a platform'. In D. Lathrop and L. Ruma (eds.), *Open Government: Collaboration, Transparency, and Participation in Practice*. O'Reilly Media.

Rajan, N. 2016. '@narendramodi, the social media star, shows way for cabinet'. Indian Express. Available at http://indianexpress.com/article/technology/social/modi-the-social-media-star-shows-the-way-for-nda-cabinet-twitter-facebook/. Accessed 4 July 2016.

Schellong, A. 2006. 'Citizen relationship management: understanding, challenges and impact'. In *Proceedings of the 2006 International Conference on Digital Government Research* (p. 490). Digital Government Society of North America.

Shaikh, R. and M. R. Khan. 2014. 'Citizen relationship management: a decisive parameter of G2C e-governance web portals of Maharashtra, India'. *International Journal on Recent and Innovation Trends in Computing and Communication*, 2(8), p. 2234–2239. ISSN: 2321-8169

Sharma, S. K., V. Lama and N. Goyal. 2016. 'Digital India: a vision towards digitally empowered knowledge economy'. *Indian Journal of Applied Research*, 5(10), p. 330–336, ISSN - 2249-555X (DOI: 10.15373/2249555X)

Sinderman, Z. 2011. 'How governments are using social media for better & for worse'. Mashable India. Available at http://mashable.com/2011/07/25/government-social-media/#MuJC6zCmPgqC. Accessed 4 July 2016.

Srivastava, M. (2013). Social media and its use by the government. *Journal of Public Administration and Governance*, 3(2), p. 161–172.

Thomas, P. N. 2012. *Digital India: Understanding Information, Communication and Social Change*. SAGE Publications India.

2

ACADEMIA GOES SOCIAL MEDIA, MOOC, SPOC, SMOC AND SSOC

The digital transformation of higher education institutions and universities

Andreas Kaplan

Introduction

Social media are commonly defined as 'a group of Internet-based applications that build on the ideological and technological foundations of Web 2.0, and that allow the creation and exchange of user-generated content' (Kaplan and Haenlein 2010, p. 61). They include a variety of applications, including collaborative projects (e.g. Wikipedia; cf. Kaplan and Haenlein 2014), content communities (e.g. YouTube), micro-blogs/blogs (e.g. Twitter; cf. Kaplan and Haenlein 2011a), social networking sites (e.g. Facebook) and virtual worlds (e.g. World of Warcraft; cf. Kaplan and Haenlein 2009).

Since the inception of social media technology, many corporations and institutions have adopted and applied it successfully, displaying the power of these applications to lead to remarkable outcomes. In the entertainment industry, pop stars such as Britney Spears have developed their marketing activities entirely around social media (Kaplan and Haenlein 2012). In politics, social media communications and viral marketing activities (Kaplan and Haenlein 2011b; Kaplan 2012) led to Barack Obama's first presidential election in 2008, and nowadays they are indispensable in any political campaign. Several governments and public administration bodies make ample use of Twitter, Instagram and other social media platforms. One of the declared objectives of the European Union, for example, is to foster a feeling of European identity among its citizens through the use of social media (Kaplan 2014a).

In recent years, the higher education sector has also begun to undergo an important transformation, triggered by the arrival of social media in particular and the expansion of the digital sphere in general (Kaplan and Haenlein 2016; Pucciarelli and Kaplan 2016). Social media marketing is a key element in the recruitment strategies of higher education institutions and is a means not only of attracting potential students but also of maintaining strong relationships with alumni and other stakeholders. In addition to focusing on relationships with students *before* and *after* their studies, social media are increasingly being used *during* students' time at the university. The current generations of freshmen who are entering university class-rooms are digital natives and expect social media and user-generated content to be incorporated into their learning experiences. In fact, many of these students are comfortable replacing traditional in-person lectures with MOOCs (massive open online courses) or SPOCs (small private online courses). Accordingly, it is impor-tant for higher education institutions to be able to market themselves as being up-to-date on pedagogical innovations that integrate social media and online features.

Despite the fact that research on the intersection of social media and higher edu-cation is at an early stage (Junco, Heiberger and Loken 2011), an increasing num-ber of scientific articles on this topic are available. The majority of this literature analyses the micro-blogging service Twitter, which is commonly used in a class-room setting (e.g. Chen and Chen 2012; Ebner, Leinhardt, Rohs and Meyer 2010; Junco, Elavsky and Heiberger 2012). Nevertheless, there are also studies focus-ing on other social media applications and their usefulness in higher education such as collaborative projects (Daspit and D'Souza 2012), blogs (Gray 2016), con-tent communities (Steffes and Duverger 2012), social networking sites (Ractham, Kaewkitipong and Firpo 2012) and even virtual worlds (Dreher *et al.* 2009).

This book chapter takes a close look at the potential of social media applications in the three main phases of a student's interaction with the university: before enroll-ment, i.e. for marketing and recruitment purposes; during his/her studies, i.e. for augmenting the student's learning experience; and after graduation, i.e. for alumni relationship management. Additionally, online distance learning in its different for-mats (MOOC, SPOC, SMOC (synchronous massive online course), SSOC (syn-chronous small online course)) will be explained and analysed with a special focus on so-called cMOOCs (connectivist MOOCs), in which social media applications are a cornerstone, since they enable MOOC participants to develop their own peda-gogical content that can then be further commented on and improved by others.

Higher education and its key challenges

The future of higher education is, and will continue to be, uncertain and challeng-ing. Some scholars are rather optimistic, whereas others view this evolution with a great deal of pessimism. Pucciarelli and Kaplan's (2016) SWOT (strengths, weak-nesses, opportunities, and threats) analysis of the higher education sector identifies three core challenges, referred to as the 'Three E's for Education': (1) Enhancing higher education institutions' prestige and market share; (2) Embracing a deeper entrepreneurial mindset; (3) Expanding links, interactions and value co-creation with key stakeholders. Each of these challenges is discussed briefly in what follows.

Enhancing prestige and market share

Globalization and digitization have increased the level of competition in the higher education sector and have forced universities in general, and business schools in particular, to expand their market shares to encompass new and untapped populations of students. Institutions have achieved such expansion by diversifying and expanding their portfolios. The London Business School, an example of a traditional MBA school, recently launched a Masters in Management programme targeting students without any professional experience. Other players who used to focus exclusively on the graduate segment have expanded into the undergraduate market. ESCP Europe Business School, for example, with its six campuses in Berlin, London, Madrid, Paris, Turin and Warsaw, started a three-year and three-country Bachelor programme in 2015.

Notably, the possibilities of the digital sphere have lowered and sometimes even completely eliminated entry barriers to new players in the education sector. Thus, long-standing and well-known universities are finding themselves in competition with newly-established private online schools, as well as with MOOCs produced by top players such as Harvard or Stanford. Anybody, even students on the other side of the world, can participate in such MOOCs. In this landscape of strong competition, it becomes all the more important for a university to be clearly positioned and to build prestige and a strong brand in a precise area. For example, while future investment bankers prefer Wharton, a lawyer's first pick would most likely be Yale, and aspiring cross-cultural managers would probably choose ESCP Europe.

Embracing an entrepreneurial mindset

To cope with a competitive environment, academic institutions need to adopt an entrepreneurial mindset and a managerial approach that enables them to rapidly adapt to new markets and demands. In the executive education market, for example, institutions must cater to demand for online training – demand that has increased as a result of tight budgets and the fact that companies are reluctant to let their managers be away from their desks for an entire day, preferring the idea of more flexible distance learning. Moreover, it may be insufficient to develop one standard educational programme, as both students and high-paying clients are increasingly requesting customized solutions. Adaptive learning environments relying on mass-customization techniques (Kaplan and Haenlein 2006) as well as the power of communication via social media can be of high interest in this regard.

The principle of embracing an entrepreneurial mindset means that professors must evolve towards becoming managers. Specifically, although these individuals will continue to contribute to the academic standing and prestige of their universities mainly through research activities and teaching, they will also be required to show stronger engagement with the management of their institutions. Such engagement entails, for example, marketing themselves and their research projects in order to develop their own resources and build up stronger relationships with other universities and corporate partners, as well as with former students. Social media can be highly useful in this context. Cambridge University, for example, has begun encouraging its faculty members to set up accounts on social media that clearly display their link to Cambridge, for presentation and marketing purposes. Following this move, Cambridge University increased its number of Facebook followers by 400%.

Expanding interaction and value co-creation

Responding to higher education's third challenge, that is, expanding interactions and co-creating value with main stakeholders, means completely reshaping and rebuilding a variety of relationships with several different partners. Of particular interest are the relationships with alumni, who are playing an ever-more vital role for the institutions with which they are affiliated: Alumni are the best advocates for a university's brand and serve as its most loyal supporters, acting as potential donors with respect to fundraising, as advertisers via their positive word-of-mouth communications, or simply as highly-valued experts with regard to their *alma mater*. By maintaining communication channels with alumni via social media applications, universities can keep them informed of new developments and current events – thus, the message that alumni share will not only be positive but also up-to-date.

The potential of a higher education institution to cope with this third challenge depends primarily on the degree to which it makes use of new information technologies in general and social media in particular. If one takes a close look at Peking University's Twitter feed, for example, one immediately sees that the university retweets a large number of posts by engaged alumni. This is a perfect way to stay close to your fan base and community while at the same time displaying your institution's prestige and influence.

Social media as a means of overcoming the challenges threatening higher education

Social media in contrast to more traditional media are 'mainly conceived of as a medium wherein "ordinary" people in ordinary social networks [...] can create user-generated "news"' (Murthy 2012, p. 3). They enable a broad range of participants, an easier two-way conversation and therefore are considered emancipatory (Castells 2007). According to Hansen, Shneiderman and Smith (2011), social media have created entirely new ways of interacting and facilitate a transparent and authentic exchange, potentially leading to more informal, closer relationships between organizations and individuals. The differences between traditional and social media empower the latter to play a vital role in each of the three main challenges that the higher education sector currently faces. When used correctly, social media can enhance a university's brand and market share, adapt learning and teaching to an increasingly diverse student population, and facilitate contact with precious alumni and other stakeholders (cf. Table 2.1).

Attracting potential future students

Social media can play a vital role in increasing the market share of a higher education institution, as well as enhance its prestige. With respect to market share, social

TABLE 2.1 Social media as a means of overcoming higher education's three core challenges

Attracting future students	• *ESCP Europe Business School*: Enhancing a university's brand, reputation and prestige via differentiated use of social media applications • *University of Southern California*: Increasing market share through a strengthened direct marketing and word-of-mouth approach
Augmenting current students' learning experience	• *Berkeley, University of California*: Empowering interactivity in big size classes by projecting live Twitter feeds from students on the wall and incorporating these tweets into the course • *Colorado Technical University*: Adopting adaptive learning and teaching environments to customize course content and sequences
Amplifying relationships with past students (alumni)	• *Harvard Business School*: Increasing alumni engagement via hyper-targeting efforts • *Ohio State University*: Expanding interactions with alumni through careful listening to, and learning from, their social media conversations

media can serve as an effective means of attracting potential students. For example, Juntae DeLane, Digital Brand Manager at the University of Southern California, has made social media an inherent part of his general effort to strengthen digital communications for recruiting purposes. He points out that social media are vital to several steps of the recruitment funnel: acquiring prospects, engaging with them, driving them to apply and ultimately converting them into actual students. As a step towards achieving these goals, the University of Southern California produced a YouTube series, inspired by MTV's *Cribs*, in which each video presented a distinctive dorm. Viewers could vote on their favorite dorm, creating further engagement and word-of-mouth. DeLane states that this campaign 'was created based on social listening', given that university managers recognized that campus housing was a recurring question from prospects (Foulger 2014). Similarly, England's Cambridge University regularly shares time-lapse videos on its social media channels (e.g. one called 'A Winter Waltz in Cambridge') to display what life could look like for a future student. These videos are often very cost-efficient, with Barney Brown, the university's head of digital communications, pointing out that 'the answer isn't always to throw money at it'; instead, 'we have to make things work' (Milbrath 2015).

Social media can also play an important role in enhancing a university's brand, reputation and, finally, prestige. For example, ESCP Europe, the world's first business school, has adopted the goal of ensuring, via its social media activities, that its brand is considered dynamic, innovative and modern. This goal is particularly important given that ESCP Europe, established in 1819, has been around longer than any other business school and wants to avoid being seen as old-fashioned. Furthermore, the school's 'overall objective is to position [itself] as an expert on European, cross-cultural management' says Andria Andriuzzi, Community manager at ESCP Europe (Kaplan 2014b). One of the school's viral marketing videos, applying the stop-motion technique, was a real success, with more than 300 students acting together to express the values and spirit of ESCP Europe in a fun, imaginative and entertaining way. Quickly after its launch, the video attracted over half a million views on ESCP Europe's YouTube channel, with viewers located all over the world.

Augmenting students' learning experience

Social media can help higher education institutions respond to students' demand for universities that are technologically savvy and that provide augmented educational experiences (McHaney 2011). Likewise, social media technologies can enable these institutions to adapt teaching and learning for increasingly diverse populations, comprising students from a variety of cultural, ethnic, geographical, religious and social backgrounds. An early adopter of adaptive learning is the Colorado Technical University, which is committed to making adaptive learning and teaching part of its general academic and pedagogical strategy.

A university's social media capabilities are also an important marketing factor, since digital natives act as rational and informed customers when selecting their future *alma maters* (Temple and Shattock 2007).

Millennials approach learning through social networking sites and other forms of multimedia- and digitally-based delivery systems that facilitate instantaneous and customized student-teacher interactions (Budde-Sung 2011). As a result of demand for such interactions, social media and user-generated content are increasingly being used for pedagogical purposes, to enhance learning, communication and student engagement. For example, micro-blogging platforms such as Twitter (Kaplan and Haenlein 2011a) enable students to continue in-class discussions outside the classroom and to express their opinions regarding all sorts of course assignments. Professors also use social media applications to hold virtual review sessions for their respective courses, thereby freeing up time in face-to-face classes. Moreover, the use of social media platforms for course discussions can start a dynamic in which students are encouraged to ask their peers for help, and peers are willing to assist because their efforts become highly visible, both to their classmates and to their instructors. Another example can be found at the University of California Berkeley. Here professors teaching very large class sizes (more than 800 students) have the option of a live Twitter feed shown on screen behind them. This can be used during the course in order to enable interactivity despite high student numbers. Indeed, an analysis by Hoffman (2009) shows that incorporation of social media into teaching yields numerous benefits, including collaborative learning, retention, sense of control and ownership, socialization and increased student engagement. Yet, it is still unclear how the availability of course material on public channels is going to impact such notions as academic freedom, intellectual property rights and privacy laws – a concern that decelerates this development but clearly does not stop it.

Amplifying relationships with alumni

As discussed above, alumni are key stakeholders with whom higher education institutions should seek to preserve relationships. Alumni are becoming ever-more important, not only in terms of fundraising, but also – and this is where social media come in – in terms of communication and marketing activities. Obviously, social media and viral marketing are used to encourage word-of-mouth communication. When applied correctly with alumni, social media can be very beneficial. Robert Bochnak, for example, Social Media Manager at Harvard Business School's alumni office, increased alumni engagement on social media by nearly 300 per cent within a single month. Specifically, HBS made efforts to hyper-target alumni by creating specific alumni lists on Twitter, taking into account users' personal and professional interests, graduation year and additional demographic data such as city of residence. Each piece of news that HBS shared on Twitter specifically targeted the alumni who would potentially be interested in it – thus creating high involvement and engagement, and encouraging retweets.

Ohio State University undertook a similar effort. When it started its Facebook page, the main objective was to communicate with students. However, it turned out to be alumni, who were nostalgic about their days at the university, who were the most involved and interactive members of this social media application. Kristen Convery, Director of Multimedia Content, thus experimented with ways of further engaging with alumni. One of Ohio State's Facebook campaigns involved posting pictures of the university's dorms and encouraging alumni to share anecdotes and to tag themselves if they had lived in the featured building. Kristen Convery states that 'One of the things we really do at the University of Ohio State is to listen to our audiences and learn, and try to use that to form our relationships' (Foulger 2014).

The role of social media in the digital transformation of academia

Like the tourism and entertainment industries some time ago, academia is undergoing a steep transformation process due to a digital revolution within the sector. In particular, the arrival of MOOCs, SPOCs, SMOCs and SSOCs has the potential to profoundly change higher education. In what follows, we first provide a brief overview of these different forms of online distance education, as well as a short historical sketch of their evolution. We subsequently focus on the important role of social media in digital forms of higher education in general, and in so-called connectivist MOOCs in particular (Kaplan and Haenlein 2016).

Defining and classifying digital courses: MOOCs, SPOCs, SMOCs, SSOCs

In line with Kaplan and Haenlein (2016, p. 441), we define distance learning as any form of 'providing education to students who are separated by distance and in which the pedagogical material is planned and prepared by educational institutions'. Two key categories of online distance learning courses are MOOCs and SPOCs, mentioned briefly above. Kaplan and Haenlein (2016, p. 443) define MOOCs as open-access online courses that allow for unlimited (massive) participation, and SPOCs as online courses in which class size is limited, such that students must formally enroll. In MOOCs and SPOCs, students might be separated not only by space but also by time. In asynchronous distance learning, students study according to their own schedule and speed, whereas synchronous distance learning refers to students who follow a course simultaneously and in real time.

Applying the two dimensions of 'time distance' and 'number of participants' enables one to classify online distance courses into four groups: MOOCs, which are unlimited in the number of participants, usually welcome students who are separated by both space and time, enabling them to learn asynchronously at their own pace; SMOCs , in contrast, are massive online courses in which students participate synchronously and in real-time; similarly, in SPOCs, where the number of students is limited, learning takes place in an asynchronous manner; whereas SSOCs require participants to follow the lessons in real time.

Precursors of MOOCs and online distance learning

The development of distance learning can be separated into three distinctive periods, each corresponding to a specific medium for dissemination of material: i.e. print, audiovisual channels and the Internet (Kaplan and Haenlein 2016). Distance learning started in 1728 when the Boston Gazette printed an ad for a weekly stenography course that participants would follow using traditional mail. In the second period, radio and television replaced printed materials as the main media channels. A cornerstone of this second era was the establishment of the Open University in 1969. The Open University was the first higher education institution that made use of television for distance learning purposes, providing a mix of residential courses as well as supporting lessons at different physical locations.

The third era of distance learning began with the advent of the Internet and its incorporation into higher education. An important milestone in this era was the creation of an entire online campus by the University of Phoenix in 1989, proposing a portfolio of online undergraduate and graduate programmes. In 2008, the term MOOC was used for the first time by Dave Cormier to refer to a course titled 'Connectivism and Connective Knowledge'. This course integrated mass social media such as blogs, forums and wikis, social networking sites such as Facebook, and even the virtual social world 'Second Life'. The year 2012 was declared by the New York Times to be 'The Year of the MOOC', marking the arrival of several major MOOC platforms and providers, including Coursera, edX and Udacity.

Social media + MOOCs = cMOOCs

While the majority of MOOCs are based on traditional lecture formats, the first MOOC, mentioned above can be considered a cMOOC (connectivist MOOC).

In cMOOCs, social media form an essential part of the learning experience, with participants creating their own pedagogical materials via blogs, tweets and the like. Such user-generated pedagogical content can then be commented on and discussed by other participants in the online course. Compared with traditional MOOCs, cMOOCs are more focused on collaboration and cooperation among participants, with the instructor facilitating interactions between students instead of merely transmitting knowledge along the lines of a formal curriculum.

Students who evolve into pedagogical content developers deeply change the traditional professor/student model, which is characterized by a clear relationship of authority and subordination. Lee and McLoughlin (2007, p. 31) state that 'these changes are inevitable and unavoidable, given the morphing nature of higher education', confirming the current and especially future importance of social media in the higher education sector.

Conclusion

This chapter started by outlining three core challenges higher education currently faces (the Three E's for Education): (1) enhancing prestige and market share; (2) embracing an entrepreneurial mindset; and (3) expanding interaction and value co-creation. We then showed how social media can play a vital role in overcoming these challenges by (1) attracting *future* students, (2) augmenting *current* students' learning experience, and (3) amplifying relationships with *past* students (alumni). Finally, we looked at the role of social media in academia's digital transformation process by (1) defining and classifying online courses into MOOCs, SPOCs, SMOCs and SSOCs, (2) briefly sketching out the history of MOOCs and distance learning, as well as (3) analysing connectivist MOOCs (cMOOCs) as open online courses which are heavily supported by, and based on, social media applications.

Though the title of this chapter is 'Academia goes social media', one should remember that some of the most important inventions in the social media landscape originated within higher education institutions. One only needs to think of Mark Zuckerberg, who was a Harvard sophomore when he developed Facebook in 2003 – which essentially started as an online 'face book' of Harvard students. Similarly, the mobile social media application Foursquare (Kaplan 2012) effectively grew out of a graduate thesis written about a similar platform, Dodgeball, developed by Dennis Crowley, who graduated from New York University in 2004. One might say that these students were ahead of their universities in creating and developing new means of communication, and that nowadays these same applications are re-entering academia – both for teaching and learning purposes, and as highly effective tools for marketing and communication.

References

Budde-Sung, Amanda. 2011. 'The increasing internationalization of the international business classroom: Cultural and generational considerations', *Business Horizons*, 54(4): 365–373.

Castells, Manuel. 2007. 'Communication, power and counter-power in the network society', *International Journal of Communication*, 1(1): 238–266.

Chen, Liwen and Tung-Liang Chen. 2012. 'Use of Twitter for formative evaluation: reflections on trainer and trainees' experiences', *British Journal of Educational Technology*, 43(2): 49–52.

Daspit, Joshua J., Errick E. D'Souza. 2012. 'Using the community of inquiry framework to introduce Wiki environments in blended-learning pedagogies: Evidence from a business capstone course', *Academy of Management Learning & Education*, 11(4): 666–683.

Dreher, Carl, Torsten Reiners, Naomi Dreher and Heinz Dreher. 2009. 'Virtual worlds as a context suited for information systems education: discussion of pedagogical experience and curriculum design with reference to second life', *Journal of Information Systems Education*, 20(2): 211–224.

Ebner, Martin, Conrad Lienhardt, Matthias Rohs and Iris Meyer. 2010. 'Microblogs in higher education – a chance to facilitate informal and process-oriented learning', *Computers & Education*, 55(1): 92–100.

Foulger, Matt. 2014. 'Higher education success stories: how 3 leading universities use social media', Hootsuite.

Gray, Glen L. 2016. 'Blogs as research and teaching resources for accounting academics', *Journal of Information Systems*, 30(2): 183–202.

Hansen, Derek, Ben Shneiderman and Marc A. Smith. 2011. *Analyzing social media networks with NodeXL: insights from a connected world*, Elsevier: Boston.

Hoffman, Ellen. 2009. 'Social media and learning environments: shifting perspectives on the locus of control', in *Education: exploring our connective educational landscape*, 15(2): 23–38.

Junco, Raynol, Michael C. Elavsky and Greg Heiberger. 2012. 'Putting Twitter to the test: assessing outcomes for student collaboration, engagement and success', *British Journal of Educational Technology*, 44(2): 273–287.

Junco, Raynol, Greg Heiberger and Eric Loken. 2011. 'The effect of Twitter on college student engagement and grades', *Journal of Computer Assisted Learning*, 27(2): 119–132.

Kaplan, Andreas. 2012. 'If you love something, let it go mobile: mobile marketing and mobile social media 4×4', *Business Horizons*, 55(2): 129–139.

Kaplan, Andreas. 2014a. 'European management and European business schools: insights from the history of business schools', *European Management Journal*, 32(4): 529–534.

Kaplan, Andreas. 2014b. 'Social media and viral marketing at ESCP Europe, the World's First Business School (est. 1819)'. European Case Clearing House.

Kaplan, Andreas and Michael Haenlein. 2006. 'Toward a parsimonious definition of traditional and electronic mass customization', *Journal of Product Innovation Management*, 23(2): 168–182.

Kaplan, Andreas and Michael Haenlein. 2009. 'The fairyland of second life: about virtual social worlds and how to use them', *Business Horizons*, 52(6): 563–572.

Kaplan, Andreas and Michael Haenlein. 2010. 'Users of the world, unite! The challenges and opportunities of social media', *Business Horizons*, 53(1): 59–68.

Kaplan, Andreas and Michael Haenlein. 2011a. 'The early bird catches the news: nine things you should know about micro-blogging', *Business Horizons*, 54(2): 105–113.

Kaplan, Andreas and Michael Haenlein. 2011b. 'Two hearts in three-quarter time: how to waltz the social media/viral marketing dance', *Business Horizons*, 54(3): 253–263.

Kaplan, Andreas and Michael Haenlein. 2012. 'The Britney Spears universe: social media and viral marketing at its best', *Business Horizons*, 55(1): 27–31.

Kaplan, Andreas and Michael Haenlein. 2014. 'Collaborative projects (social media application): about Wikipedia, the free encyclopedia', *Business Horizons*, 57(5): 617–626.

Kaplan, Andreas and Michael Haenlein. 2016. 'Higher education and the digital revolution: about MOOCs, SPOCs, social media and the Cookie Monster', *Business Horizons*, 59: 441–450.

Lee, Mark and Catherine McLoughlin. 2007. 'Teaching and learning in the Web 2.0 era: empowering students through learner-generated content', *International Journal of Instructional Technology & Distance Learning*, 4(10): 21–34.

McHaney, Roger. 2011. *The new digital shoreline: how Web 2.0 and millennials are revolutionizing higher education*, Sterling, VA: Stylus Publishing.

Milbrath, Sam. 2015. '3 successful higher education social media campaigns'. Hootsuite.

Murthy, Dhiraj. 2012. 'Towards a sociological understanding of social media: theorizing Twitter', *Sociology*, 46(6): 1–15.

Pucciarelli, Francesca and Andreas Kaplan. 2016. 'Competition and strategy in higher education: managing complexity and uncertainty', *Business Horizons*, 59: 311–320.

Ractham, Peter, Laddawan Kaewkitipong and Daniel Firpo. 2012. 'The use of Facebook in an introductory MIS course: social constructivist learning environment', *Decision Sciences Journal of Innovative Education*, 10(2): 165–188.

Steffes, Erin M. and Philippe Duverger. 2012. 'Edutainment with videos and its positive effect on long term memory', *Journal for Advancement of Marketing Education*, 20(1), 1–10.

Temple, Paul and Michael Shattock. 2007. 'What does branding mean in higher education?' In B. Stensaker and V. d'Andrea (eds), *Branding in Higher Education: Exploring an Emerging Phenomenon*, EAIR: Amsterdam, 73–82.

3

INTEGRATING COMMUNITY AND RELATIONSHIP BUILDING INTO UNIVERSITIES' SOCIAL MEDIA MARKETING

Implications from a case study

Jenny Hou

Introduction

Social media are a game changer in the contemporary marketplace. As a relatively new terrain, social media marketing has attracted attention from both marketers and researchers. The mainstream literature ascribed to for-profits has explored social media for various marketing benefits including marketing positioning, segmentation and planning (Mangold and Faulds 2009). Non-profit higher education systems have only recently experimented with social media marketing in response to the mounting global education competition (Hemsley-Brown and Oplatka 2006). While marketers applauded the immediacy, proximity and easy access of social media, which is unmatched by traditional media (Agnihotri, Kothandaraman, Kashyap and Singh 2012), they overlooked the underlying conflict between the relational and participatory philosophy inherent in social media and the promotional nature of marketing (Motion, Heath and Leitch 2016). Today's publics, especially technology-savvy college students, appear to resist corporate intrusion into the public sphere, such as intrusion into social media and companies' exploitation of online marketing (Bal, Grewal, Mills and Ottley 2015).

The clash between corporate-driven marketing and public participation on social media invites us to refocus on the value and necessity of community-based relationship marketing. Marketers need to be aware that they are playing in other folks' playgrounds (i.e. social media), so they cannot behave deterministically. Community is not foreign to marketing strategies, and social media are deemed ideal avenues for community building and relationship marketing due to their collaborative and interactive nature. Moreover, relationship marketing seems to suit higher education institutions which, in addition to surviving economically, need to fulfil public expectations of creating 'social benefits including emotional satisfaction, spiritual values and the sharing of humanitarian ideals' (Arnett, German and

Hunt 2003, p. 91). For relationship marketing to be truly effective, universities should act like a neighbour immersed in wider communities (Juarez, 2011).

Literature on strategic issues, case studies and best practices of social media marketing specific to a university context is limited. Extant research (e.g. Belanger *et al*. 2014; McAllister 2012; Raciti 2010) reveals that universities mainly use social media for one-way newsfeeds, information delivery, publicity and advertising campaigns to present universities in the best light possible which, arguably, constitutes an instance of hyper-real identity assemblage (Ramirez and Palu-ay 2015). Little is known about how social media can be employed for community engagement and relationship marketing in universities that operate on a *collaborative*, rather than a *consumptive*, model (Gibbs 2002). To fill this gap, this case study aims to investigate whether and how three popular social media platforms (Facebook, Twitter, YouTube) are being employed in a New Zealand university to build relationships and student communities.

New Zealand was chosen as a case study as it is ranked fifth in higher education exportation markets (following the US, UK, Canada and Australia) (Hemsley-Brown and Oplatka 2006) and enjoys a high adoption rate of social media (Pham 2011). Since the 1990s, when government reduced funding on a large scale, New Zealand universities have attempted to recruit external students and forge international relationships. To tackle the issue of social media use in university community building and relationship marketing, what follows is a theoretical review that draws literature from three aspects: marketing universities on social media, relationship marketing and community building, and social media engagement. This chapter then describes data collection and analysis, based on which major findings will be presented by themes. Both theoretical and practical implications will be discussed at the end of the chapter.

Marketing universities on social media or not?

The idea of marketing educational institutions has been controversial and often gained limited support given the concern that commercialisation might undermine academic quality and excellence (Gibbs 2002). Nonetheless, it is increasingly accepted that 'educational institutions are considered as a service provider, students as potential customers and the parties to a mutually interactive process, and training has a marketable service quality' (Ozkanal and Uygucgil 2016, p. 91). A trend of marketing universities has emerged to not only adopt corporate-like marketing techniques such as distributing promotional materials and appealing advertisements, but also to venture into the realm of social media marketing.

According to extant studies (see Table 3.1 for a summary), social media marketing in universities is still in its infancy (Constantinides and Zinck Stagno 2011) and its main application can be divided into four stages. Stage I is to adopt and present on social media 'just for the sake of it' (Belanger *et al*. 2014, p. 27), or 'because everyone else has [a social media account]' (Charlesworth 2014, p. 329). Those universities that do not take advantages of social media are 'missing out

TABLE 3.1 Extant studies addressing social media in higher education institutions

Research streams	Issues examined	Primary methods	Main findings	Examples
1. Social media adoption	Whether and to what extent social media are adopted in universities	Surveys	Social media (e.g., Facebook, Twitter) have been increasingly adopted in universities (e.g. 68% in Canada; 80% in US)	Belanger et al. (2014); Kelleher & Sweetser, (2012); Raciti (2010), 68
2. Social media for branding promotion	How universities use social media for branding and promotion	Content analysis; Case studies	Social media are instrumental for branding through publicity, one-way information delivery and marketing segmentation.	Constantinides & Zinck Stagno (2011); Sandlin & Pena (2014); Waters et al. (2009)
3. Social media for learning improvement	How universities use social media for pedagogical purposes	Experiments; Comparative case studies	Social media are used as online teaching tools to improve student engagement	Abe & Jordan (2013); Neier & Zayer (2015); Wankel (2009)
4. Social media for relationship building and marketing	How universities use social media to build relationships	Surveys; Interviews	A low percentage utilises social media interactive features to foster dialogue and relationships	McAllister (2012); Rossmann & Young (2015); Sison & Brennan (2012)

on marketing and recruitment opportunities' (Greenwood 2012, p. 27). Stage II is to use social media for branding and projecting university images that are often loosely connected to physical bodies; as Ramirez and Palu-ay (2015) commented, 'You don't look like your profile picture' (p. 139). Stage III involves using social media for pedagogical purposes such as engaging and improving student learning, whereas stage IV, also an underdeveloped one, is to manage social media for relationship building and marketing.

Noticeably, Table 3.1 shows that the participatory and interactive potential of social media has not yet been fully explored, nor their strategic function of relationship marketing, which, arguably, fits best with higher education institutions (Gibbs and Murphy 2009). Many universities are not yet ready for dialogue online or prepared to build communities based on value exchange between universities and students, or among students themselves. What is even more pressing is what Hemsley-Brown and Oplatka (2006, p. 18) conclude, that "The current literature on university marketing is incoherent, even inchoate, and lacks theoretical models that reflect upon the particular context of higher education and the nature of their services." Universities lack research-based guidance on how to navigate social media for community building and relationship marketing that appears to be more effective than traditional transactional marketing. To combat this deficiency, a close look at the nature of community-based relationship marketing is needed, and is detailed in what follows.

Why relationship marketing and community building?

Emerging from the context of services marketing in the early 1980s, relationship marketing has no unified definition due to having had a short lifetime in which to develop a fully-formed paradigm (Moller and Halinen 2000). Nonetheless, a review of literature shows that Grönroos' (1994, p. 6) definition, which defines 'relationship marketing' as 'an interactive process in a social context where relationship building is a vital cornerstone to marketing', gains the most popularity in the field. Relationship marketing represents a paradigm shift from the transactional model of sending brochures or emails to an interactive and participatory process involving relationships. Harker (1999) summarized seven conceptual categories that underpin relationship marketing: creation, development, maintenance, interaction, long term, emotional content and output. Recently, Lehtinen (2011) proposed an integrated approach, a RELMIX (RELationship-MIX) framework, to combine the use of relationship marketing (e.g. exchange both transactions and relationships) and a transactional model (e.g. marketing mix of the 4Ps), as the two are not necessarily contradictory but rather complementary to one another.

Since relational exchange involves interaction between human beings, social bonds, along with emotional attachment or mutual liking that develop between parties, are an important feature of relationship marketing (Sashi 2012; Szmigin, Canning and Reppel 2005). To craft and strengthen the social bonds, modern relationship marketing literature has theorized four key virtues that are vital to relationship quality: trust (Veloutsou, Saren and Tzokas 2002), commitment (Moorman, Zaltman and Deshpande 1992), conflict handling (Ndubisi and Chan 2005) and communication (Arnett and Badrinarayanan 2005).

Although the above factors are widely cited in subsequent studies, the current scholarship is still criticized for several reasons. Firstly, it provides a narrowed and simplified understanding of 'relationships' by only focusing on the firm-customer relationship, which is not applicable to other organizational contexts like universities. Universities are not firms in a rigid sense but instead have the dual needs of marketing to and serving wider communities. Secondly, most empirical studies emphasize the 'effect' or 'impact' of relationship marketing on customer satisfaction and loyalty (e.g. Laroche, Habibi, Richard and Sankaranarayanan 2012; Negi and Ketema 2010), with the result that there is lack of knowledge on the 'process' and 'strategies' of relationship marketing. Thirdly, current relationship marketing theories seem to be at a lip-service stage without providing much insight into its practicality and operationality. Many organizations use relationship marketing to create a firmer grip on customers 'much like the fisherman's relationship to the fish' (Harker and Egan 2006, p. 228).

Given the above theoretical and empirical gaps in the field, a broader and more integrated perspective that goes beyond the classical firm-customer relationship is needed. Community is such a useful instrument for relationship marketing. According to Rossmann and Young (2015), communities are characterized by connections, interaction, self-organising and consensus-building. Compared to one-way marketing promotion, community-based relationship building has a better chance of success through improved communication and customer engagement, and increased brand loyalty. Generally, the idea of community building is to develop a sense of belonging and emotional attachment among the members of a community (Charlesworth 2014).

In recent years, some researchers (e.g. Chaston and Mangles 2001) have introduced 'brand communities' as a solution to serving customers in the wake of internet technologies. Laroche *et al.* (2012) also find that brand communities support sharing information, perpetuating the history and culture of a brand, and providing assistance to consumers. Community-based relationship marketing is deemed important and suitable to a social media environment where sociality plays out in the marketing process. However, there are no systematic efforts to examine how social media can support university community building and relationship marketing. For this reason, we need to better understand social media characteristics as well as how social media can enable community-based relationship marketing in practical ways.

How can social media help?

Social media, also called 'Web 2.0' or 'social networking sites (SNS)', refer to 'a set of technology tools that are just as they sound—mediated opportunities for bringing people together and encouraging social networking and dialogic communication' (Sweetser and Lariscy 2008, p.180). Macnamara and Zerfass (2012, p. 293) summarized two defining features of social media environments: (1) the 'openness for *participation* and *interactivity* involving dialogue, conversation, collaboration, and co-creativity harnessing collective intelligence'; and (2) *relinquished control* that 'characterises one-way, top-down information distribution models, as well as a requirement for authenticity instead of pre-packaged content'. Social media users have increased expectations of appropriate communication online and also have a space to voice such expectations at volume. This is especially true with cynical college students, in Tapscott's (2009) term, the 'net generation', who were born after 1990 with an unprecedented level of exposure to modern technologies and social media.

One radical change brought about by social media is from spectatorship – customers as passive audience waiting for sales representation responses – to participation, whereby they have agency in information creation, sharing and mutually influencing each other's purchase decisions. The central spirit of conversation and interaction online is critical to community building as well as to remind marketers of going beyond just pushing message awareness. As such, scholars (e.g. Baird and Parasnis 2011; Malthouse, Haenlein, Skiera, Wege and Zhang 2013) have recently coined a new term 'social CRM' (social customer relationship management) to recognize the influence of social media on relationship marketing. However, this term is partially problematic because it confuses customers with online community members. To clarify this confusion, Ang (2011) proposed an alternative term, 'CoRM' (community relationship management), to accurately reflect what people do in online communities – connect, converse, create and collaborate.

The community thinking on social media provides at least two implications for relationship marketing. One is to extend the traditional firm-customer relationship, namely market-based relationship marketing, to what Moller and Halinen (2000, p. 16) called 'network-based relationship marketing', which examines multi-way relationships in a networked environment. The other is to expand the predominant focus on the 'end' of relationship marketing (i.e. relationship quality, sales volumes) to include Harker and Egan's (2006, p. 226) 'means-end equation', namely, both means to, and end of, relationship marketing are important. The rationale can be better understood in today's social media environment with Berry's (1995, p. 242) explanation that "companies must establish relationships with non-customer groups (the means) in order to establish relationships with customers (the end)."

In line with community-based relationship marketing thinking, engagement is another key theme in many marketing studies (e.g. Sashi 2012; Szmigin *et al.* 2005), although few have clearly defined what it is. According to Rowe *et al.* (2004, p. 512), engagement refers to "the practice of consultation and involving members of the public in the agenda-setting, decision-making, and political forming activities of organisations." The central notion of engagement is joint, which implies two-way communication and a balanced power relation between marketers and consumers. However, John (2013) realized that most engagement online is *distributive* through generating and circulating content, rather than *communicative* through enabling relational practices of value exchange. In order to achieve the latter, Motion *et al.* (2016) summarized five social media engagement techniques: (1) Appeal to multiple values; (2) Connect with everyday meanings and practices; (3) Develop a network of advocates; (4) Inspire change by a governance (not control) approach; (5) Seed online conversations by listening and responding to online comments in a timely manner.

In a university context, Belenger *et al.* (2014) find that the more engaged students become online, that is, the more they comment, like, share or otherwise interact with a university, the more receptive and sympathetic they will become to institutional branding. Hence, engaging online students requires building digital communities where like-minded students congregate on social media as they might in a club. Belanger *et al.* (2014) also identified three approaches to engaging students online: (1) news feed and content production, particularly encouraging user-generated content (UGC) that allows peer-to-peer communication; (2) student-university interaction, mainly targeting a specific audience such as sports teams or interest groups, and urging discussions among the cohort or soliciting feedback on the university; (3) a hybrid approach combining these two.

To sum up the preceding literature, we can clearly identify that many universities tend to rely on social media for one-way promotion and transactional marketing, whereas relationship marketing from a broader community perspective is better suited to both higher education institutions and the social media environment. Although considerable efforts have been made to address the end and effect of relationship marketing, a large gap exists in the process, strategies, techniques and tactics of community building and relationship marketing on social media for universities. This gap will be addressed by the current case study.

Methods

Given its exploratory nature, this research applied a case study approach (Yin 2009) to exploring the state and strategies of using social media for university community-based relationship marketing. A public New Zealand university was chosen for two reasons. Firstly, it has the largest number of students enrolled in multiple campuses across three different cities in New Zealand, with one third being international students, while at the same time facing the pressure of retaining domestic students. Secondly, the university has actively used social media by embedding Facebook (with 52,230 likes), Twitter (with 10,800 followers) and YouTube (with 10,000 subscribers) into its main website.

Two sets of qualitative data were collected. One is eighteen in-depth interviews with the university's marketing team to gain insights into the overall online marketing strategies and the rationale of decision-making. The semi-structured interview guide covered issues such as the perceived importance of community building among marketers, ideal relationships with students, and social media engagement strategies and tactics. The other data set was gathered through content analysis of the university's Facebook pages, Twitter posts and YouTube videos for a semester span starting from 29 February to 3 June 2016 which, as justified by Belanger *et al.* (2014), is a reasonable time frame to capture the real-time social media usage in a full semester.

Two hundred and sixty-two pages of interview transcripts were analysed through inductive thematic analysis. Braun and Clarke (2006, p. 86) define 'thematic analysis' as 'searching across a data set…to find repeated patterns of meaning' and to link the synthesized data back to research questions and the theoretical framework. The social media content was analysed by using basic descriptive statistics, such as gauging the number of posts pertaining to a particular topic (e.g. paper offerings, course materials, success stories, research highlights, executive activities, events) and the number of student reactions (e.g. likes, shares, retweets, comments, views). To improve the research validity, a member-checking technique was applied by reporting the interview results back to the participants and asking them to verify the accuracy (Creswell 2009). Both interview data and content analysis were then cross-validated.

Lack of social media marketing strategies and the reasons behind this

The first major finding derived from the data is that the university has yet to develop a full social media marketing strategy in general, and a relationship marketing protocol in particular. Most participants shared that the current use of social media is tactical, fragmented and largely experimental. There are no clear guidelines as people are learning by doing. For example, one digital officer said, "It must be quite shocking to hear that we don't have a strategy but that's true." Another marketing officer added, "I think the university is a bit young when it comes to social media. We do it because it's trendy, but there hasn't been a strategy or any real thought into how we should do it and get value out of it." However, the participants held a strong belief in the value of social media and appeared keen to build a marketing strategy based on it and develop relationship and community building around the university. As one marketing executive explained:

> Eventually we want to build a community, provide a sense of belonging and make students feel part of the university by using social media, as opposed to a post that just says here is a brand. We are selling students not only a brand, but also a multi-faceted life, a living thing, a community.

The data continued to reveal several reasons for the absence of an overarching social media marketing strategy. One is lack of ownership of this new terrain of social media from the senior leadership team (SLT). In one participant's words, "It's unclear who takes leadership over this new land." The marketing team has hoped the SLT can be more visionary and drive a strategy from the top down, but they found even senior executives have no idea of how to do it. One participant said, "The SLT seems to be willing to invest serious amounts of money for new buildings to attract new students, but they won't invest small money like building a social media strategy."

Another reason for this lack of strategy relates to different views held by different clusters of professionals (e.g. marketing, recruitment, PR) about what it means to be 'strategic' in social media marketing – to present the university in the best light possible or to engage with wider communities. One participant explained, "Strategy is a contingent thing. My desired version of strategy might not be what others want."

A third reason was found relating to the internal resistance to social media technologies as the appetite for in public institutions is often not enormous. As one marketing practitioner described the situation, "People still feel nervous about social media and don't see them as a priority so marketing campaigns just start to go digital like everywhere else."

Content production is still king

Due to the absence of a social media marketing strategy, this study further found content production was used as a main approach to growing student communities and engaging them in a marketing process. An explicit emphasis has been put on delivering one-way information that either projects a positive image of the university or raises people's awareness of particular promotional materials. As shown in Table 3.2, the information online has covered a range of topics from course/programme promotion, campus life, faculty achievements, student success, events/workshops and SLT visiting activities.

According to the marketers' experience, while they tend to post practical information such as programme and course introductions, they realized the most well-received content (by counting the number of likes, shares, reposts) is about campus life, student success and events/workshop activities in which students can participate. This popular content shares common features such as originality,

TABLE 3.2 Content themes on three social media platforms between 29 Feb and 3 Jun 2016

Content themes	Facebook (posts)	Twitter (posts)	YouTube (posts)
Course/program promotion	44	56	16
Campus life	30	44	10
Faculty achievement	19	39	8
Student success	18	35	7
Events, activities, workshop	15	26	6
International collaboration	12	24	4
Senior leaders' activities	11	18	3
Industrial collaboration	9	14	2
Others	4	12	1
Total posts produced	**162**	**268**	**57**

authenticity, relevance, personality and fun, creating a strong emotional appeal. For example, as a content editor emphasized, "It's all about content, true stuff. Students nowadays can easily tell whether this is advertising. So we'd better write our own posts, take original photos, rather than duplicate the information that has already existed online."

Content on student success adds relevance and creates coalitions among students. As the content editor explained, "Students don't want big stories about impactful research but instead they like news about themselves and their peers." This was verified by the content analysis which found, for example, that a story about a distance learning student who studied extramurally for seven years and finally obtained a masters degree, was shared by 485 people on Twitter. In addition, personalized content based on popular culture also enjoyed support from students. A typical example is the 'Running Man' activity on Facebook, which called students from three campuses to dance in a Running Man style and then nominate peers to beat their moves. The marketing executive commented, "this is really engaging as we show future students there is a life on campus, rather than just showing them a product, say, an accredited program."

In addition to this type of self-produced content, the marketing team also tried to energize and invite present students to contribute user-generated content that, preferably, is favourable to the university. As well as this, marketers invited students to either provide positive comments and reviews under the university posts, or to upload personal narratives and stories to the official accounts. For example, a number of videos about students' overseas exchange experiences to promote the 'Study Abroad' programme were found on the university's YouTube channel, with 2,903 viewers.

Further, the university enlisted a team of student advocates as social media interns to provide fun, interesting and engaging content from a student perspective. The marketing director explained, "Posting student-generated content can provide a more authentic and vivid depiction of the university experience to future students than can pamphlets, brochures, and other traditional recruitment materials." Although the full potential of social media engagement (e.g. forums, chatrooms) has yet to be applied, the marketing director justified the value of one-way content production: "Content is still king because good content can at least help to build a consumer base to engage with."

Emerging tactics of community building

Although the preceding findings showed that there was no overarching strategy to social media use and that the university relied on content production for marketing, both interview and content analysis data indicated emerging tactics of building student communities as a foundation of relationship marketing. According to the participants, community-based marketing means two relationships that the university aims to establish. One is the relationship between the university and students, being alumni, current and prospective, in order to create a sense of belonging and attachment to the university. The other is to inspire students to develop their own communities around common interests, in order to pave a way for improved recruitment and retention through helping future students connect to their soon-to-be peers. The marketing manager articulated this situation as follows:

> Students need to feel that they belong to a community and if our social media are bland they don't get that feeling. So we want people to feel that it's a bit of a club that they belong to, and we deliver stuff that is tailored to them.

To this end, the data disclosed three tactics of community building for marketing benefits, including role model motivation, social network support, and top-down empowerment. Marketers employed role model motivation by selecting influential student representatives to share their learning experience online, tell how they overcame various hurdles or describe why they enjoy what they are doing. For instance, one disabled PhD student was established as a role model for pursuing his dream with commendable courage and perseverance. His story was then widely distributed on Facebook and Twitter so that a page, 'PhDs@Uni', was created as an inspiration for both current and future students having adventures within the university.

STARTSocial networks support refers to the university tends to attract and retain students by establishing social support systems. This is mainly done by embracing diverse cultures in the university and seeking every opportunity to celebrate different cultural festivals. For example, the Maori (a minor ethnic group in New Zealand) marketing officer shared her experience of engaging with Maori students:

> We really need to engage with Maori and Pacific students' extended families and communities. We want Facebook to actually speak to the whole family, not just to the students. We want to show Maori student achievements to their ethnic group and the whole country.

A third tactic of top-down empowerment refers to the endorsement from the senior management to empower a participatory approach to interacting and engaging with students. For example, the Vice-chancellor created his own Twitter account to post original contents or opinions, rather than reposting the template-like information prepared by the marketing office. He also retweeted student achievements or solicited public feedback on a university policy or initiative. This power sharing signalled a shift from the organisational deterministic approach to marketing, to a participatory mode of co-promoting the university brand. However, this top-down empowerment has not yet reached a critical mass. The university has yet to explore the full interactive potential of social media for the community-based relationship marketing.

Discussion and conclusion

The big-picture takeaway from this case study is that community-based relationship marketing, albeit considered important, is not yet largely practiced on the university social media. Inline with earlier studies (e.g., Fitch 2009; Macnamara & Zerfass 2012), this research found no overarching social media strategy even though the university embraces large followers probably "due to the prestige or brand recognition of the institution" (O'Hallarn, Morehead & Pribesh 2016, p. 40). Apart from the newness and changeable landscape of social media, this study revealed several reasons for the missing social media strategy. Unlike large firms with a clearly-structured and dedicated marketing team, there is a lack of ownership within the university as to who takes leadership over the new terrain of social media. Different perceptions of either earning quick gains or building long-term relationships, along with internal resistance to new technologies, hindered social media marketing towards a strategic level.

This study offers both practical and managerial implications for higher education institutions on social media content production which can serve as a starting point to grow student communities. Specifically, developing authentic and relevant content for prospective students will enable them to gain insights into the everyday campus life, form an emotional attachment to the university, increase their willingness to listen, and eventually transform their online behaviours (e.g., browsing, sharing) to offline action (e.g., paying tuition fees for enrolment). Personality-rich and fun contents deriving from popular culture with a link to "the everyday, the intimate, the immediate..." (Jenkins et al. 2002, p. 3) can show future students a real dynamic life that they might desire to join. Additionally, integrating student-generated content into social media can encourage future students to trust their soon-to-be peers' opinions more than advertising when making purchase decisions. Marketers should hence bear in mind producing high converting social media profiles that function to transform community members to potential customers.

Further, this study informs that community-based relationship marketing can only be successful when the social media engagement transcends from being *distributive*, pushing message awareness, to being *communicative*, enabling relational practice of value exchange. The findings identified a few techniques to achieve this communicative engagement. Role-model motivation, by leveraging peer influence, can not only inspire prospective students to pursue their dreams with a university, but also retain current students to learn from like-minded peers. Developing social networks support by engaging with students' families, ethnic groups and communities can attract and retain students, whose choices of universities are often shaped by their significant others. Additionally, the top-down empowerment from the senior leadership is critical to fostering dialogue and participatory culture online, which is the cornerstone to relationship marketing. This is particularly important for a public institution that has low risk-taking but high bureaucracies in innovating.

In conclusion, this study has offered the following insights and contributions:

- Refocusing on the value of community building and relationship marketing to address the overlooked conflict between the promotional nature of marketing and the participatory culture of social media. Social media marketing is no longer a "spectator sport" with excessive emphases on pushing message awareness to attract attention. An integrated community-based relationship marketing approach necessitates viewing customers as partners, contributors, and facilitators of social media marketing.
- Addressing the shortcomings of traditionally linear, promotional marketing by advancing social media engagement from a distributive to a *communicative* level. At this level, community-based relationship marketing should have participation and empowerment as its core to leverage the agency and creativity from wider communities.
- Providing a contextual understanding of how to steer social media, both strategically and operationally, to market universities that are nowadays prevalently being commercialised but still expected to fulfil social expectations.

References

Agnihotri, R., Kothandaraman, P., Kashyap, R. and Singh, R. (2012). Bring "social" into sales: The impact of salespeople's social media use on service behaviours and value cretion. *Journal of Personal Selling & Sales Management*, 32(3), 333–348.

Ang, L. (2011). Community relationship management and social media. *Journal of Database Marketing & Customer Strategy Management*, 18, 31–38.

Arnett, D. B., and Badrinarayanan, V. (2005). Enhancing customer-needs-driven CRM strategies: Core selling teams, knowledge management competence, and relationship marketing competence. *Journal of Personal Selling & Sales Management*, 25(4), 329–343.

Arnett, D. B., German, S. D., and Hunt, S. D. (2003) The identify salience model of relationship marketing success: the case of non-profit marketing. *Journal of Marketing*, 67, 89–105.

Baird, C. H., and Parasnis, G. (2011). From social media to social customer relationship management. *Strategy & Leadershp*, 39(5), 30–37.

Bal, A. S., Grewal, D., Mills, A., and Ottley, G. (2015) Engaging students with social media. *Journal of Marketing Education*, 37(3), 190–203.

Belanger, C. H., Bali, S., and Longden, B. (2014). How Canadian universities use social media to brand themselves. *Tertiary Education and Management*, 20(1), 14–29.

Berry, L. L. (1995). Relationship marketing of services: Growing interst, emerging perspectives. *Journal of the Academy of Marketing Science*, 3(4), 236–245.

Braun, V. and Clarke, V. (2006) Using thematic analysis in psychology. *Qualitative Research in Psychology*, 3, 77–101.

Charlesworth, A. (2014). *Digital marketing: A practical approach* (2nd ed.). London & New York: Routledge.

Chaston, I., and Mangles, T. (2001). E-commerce and small UK accounting firms: Influence of marketing style and orientation. *The Service Industries Journal*, 21(4), 83–99. doi: 10.1080/714005049

Constantinides, E., and Stagno, M. C. Z. (2011) Potential of the social media as instruments of higher education marketing: A segmentation study. *Journal of Marketing for Higher Education*, 21(1), 7–24.

Creswell, J. W. (2009) *Research design: Qualitative, quantitative and mixed methods approaches* (3rd ed.). Los Angeles: Sage.

Fitch, K. (2009) Making friends in the wild west: Singaporean public relations practitioners' perceptions of working in social media. *PRism*, 6(2). doi: http://www.prismjournal.org/fileadmin/Praxis/Files/globalPR/FITCH.pdf

Gibbs, P. (2002). From the invisible hand to the invisible handshake: Marketing higher eudcation. *Research in Post-compulsory Education*, 7(3), 325–338.

Gibbs, P., and Murphy, P. (2009) Implementation of ethical higher education marketing. *Tertiary Education and Management*, 15(4), 341–354

Grönroos, C. (1994), From marketing mix to relationship marketing: towards a paradigm shift in marketing, *Management Decision*, 32(2), 4–20.

Greenwood, G. (2012). Examining the presence of social media on university web sites. *Journal of College Admission*, 216, 24–28.

Harker, M.J. (1999) Relationship marketing defined? An examination of current relationship marketing definitions. *Marketing Intelligence & Planning*, 17(1), 13–20.

Harker, M. J., and Egan, J. (2006). The past, present and future of relationship marketing. *Journal of Marketing Management,* 22, 215–242.

Hemsley-Brown, J. V., & Oplatka, I. (2006) Universities in a competitive global marketplace: A systematic review of the literature on higher education marketing. *International Journal of Public Sector Management*, 19(4), 316–338.

Jenkins, H., McPherson, T., Shattuc, J., and Durham, N. C. (2002). *Hop on pop: The politics and pleasure of popular culture*. Durham: Duke University Press.

John, N. A. (2013). Sharing and web 2.0: The emergence of a keyword. *New Media & Society*, 15(2), 167–182.

Juarez, F. (2011). A critical review of relationship marketing: Strategies to include community into marketing in development contexts. *African Journal of Business Management,* 5(35), 13404–13409.

Laroche, M., Habibi, M., Richard, M., and Sankaranarayanan, R. (2012). The effects of social media based brand communities on brand community markers, value creation practices, brand trust and brand loyalty. *Computers in Human Behaviour,* 28, 1755–1767.

Lehtinen, U. (2011). Combining mix and relationship marketing. *The Marketing Review,* 11(2), 117–136.

Malthouse, E. C., Haenlein, M., Skiera, B., Wege, E., and Zhang, M. (2013). Managing customer relationships in the social media era: Introducing the social CRM house. *Journal of Interactive Marketing,* 27, 270–280.

McAllister, S. M. (2012). How the world's top universities provide dialogic forums for marginalized voices. *Public Relations Review*, 38, 319–327.

Macnamara, J. and Zerfass, A. (2012) Social media communication in organisations: The challenges of balancing openness, strategy and management. *International Journal of Strategic Communication*, 6(4), 287–308.

Mangold, W.G. and Faulds, D.J. (2009) Social media: The new hybrid element of the promotion mix. *Business Horizons* 52, 357–365.

Moller, K., and Halinen, A. (2000). Relationship marketing theory: Its roots and direction. *Journal of Marketing Management,* 16, 29–54.

Moorman, C., Zaltman, G., and Deshpande, R. (1992). Relationships between providers and users of market research: The dynamics of trust within and between organisations. *Journal of Marketing Research,* 29(3), 314–328.

Motion, J., Heath, R. L., and Leitch, S. (2016). *Social media and public relations: Fake friends and powerful publics*. London and New York: Routledge.

Ndubisi, N. O., & Chan, K. (2005). Factorial and discriminant analyses of the underpinnings of relationship marketing and customer satisfaction. *International Journal of Bank Marketing,* 23(7), 542–557.

Negi, R., and Ketema, E. (2010). Relationship marketing and customer loyalty: The Ethiopian mobile communications perspective. *Internationl Journal of Mobile Management,* 5(1), 113–124.

Ozkanal, B., and Uygucgil, G. (2016). Based on social media relationship marketing approach: A study on Anadolu University open education system website and the facebook network. *International Journal on New Trends in Education and Their Implications,* 7(2), 90–108.

O'Hallarn, B., Morehead, C. A., and Pribesh, S. L. (2016). Gaining S-T-E-A-M: A general athletic department social media strategy. *Journal of Issues in Intercollegiate Athletics,* 9, 39–61.

Pham, M. L. (2011). Social media as a marketing communication tool for non-profit organisations. (Master Thesis), Massey University, Albany, New Zealand.

Ramirez, G. B., and Palu-ay, L. (2015) "You don't look like your profile picture": The ethical implications of researching online identities in higher education. *Educational Research and Evaluation,* 21(2), 139–153.

Raciti, M. (2010). Marketing Australian higher education at the turn of the 21st century: A precis of reforms, commercialisation, and the new university hierarchy. *E-Journal of Business Education & Scholarship of Teaching,* 4, 32–41

Rossmann, D. and Young, S. W. H. (2015) Using social media to build community. *Computers in Libraries,* 18–22.

Rowe, G., Marsh, R. and Frewer, L. J. (2004) Evaluation of a deliberative conference. *Science, Technology & Human Values,* 29(1), 88–121.

Sashi, C. M. (2012). Customer engagement, buyer-seller relationships, and social media. *Management Decision,* 50(2), 253–272.

Sweetser, K. D. and Lariscy, R. A. W. (2008) Candidates make good friends: An analysis of candidates' use of Facebook. *International Journal of Strategic Communication,* 2, 175–198.

Szmigin, I., Canning, L., & Reppel, A. E. (2005). Online community: Enhancing the relationship marketing concept through customer bonding. *International Journal of Service Industry Management,* 16(5), 480–496.

Tapscott, D. (2009) *Grown up digital: How the net generation is changing your world*. New York, NY: McGraw-Hill.

Veloutsou, C., Saren, M., and Tzokas, N. (2002). Relationship marketing: What if...? *European Journal of Marketing,* 36(4), 433–449.

Yin, R. K. (2009) *Case study research: Design and methods* (4th ed.). Thousand Oaks, CA: Sage.

4

SOCIAL MEDIA MARKETING FOR B2B

From information to decision to retention

Roisin Vize and Monique Sherrett

Introduction

Social networks in a business context are referred to as two or more connected business relationships, where an 'exchange' exists between business partners. The concept of a 'network' is based on the establishment of ties between individuals, groups of people, organizational departments or corporations that lead to the creation of social networks (Michaelidou *et al.* 2011: 1,154). Advances in web-based technology and innovation have changed the nature of social networks. Where traditional social networks involve personal and social interaction between people, these interactions are now mediated by computers and web-connected devices such as mobile phones, laptops and e-notebooks. Social media marketing has fundamentally changed the way marketers communicate, interact, consume and create, both within and outside the firm. This form of marketing represents one of the most transformative impacts web technology has had on companies since the advent of the Internet (Dou *et al.* 2013). The growth of social media sites has revolutionized the way businesses relate to the marketplace, opening up new and exciting possibilities but also creating unprecedented challenges (Aral 2011; Kaplan and Haenlein 2010). As social media marketing has proliferated significantly from a B2C context, its uptake as a marketing tool in the B2B context is relatively meagre by comparison (Swani *et al.* 2014).

This chapter explores the benefits and challenges of social media marketing from a B2B perspective. It synthesizes theoretical and practitioner frameworks for understanding and resolving challenges relating to social media strategy development, tactical implementation and performance measurement. Practical recommendations along with best practice case examples highlight strategies a marketer can consider as they design, plan and integrate social media content for the modern, socially connected B2B buyer.

Social media marketing adoption: the benefits and challenges from a B2B perspective

B2B adoption of social media has been driven by new technologies and evolving buyer expectations for more consumer-like experiences. The changing nature of the connected consumer has striking implications for the business market (Kumar 2015) and, as B2C marketers have discovered already, it is not enough to be on social; the benefits are in *being* social.

Despite the relative novelty of social media marketing from a B2B perspective, empirical evidence shows that social media sites can be effectively used for a number of B2B marketing activities. Those include e-WOM (electronic word of mouth) opportunities facilitating brand exposure on a scale far greater, and more cost effectively, than the more traditional marketing methods. The social networking characteristics inherent in social media sites enhance communication, interaction and collaboration; for example, social media can be utilized to identify and attract new business partners (Siamagka *et al.* 2015). Social media can be used as an effective marketing communications tool to reach and engage with existing consumers, which industrial partners value. Such online interactions enable marketers to obtain valuable feedback in the form of comments, interactions and reactions online about products, services and the brand message (Michaelidou *et al.* 2011), which, when analyzed, allow them to better tailor a firm's offering to their business partners' needs. This in turn is directly related to an increased sales performance and greater return on investment. This marketing communications channel effectively allows B2B marketers to deepen relationships with their business partners, thus facilitating greater trust and loyalty between both parties (Agnihotri *et al.* 2016). It is therefore not surprising to hear that many B2B companies plan to double their social media marketing budgets within the next five years (CMI 2015).

Notwithstanding the numerous advantages arising from the use of social media sites by B2B professionals, Swani *et al.* (2014) suggest that one of the key challenges is the struggle to implement successful social media strategies. This is partly due to a poor understanding of how to use these sites for B2B marketing purposes as well as a perception that social media sites cannot support B2B marketing goals and objectives (Lacka and Chong 2016). Negative attitudes of marketing professionals towards the usefulness and usability of social media sites hinders the adoption of those sites in the B2B business environment. In addition to a lack of understanding of how to use social media sites in B2B marketing, a lack of control over communications is also a deterrent in its adoption as a B2B marketing tool (Michaelidou *et al.* 2011). There is an increased perception of risk due to marketers being unable to control the exchange of information online and fearing confidential information disclosure that may have a profound impact on future B2B business (Simula *et al.* 2013). As such, the two-way communication channel recognized earlier as a benefit of social media sites in the B2B sector may actually be perceived as a disadvantage, which seriously affects marketers' perception of social media sites' usability in the B2B environment.

Research also asserts there is a common belief among marketing professionals that social media sites do not fit with the nature of the B2B sector, where industrial partners are highly involved in the buying process, which requires face-to-face interaction and an individual, personal approach to building business relationships, something that cannot be achieved in an environment that is intangible and dynamic such as the web (Habibi *et al.* 2015; Michaelidou *et al.* 2011). The impersonal nature of the online environment is therefore yet another factor that creates a negative perception of the usability of SMM and hinders the adoption of social media sites in B2B marketing. Finally, there are also difficulties in assessing financial gains from these emerging digital channels coupled with a lack of suitable case evidence to help guide decision making. Fulfilling revenue expectations and identifying profitable leads comes under the direct influence of marketing. It is vital for marketers to focus on maintaining an ever productive marketing arm but this is a challenging task.

Understanding the factors that influence social media adoption from a B2B perspective is important as they can provide insight into key issues that need to be considered when a firm decides to utilize social media as a means to connect, communicate and collaborate with other businesses online. In so doing, managers are better equipped to make informed, strategic and timely decisions relating to campaign planning, development and execution. Decisions relating to identifying and implementing the appropriate tactical and measurement options to address goals and objectives are essential to facilitating satisfactory SMM campaign outcomes.

To date, a variety of models have been utilized to identify factors influencing user adoption of web-based technologies including the Theory of Planned Behaviour (TPB) (Ajzen 1991), the Unified Theory of Acceptance and Use of Technology (UTAUT) (Venkatesh, Thong and Xu 2012) and Technology Readiness (Vize, Coughlan, Kennedy and Ellis-Chadwick 2013) to name a few. This chapter employs the Technology Acceptance Model (TAM) (Davis 1989) as the framework to explore factors that facilitate and inhibit adoption of social media sites in a B2B context. This framework has been successfully utilized in recent research exploring social media adoption by B2B companies (Siamagka, Christodoulides, Michaelidou and Valvi 2015). The following section explores TAM in the context of B2B Web 2.0.

Technology acceptance model: a B2B Web 2.0 perspective

Rogers (2003) describes adoption as a decision by an individual or organization to fully utilize an innovation. The Technology Acceptance Model (TAM) (Davis 1989) has been used extensively to investigate and identify factors motivating a user's adoption of digital technologies. Rooted in the Theory of Reasoned Action (TRA) (Ajzen 1980), TAM is a specific and parsimonious framework for predicting and explaining people's adoption of new technologies in the workplace. Intention-based models such as TRA and TAM demonstrate that user behaviour can be effectively predicted by intentions, and intentions are determined by attitudes towards the behaviour in question (Lin, Shih and Sher 2007). TAM postulates that a user's acceptance of a new technology is determined by their intention to use the technology, which is influenced by their beliefs about the technology's perceived usefulness and perceived ease of use (Davis, Bagozzi and Warshaw 1989). The TAM relies on two fundamental variables to explain behaviour. These two variables are *perceived usefulness* of technology and *perceived ease of use*, which influence attitudes and usage intention, subsequently leading to adoption and usage behaviour of a specific technology (Davis *et al.* 1989). Perceived usefulness (PU) is defined as the degree to which one believes that using the technology will enhance his/her performance, while perceived ease of use (PEU) refers to the degree to which one believes that using the technology will be free of effort.

Web 2.0 is a relatively new concept, defined as 'technologies that enable users to communicate, create content and share it with each other via communities, social networks, and virtual worlds' (Jussila, Kärkkäinen and Leino 2011: 168). With advancements in web technology, particularly Web 2.0, users can set up a significantly more complex web presence in the form of, for example, a blog or a social media website, without having to consider the technological aspects of it. The rise of social media can be readily explained using the original TAM variables. The TAM suggests that perceived ease of use has a significant effect on perceived usefulness. Hence, the easier it is to use a specific technology, the more likely the users will find it useful. Siamagka *et al.* (2016) argue that the extent to which B2B organizations find social media easy to use positively impacts perceptions of usefulness in deciding to adopt social media as a marketing tool.

As indicated in Figure 4.1, a number of other key predictors of TAM have been suggested as influencing adoption of social media sites including

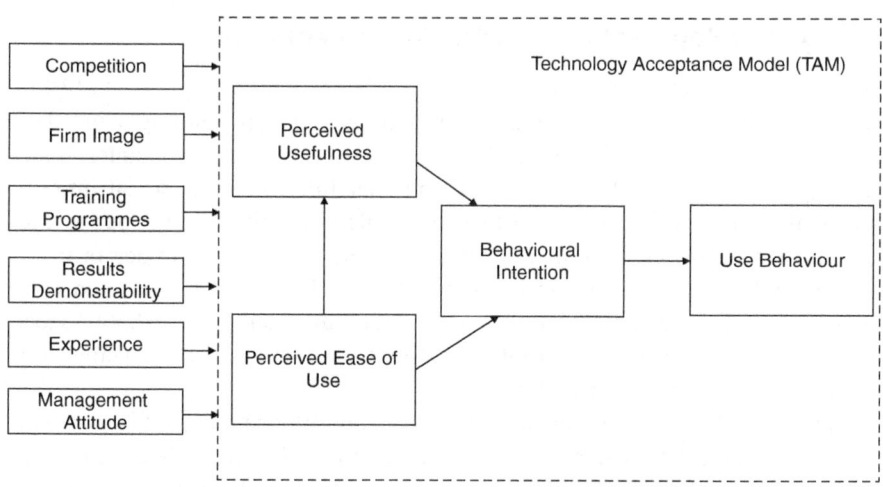

Technology Acceptance Model: Adoption of Social Media in a B2B context
(Adapted from Davis, 1989; Lacka & Chong, 2016; Siamagkaet al., 2016)

FIGURE 4.1 Social media marketing: strategy development, tactics and performance measurement.

managerial attitude and previous experience with the innovation, training programmes, results demonstrability and firm image. B2B firms that intend to adopt social media should seek to enhance their managers' perceptions about the usefulness of social media, address the perceived barriers through training programmes that will enhance employees' skills in social media and identify the importance and relevance of social media within their organizations (Siamagka *et al*. 2016). Previous experience with adopting new technological platforms for marketing purposes can influence positive attitudes towards the innovation and ultimately influence adoption behaviour. Research shows that those with more experience will have more realistic expectations and be better able to exploit the benefits of web-based platforms such as social media sites (Vize *et al*. 2013). Results demonstrability refers to the extent to which the results of using social media as a marketing tool are apparent, as well as one's ability to communicate the results to others within the firm. This is critical as conversion data is key to informing the future strategic direction of online marketing campaigns (Leeflang *et al*. 2014). Similarly, image captures the firm's perceptions about the prestige and status involved in using a specific technology and social media sites, which in turn influences perceptions about whether the technology is useful and effective in achieving objectives. Siamagka *et al*. (2016) argue that image is relevant to perceived usefulness of social media as an effective marketing tool.

The following section details elements management needs to consider when taking a structured approach to the strategic planning and tactical implementation of B2B social media marketing.

Strategy development and tactical implementation

Social media in a B2B context is of widespread interest, with 93 per cent of B2B marketers purporting to use social media as a marketing tactic, putting it ahead of other, more traditional tactics (CMI 2016) such as trade shows, catalogues, trade magazine advertising and direct mail. Firms that fully integrate social into all aspects of the enterprise use social listening tools to monitor market trends and shifts in attitude towards offerings. Their sales units use YouTube to demonstrate products and provide training to business partners. Customer success and customer support use social media tools to onboard partners and troubleshoot issues, and HR units use Facebook and LinkedIn groups, Twitter, and Slack channels for employee recruitment and retention.

Regardless of how social media is integrated, the value and impact is most felt by firms that take a S.M.A.R.T. approach to creating objectives. See Figure 4.2 for a breakdown of the S.M.A.R.T framework. Throughout the planning process, specific, measurable targets are set that must be achievable and realistic within given time frames.

The key to creating business value from social media is in planning and building strategies based on the buyer decision journey. This audience-centric approach

S.M.A.R.T

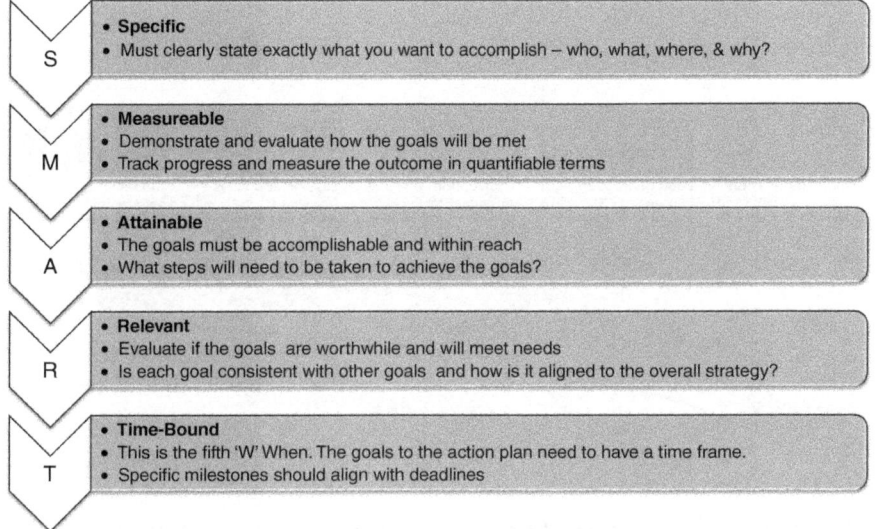

FIGURE 4.2 S.M.A.R.T framework.

Source: Author's own.

ensures that firms post and curate social media content that is of value to their business partners.

Stages of the buyer decision journey

As per Figure 4.3, the buyer decision journey is often portrayed as a funnel to help marketers understand what factors move buyers from information to decision to retention. In reality, the communication path is far from linear (Agnihotri *et al.* 2012) but the framework helps marketers effectively use social media for demand generation, lead generation, conversion optimization, customer success and customer satisfaction.

Stage one: awareness

With 89 per cent of B2B decision makers using the Internet during their research process (Google/Millward Brown Digital 2014), it becomes increasingly important for marketers to develop educational materials that can attract the attention of B2B researchers in the early stages of their journey and generate demand for further information. Edutainment content – material intended to educate and entertain – such as infographics and videos, is cited by business partners as the social media content they often share with colleagues responsible for purchase decisions (Google/Millward Brown Digital 2014).

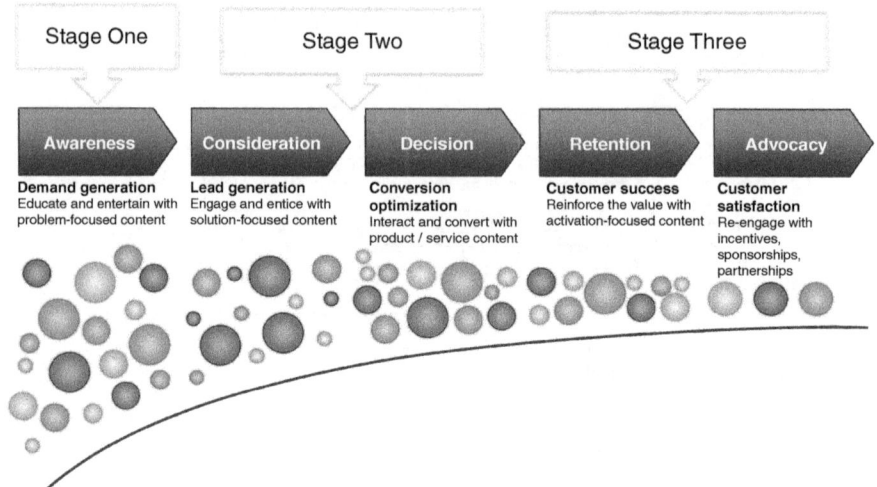

FIGURE 4.3 The buyer journey: from information, to decision, to retention.

Source: Author's own.

Tactical approaches to building brand awareness with edutainment

Edutainment content shared to social networks can gain vast exposure when supported by social media mentions and social advertising that targets specific profile types, topics or interests.

Case study: CSX Corporation

In 2015 CSX, the largest freight rail company in the eastern US, needed to increase awareness and generate demand for its intermodal services, a lower-cost, lower-emissions form of freight transportation that uses multiple modes (rail, ship and truck). Edutainment materials were used to educate two key audiences: logistics professionals and engaged citizens (an influential subset of the general population).

Strategy: CSX and Agency MullenLowe Winston Salem created 'The Intermodals', a highly entertaining campaign using sixteen sitcom-inspired videos and an 8-bit video game that allowed visitors to learn about intermodal from the driver's seat (theintermodals.com). The campaign was widely distributed on social media and earned substantial media attention, which drummed up civic support for, and commercial interest in, a valuable yet unknown transportation system.

Results: The Intermodals campaign positioned CSX as an industry leader, drove commercial interest in the service and gained support from the general public.

Social media channels and publicity drove traffic to The Intermodals' microsite, with Facebook and Twitter reportedly generating 3.9 million video views (adapted from http://shortyawards.com/8th/csx-the-intermodals).

Stage two: consideration and decision

The need for direct conversation between business partners and sales varies according to the complexity of the offering and the quality and quantity of available information. Practitioner-led research suggests that business partners are evaluating offerings using more video and more social media (Zimmerman and Blythe 2013; Google/Millward Brown 2014). Business partners engaged in social networking encounter invitations to download case studies and whitepapers, or to join webinars and other virtual events that put them in contact with subject-matter experts.

Tactical approaches to generating interest through thought leadership

Showcasing expertise through thought leadership and participation in community conversations increases reputation and ensures that business partners encounter a firm's offering at the early stages of their research.

Case study: Airbus

Leading aircraft manufacturer Airbus launched Airspace in early 2016, a new cabin design purportedly inspired by customer feedback on social media. Although aircraft sales are an industrial good, the cabin is a consumer-influenced product. Passengers review and compare the details of the on-board experience on social media and this has an impact on the airlines that purchase aircraft from Airbus. Airbus credits social media reviews for providing their designers with insights into the cabin experience, and that customer preference information is used in the sales process to persuade airlines that Airspace is the flyer-preferred option (Garcia 2016).

Stage three: retention and advocacy

A social media strategy is not complete once the transaction is finalized. Activation- and engagement-oriented content on social media can reinforce the value of the offering, increase satisfaction with the product and empower business partners to seek support from a network of peers.

Tactical approaches to retaining customers through service excellence

Customer experience is a key differentiator for firms. It is the business partner's perception of the product/service experience, and all the processes and interactions with the firm. A customer experience strategy integrated with social media can deepen and sustain business relationships.

Case study: Amex OPEN

Objective: American Express regularly produces marketing education programmes aimed at helping its business partners drive business growth. They learned from commissioned research that small businesses see greater results when they advertise that they accept the card, yet many fail to do so. The objective of the 'Love My Store' campaign, created by Agency Attention Global and American Express, was to increase orders and placement of Amex signage among small businesses across the US.

Strategy: Amex collaborated with celebrity designers and retail experts to offer merchants insights into store design. The campaign included a series of videos showcasing how various types of small businesses use their store design and signage to bring in more customers. The #LoveMyStoreAmexContest on Twitter and Instagram ran in conjunction with the programme and offered merchants a chance to win $10,000 towards a storefront redesign and a one-on-one design consultation (Amex 2015).

Results: Amex leveraged the influence of participating design experts to generate broad awareness of the campaign, engagement with the educational content, participation in the social media contest and orders requests for the new, fashionably designed Amex decals (Shorty Awards 2015).

- Awareness: campaign content from participating design experts and Amex social channels drove 5 million impressions.
- Behaviour: those impressions earned over 50,000 social engagements from small business owners.
- Outcomes: over 400,000 Love My Store decals were distributed, making the series the most-ordered of all available Amex decals.

Performance measurement

As social media adoption by B2B firms increases so too does the interest in social media monitoring and analytics. Social analytics refers to the tools a marketer can avail of to monitor the effectiveness of social media. Monitoring includes listening, interacting, influencing and reflecting on the positive, neutral and negative expressions about a firm's product and services. Social media is an emerging channel and so the tools used continue to evolve. In general, metrics are grouped according to outcomes, or key performance indicators (KPIs), along the inbound marketing funnel.

- **Acquisition metrics** such as total fans or followers, and ad impressions for paid media, are about measuring how well a tool is doing at reaching the firm's largest, addressable audience.

- **Behaviour metrics** such as post likes, comments and shares, and click-through rates for paid media, qualify how well a tool is doing at engaging the audience, not just reaching it.
- **Conversion metrics** like leads or lead conversion rate, or cost per lead for paid media, are used to track higher levels of commercial intent and are associated with non-revenue generating actions such as email subscriptions, downloads, form completions or other types of content engagement like viewing a video to completion. Revenue-generating actions such as ecommerce purchases are measured by tracking total transactions, total revenue and average order value. Cost-per-conversion and revenue-per-click metrics report on the efficiency of paid campaigns.
- **Retention** metrics such as lifetime value and referrals can be integrated with other sales and customer data systems to track customer health and advocacy.

Measuring ROI: social media and sales

Measuring the return on investment (ROI) of social media has been a long-standing blind spot for many marketers. Actionable intelligence requires robust data sets, analysts and IT support; nevertheless, even a basic combination of website and social analytics can provide marketers with data that drives decision making related to marketing spend. Manually combining website and social analytics, or using tools like *True Social Metrics,* as seen in Figure 4.4, offer four metrics that help a firm determine their share of conversation, reach, relevance and financial impact: conversation rate, amplification rate, applause rate and economic value.

The metrics are calculated as follows and can be used in varying ways to determine resource allocations (Kaushik 2011).

Conversation rate = # of audience comments (or replies) per post

Conversation rate in combination with sentiment analysis (or opinion mining) tracks the volume and tone of conversations. A high conversation rate with positive sentiment suggests high engagement with the content, while a high conversation rate with negative sentiment offers insights into areas for discussion or improvement.

Amplification rate = # retweets or shares per post

Amplification rate is used to understand what types of content get shared most. The more sharing the better as this peer-to-peer action represents valuable eWOM (electronic word of mouth), which helps firms expand their networks.

Applause rate = # of favourites (likes or +1s) per post

Applause, like in real life, is a sign of approval. When followers like or favourite content it is effectively an endorsement, or sign of relevancy, which is visible to that person's followers.

	Conversation rate↓↑	Amplification rate↓↑	Applause rate↓↑	Economic value↓↑	Posts↓↑	Comments↓↑	Shares↓↑	Favorites↓↑
Twitter	2.77	17.03	14.35	0.24	178	493	3032	2555
Facebook Page	58.02	201.82	2800.14	0.0 0	56	3249	11302	156808
Google+	1.80	7.23	21.25	0.0 ⑦	185	333	1338	3931
Blog	80.00	2658.67	434.00	0.23	3	240	7976	1302
YouTube	11.29	14.29	69.43	0.0 ⑦	7	79	100	486
LinkedIn	0.00	0.00	0.00	0.0 0	0	0	0	0
Tumblr	0.81	9.91	41.96	none ⑦	103	83	1021	4322
Instagram	150.67	14.16	14461.65	none ⑦	43	6479	609	621851
SlideShare	12.50	131.71	614.50	none ⑦	14	175	1844	8603

FIGURE 4.4 Social media metrics dashboard.

Source: True Social Metrics, https://www.truesocialmetrics.com.

Effective social media also moves followers beyond engagement within social tools and to the firm's website where further interactions occur, such as email sign up, whitepaper download or click to call. B2B marketers actively using data-driven decision-making assign a value to those actions in their web analytics programme in order to calculate economic value or value per visitor.

Economic value = sum of short- and long-term revenue and cost savings

It is the economic value metric that differentiates the channels that are most effective for converting business partners at the purchase stage of the funnel, whereas conversation, amplification and applause rates indicate the channels that are effective for those at the awareness, consideration and retention stage.

Measurement across social media, apps and websites requires integration of several sources of data:

- web and app tracking platforms track app and website traffic (e.g. Google Analytics, Kissmetrics, Adobe Analytics, Mixpanel, IBM Digital Analytics)
- social media analytics help marketers assess their audience size and engagement rates (e.g. analytics.twitter.com, Facebook Insights)
- third-party analytics in combination with the above two analytics platforms offer additional insights into audience size and engagement, as well as comparative insights on industry benchmarks and competitors (e.g. Simply Measured, Radian6)

It is essential to understand social analytics. Firms not ready to adopt social media can focus on social listening and monitoring while those more active on social media can focus on increasing their firm's visibility, deepening relationships and generating business value, all of which can be tracked and measured using social analytics.

Conclusion

This chapter has looked at social media marketing from a B2B perspective. A thorough discussion of the factors that facilitate and inhibit SMM adoption within the firm highlighted key issues marketing managers need to address when considering utilizing the emerging social media space as a marketing tool. The use of the Technology Adoption Model provides a theoretical perspective into key issues the modern firm faces when considering adopting and using social media marketing.

The key points from this chapter are:

- Social media sites can support B2B marketing goals and objectives when attention is paid to strategic planning and integration of social media in the sales cycle.

- The buyer journey offers an important framework for strategically planning content and promotions that effectively move buyers from information to decision to retention.
- Social media is rapidly changing the B2B market and firms positioned to leverage these new communication tools for demand generation and customer satisfaction are outpacing their peers.

References

AMEX. 2015. 'Make Your Storefront Stand Out with #LoveMyStore'. Available at https://knowledgecenter.americanexpress.com/love-my-store-overview/. Accessed 5 October 2016.

Agnihotri, R., R. Dingus, M. Y. Hu and M. T. Krush. 2016. 'Social media: influencing customer satisfaction in B2B sales'. *Industrial Marketing Management*, 53: 172–180.

Agnihotri, R., P. Kothandaraman, R. Kashap and R. Singh. 2012. 'Bringing "social" into sales: the impact of salespeople's social media use on service behaviors and value creation'. *Journal of Personal Selling & Sales Management*, 32: 333–348.

Aral, S. 2011. 'Commentary-identifying social influence: a comment on opinion leadership and social contagion in new product diffusion'. *Marketing Science*, 30: 217–223.

Ajzen, I. 1991. 'The theory of planned behavior'. *Organizational Behavior and Human Decision Processes*, 50(2): 179–211.

Content Marketing Institute (CMI). 2015. '2016 Benchmarks, Budgets, and Trends—NorthAmerica'. Available at http://contentmarketinginstitute.com/wpcontent/uploads/2015/09/2016_B2B_Report_Final.pdf ed. Accessed 22 June 2016.

Davis, F. D. 1989. 'Perceived Usefulness, Perceived Ease of Use, and User Acceptance of Information Technology'. *MIS Quarterly,* 13: 319–340.

Davis, F. D., R. P. Bagozzi and P. R. Warshaw. 1989. 'User acceptance of computer technology: a comparison of two theoretical models'. *Management Science,* 35: 982–1,003.

Dou, Y., M. F. Niculescu and D. J. Wu, D. J. 2013. 'Engineering Optimal Network Effects via Social Media Features and Seeding in Markets for Digital Goods and Services'. *Information Systems Research,* 24: 164–185.

Garcia, M. 2016. 'Airbus unveils the air cabin that social media built'. Available at http://mashable.com/2016/03/24/airbus-airspace-cabin-design. Accessed 22 June 2016.

Google and Millward Brown Digital. 2014. *B2B Path to Purchase.* Available at https://www.millwardbrowndigital.com. Accessed 22 June 2016.

Habibi, F., C. A. Hamilton, M. J. Valos and M. Callaghan. 2015. 'E-marketing orientation and social media implementation in B2B marketing'. *European Business Review,* 27: 638–655.

Jussila, J., H. Kärkkäinen and M. Leino. 2011. 'Benefits of social media in business-to-business customer interface in innovation'. *MindTrek '11 Proceedings of the 15th International Academic MindTrek Conference: Envisioning Future Media Environments*, 167–174.

Kaplan, A. M. and M. Haenlein. 2010. 'Users of the world, unite! The challenges and opportunities of social media'. *Business Horizons*, 53(1): 59–68.

Kaushik, A. 2011. 'Best social media metrics: Conversation, amplification, applause, economic value'. Available at http://www.kaushik.net/avinash/best-social-media-metrics-conversation-amplification-applause-economic-value. Accessed 22 June 2016.

Lacka, E. and A. Chong. 2016. 'Usability perspective on social media sites' adoption in the B2B context'. *Industrial Marketing Management,* 54: 80–91.

Leeflang, P. S., P. C. Verhoef, P. Dahlström and T. Freundt. 2014. 'Challenges and solutions for marketing in a digital era'. *European Management Journal,* 32: 1.

Lewis, J., P. Whysall and C. Foster. 2014. 'Drivers and technology-related obstacles in moving to multichannel retailing'. *International Journal of Electronic Commerce,* 18: 43–68.

Lin C. H., H. Y. Shih, and P. Sher. 2007. 'Integrating technology readiness into technology acceptance: the TRAM model'. *Psychology & Marketing,* 24(7): 641–657.

Michaelidou, N., N. T. Siamagka and G. Christodoulides. 2011. 'Usage, barriers and measurement of social media marketing: an exploratory investigation of small and medium B2B brands'. *Industrial Marketing Management,* 40: 1,153–1,159.

Rogers, E. M. 2003. *Diffusion of innovations.* New York.

Shorty Awards. 2015. 'Love my store campaign – the Shorty Awards Finalist in Business to Business. Available at http://shortyawards.com/8th/love-my-store-campaign. Accessed 22 June 2016.

Siamagka, N. T., G. Christodoulides, N. Michaelidou and A. Valvi. 2015. 'Determinants of social media adoption by B2B organizations'. *Industrial Marketing Management,* 51: 89–99.

Simula, H., A. Töllinen and H. Karjaluoto. 2013. 'Crowdsourcing in the social media era: a case study of industrial marketers'. *Journal of Marketing Development and Competitiveness,* 7: 122.

Swani, K., B. P. Brown and G. R. Milne. 2014. 'Should tweets differ for B2B and B2C? An analysis of Fortune 500 companies' Twitter communications'. *Industrial Marketing Management,* 43: 873–881.

Venkatesh, V., J. Thong, and X. Xu. 2012. 'Consumer acceptance and usage of information technology: extending the unified theory of acceptance and use of technology'. *MIS Quarterly,* 36(1): 157–178.

Vize, R., J. Coughlan, A. Kennedy and F. Ellis-Chadwick. 2013. 'Technology readiness in a B2B online retail context: an examination of antecedents and outcomes'. *Industrial Marketing Management,* 42: 909–918.

Watson, G. F., J. T. Beck, C. M. Henderson and R. W. Palmatier. 2015. 'Building, measuring, and profiting from customer loyalty'. *Journal of the Academy of Marketing Science,* 43: 790–825.

5

SOCIAL MEDIA STAKEHOLDER CO-CREATION OF CELEBRITIES AS HUMAN BRANDS

Dave Centeno

Celebrity sponsorship and advertising in social media as a context of marketing communication are an apt venue for studying how different stakeholders – advertisers, press, talent management, broadcast networks, consumers/fans and celebrities themselves – are gathered together in an assemblage of service in co-creating human brand identities, which in turn provide service back to these stakeholders' own incentives. With the advent of social media as a rich avenue of social reality, the outlets for co-creation have become discursive and dynamic for celebrity stakeholders to create, re-create, persuade and negotiate identities for social and economic purposes (Burgess and Green 2009; Boffard 2014). This paper explores the role of social media in understanding the co-creation processes that occur in human brand identities in celebrities among stakeholder-actors. The hybrid term 'stakeholder-actor' refers to the combined functions of a 'stakeholder' who can affect and is affected (Freeman 1984) by the objectives of the celebrity human brand, and an 'actor' who may not strictly be a stakeholder (according to the criteria set by the stakeholder theory) but, in a more sociological sense, has agency according to Giddens' structuration theory (1984) and Latour's actor-network theory (1988). In other words, a stakeholder-actor is defined as a proactive identity that acts on a creation and receives the benefits of the creation.

Celebrities are human brands – their performances on- and offstage, off- and online, in public or private, are marketing and branding exercises. Their everyday life choices and values, which are intrinsically private, performed in public, become brands and branding identities. Consequently, these created human brand identities sell product brands through endorsements and persuasions by giving personality qualities to inanimate brands, and they encourage consumption through being an idealized consumer and a commodity vessel (Holmes and Redmond 2014).

This paper extends 'human brands' as 'any well-known persona who is the subject of marketing communication efforts' (Thomson 2006: 104) by analysing their identities as a 'multi-dimensional classification or mapping of the human world and our places in it, as individuals and as members of collectivities' (Jenkins 2014: 5). The recent development in branding literature shifts from merely focusing on brand image or brand differentiation to include brand identity in the total brand equity (Keller 2003). The early definition of brand identity (Aaker 1996) describes it as a unique set of brand associations that a brand strategist aspires to create or maintain. These combined definitions of human brand and identities make it apt to study a celebrity's human brand identity as a multidimensional classification and mapping of human concepts on 'who they are, and who they are *seen* to be ... and who they are in our lives' (Jenkins 2014: 3), both as individuals and as members of communities that can be relevant to marketing efforts. Human brand identities take place in a collective and collaborative notion of a social co-creation process by multiple providers of identity as stipulated by Service-Dominant (S-D) Logic, as adopted by the evolving brand logic (Merz, He and Vargo 2009). Complementarily, the stakeholder paradigm in co-creation is inherently compatible with the framework of the human brand identity co-creation process, which is understood as a set of interrelationships among groups that have a stake in the activities that make up a business – here, celebrity human brand identity co-creation. Although celebrities may be in various forms of public identity formation and consumption, such as the popularity of 'microcelebrities' and 'instacelebrities' in social media, this research focuses on the traditional definition of a celebrity – individuals who are popular in mainstream media entertainment. This systematically illustrates a stakeholder-actor paradigm in co-creation.

Service-Dominant Logic in human brands

Co-creation has recently emerged as a central component in contemporary businesses and marketing (Ramirez 1999). It refers to the processes in which both consumers and producers participate, collaborate and co-produce value (Vargo and Lusch 2004). There are two emerging perspectives in understanding co-creation: S-D Logic (Vargo and Lusch 2004) and working consumers (Cova and Dalli 2009; Zwick *et al.* 2008). From the S-D Logic perspective, all parties in the market are eligible and always co-creating (value) through service, and they gain benefits in a harmonious relationship in which all parties are viewed as partners (Lovelock and Gummesson 2004; Lusch and Vargo 2006). Meanwhile, the working consumers perspective sees the immaterial labour of consumers as doubly exploited: consumers are not paid for the co-creation, and they are asked to pay a premium for the 'fruits' of their co-creation (Cova and Dalli, 2009; Zwick *et al.* 2008). However, Pongsakornrungsilp and Schroeder (2011) argue that double exploitation need not necessarily threaten value co-creation; rather, it activates consumer empowerment and sacrifice. To the extent that this claim applies to the current research, the human brand identity co-creation process takes on the former perspective, as stakeholders are co-creating parties that have their own stake in co-creation activities. While the human brand identity follows the S-D Logic co-creation para-digm, it further extends propositions of the logic from its extensive literature.

The S-D Logic, meanwhile, as an emerging school of thought within market-ing, is open for further elaboration, refinement and development (Edvardsson, Tronvoll and Gruber 2011). This logic advances the idea that all providers in a business are essentially service providers of value (Vargo and Lusch 2004). Service is defined as the use of resources for the benefit of another party, which forms the basis for all exchanges (Vargo and Lusch 2008c). In a recent work, Lusch and Vargo (2014) summarize the S-D Logic into four axioms based on its few years of development: (1) service is the fundamental basis of exchange, (2) the customer is always a co-creator of value, (3) all economic and social actors are resource integrators, and (4) value is always uniquely and phenomenologi-cally determined by the beneficiary. These axioms are inherently open for further development and refinement of the logic as possibilities are called for to advance the basic premises of the S-D Logic (Lusch and Vargo 2014). In particular, although the S-D Logic suggests that dynamic and adaptive resource integrations (i.e. 'adaptive competence') take place in the value co-creation process, further refinement of this aspect can contribute to developing the idea of co-creation in the service paradigm (Lusch *et al.* 2007; Vargo *et al.* 2008). Specifically, we aim to demonstrate an adaptive brand identity stakeholder co-creation where parties involved can adapt to and proactively influence the dynamic social and cultural realities that make up a human brand identity.

Moreover, although the above-mentioned axioms are primarily drawn on *value* co-creation *per se*, mostly based on institutions, goods and services (offerings), co-created *brand identity* beyond value is scarce in empirical investigation except for a few related works assuming the perspective of the S-D Logic in brands (e.g. Merz, He and Vargo 2009) and identifying the multi-stakeholder view in the co-creation of brand meaning (Kornum and Mühlbacher 2013; Vallaster and von Wallpach 2013). However, research has not been conducted to explicitly utilize the S-D Logic in understanding human brand identity co-creation using a multi-stakeholder approach, nor, in particular for our interests, through social media co-creation resources.

Social media in co-creation

The advent of new social media technologies and platforms paves the way to a more open-access multi-stakeholder engagement and interactions that could be publicly performed (Asmussen *et al.* 2013). The availability and nature of social media interactions enable stakeholders to become more 'engaged and cultur-ally adept social actors' to co-create with other actors with a range of social and economic interests (Handelman 2006: 107). Therefore, social media serve as an avenue and medium of stakeholder co-creation, and in particular, human brand identities in celebrities. Logan (2015) asserts that through social media ethnogra-phy, celebrities can be observed and interacted with directly.

How then does the social media perform human brand identity co-creation? Because social media require mostly written language to practise and participate in brand identity co-creation, linguistic and hermeneutic approaches make it possible for research to study brand identity co-creation (cf. Hatch and Rubin 2006). One basic assumption that underlies this approach is that language use is a social practice that constructs aspects of social reality among actors (Cherrier 2009). Through a discourse that is constantly enriched through evolving interactions and interpretations among multiple stakeholders, social media represent textual expressions of the stakeholders' *intended* reality that builds up an identity (Muehlbacher and Hemetsberger 2008). Stakeholders co-create human brand identities in the celebrity by their integration of their own knowledge, elaborations, expectations, evaluations and appreciations. In other words, social media develop and encourage a discursive social process where stakeholders can participate freely and willingly to directly or indirectly contribute to the written text of human brand identity aspects based on the resources that stakeholders integrate throughout the process (Muehlbacher and Hemetsberger 2008). Also, through social media participation, stakeholders gain their own 'stake' for their participation, be they social or economic benefits.

Research gaps and calls for theory development support the goal of the present study to theorize on the social media co-creation process of human brand identities. The present study seeks to broaden the current thought on service exchange and the identity co-creation process by understanding a set of interrelationships among parties that have a win-win stake in the activities that make up a business; here, a celebrity human brand identity co-creation happening in the terrain of social media. Thus, the first research question is: how does human brand identity co-creation happen in a multi-stakeholder-actor approach? Moreover, we extend the S-D Logic by demonstrating that the service exchanges and stakeholders' roles in the co-creation process are dynamic in adaptive identity co-creating service systems founded in the prevailing consumer culture mirrored in the social media interaction. To explicate this theoretical development proposition, the second research question is: what sociocultural codes guide stakeholders in their co-creation of celebrity human brand identities?

Research inquiry

Research approach

Netnography, or Internet ethnography, is used in this research to understand how social media interactions form human brand identities among celebrities involving different stakeholders. Netnography is defined as a specific set of related data collection, analytical, ethical and representational research practices where a significant amount of the data collected and participant-observational research conducted originates from, and manifests through, digital communication data

(Kozinets 2015). In this paper, the researcher explores the Philippines' celebrity culture, both as a scholar and as a part of the audience's culture (i.e. 'autoethnography', cf. Holmes, Ralph and Redmond 2015), in observing how different social media actors (i.e. stakeholders) interact with, reformulate and stabilize celebrity human brand identities. The researcher, though unobtrusive, is a real-time observant of Facebook and Twitter social media interactions and an active YouTube user and viewer. This real-time observational research tool reflexively places the researcher in both an emic (insider) and an etic (outsider) point of view. Archival netnographic data provide a cultural baseline for analysis, offering a large amount of data, and categories for interpretation emerge from the ground up (Kozinets 2015). Through the Internet, celebrities themselves, or the agents that handle them, namely outside corporate streams, can directly negotiate their fame and brand presentation. The flow of negotiation is a complex one that allows for media mobility, interactivity and archivability of past records of interactions, akin to an online public diary (Trammel and Keshelashvili 2005). Online brand communities have become an accepted and stable avenue for rich resources of brand creations (Vallaster and von Wallpach 2013). This happens because such a naturally qualitatively data-rich reservoir provides an unparalleled platform in less restrictive, more realistic and engaging online presentations of identity, authenticity, power and value (Vallaster and von Wallpach 2013). This technique offers ways of documenting and analysing the co-creating parties in their natural environment. Netnography has shown to be a capable and reliable tool for branding research (Giesler 2006).

The empirical study considers four celebrity human brand identities as a case study of the stakeholder co-creation processes, from the social media platforms most popular in the Philippines (i.e. Facebook, Twitter and YouTube), giving a glimpse of the complex phenomenon of stakeholder co-creations. The research context, the Philippines, provides an exemplary social media usage, with reports that it is one of the highest in both Asia and the world in recent years (Mander, 2014). According to statistics, in 2014 alone, 39 per cent of the 100-million-strong population of the Philippines are social media users: 30 million have Facebook accounts, 4.9 million have Twitter accounts, and 24 million have accessed YouTube (*Digital Marketing Philippines* 2014). These figures project salience in the social reality among stakeholders and the celebrity identities where the co-creation happens. In addition, the Philippines is considered one of the Asian societies where celebrity culture is integrated into the social, economic and political activities of many stakeholders (Schmitt 2014). Finally, since the Philippines has a highly collectivistic culture, social media are a popular everyday socialization tool among individuals and many businesses in the country (Smith and Zook 2011).

Three social media platforms were selected as the most popular participatory resources of co-creation inputs from stakeholders, namely, Facebook, Twitter and YouTube. A two-week time frame for observations of social media interactions among the four celebrity exemplars was set for Facebook and Twitter platforms, from 11 to 25 March, 2015. This short time frame provides a rich archival dataset for the two social media platforms for their active usage and salience among users. The 'official' Facebook and Twitter accounts of the celebrity exemplars served as data touchpoints from where account information, posts and comments were extracted. Meanwhile, a five-year data time frame from March 2011 to March 2015 was given to study YouTube video posts from different sources and comments elicited among the viewers. The topics vary accordingly, illustrating how various stakeholders apparently participate in celebrity identity co-creation. In total, the data sample from the social media archive comprises 304 posts with 34,767 aggregated comments (and 'retweets' on Twitter). Apparently, these social media outlets have become discursive and dynamic platforms for celebrity stakeholders to create, re-create, persuade and negotiate identities for social and economic purposes (Burgess and Green 2009).

The data utilized come from a collection of archival netnographic data containing social media communal interactions in the past that were unaffected by the actions of the researcher (or netnographer) (Kozinets 2015). A linguistic and hermeneutical approach is used to analyse stakeholder brand identity co-creations (Hatch and Rubin 2006; Holt 2002; Vallaster and von Wallpach 2013; Pongsakornrungsilp and Schroeder 2011). This analytical approach is also consistent with the methodological guidance offered by Belk *et al.* (2013).

Compared with the typical Internet ethnographic (netnographic) data, archival netnographic data are non-elicited and unaffected by the actions of the netnographer, akin to historical archival methods (Kozinets 2015). Archival netnographic data provide a cultural baseline for analysis, offering a large amount of data, and categories for interpretation emerge from the ground up (Kozinets 2015). Through the Internet, celebrities or the agents that handle them, outside the corporate streams, can directly negotiate their fame and brand presentation. The flow of negotiation is a complex one that allows for media mobility, interactivity and archivability of past records of interactions, akin to an online public diary (Trammel and Keshelashvili 2005). Online brand communities have become an accepted and stable avenue for rich resources of brand creations (Vallaster and von Wallpach 2013). This happens because such a naturally qualitatively datarich reservoir provides an unparalleled platform in less restrictive, more realistic and engaging online presentations of identity, authenticity, power and value (Marwick 2005; Men and Tsai 2013; Vallaster and von Wallpach 2013). This technique offers ways of documenting and analysing the co-creating parties in their natural environment. Netnography has shown to be a capable and reliable tool for branding research (Avery 2007; Giesler 2006; Mathwick *et al.* 2008). For example, Dolbec and Fischer (2015) utilized the archival netnographic data collection approach as a part of their methodology to track the dynamic connections between consumers and institutions in the fashion market. Archival netnographic research is a cultural baseline for understanding communal interactions, providing the netnographer with a bank of observational data stretching back years (Kozinets *et al.* 2010).

Findings

Human brand identity co-creation always resides in the intersections connecting actors during resource integration. The co-creation process happens in both direct and indirect exchanges among stakeholder-actors (Lusch and Vargo 2014). This is akin to the actor-network's claim that the social translation of projects happens through 'negotiations, intrigues, calculations, acts of persuasion … to which an actor or force takes on, or an authority to speak or act on behalf of another actor or force' (Callon and Latour 1981: 279).

As Figure 5.1 illustrates the interrelationships among stakeholders of celebrity identity, the arrows also show that the co-creation sub-processes intersect the stakeholders in their participation and benefits in celebrity identity co-creation. Based on the large amount of data gathered and the retracing of literature, I next present the underlying sociocultural codes using a hermeneutic approach, identifying the themes that stakeholders take in their resource integrations during co-creation.

This section describes the intersections and social translations among the actors that make up the human brand identity co-creation. I describe the online human brand identity co-creation as a result of sociocultural codes and mechanisms. (Due to space limitations, representative netnographic quotes are not available in this chapter but are available at this link: https://socialmediacocreation.wordpress.com)

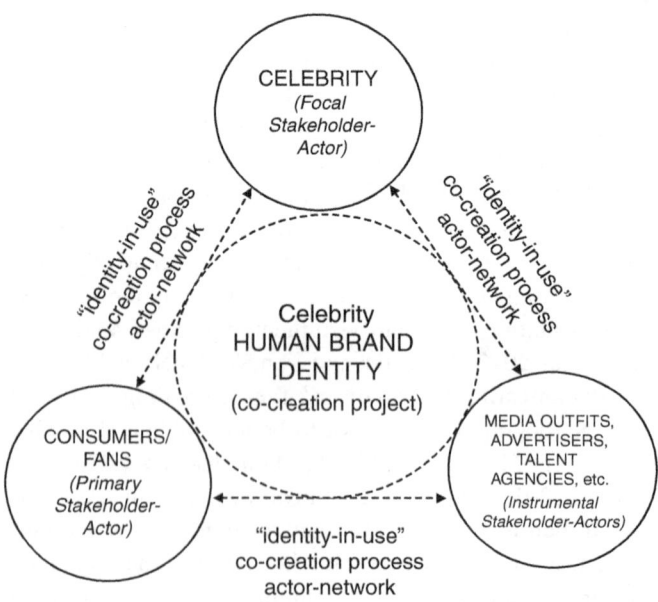

FIGURE 5.1 Stakeholder-actor co-creation of human brand identity.

Negotiation and social construction

Human brand identities are formed through a collaborative (Holt 2004) yet indeterminately orchestrated co-creation of human brand identities, constructed as stories and conversations about the celebrity collide. Stories and active engagement and participation by stakeholders are apparent in human brand identity co-creation. Interestingly, celebrities themselves seem to actively participate in the co-creation social project of brand identity. In his daily posts on Twitter, Manny Pacquiao co-creates his idealized identity, which can be easily appreciated by his followers: a fighter for the country, a God-fearing person and a man with norm-based wisdom. These posts manifest the active participation of Manny himself in the co-creation of his identity.

A greater impact of an instrumental stakeholder's participation in the co-creation, however, may manifest from more legitimate press or media content such as television news and documentaries. The Biography channel, for instance, creates content featuring distinguished personalities from across the globe and eventually posts such content online. In the same way, television content posted on social media makes more credible social construction and negotiation of brand identity through its cultivation effects (Gerbner 1998).

This collective understanding of the identity negotiated for a celebrity constitutes the human brand identity validation process. Although several stories and narratives (i.e. resources) compose the overall identity, the identity created for the celebrity serves as an essence of content and utility ('identity-in-use') of the human brand according to the iterative nature of the stakeholder co-creation. Through repetition and the responsiveness of stakeholders to the events and stories that are told and retold by the actors themselves, identity myths are formed. In the example, the socially constructed and negotiated brand identity for the sports icon and politician Manny Pacquiao constitutes his being a 'modern national hero, aspirational, and mass icon and national idol' in his country. As Giddens (1991) puts it, brand identities' 'becoming' is a result of the social construction involved in their creation through repeated interactions and negotiation with different actors.

Utilization of human brand identities

Reflexivity of identities means that varying dynamic images of celebrities co-created as human brand identities exist, depending on the context, such as stage performances, product category nature and employed creative design (Schroeder 2005). Further, according to Giddens' conception of postmodern identities, self-identity presumes reflexive construction, and so do human brand identities, depending on the context at play. Such reflexive identities are strategically positioned in relation to an overall utility of human brand identity.

Reflexivity in identities is co-created by stakeholders reflecting contexts and rhetorical strategies of the said contexts. Reflexivity is but a result of making human brands as 'identities in use' in the co-creation. But the deeper sense and mechanism of reflexivity rely on the sociocultural norms and acceptable behaviours that the celebrity is able to showcase (resource to integrate) *a priori* to the production of meanings in the context that calls for reflexivity (Schroeder 2005). Thus, these reflexive identities that are able to be utilized depends upon the social legitimacy the identities carry.

Legitimization

Legitimacy is a social fitness indicator, 'a generalized perception or assumption that the actions of an entity (e.g. celebrity) are desirable, proper, or appropriate within some socially constructed system of norms, values, beliefs, and definitions' (Suchman 1995: 574). Institutional theories (Scott 2008) provide the notion of social acceptability or legitimacy through cultural and normative institutions (along with regulatory). The case of human brands also undergoes such a legitimization process underlying normative and cultural fitness formed through a collective memory (Humphreys 2010). These fitness indicators manifest through human brand identities in ways of talent/skill desirability, dominant social norms, shared values, national ideologies and class-and-gender nuances.

Traditional definitions of a celebrity often include the ability to perform in a site-specific talent arena such as television, concert halls or movie theatres. This basic requirement still holds value for celebrity human brands. Stakeholders' co-creation resources in (social media data) discourses are sizable in encapsulating remarkable celebrity skills.

For example, Sarah Geronimo is often cheered for her tasteful singing and Manny Pacquiao for his eventful boxing performances. Sharon Cuneta is still remembered for her melody in the past decades, and Kris Aquino, though not known for any artistic talent, is ubiquitously trivialized in her personal current affairs and the gossip surrounding these. Talents and skills may be fundamental criteria for a person to carry a cultural, social and economic worth; however, other themes emerged to further legitimize the human brand in celebrities. For example, a country's reputable social media news organization, Rappler.com, publishes a video (linked to YouTube and Facebook) that features a new Disney project for Sarah Geronimo, implying that the celebrity has a talent worthy of attention from an international franchising company. The news organization describes the video as an act of Sarah's genuine talent.

Such co-creation between the news organization and the celebrity suggests that, apart from skills and talent, some other mechanisms of legitimization come from the peripheral embodiment of celebrities' personal lives. Thus, through such embodiment of stakeholders' shared vision, dominant cultural ideology and social moral imperatives, human brand identities are co-created and legitimized. Common themes of social and cultural legitimizations are being family and socially oriented, success driven and morally inclined, as well as projections of humility, sociability and skillfulness. Interestingly, the moral and religious facets of a culture are also standard criteria of human brand legitimacy.

Parasocialization

Social interface in the co-creation process is enhanced through relational mechanism and content on identification and 'parasocialization' where social distances are reduced (So and Nabi 2013). *Identification* refers to perceptions of similarities in self-identities (Bandura 1986). *Parasocialization* refers to a sense of social intimacy and relatedness (Horton and Wohl 1956), which are *interactions* in the social media engagements of stakeholders where conversations, modifications and discussions of identities are performed.

Celebrities, beyond their skills and talents, are valued more in their parasocial identities. Expressions of love, hatred, intimacy and interpersonal distances make up the human brands where identity and identification are substantially anchored on. Unlike in the United States, the celebrities on Philippine television are also the celebrities across other media platforms such as films and recording industries. Through these multimedia avenues for celebrities, the parasocial effects of television on the celebrity human brand are carried over across audiences of/in different media. Thus, this scheme provides a bigger and richer venue for the ordinariness of celebrity brand identities being constructed by consumers, and projected, sustained and co-created by other stakeholders.

The representation and construal of celebrities as friends, family members and other significant others are salient in the social media data of this study. Most of the time, celebrities frame themselves as simple, ordinary, authentic and 'real' human beings. For example, Sharon Cuneta writes this on her Twitter profile: 'The one and only. :-) Proud wife to Kiko, happy mommy to Kristina, Simone, Mariel & Miguel.'

Projection of influence

This co-creation code refers to stakeholders' attributions and emphasis on the social, cultural (e.g. role models and icons), political (e.g. voting preferences and behaviours) and economic (e.g. purchase behaviours) roles and influences of celebrities. The influence or power that celebrities possess is culturally rooted in the social world among primary stakeholder consumers. Celebrities are seen to have worked to the rationalization of audiences to give legitimate cultural value and meanings to the representations these personalities have in their lives. Moreover, celebrities are a representation of something else other than themselves: personae or identities that are given heightened cultural significance in the social world (e.g. heroes, idols or even villains). Finally, celebrities' cultural power comes from the subjectivities that audiences feel for them as close affinities in social categories (e.g. friends, acquaintances, etc.).

Such 'cultural power', employed and given to celebrities by stakeholders, refers to the power of persuasion through ideas, cultures and interpersonal politics, generally referring to the culture and values of social entities that can employ persuasion in outward relationships to change attitudes and behaviours (McCracken

1989). As largely discussed in the literature of celebrity endorsements, the images that celebrities project, such as source credibility, likability and attractiveness, have some behavioural influences on consumers. Such behavioural effects from celebrities are rooted in their human brands and the identification, relationship and connection consumers can perceive from them. In this study, manifestations of behavioural followings surfaced. The sheer number of comments and reactions in each post of the celebrities and other instrumental stakeholders suggest that the attraction that celebrity human brands radiate is worthy of consumers' expressions of attitudes. The activating power of human brands that translates words and images into behaviours, or at least behavioural intentions, is deeply ingrained into the relational capacity of the celebrity. Consumers express their behavioural intent to purchase a product endorsed by celebrities in the way they talk to a referent other in their social circle.

Summary and conclusions

The stakeholder ecology works towards celebrity human identity co-creation in a mutually engaging and beneficial landscape of resource integrations. This co-creation process is a joint exchange of experiences, perceptions and insights that emanate from the stakeholders' incentives for participating in the process. It is dynamic and adaptive and yet simultaneous, undirected and clustered across time and space, both online in social media as an avenue of co-creation and offline through traditional media consumption. The overall nature and dynamics of social media interactions characterize the resource integration happening in this kind of brand identity co-creation.

Stakeholder participations play hand in hand through social interactions, engagement and amplification of human brand identities through fast-paced, dynamically interconnected physical and virtual environments. Through social media as an avenue of co-creation, human brand identities are negotiated through a function of media experiences (with celebrities on TV shows, films and commercials), second-hand information (gossip, hearsay and hand-me-down historical accounts) and even personal (face-to-face) encounters with celebrities. Social media engagement enables all stakeholders to amplify such offline social encounters and further shape human brand identities.

Democracy-enabled co-creations are empowered by the less strict, digitally engaging nature of the social media and the freedom of expression in the country of this study. By combining these forces of a democratic environment, human brand identities in celebrities gain further incarnation of the mythologies of previously-regarded-as-distant superstars (Mosco 2005). Stakeholders are collaborated, converged and grounded more in their participation in identity meaning-making. Although in this study, social class and gender are seen as relatively conventional in human brand identities, online avenues may challenge such dominant ideology and offer new opportunities to question prevailing discourses of social positions.

This paper examines human brands, which are atypical brands often regarded as only peripheral (such as in celebrity endorsements) in marketing management. In the dialogue of brand identity, theoretical development should consider human brands in constructing assumptions about brand identity concepts. Human brand identities can be co-created by multiple stakeholders, including the 'human' itself. Thus, the dialectical tensions between upward (consumer-driven) or downward (marketer-driven) and dual combinations are challenged as stakeholder logic embraces a new understanding of the concept of brand identity.

Implications for brand management can be drawn from this study. Celebrities as both human brands and endorsers of brands may need to be managed as well. Firms that are economically motivated and socially responsible for celebrity identity are often faced with issues of desirability and the persuasions employed by human brands. However, as discussed in this paper, several stakeholders are responsible for human brand identities, and the online and offline avenues for human brand identity co-creation are extremely dynamic, implying complexity of manageability. Therefore, strategic approaches should be carefully designed in flexible and adaptive executions of human brand elements by understanding social and cultural codes and the possible tensions and impact of celebrity human brands in the overall brand equity of both the firm, and the product and/or service it offers (Madhavaram, Badrinarayanan and McDonald 2005; Hatch and Schultz 2010).

This paper constitutes exploratory research into understanding celebrity human brand identity co-creation among stakeholders. Future directions include a more longitudinal, immersive study where there is elicitation of insights from the researcher himself to enrich participation in the community. Since the main premise of the paper implies stakeholder co-creation, a larger-scale partnership with firms, celebrities and other related stakeholders may be sought to further construct the understanding of the entire co-creation process.

Finally, while this paper mainly examines popular celebrities in a traditional, collectivistic society, future research may investigate human brands in other personae such as company CEOs, employees and other workers who have roles in, and contributions to, a firm's reputation (Parmentier, Fischer and Reuber 2013). Marketing and communication strategies on anthropomorphism can also relate to human brand research. Interestingly, the increasing popularity of social media celebrities – 'instacelebrities' and 'microcelebrities' – also suggests new definitions of social media influencers that translate into attitudes and behaviours among stakeholders. Additionally, human brand identity co-creation can be further explored by tracing its life cycle to symbolically determine its evolution, adaptation and re-creation. Given a wide array of possibilities in extending human brand identity research, this paper advances the stakeholder-focused brand identity co-creation in celebrities. Although co-creation studies in social media and human brands explicitly suggest qualitative explorations, quantitative approaches may answer questions that address analytics-based studies in this subject matter. For example, testing hypotheses that address the magnitude (amount of insights – comments and reactions) and direction of sentiments (i.e. positive or negative) to a human brand can be tested using scales driven by the mechanisms discussed above, such as identification, parasocial interaction, legitimization and measures on attitudes and behaviours. These scales can be appropriated in the comparative viewpoints of each stakeholder. In the end, convergence and divergence of the formation of human brands can be realized quantitatively.

References

Aaker, D. A. 1996. 'Measuring brand equity across products and markets'. *California Management Review*, 38(3): 103.

Asmussen, B., S. Harridge-March, N. Occhiocupo J. and Farquhar. 2013. 'The multi-layered nature of the internet-based democratization of brand management'. *Journal of Business Research*, 66(9): 1473–1483.

Avery, J. J. 2007. 'Saving face by making meaning: the negative effects of consumers' self-serving response to brand extension', PhD Dissertation. Boston, MA: Harvard University.

Bandura, A. 1986. *Social Foundations of Thought and Action: A Social Cognitive Theory*. Englewood Cliffs, NJ: Prentice-Hall, Inc.

Belk, R., E. Fischer and R. V. Kozinets. 2013. *Qualitative Consumer and Marketing Research*. London: Sage.

Burgess, J. E. and J. B. Green. 2009. 'The entrepreneurial vlogger: participatory culture beyond the professional-amateur divide'. *The YouTube Reader*: 89–107.

Boffard, R. 2014. 'The value of celebrity endorsements'. *BBC News Business*. Available at http://www.bbc.com/news/business-30392829. Accessed 3 February 2016.

Callon, M. and B. Latour. 1981. 'Unscrewing the big Leviathan: how actors macro-structure reality and how sociologists help them to do so' by Karin Knorr Cetina and A.V. Cicourel (Eds), *Advances in Social Theory and Methodology: Toward an Integration of Micro- and Macro-Sociologies*. London: Routledge: 277–303.

Cherrier, H. 2009. 'Anti-consumption discourses and consumer-resistant identities'. *Journal of Business Research*, 62(2): 181–190.

Cova, B. And D. Dalli. 2009. 'Working consumers: the next step in marketing theory?', *Marketing Theory*, 9(3), 315–339.

Digital Marketing Philippines. 2014. *10 Reasons Why Local Filipino Companies Should Use the Internet for Business Promotion* Available at http://digitalmarketingphilippines.com/10-reasons-why-local-filipino-companies-should-use-the-internet-for-business-promotion-infographic/. Accessed 10 February 2016.

Dolbec, P. Y. and E. Fischer. 2015. 'Refashioning a field? Connected consumers and institutional dynamics in markets'. *Journal of Consumer Research*, 41(6): 1447–1468.

Edvardsson, B., B. Tronvoll and T. Gruber. 2011. 'Expanding understanding of service exchange and value co-creation: a social construction approach'. *Journal of the Academy of Marketing Science*, 39(2), 327–339.

Freeman, R. 1984. *Strategic Management: A Stakeholder Approach*. Marshall, MA: Pittman.

Gerbner, G. 1998. 'Cultivation analysis: an overview'. *Mass Communication and Society*, 1(3–4), 175–194.

Giddens, A. 1984. *The Constitution of Society: Outline of the Theory of Structuration*. Berkeley, CA: University of California Press.

Giddens, A. 1991. *Modernity and Self-Identity: Self and Society in the Late Modern Age*. Stanford, CA: Stanford University Press.

Giesler, M. 2006. 'Consumer gift systems'. *Journal of Consumer Research*, 33(2): 283–290.

Handelman, J. M. 2006. 'Corporate identity and the societal constituent'. *Journal of the Academy of Marketing Science*, 34(2): 107–114.

Hatch, M. J. and J. Rubin. 2006. 'The hermeneutics of branding'. *Journal of Brand Management*, 14(1): 40–59.

Hatch, M. J. and M. Schultz. 2010. 'Toward a theory of brand co-creation with implications for brand governance. *Journal of Brand Management*, 17(8): 590–604.

Holmes, S. S. and Redmond. 2014. 'Socialising celebrity'. *Celebrity Studies*, 5(3): 223–224.

Holmes, S., S. Ralph and S. Redmond. 2015. 'Swivelling the spotlight: stardom, celebrity and "me"'. *Celebrity Studies*, 6(1): 100–117.

Holt, D. B. 2002. 'Why do brands cause trouble? A dialectical theory of consumer culture and branding'. *Journal of Consumer Research*, 29(1): 70–90.

Holt, D. B. 2004. *How Brands Become Icons: The Principles of Cultural Branding*. Boston, MA: Harvard Business School Publishing Corporation.

Horton, D. and R. Richard Wohl. 1956. 'Mass communication and para-social interaction: observations on intimacy at a distance'. *Psychiatry*, 19(3): 215–229.

Humphreys, A. 2010. 'Megamarketing: the creation of markets as a social process'. *Journal of Marketing*, 74(2): 1–19.

Jenkins, R. 2014. *Social Identity*. New York, NY: Routledge.

Keller, K. L. 2003. 'Understanding brands, branding and brand equity'. *Interactive Marketing*, 5(1): 7–20.

Kornum, N. and H. Mühlbacher. 2013. 'Multi-stakeholder virtual dialogue: introduction to the special section', *Journal of Business Research*, 66(9): 1460–1464.

Kozinets, R. V. 2015. *Netnography Redefined*. London, UK: Sage.

Kozinets, R., A. C. Wojnicki, S. J. Wilner and K. De Valck. 2010. 'Networked narratives: understanding word-of-mouth marketing in online communities'. *Journal of Marketing*, 74 (March): 71–89.

Latour, B. 1988. *The Pasteurization of France*. Cambridge, MA: Harvard University Press.

Logan, A. 2015. 'Netnography: observing and interacting with celebrity in the digital world'. *Celebrity Studies*, 6(3): 378–381.

Lovelock, C. and E. Gummesson. 2004. 'Whither services marketing? In search of a new paradigm and fresh perspectives'. *Journal of Service Research*, 7(1): 20–41.

Lusch, R. F. and S. L. Vargo. 2006. 'Service-Dominant Logic: reactions, reflections and refinements', *Marketing Theory*, 6(3): 281–288.

Lusch, R. F. and S. L. Vargo. 2014. *The Service-Dominant Logic of Marketing: Dialog, Debate, and Directions*. Oxon, OX: Routledge.

Lusch, R.F., S. L. Vargo and M. O'Brien. 2007. 'Competing through service: insights from Service-Dominant Logic', *Journal of Retailing*, 83(1): 5–18.

Madhavaram, S., V. Badrinarayanan and R. E. McDonald. 2005. 'Integrated marketing communication (Imc) and brand identity as critical components of brand equity strategy: a conceptual framework and research propositions'. *Journal of Advertising*, 34(4): 69–80.

Mander, J. 2014. Global Web Index Social 2014. Available at www.insight.globalwebindex. net. Accessed 11 February 2016.

Marwick, A. E. 2005. '"I'm a lot more interesting than a Friendster Profile": identity presentation, authenticity and power in social networking services'. *Association of Internet Researchers*, 6.

Mathwick, C., C. Wiertz and K. de Ruyter. 2008. 'Social capital production in a virtual P3 community', *Journal of Consumer Research*, 34(6): 832–849.

McCracken, G. 1989. 'Who is the celebrity endorser? Cultural foundations of the endorsement process'. *Journal of Consumer Research*, 16(3): 310–321.

Men, L. R., and W. H. S. Tsai. 2013. 'Beyond liking or following: understanding public engagement on social networking sites in China'. *Public Relations Review*, 39(1): 13–22.

Merz, M. A., Y. He, and S. L. Vargo. 2009. 'The evolving brand logic: a service-dominant logic perspective'. *Journal of the Academy of Marketing Science*, 37(3): 328–344.

Mosco, V. 2005. *The Digital Sublime: Myth, Power and Cyberspace*. Cambridge, MA: MIT Press.

Parmentier, M. A., E. Fischer and R. Reuber. 2013. 'Positioning person brands in established organizational fields'. *Journal of the Academy of Marketing Sciences*, 41(3): 373–387.

Pongsakornrungsilp, S. and J. E. Schroeder. 2011. 'Understanding value co-creation in a co-consuming brand community'. *Marketing Theory*, 11(3): 303–324.

Ramirez, R. 1999. 'Value co-production: intellectual origins and implications for practice and research'. *Strategic Management Journal*, 20(1): 49–65.

Schmitt, B. 2014. *The Changing Face of the Asian Consumer: Insights and Strategies for Asian Markets*. Singapore: McGraw Hill Education.

Schroeder, J.E. 2005. 'The artist and the brand'. *European Journal of Marketing*, 39: 1291–1305.

Scott, W. R. 2008. 'Approaching adulthood: the maturing of institutional theory'. *Theory and Society*, 37(5): 427–442.

Smith, P. R. and Z. Zook. 2011. *Marketing Communications: Integrating Offline and Online with Social Media*. London: Kogan Page Ltd.

So, J. and R. Nabi. 2013. 'Reduction of perceived social distance as an explanation for media's influence on personal risk perceptions: a test of the risk convergence model'. *Human Communication Research*, 39(3): 317–338.

Suchman, M. C. 1995. 'Managing legitimacy: strategic and institutional approaches'. *Academy of Management Review*, 20(3): 571–610.

Thomson, M. 2006. 'Human brands: investigating antecedents to consumers' strong attachments to celebrities'. *Journal of Marketing*, 70(July): 104–119.

Trammell, K. D. and A. Keshelashvili. 2005. 'Examining the new influencers: a self-presentation study of A-list blogs'. *Journalism & Mass Communication Quarterly*, 82(4): 968–982.

Vallaster, C. and S. von Wallpach. 2013. 'An online discursive inquiry into the social dynamics of multi-stakeholder brand meaning co-creation'. *Journal of Business Research* 66(9): 1505–1515.

Vargo, S. L. and R. F. Lusch. 2004. 'Evolving to a new dominant logic for marketing', *Journal of Marketing,* 68 (January), 1–17.

Vargo, S.L., P. P. Maglio and M. A. Akaka. 2008. 'On value and value co-creation: a service systems and service logic perspective', *European Management Journal* 26: 145–152.

Zwick, D., S. K. Bonsu and A. Darmody. 2008. 'Putting consumers to work: co-creation and new marketing govern-mentality', *Journal of Consumer Culture,* 8(2): 163–196.

6

SOCIAL RECRUITMENT

Investing in social currency

Arti Sharma and Arunava Ghosh

Introduction

> 'Everyone is a brand ambassador, everyone is a recruiter'
>
> *Lars Schmidt*

The dynamic business environment is posing serious challenges for organizations' challenges in hiring employees. The Internet has revolutionized global business operations by making many organizations boundary-less, enabling them to function beyond a brick and mortar structure. It has also affected recruitment and hiring practices and is providing easy access to skilled employees (Joos 2008). For this reason, many organizations are adopting social recruiting as a dominant recruitment strategy for hiring their employees. Social recruiting is when companies and recruiters use Facebook, LinkedIn, Twitter and other social media sites to source and recruit candidates for employment (Tony 2014). It is a *concept*, not a defined technique, and breaks down the three primary activities of social recruiting into push, pull and being genuinely social (Doherty 2010). These relate to the idea that consistent social media presence is required from organizations to 'push' their organization's image, to 'pull' potential employees into the act of being 'social' on social media networks. Social recruiting is defined as a process of recruiting candidates by using social media networks for communicating, promoting and advertising the job requirements. It is an intelligent blending of recruitment exercises and social media platforms. It is an effective mode of branding, customer interaction, creating a talent database, mobile engagement and video advertising and promotions. Social hiring is sourcing the right candidates according to an organization's specific requirements via social media networking channels. The candidates are not only pooled through social networks but also reference checked by the potential hirers. This helps the organizations to have *a priori* information about the personal, professional and technical skills of an employee for being appointed to the post that will utilize the best of his or her capabilities (Kaplan and Haenlein 2010).

Social recruiting is the 'new' and 'promising' strategy for hiring candidates. It's the new 'it' thing in the land of recruiting (Smith 2012). Each person is so engrossed in technologies these days that ignoring the power of social media would be suicidal for an organization. Snow, Zurcher Jr. and Ekland Olson (1980) linked differential recruitment with differential social movements accounting for structural proximity, availability and effective interaction between members. With the increasing reach of high-end smartphones and cheaper Internet plans, social currency is gaining wider importance globally. Not earlier than 2009, social media platforms were thought to be more help for marketing and branding concerns. The buzz around social recruitment came in late 2009 and has evolved rapidly in recent times. By 2011, about 80 per cent of the total 600 employers surveyed responded positively regarding the use of social media for recruitment purposes (Jobvite 2015).

Understanding social media

Social media are modern age digital technology mediated tools that provide an interface for people to interact by creating, sharing or exchanging ideas, information, pictures, videos and audio within a virtual community. They are mobile- and computer-technology-based, highly interactive media to create, discuss, share or modify user generated information. Kaplan and Haenlein (2010) define social media as 'a group of Internet based applications that are built on the ideological and technological foundations of Web 2.0, and that allow the creation and exchange of user generated content'. Social media have become the modern method of faster, easier and cheaper communication among individuals, organizations, societies and communities. The instant interaction facility in comparison to traditional monologue communication modes is making social media increasingly popular. Social media provide a platform on a web network to engage users to initiate, discuss and participate in exchanging their views, opinions and ideas with fellow users and all other virtual participants.

The power of social media networks

Social media networks or social websites are interactive platforms that allow a user to make social connections or social relations among people sharing common interests, backgrounds, attitudes and real life relations. According to Boyd and Ellison (2008), social network sites are web based platforms that allow an individual to represent by creating a profile connected with a list of users to share and view the content across the connections within the network. This provides new information and content to users who can interact through in-built networking features like chat, messaging and emails. They have become popular media of the digital age to communicate and share ideas. More and more Indian users are registering into different social media platforms, predominantly Facebook, Twitter and LinkedIn. Owing to its phenomenal growth rate in 2013, India has attained a position among the top ten countries in 2017 with Indonesia, Philippines, Mexico and Brazil of significantly higher social media usage in contrast to US, UK and other European nations (Chaffey, 2017).

Social media networks are often confused with online communities. Social media networks are individual-centric websites and applications allowing users to share ideas, information, links, pictures, videos, audio, interests, events, activities and posts in their networks (Zaglia 2013). For example, Academia.edu is a social media networking site for academics that helps researchers share their research articles and pursue research in a certain field. Online communities are formed when individuals with common interests come together to form a community and utilize the Internet to cooperate and work together to accomplish their interests (Preece 2001). Online communities are group oriented in their approach. Another example is Stack Overflow, which is an online community for programmers to share their programming skills, which helps them in debugging their programmes. These days, social professional networks are the preferred channels for promoting talent brand. The term 'talent brand' can be used to signify the best representation of one's own talent by social media users (Akiode 2013).

Theoretical framework of social recruiting

Social networks have emerged as a powerful tool for community building and technologically-mediated communication. With the passage of time, the online communities expanded and adopted new features with the developing new technology and has led to the evolution of social media platforms. The emergence of social media is not based on any theoretical background; see, for example, how Facebook emerged as the brainchild of a Harvard undergraduate student who wanted to connect with his classmates (Mezrich 2010). Twitter had similar origins, as a result of a brainstorming session by its founder Evan Williams. The Internet and social media are becoming increasingly popular and a concrete theoretical framework is required to understand and fully tap the potentialities of this medium. Theories could help us to identify and interpret the dynamics of social media. There has been extensive research into finding out the underlying theoretical framework of social networks. Social media networks are web-structured communities formed by content sharing among users. For the purpose of our research, we explored the various theories pertaining to socialization and communication in a network. Pan and Crotts (2012) have segregated social media theories into three segments: firstly, as 'micro theories', which explain the dynamics of contribution of online information and communication patterns of individual social actors; secondly, as 'macro theories' which present the understanding of the structure and dynamics of social actors' social media content on the basis of global and abstract opinions; thirdly, as 'pseudo theories' which include all of the social media concepts proposed recently by non-academicians. Pseudo theories are those that are the outcome of practical experience but have yet to be tested empirically using scientific methodology; we have made an attempt to extend the classification made by Pan and Crotts (2012) and propose the inclusion of self-categorization theory under micro theories, and social identity theory under macro theories. The earlier theoretical classification by Pan and Crotts (2012) is given briefly below with our inclusion of the aforementioned theories. We propose the contribution of self-categorization theory and social identity theory to the existing theory to enrich the theoretical base for social recruiting.

Micro theories

i) Psychological Ownership Theory and Perceived Control – Psychological ownership refers to the feeling of something 'belonging' to you (Pierce, Kostova and Dirks 2001). The information shared and communicated by relatives and friends is considered to be more reliable, credible, trustworthy and honest in contrast to reviews claimed by the organization.

ii) Social Exchange Theory – Social media networks are web-structured communities formed by content sharing among the users. The users are responsible for providing the content, which can be understood with reference to social exchange theory. The theory is an extensive framework analysing the dynamics of human relations by using cost-benefit analysis and comparing alternatives to deduce how human beings build relationships and communities through communication exchanges (Homans 1958). According to this theory, social behaviour is an outcome of an exchange process, with an objective of reaping maximum benefits with minimum costs. The benefits are the rewards of the relationship that an individual gets in the form of social security, support, companionship or friendship. The rewards are not monetary. Similarly the benefits are largely social such as security, opportunity, conformity, prestige or social acceptance (Emerson, 1976). The relationships on social media networks are also based on social exchange theory. People engage in a social exchange relationship for a perceived gain in reputation and influencing ability, an anticipated response on the part of others, altruism and direct reward (Pan and Crotts 2012).

iii) Social Penetration Theory – Social penetration theory, also known as the 'onion analogy', posits that during the development of relationships, interpersonal communications transform from a superficial, shallow, non-intimate stage to a deeper, more engrossed, more intimate stage (Griffin *et al.* 2010). The theory, as suggested by Altman and Taylor (1973), places an emphasis on the individual and dyadic levels in interpersonal communication. According to this theory, self-disclosure enhances the proximity in a human relationship. The theory uses the analogy of peeling an onion layer by layer as an individual discloses their identity gradually from public self to private self through a continuous process to reveal their inner self (Altman, Vinsel and Brown 1981). The communication initiates from general, superficial and visible information (gender, ethnicity and more) and moves to a more intimate, deeper level (sharing of ideology and beliefs).

iv) Self Categorization Theory – This theory explains the situations in which an individual will perceive an aggregate of people (forming themselves) as a group, along with the consequences of perceiving other people in the form of a group (Haslam, Oakes and Turner 1996). The theory is well understood to explain the role of the categorization process by an individual in the context of social perception. It is further elaborated to explain the categorization of 'self' by an individual under different levels of abstraction. We propose this theory as a micro theory of social media frameworks. One can see different people are quite selective in choosing their mode of social media presentation. It is a manifestation of self-categorization in a virtual world where an individual is perceiving being themselves as part of one virtual community as well as thinking about the consequences of an online presence. We further state that this theory is useful in explaining individual behaviour on social networks with their categorization of their own profiles, friends and other online communities. Managers should understand this theory to scrutinize the applications of the persons that are selected through social media networks. It provides a handy base to understand the self-concept of a person through her online profile, which can later be used to ascertain her hiring status.

Macro theories

i) Social Networking Theory – The Social Networking Theory is the study of the interaction of people, groups and organizations within their network. The theory, propounded by Wasserman and Faust (1994), identifies the community of individuals in a network as connected actors, presenting their evolution, composition, formation and structure on the basis of mathematical models. Social network analysis uses specific terminology to describe the social relations in a network. It refers to individuals as 'actors' connected in a community as 'nodes' and communication between these actors is called 'ties', 'links', 'connections' or 'edges'. A social network can be formed at various levels, ranging from the individual level to friends, relatives, families, communities and across nations. Social network is 'the structure of relationships linking social actors' (Marsden, 2000).

ii) Theory of Rumour Transmission – Buckner (1965) propounded the theory on rumour transmission stating that the accuracy and speed of spreading a rumour were determined by the structural set up of a network and the state of mind of the participating individuals as actors in the network.

iii) McLuhan's Media Theory – McLuhan (1994) argued that it is communication medium that has the capacity to transform people and society rather than the content of the medium, stating, 'The medium is the message'. According to this theory, people's communication remains similar across different media but their behaviour is modified completely due to the interaction and frequency of communication on new media.

iv) Social Identity Theory – Another theory proposed by Turner and Oakes (1986) should be considered in the theoretical grounding of social media theory under the heading of macro theories. According to this theory, a part of an individual self is derived from the group to which she belongs. This theory explains the social selves of the individual (Haslam *et al.* 2010) and the phenomenon of intergroup behaviour on the basis of perceived group status differences, resulting in the formation of 'in groups' and 'out groups'. This theory can be used by organizations to formulate their social recruitment strategy in an effective and efficient manner. The organization can devise the strategy in such a manner that it creates an 'in group' phenomenon for the organization, attracting maximum recruitment applications. This can further be extended by projecting the organization's image, as not only the potential employees but also the current employees may identify with the organization.

Pseudo theories

The face of social media is changing rapidly with advancements in digital technology. There is a lack of academic background to the concept and this creates a significant lag in the subject. The concrete research and its allied theories are not much worked upon by the academic fraternity because of a disconnection between industry and academics. Marketers and different organizations are filling this gap by providing some practical frameworks.

Need for social recruitment

Social recruitment is gaining a status as the dominant recruitment strategy in the present business scenario. It is serving as the most promising and most effective tool in hiring and recruitment. The reason for the shift from traditional recruitment strategies to social media recruitment lies in the changing demographic characteristics of the population. The current generation is technology savvy, computer literate and addicted to screens (Joos 2008), preferring socializing on social media over face to face interactions. Hence, it becomes quite easy for organizations to project their image on social networks to attract the best of talent to work for their organization. Social recruitment is needed for the following reasons:

1. The 'connected' generation – Digital youngsters have a huge presence on social media networks. They like to be in continuous conversation with the world. They like to share their opinions and views on various issues. Thus, it becomes very easy to find employees as required by organizations.
2. Quick access to talent pool – The younger generation spends a considerable amount of time on online activities. They have become largely dependent on the Internet for their most of their information and communication needs. They usually become members of various online communities and social networks related to their interests. This provides handy access to organizations looking to find a similarly skilled set of people instantly.

3. The 'mobile' generation – According to a recent survey (Mallaya 2015), India was expected to reach 314 million mobile Internet users by 2017, making it the third largest smartphone market globally. Besides this, the mobile app market is also expanding rapidly. The current generation rely heavily on apps and mobile accessories. The functions of these apps can range from keeping track of expenses to looking for directions, booking a cab, reading news updates or following an organization to find their dream job.

4. The 'netizens' revolution – Mobile usage frequency is increasing at a rapid rate. Indian smartphone users are found to spend an average of 169 minutes daily on their smartphones (Mallaya 2015). This makes it easier for a person to be connected to other people on a virtual network. Using the Internet on mobile makes it more accessible. An average user opens ten apps per day (Spence 2014) and this unfolds the potential market of apps. This necessiates the adoption of the practice of social recruitment in place of traditional recruitment policies.

5. Need of the hour – The advancement of technology, information and communication makes it essential for organizations to take this medium of recruitment seriously. If not, organizations will face difficulty in finding the best employees and will lag behind in the competition for talent.

Table 6.1 emphasizes the differences between traditional recruitment methods and social recruitment methods.

Trends in social recruiting

Finding expert talent at lower costs is becoming an increasing challenge for big brands as well as for start-ups. According to LinkedIn's Annual Recruitment Trends for 2015, companies have shifted to digital marketing and social recruitment through social media. Based on the LinkedIn survey of more than 4,125 talent acquisition leaders across the globe, which included 300 plus in India across fourteen industries, India stands in the global top three (ET).

Figure 6.1 clearly shows an increase in social professional networks in India. A significant increase has been noted between 2011 and 2014. The online network of professionals has made talent more accessible than ever.

Tools of social recruiting

i) *LinkedIn*

LinkedIn was launched on 5 May 2003. Its mission was to connect the world's professionals to make them successful and productive. In 2004, LinkedIn added the address book facility to make it possible to invite one's colleagues to the service and thus to build communities. In 2005, LinkedIn had a membership of 4,192,941 In 2015, LinkedIn had registered thirty million users marking a 50 per cent growth in the nation (Press Trust of India, 2015). The following companies recruit through LinkedIn:

TABLE 6.1 Differences between traditional recruitment methods and social recruitment methods

Reference	Traditional Recruitment Method	Social Recruitment Method
Based on online systems	At present, traditional recruitment involves online work like the collection of resumes in digital format and then manually going through each and every resume.	Social recruitment can be connected to online recruitment software. Online recruitment software will use a web based algorithm that will automate the communication between the recruiter and the candidates. All processes will be done electronically. The software will automatically fill in the vacancies with the next suitable candidate. In India, IIMJOBS.com uses online recruitment software.
Time frame	In traditional recruitment, jobs are posted in newspapers, and then candidates send their biographical data via courier. After that the process of sorting of applications can start.	Social recruitment methods are fast, efficient and reduce the time gap between calling for, and receiving, applications. Job openings can be published instantly, and responses can be received in real time. The recruitment algorithm would do the sorting of the received applications.
Money factor	It is expensive to place ads in newspapers. Once published, the ad can't be edited.	It is cheaper to post jobs ads on websites. Additionally, the recruiter can edit the ads based on circumstances.
Success rate	The ad is advertised once in a newspaper. Any potential candidate who hasn't purchased that newspaper misses out on the ad. So, the ad becomes restricted to those who have read the newspaper in which the ad has been published.	An ad published on a website or on a page linked to Facebook, LinkedIn, etc. remains on the site for a long time. A candidate can browse through the ads at any time. Therefore, the response rate increases significantly. Ads also have a wider reach.
Depth and detail	Other than the eligibility criteria, no other skills of the candidate can be accessed.	Here, other skills of the candidate can be accessed. Google conducts an online coding test to access the coding skills of the candidates applying.
Personal touch	A high amount of human interaction occurs between candidate and recruiter during recruitment interviews.	There is a lack of human interaction. The recruitment process is mostly carried out by artificial intelligence.
Competition	The slower response to newspaper advertisements will give an advantage to companies advertising online.	The faster response to online advertisements will help in quicker recruitment of the right candidate.

Source: http://content.wisestep.com/traditional-vs-non-traditional-recruiting-methods-comparison/. Accessed 3 October 2016.

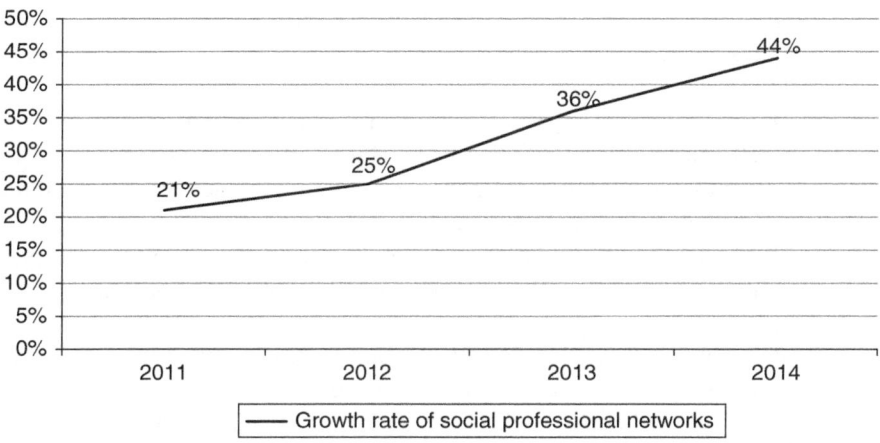

FIGURE 6.1 Social media network trends in India.

Source: Business LinkedIn; accessed 26 June 2016.

a) Deloitte: Deloitte uses LinkedIn to source experienced candidates. The recruitment team looks for professionals who are connected to their network or are shown as recommendations. Deloitte also maintains a LinkedIn group where it posts its vacancies. two per cent of Deloitte's hires are through social media but the benefits of social media are much higher (Brouat 2011).

b) L'Oréal: The L'Oréal group is the world's largest cosmetics beauty company with a presence in 130 countries. In India and the Philippines in particular, they use social recruitment. The UK and US L'Oréal jobs website links to the L'Oréal LinkedIn page. L'Oreal has one LinkedIn company page with a branded 'Careers' tab to match. This page introduces new applicants and also contains a YouTube page with video testimonials from past employees (Florence 2014).

ii) *Facebook*

Facebook was launched on 4 February 2004 by Mark Zuckerberg. Today, Facebook has 1.55 billion users around the world. Facebook calculates its revenue through ad impressions and the sale of virtual goods from its platform developers (Nair 2014). The company was listed on 17 May 2012 at a share price of $38 (Nielson 2014). In 2015, Facebook's US user base grew 3.7 per cent compared to the previous year (Statista 2016). Facebook is being used by the following organizations:

a) Accenture: Dell provides job seekers with customized job recommendations directly through a Facebook page. This page also shows recruitment events and also promotes virtual gatherings.

b) Marriott: Posting content three to four times a day highlighting what it's like to work at the Marriot has increased the number of Likes on the official Marriot Facebook page more than that of Facebook's own career page. Career Chats on the Marriot's Facebook page answer users' questions in real time and offer career advice.

c) Dell: Dell's career page has more likes than Facebook's career page. Dell's Facebook page highlights employee achievements and also allows users to apply through the page while promoting the company's culture through pictures of various events held.

d) Unilever: Unilever breaks their Facebook job postings into 'Early Career' and 'Professional Career' for easier targeting of jobs by applicants.

iii) *Twitter*

Twitter enables users to send and read short messages called 'tweets'. It can be accessed through desktop, mobile app and also by SMS. Twitter was created by Evan Williams, Noah Glass, Jack Dorsey and Biz Stone in March 2006. It became popular in 2012 when more than 100 million users started posting 340 million tweets each day. In 2013, one of the most visited websites was Twitter and it has been dubbed 'the SMS of the Internet'. Twitter's year-on-year user growth was 11.8 percent (Statista 2016). The following companies recruit through Twitter:

a) Walt Disney: Walt Disney recruits through Twitter. It has a separate Twitter handle for recruitment tweets.

b) IBM: IBM personalizes its recruiting profiles to make job seekers feel like they are interacting with individuals. IBM lists the personal handles of the recruiters that maintain @IBMUSJobs in its profile description so that job seekers can see who they're interacting with (Westfall 2015).

c) Individual recruiters also use Twitter to build trust for the clients and companies they work for (Akiode 2013).

iv) *YouTube and Google Plus*

YouTube is used primarily to share videos. It is headquartered in California, United States. It was established in February 2005. In 2006, Google bought it for US$1.65 billion. Individuals and media corporations offer their content through YouTube. Google Plus is owned and operated by Google. Launched in 2011, the main feature is the ability to post photos and videos and status updates to specific interest communities. Using YouTube as a major recruitment tool, job postings with video descriptions get a higher response rate. Sharing the details of a company is easier than sharing through text. Companies like Google, Apple and Microsoft have their recruitment videos online. Using videos, it is easy to expose the prospective candidates to company culture. This famous Google recruitment video from 2006 does a great job by highlighting all the awesome perks of being a Google employee, from free childcare to food so good people gain the 'Google 15' while working there (Medved 2014). Companies also ask prospective candidates to upload their own introductory videos to YouTube as part of the application process during recruitment season.

Using Google Plus as a recruitment tool helps to locate people with the required educational background and work experience for the job opening. In addition, a company can skim through the posts and comments published on Google Plus as a part of the personality test for the applicant. One can contact Google Plus users even if they don't know their email IDs. Additionally, the company's HR department can conduct a Google Hangout interview with applicants (Recruiting 2014).

Advantages of social recruiting

i) Accessibility – Social media networks provide greater access to a pool of potential employees than is provided by traditional recruiting methods.
ii) In-depth filtering of candidate profiles – Traditional recruitment methods involve the process of scrutinising the application provided by candidates. But social media networks provide access to information beyond the applications submitted by candidates. They can provide interests, likes and other aspects of the candidate's personality.
iii) Cost and time saving – If the company keeps track of potential employees on social media networks, it assists the company in making a quick hire in case of sudden vacancies, thereby saving both cost and time.
iv) Brand impact – Companies use social media networks to advertise on platforms like Facebook, Twitter and LinkedIn. Posting of company success stories and their employees' testimonials boosts the image of the company as a good employer.
v) Online interactive notice board – Important company information can be posted on company profiles maintained on Facebook, Twitter and LinkedIn. Information related to job vacancies can be circulated through social media networks at a negligible cost. American Express India uploads video job descriptions on the social media networks in which employees provide their video testimonials about the working environment of the company.
vi) Easy update of profiles – Candidates can update their accomplishments on their LinkedIn or Facebook profiles. Social media networks can notify the company about the candidate's profile update in the case that the company is following the candidate's profile.

Challenges in social recruiting

There is an absence of government guidelines for social recruiting. Educating staff on how social media can impact the business of an organization is difficult. The biggest drawback of social recruiting is the inadequacy of information that is available to an organization. Based on the restricted information made available by the user due to privacy issues, an organization may not be able to make decisions based on the information provided on a social media forum by the user. In addition, fake profiles created by many users add to the problems faced during social recruitment for organizations (Rajput 2014).

Discussion

Social media networks are gaining wider popularity among organizations as a major tool for communication, branding and recruitment purposes. The presence of a huge talent pool at a mere click make these networks extremely attractive for recruitment. Social media are shaping a new face for organizations and acting as a new force in organizations. According to a report by Cristina Castronovo and Lei Huang (2012), social media have become an integral tool in devising marketing and communication strategies in business organizations. Social media have become a part of business strategies and can act as a reservoir for recruitment. What sets social media apart from recruiting through traditional recruitment practices is the 'interactionist' nature of this medium. For instance, LinkedIn and Facebook facilitate quick and easy communication between the prospective employee and employer. Besides this, they also provide a glimpse of the employee as a person to the employer. The sharing of posts, comments and various activities by prospects may help the HR analyst to make a wise decision on hiring. Organizations can zero in on potential candidates based on certain online competition or forum activity and then can call to further the recruitment process. However, this holds the underlying assumption that the posted content and information is accurate and truly reflects the potential candidate. This assumption may not always be right as we often come across fake social media accounts. This poses the biggest challenge for recruiters to distinguish fake accounts from true accounts while sorting the talent pool and calling for recruitment. On the basis of observation, we suggest that fake accounts can be avoided by cross-verifying the information of a person on different social media as manipulating the information on different platforms would be a tedious job and requires consistent effort. Additionally, having a personal interview before hiring is recommened and can be done through Skype or any other video medium to avoid the chances of an inappropriate hire.

Future directions and conclusion

Progress in information technology and communication is happening at a rapid pace. Organizations are having difficulty accessing talented employees for hiring and recruitment purposes. The traditional modes of recruitment are no longer bearing fruit and hence it becomes imperative for organizations to rethink their recruitment strategies. For this purpose, social recruiting is a promising tool where an organization attempts to invest in peoples' social networks, thereby reaping social currency. The social media network works on the principle of social exchange theory. Organizations are advised to also look at social penetration theory in alignment with social exchange theory to devise a targeted social recruitment strategy using approximate tools best suited to the purpose. We caution organizations against issues in social recruitment such as fake profiles, inadequate information and false claims made by people on their social networks. Future research directions may require researchers to probe deeper into the social media strategies that an organization can adopt. Additionally, a further gap lies in the selection of appropriate tools for social media recruitment. Further research can explore the different strategies that organizations are adopting for social recruiting and this can be further extended to the appropriate mix of traditional and social recruitment. The research can also be done with regard to the use of HR analytics in social recruitment and its related aspects. So far, the area has been explored theoretically and hence empirical studies are required to obtain a better picture of the propositions. In brief, social recruiting is a new but promising mode of hiring and recruitment that present day organizations are adopting to connect with younger generations.

References

Akiode, S. 2013. [Infographic] 'The Social Recruiting Pocket Guide'. Available at http://theundercoverrecruiter.com/social-recruitment-pocket-guide/. Accessed 20 April 2016.

Altman, I. and D. A. Taylor (1973). *Social Penetration: The Development of Interpersonal Relationships*. St. Louis, MO: Holt, Rinehart & Winston.

Altman, I., A. Vinsel and B. B. Brown. 1981. 'Dialectic conceptions in social psychology: an application to social penetration and privacy regulation'. *Advances in Experimental Social Psychology*, 14, p. 107–160.

Brouat, L. 2011. 'How Deloitte uses social media to recruit' [CASE STUDY]. Available at http://linkhumans.com/blog/how-to-use-social-media-to-recruit-deloitte-case-study. Accessed 18 May 2016.

Business LinkedIn. 2015. 'India recruiting trends'. Available at https://business.linkedin.com/content/dam/business/talent-solutions/global/en_US/c/pdfs/india-recruiting-trends-final1.pdf. Accessed 26 June 2016.

Buckner, H. T. 1965. 'A theory of rumor transmission'. *Public Opinion Quarterly*, 29(1), p. 54–70.

Castronovo, C. and L. Huang. 2012. 'Social media in an alternative marketing communication model'. *Journal of Marketing Development and Competitiveness*, 6(1), p. 117.

Chaffey, D. (2017, February 27). Global social media research summary 2017. Retrieved from www.smartinsights.com: http://www.smartinsights.com/social-media-marketing/social-media-strategy/new-global-social-media-research/. Accessed 20 April 2016.

Doherty, R. 2010. 'Getting social with recruitment'. *Strategic HR Review*, 9(6), p. 11–15.

Ellison, N. B. 2007. 'Social network sites: definition, history, and scholarship'. *Journal of Computer-Mediated Communication*, 13(1), p. 210–230.

Emerson, R. M. 1976. 'Social exchange theory'. *Annual Review of Sociology*, p. 335–362.

Griffin, E. A., J. Crossman, S. Bordia, C. Mills, S. Maras, G. Pearse, P. Kelly and D. Shanahan. 2010. *A First Look at Communication Theory*. Boston, MA: McGraw-Hill Higher Education, p. 230–265.

Haslam, S. A., P. Oakes, J. Turner and C. McCarty 1996. 'Social identity, self-categorization, and the perceived homogeneity of ingroups and outgroups: the interaction between social motivation and cognition'. In Sorrentino, Richard M. and E. Tory Higgins (Eds), *Handbook of motivation and cognition, Vol. 3: The interpersonal context*, pp. 182–222.

Haslam, S. A., N. Ellemers, S. D. Reicher, K. J. Reynolds and M. T. Schmitt. 2010. 'The social identity perspective today: the impact of its defining ideas'. In Postmes, T. and N. R. Branscombe (Eds), *Rediscovering Social Identity: Key Readings*. London: Routledge, pp. 341–356.

Hebberd, L. (2014). How L'Oreal Uses Social Media for Recruitment [CASE STUDY]. Retrieved from www.linkhumans.com: http://linkhumans.com/blog/how-loreal-use-social-media-for-recruitment. Accessed 16 May 2016.

Homans, G. C. 1958. 'Social behavior as exchange'. *American Journal of Sociology*, 63(6), p. 597–606.

IANS. 2014. 'India records highest social networking growth' [STUDY]. Available at http://www.bgr.in/news/india-records-highest-social-networking-growth-study/. Accessed 20 April 2016.

Jobvite. 2015. 'The Jobvite Recruiter Nation Survey'. Available at http://www.jobvite.com/wp-content/uploads/2015/09/jobvite_recruiter_nation_2015.pdf. Accessed 27 June 2016.

Joos, J. G. 2008. 'Social media: new frontiers in hiring and recruiting'. *Employment Relations Today*, 35(1), p. 51–59.

Kaplan, A. M. and M. Haenlein. 2010. 'Users of the world, unite! The challenges and opportunities of social media'. *Business Horizons*, 53(1), p. 59–68.

Kasper, K. (2013, September 5). The 2013 Social Recruiting Survey Results Are Here! Retrieved from www.jobvite.com: http://www.jobvite.com/blog/2013jobviteso cial recruitingsurvey/. Accessed 27 June 2016.

LinkedIn. 2014. 'The history of LinkedIn'. Available at http://thelinkedinman.com/history-linkedin/. Accessed 16 May 2016.

Mallaya, H. 2015. 'With 3rd largest smartphone market in the world, India to reach 314 million mobile Internet users by 2017'. Available at http://yourstory.com/2015/07/mobile-internet-report-2015/. Accessed 24 June 2016.

McLuhan, M. 1994. *Understanding Media: The Extensions of Man*. New York: McGraw Hill.

Mallaya, H. 2015. 'Indian smartphone users spend on average 169 minutes per day on their device and can be categorized into 6 persona'. Available at http://yourstory.com/2015/07/smartphone-user-persona-report-vserv/. Accessed 24 June 2016.

Marsden, P. V. (2000). Social networks. *Encyclopedia of Sociology*, 4, 2727–2735.

Medved, J. (2014, November 13). How to Recruit on YouTube. Retrieved from www.humanresourcestoday.com: http://www.humanresourcestoday.com/2006/2014/?open-article-id=3369986&article-title=how-to-recruit-on-youtube&blog-domain=capterra.com&blog-title=capterra. Accessed 24 June 2016.

Mezrich, B. (2009). *The Accidental Billionaires: The Founding of Facebook – A Tale Of Sex, Money, Genius, and Betrayal*. Toronto: Random House.

Nair, S. 2014. 'Must-know: assessing Facebook's revenue sources'. Available at http://finance.yahoo.com/news/must-know-assessing-facebook-revenue-170009607.html. Accessed 17 June 2016.

Nielson, S. 2014. 'Why Facebook is a leading social media player'. Available at http://marketrealist.com/2014/01/facebook/?utm_source=yahoo&utm_medium=feed&utm_content=toc-1&utm_campaign=facebook-revenue-advertising. Accessed 20 June 2016.

Pan, B. and J. C. Crotts. 2012. 'Theoretical models of social media, marketing implications, and future research directions'. *Social Media in Travel, Tourism and Hospitality*, 46, p. 73–83.

Pierce, J. L., T. Kostova and K. T. Dirks. 2001. 'Toward a theory of psychological ownership in organizations'. *Academy of Management Review*, 26(2), p. 298–310.

Preece, J. 2001. 'Sociability and usability in online communities: Determining and measuring success'. *Behaviour & Information Technology*, 20(5), p. 347–356.

Press Trust of India. (2015, May 7). LinkedIn sees 50 per cent growth in India, crosses 30 mn user mark. Retrieved from www./indianexpress.com: http://indianexpress.com/article/technology/social/linkedin-sees-50-per-cent-growth-in-india-crosses-30-mn-user-mark/

Rajput, H. 2014. 'Social recruiting: trends, opportunities and challenges in India'. *Pacific Business Review International*, p. 25–28.

Recruiting. 2014. 'How to use Google+ as a social recruiting tool'. Available at http://theundercoverrecruiter.com/social-media-recruiters-google-tool/. Accessed 16 May 2016.

Smith, P. J. W. 2012. 'Social recruiting series: an introduction & infographic'. Available at http://philipjwsmith.com/social-recruiting-series-an-introduction-infographic/. Accessed 27 June 2016.

Snow, D. A., L. A. Zurcher Jr, and S. Ekland-Olson. 1980. 'Social networks and social movements: a microstructural approach to differential recruitment'. *American Sociological Review*, p. 787–801.

Spence, Ewan. 2014. 'More people are opening more mobile apps every single day'. Available at http://www.forbes.com/sites/ewanspence/2014/04/24/more-people-are-opening-more-mobile-apps-every-single-day/#50a421a55957. Accessed 27 June 2016.

Statista, 2016. Projected annual Facebook and Twitter user growth rates in the United States from 2014 to 2020, Available at http://www.statista.com/statistics/278416/facebook-and-twitter-us-user-growth/. Accessed 27 June 2016.

Tony, Restell. 2014. 'What's social recruiting? 25 experts weigh in'. Available at https://www.smartrecruiters.com/blog/question-what-is-social-recruiting/. Accessed 8 March 2017.

The linkedinman. (2014). The History of Linkedin. Retrieved from www.thelinkedinman.com: http://thelinkedinman.com/history-linkedin/. Accessed 24 June 2016.

Turner, J. C. and P. J. Oakes. 1986. 'The significance of the social identity concept for social psychology with reference to individualism, interactionism and social influence'. *British Journal of Social Psychology*, 25(3), p. 237–252.

Wasserman, S., & Faust, K. 1994. *Social Network Analysis: Methods and Applications*. Cambridge: Cambridge University Press.

Westfall, B. 2015. 'How Fortune 500 companies engage talent on Twitter'. Available at http://www.softwareadvice.com/resources/hr-engage-talent-on-twitter/. Accessed 27 June 2016.

Zaglia, M. E. 2013. 'Brand communities embedded in social networks'. *Journal of Business Research*, 66(2), p. 216–223.

7

THE STRUGGLE OF THE SECRECY, SAFETY AND SECURITY OF SOCIAL MEDIA AND SMARTPHONES

Ronald M. Zochalski, Jr

Introduction

Social media have given marketers new tools, techniques and paradigms to change how marketers and audiences interact. Here are four examples from McKinsey:

1. McDonald's attempt at soliciting positive customer feedback via the hashtag '#McDStories' was pulled within two hours, when customers started posting derogatory tweets.
2. Oreo's tweet when the lights went out during the Super Bowl, 'You can still dunk in the dark', was retweeted 15,000 times, gained 20,000 Facebook 'likes' and 34,000 new Instagram followers.
3. Kraft launched Nabisco 100-calorie packs in response to trends in online discussions, racking up $100 million in sales within a year.
4. A European CPG company used advanced analytics of SKU data to match retail assortments with consumer preferences, achieving a higher sales growth.

A report from the Economist Intelligence Unit describes what organizations should do to effectively harness data from digital platforms. The report says that 'the most competitive organizations deliver superior experiences that keep their customers engaged across all channels'. This requires the ability to personalize marketing, which is the essence of what makes digital marketing superior to traditional marketing. A CIO is cited as saying that mobile technologies and social media have transformed customer interaction dynamics. One analyst is cited as saying the traditional '4Ps' of marketing have been abstracted by mobile devices (Jayaram, Manrai and Manrai 2015).

So why do we love our smartphones loaded with our favorite social media apps while simultaneously demanding our privacy, yet when there is a terrorist attack our safety becomes a priority?

> The most important concern of customers when it comes to successful online brand management, is to respect their privacy by letting them control the use of their personal information.
>
> *(Bandyopadhyay 2009: p. 11)*

President Obama took the side of the FBI at South by Southwest, a conference in Austin, Texas: 'If there's no way to gain access to new communications devices, the president asked, how do we solve or disrupt a terrorist plot? What mechanisms do solve to even do things like tax enforcement … If government can't get in, then everyone's walking around with a Swiss bank account in their pocket' (Crovitz 2016).

The public do not want their personal privacy violated by the government or technology companies, yet law enforcement needs access to mobile devices and applications to gather digital evidence in the interest of public safety.

There were shifting concerns, as per a Pew Research Survey from 8–13 December 2015, from the American public on security and civil liberties regarding the terrorist shootings in San Bernardino and Paris in late 2015. One day fifty-eight respondents said the government had not gone far enough to protect the country, with twenty-seven saying the government had gone too far in restricting liberties. Another day, forty-seven respondents said the government had not gone far enough to protect the country, with thirty-five saying the government had gone too far in restricting liberties.

The struggle for the secrecy, safety and security of smartphones and social media apps (like Facebook, Instagram, Twitter, Snapchat, Kik, Tumblr, Pinterest, Vine, YikYak, WhatsApp, Telegram, Vent, YouTube, Skype and ooVoo) is overwhelming.

Academic research exists for technology security, ethics and public safety but smartphones, combined with the new encrypted social media apps, present new challenges that have yet to be addressed. The technology is moving so fast, no one can keep up. Software that used to take years to develop is now launched within months or even faster. Consumers have a basic understanding of data security but they don't know how much encryption they really need. The consumer expects the hardware and social media app companies to protect their information. Look, for example, at the Target customer and financial data that was accessed through the HVAC system, essentially through social engineering. Customers got scared and wondered why their financial data wasn't being protected.

We are all having a tough time grasping the privacy versus security issues. It is difficult to understand because there are no real guidelines or framework that social media apps or hardware are required to follow legally. We need to be protected but we want to protect our privacy at the same time. We also need to understand hackers primarily hack to steal information or money, while some do it for fun or others to disrupt.

Based on my informal surveys of co-workers and students, the top four areas which they believe need to be protected in order of importance are:

1. social security number
2. credit card numbers
3. mobile phone number
4. driver's license number

Respondents indicate a relatively high level of awareness in relation to their privacy-related rights, with a lower level of awareness related to the right not to be subject to individual decisions regarding personal data, while in the case of the right to be informed about processing, there was the highest level of awareness among respondents, at 94.8 per cent (Orzan, G., C. Vegheş, C. Silvestru, M. Orzan and R. Bere 2012).

Cybersecurity: FBI vs Apple – the public safety vs privacy battle begins

It started with a simple FBI request to have Apple unlock the iPhone 5c of San Bernardino shooter Syed Rizwan Farook to access its data. On 16 February 2016 (Cook 2016), Tim Cook, Apple CEO published a 'Message to Our Customers' on the Apple website stating, 'We oppose this order, which has implications far beyond the legal case at hand'. Apple stood its ground on privacy, refusing to comply, and the battle began.

Why did Apple take this issue public? The Apple PR machine positioned it as being about free speech and privacy, 'the two things Americans value above all else' (Greenburg 2016).

The FBI posed a key question to Congress (Crovitz 2016): 'Either the Fourth Amendment permits reasonable, warranted searches in the digital era or Internet companies can design systems to defeat court orders, putting themselves and criminals, including terrorists, above the law'.

Every time apple releases a new iPhone there are a number of interesting individuals lining up to test it like hackers, other government agencies, foreign spies, cyber criminals and terrorists.

Interestingly enough, 51 per cent of the population polled believe Apple should unlock the device for the FBI, according to the Pew Research Center.

Here is the law enforcement criminal data acquisition process work, according to www.aei.org (Ries, March 2016). You can see that social media app and secure messaging application companies cannot decrypt their own data. As a result, the FBI is forced to ask the hardware company, in this case Apple, to unlock the device to get to the original data before it was encrypted.

However, the FBI asked for an eleventh hour postponement after the Tuesday, 22 March 2016 bombing in Brussels, saying an outside company had offered to help. A day later, it was announced the Israeli digital forensics firm, Cellebrite, had offered to help (Weise and Swartz 2016).

The debate continues. There are numerous critics and much speculation that the FBI should have tried harder before it went to the courts. According to Williams (2016), it costs more to hack into a device using internal resources than with a contractor. The FBI has used Cellebrite before, generating $2 million in purchase orders since 2012. Others think the FBI is trying to get $38 million in funds, 23 per cent more than last year, to purchase tools to access encrypted data.

If you look at it from both sides, further investigation is required to find out what the real motivation is for both Apple and the FBI.

Social media and hardware encryption: how are your data used and who do you trust?

Who do you trust with your data? Smartphone manufacturers like Apple, Samsung, Google, LG, Microsoft, Blu and Alcatel? Or social media and other apps? Can you control it?

Social media apps have been one of the ways hardware manufacturers have been able to get the general public to actually purchase a smartphone. It is claimed that half of all crimes in Britain, particularly rape and death threats, are now committed online using Facebook and need to be taken seriously (Fishleigh 2015).

Looking at the percentage of adult ownership of smartphones by country, 43 per cent is the global median:

We then compare this with the use of social networking sites over time by age group to understand social media use on smartphones:

So 90 per cent of all adults eighteen to twenty-nine, essentially all of the Millennials (Millennials are classed as being between the ages of eighteen and thirty-three) are using social media applications. There might be some correlation between this data and ISIS recruits.

Social media apps were used by ISIS terrorists in the Brussels terrorist attack to communicate. The private messaging app, Telegram, seems to be the social media app of choice, although it has been using Twitter more recently (Ries 2016).

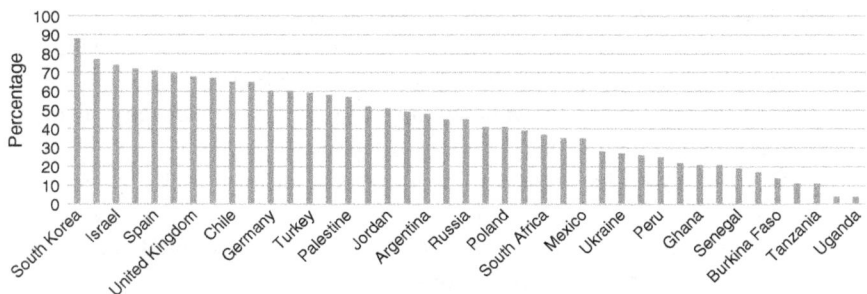

FIGURE 7.1   2015 Smartphone ownership by country.

Source: wikipedia

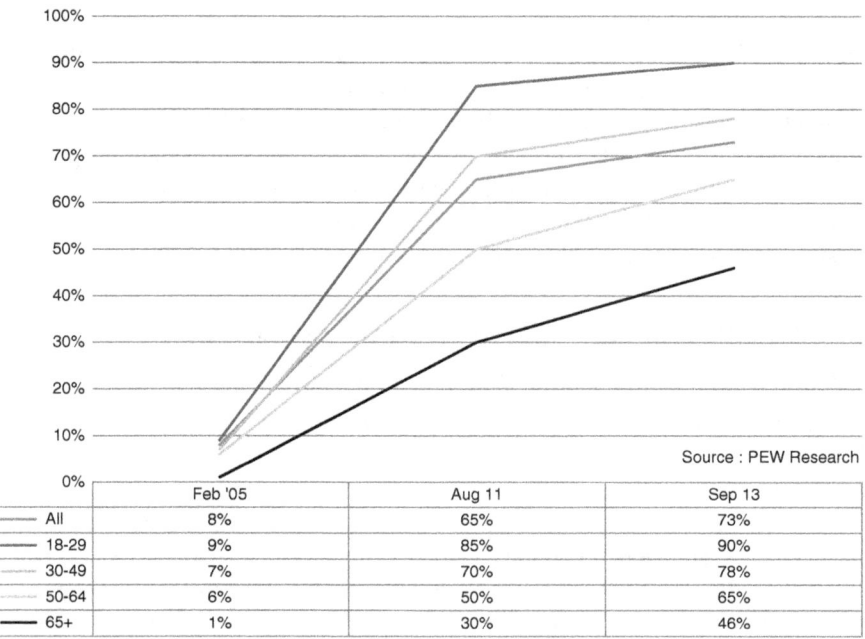

	Feb '05	Aug 11	Sep 13
All	8%	65%	73%
18-29	9%	85%	90%
30-49	7%	70%	78%
50-64	6%	50%	65%
65+	1%	30%	46%

Source : PEW Research

FIGURE 7.2 Social networking use by Age Group.

Michael S. Smith II, a principal at the counter-terrorist firm Kronos Advisory, received this message on Twitter from an invite-only ISIS Twitter group (Ries 2016):

Below were the seven tips given to Jihadists before the Tuesday attacks in Brussels (if this information is legitimate) (Ries 2016):

1. Stay away from using the Internet unless you are using encryption software such as (Tor Network – i2P Network – VPN).
2. Encrypt all of our jihadi's files and it's better to delete them permanently with Eraser or iShredder or kill the disk.
3. We highly recommend using TailsOS or Qubes OS and stay away from using any other products or systems unless you unplug the Internet.
4. Stay away from social media websites, don't share any information with your brothers right now, keep a low profile until the heat dies down.
5. Intelligence agencies will work all day and night to catch any jihadi in Belgium so be ready to act.
6. Try to change your location as soon as possible and don't tell anyone about your location.
7. Don't panic, keep calm and concentrate on your next move and don't forget to warn your brothers to take precautions.

Recently, the Electronic Frontier Foundation (EFF) found Google was mining student browsing data and sharing this data with third parties while students were using Chromebooks. The sync feature is automatically enabled in the Chrome browser. EFF then filed a complaint with the FTC. They discovered the issue through their 'Spying on Students' programme, a programme created to raise awareness of privacy risk issues with school-supplied electronic devices and software. Google has promised to disable the setting on Google Chromebooks going forward (Godbe 2015). Parents should be made aware of these privacy issues and they are not. Why? Who is protecting our children?

This example is no different than the fact that phone manufacturers geocode your pictures by default so anyone can find where the picture was taken if you turn location services on. This was done automatically when the first camera phones were introduced and has never been changed. These two scenarios raise ethical issues. Why are consumers not paying attention and why are phone manufacturers not clear about the data they capture, potentially putting users at risk?

The other most fascinating security and privacy risk is that of the QR code. This code, when scanned by your smartphone, takes you to a site where malware can be downloaded (Zetter 2016).

Hackers, as of October 2015 according to researchers at the French Network and Information Security Agency, can take charge of Siri and Google Now and issue it with commands as long as your headphones are plugged into your iPhone or Android device. The headphone wire acts as an antenna to receive radio waves. A hacker can do this simply by using a laptop with open source radio software, an amplifier and an antenna to send commands over radio waves. The recommended solutions are better shielding for the headphone cord or using 'wake words' to launch personal assistants (Newcomb 2015).

Social engineering hacking

The definition of social engineering hacking is an attack vector that relies heavily on human interaction and often involves tricking people into breaking normal security procedures (Google). This technique is one of the most effective ways in which hackers can gain access to a system. Social media make it even easier, because people post most of the items that make up their passwords like favourite colours, pets' names, children's names, birthday dates and so on. It is also possible to do something called number spoofing. This involves first searching on the Internet to obtain information from your victim's social media activity and any other information publically available online. After this, you can begin to use number spoofing.

Number spoofing works through a piece of software that changes the user's phone number to transmit the number of the person they want to represent. For instance, it is possible to call the victim's cell phone company and the victim's number will show up in their system instead of the number the hacker is calling from. To make the scenario even more authentic, hackers can do things like pretend they are busy with kids by playing a YouTube video of kids crying in the background, so they can imply they have a busy household. This makes it more believable to say they forgot what email address they used and typically have an email address in around thirty seconds from the customer service representative. They can continue the charade using a fake social security number and get the account set up in their own name.

It is not necessary to learn to use sophisticated software tools to hack someone's account. There are software tools out there that can gain access to your computer and smartphone, but it is easier for hackers to use simple social engineering techniques to obtain the data or money they want.

Social media policy

Companies are now being forced to develop social media policies in order not only to protect their brand but also to protect their employees from lack of common sense when it comes to using social media and their smartphones. If you were to work for a detention centre, would it be wise to post that you are going off to work today? Or state that you know some of the people detained there?

Unfortunately for companies, workers are using social media at work primarily for a mental break, but there are other reason as well. Here are the top three reason for using social media at work:

Taking a mental break from work:	34%
Connecting with friends/family:	27%
Making/supporting professional connections:	23%

(Source: Pew Research)

The graph in Figure 7.3 depicts how younger workers are using social media to find information, which either improves or lowers their opinion of a co-worker.

The most important item to note is that when a company develops an at-work social media policy, employees are less likely to use social media for personal reasons on the job.

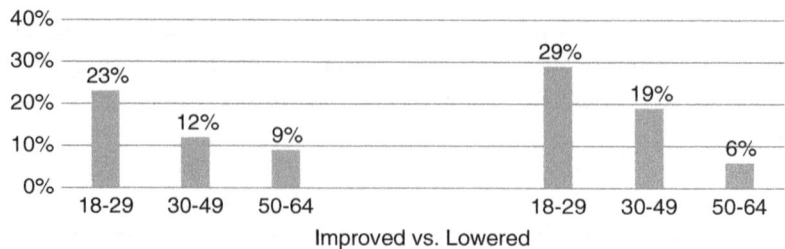

FIGURE 7.3 How Social Media has either improved or lowered opinions of their colleagues by Age Group.

Source: PEW Research

It is important for companies to define specific boundaries with regard to what is posted by employees on their social media to really protect their brand. Employees need to say that they are speaking for themselves and be reminded that the Internet is a public space and what they say online does not disappear. As time goes by, it can be predicted that more issues will arise and social media policies will need to be changed. Examples of companies that have good social media policies are Adidas, Best Buy, HP and GAP. Governments are also having to put social media policies in place, especially in the court systems, so there is no perception of partiality on the part of attorneys, judges and their staff.

What follows are some examples of interesting social media policy employee misunderstandings:

- When factory worker Ashley Heffran learned she had received a $100 holiday bonus from her company, she turned to Facebook to praise her employer. She posted: 'I was wowed by this today. Feels great to be appreciated by your job'. Before her shift ended, Heffran's supervisor informed her that she had been fired for violating the company's zero-tolerance policy for work-related social media posts (O'Connor, Schmidt and Drouin 2016).
- Similarly, when journalist Kristopher Brooks received a job offer from the *Wilmington News Journal*, he announced it on his personal Tumblr blog. Soon after, Brooks was notified that his job offer had been rescinded because he quoted his offer letter and used the company's logo when making his announcement.

The table below illustrates employees' understanding of their company's social media policy for those who knew their company has a social media policy:

	Yes	No	I don't know
Know what violates company's SM policy	50%	50%	–
Company gives practical advice for employee SM use	42%	18%	41%
Company has 'use common sense' provision	54%	10%	36%
Company requires protection of trade secrets	42%	11%	47%
Company prohibits online discussion related to work	30%	23%	48%

Note: $n = 118$ (O'Connor, Schmidt, Drouin 2016)

Social media policies, as can be seen from the above examples and data, need to be clearly written so they can be easily understood by employees.

Conclusion

Social media marketing is progressing at a rapid rate and our privacy is at stake. For example, McDonald's requests your friendship on Facebook. You visit your local McDonald's and make a purchase based on a Facebook promotion. McDonald's can keep a record of their Facebook 'friends" purchases through tracking the last four numbers on their credit or debit cards to tell how often they visit a McDonald's location, what was purchased and how, and how much money was spent. Some consumers may not be aware of this and, if they were, may not be comfortable with McDonald's having this information about them.

Our trust is being tested. See for example Figure 7.4, a standard Google message sent by email informing a user that someone has their password.

Now, here is an example of a fake Gmail alert that was used to obtain a password. The difference is almost imperceptible.

As another example, Figure 7.5 shows a fake American Express email asking the user to verify their credit card data.

Think about how much of your privacy and trust is being taken advantage of. Mobile connected devices are becoming the standard and new social media apps are being created and adopted faster that adults can learn them. Our children end up teaching us how to use the technology tools we created yet we are not considering the privacy, public safety and ethical issues before they are deployed. With the new wave of connected devices or the 'Internet of things', privacy is going to be the most important.

It is apparent that in most situations the general public is not really that educated with regard to technology. Take, for example, a Comcast commercial selling

Google

Someone has your password

Hi jane,

Someone just used your password to try to sign in to your Google Account k221iun@gmail.com.

Details:
Friday, October 21, 2016 3:35 PM (Central Daylight Time)
Crown Point, IN, USA*

Google stopped this sign-in attempt, but you should review your recently used devices:

REVIEW YOUR DEVICES NOW

Best,
The Google Accounts team

*The location is approximate and determined by the IP address it was coming from.

This email can't receive replies. For more information, visit the Google Accounts Help Center

You received this mandatory email service announcement to update you about important changes to your Google product or account.

FIGURE 7.4 Example of a fake gmail alert.

Your Card Number Begining: -37XX

Dear Valid Member,

We recently made some changes to make our valued Customers happier with better security and more benefits for staying with us. We have updated our website once more and we advice you, our valid customer to follow the Update below.

VERIFY YOU CARD

It is important you verify your card details on site to be part of the benefits as a valid memeber and avoid recurrence of any future attention with card and online access.

Thank you for your Card Membership.

Sincerely,
American Express Customer Care

FIGURE 7.5 Example of a fake American Express email alert.

the benefits of security cameras with your data accessible from the cloud. The customer probably does not think to ask the most important question: who else has access to the camera data? The social responsibility is in the hands of the technology companies and the social content is the user's responsibility. You might want to look at Kim Kardashian and ask how she felt when she was robbed at gunpoint in Paris and she flashed her $4M dollar ring on social media.

Social media users need to pay attention to what privacy they are giving away for free. Figure 7.6 shows the number of social media networks and users worldwide.

It is important for social media networks to respect user privacy and for smartphones to protect it. If the public loses trust in the privacy, safety and security of social media applications and their smartphones, the implications could be devastating. Governments would be forced to develop very restrictive regulations for marketers, smartphone manufacturers and social media networks. Depending on how restrictive government regulations become, marketers might have to resort to other channels to market their products and the public might stop using social media applications and possibly their smartphones. Is this worth the risk of not acting responsibly?

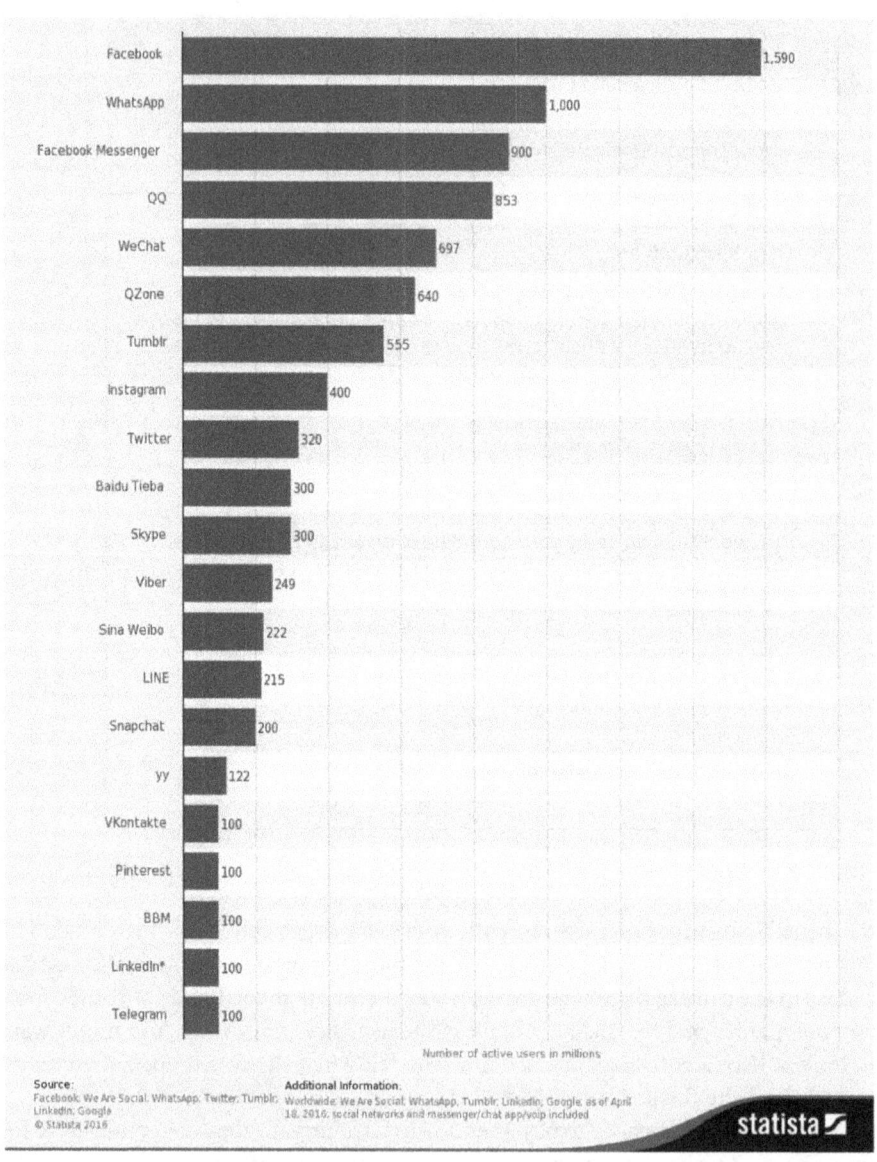

FIGURE 7.6   Leading social networks worldwide as of April 2016, ranked by number of active user (in millions).

References

Bandyopadhyay, S. 2009. *Contemporary Research in E-branding*. Hershey, PA: Information Science Reference.

Cook, T. 2016. 'Customer Letter – Apple. A message to our customers'. Apple, 16 February 2016. Available at https://www.apple.com/ie/customer-letter/.

Crovitz, G. 2016. 'FBI vs. Apple isn't over'. *WSJ*. WSJ, 27 March 2016. Available at https://www.wsj.com/articles/fbi-vs-apple-isnt-over-1459116064.

Fishleigh, J. 2015. 'Is someone watching you? Data privacy and protection: current issues'. *Legal Information Management*, 15(1): p. 61–69. Lls.

Godbe, M. 2015. 'Google deceptively tracks students' Internet browsing, EFF says in FTC complaint'. Electronic Frontier Foundation (EFF), 01 December 2015. Available at https://www.eff.org/press/releases/google-deceptively-tracks-students-internet-browsing-eff-says-complaint-federal-trade.

Greenburg, J. 'To fight the FBI, Apple ditched secrecy for openness'. Wired.com. Condé Nast Digital, 25 March 2016. Available at https://www.wired.com/2016/03/fight-fbi-apple-ditched-secrecy-openness/.

Jayaram, D, A. Manrai and L. Manrai. 2015. 'Effective use of marketing technology in Eastern Europe: web analytics, social media, customer analytics, digital campaigns and mobile applications'. *Journal of Economics, Finance & Administrative Science*, 20(39): p. 118–132, Business Source Complete.

Newcomb, A. 2015. 'How Hackers say they can silently commandeer Siri, Google Now'. ABC News, 14 October 2105. Available at http://abcnews.go.com/Technology/hackers-silently-commandeer-siri-google-now/story?id=34475819.

O'Connor, K. W., G. B. Schmidt, M. Drouin. 'Helping workers understand and follow social media policies'. *Business Horizons*, 59(2): p. 205–211.

Orzan, G., C. Vegheş, C. Silvestru, M. Orzan and R. Bere. 2012. 'Marketing implications of information society privacy concerns', *Review of International Comparative Management/Revista De Management Comparat International*, 13(5), p. 733–742, Business Source Complete, December 2012.

Rainie, L. and S. Maniam. 2016. 'Americans feel the tensions between privacy and security concerns'. Pew Research Center RSS. Pew Research, 19 February 2016.

Ries, B. 2016. 'ISIS tech team warns "brothers in Belgium" to avoid social media after Brussels attacks'. Mashable, 23 March 2016. Available at http://www.gizmodo.in/indiamodo/ISIS-Tech-Team-Warns-Brothers-In-Belgium-To-Avoid-Social-Media-After-Brussels-Attacks/articleshow/51528921.cms.

Weise, E. and J. Swartz. 2016. 'Twist in iPhone hacking puzzle leads to Israel'. *USA Today*. Gannett, 23 March 2016. Available at https://www.usatoday.com/story/tech/news/2016/03/23/report-israeli-firm-mysterious-outside-party-aiding-fbi/82157046/.

Williams, K. B. 2016. 'FBI reversal in Apple fight draws critics' ire'. *The Hill*. 27 March 2016. Available at http://thehill.com/policy/cybersecurity/274350-fbi-reversal-in-apple-fight-draws-critics-ire.

Zetter, K. 2016. 'NSA hacker chief explains how to keep him out of your system'. *Wired.com*. Condé Nast Digital, 28 January 2016. Available at https://www.wired.com/2016/01/nsa-hacker-chief-explains-how-to-keep-him-out-of-your-system/.

8

CREATING, CONTRIBUTING AND CONSUMING BEHAVIOUR

How rational and affective appeals in social media facilitate engagement

Rebecca Dolan, Jodie Conduit and John Fahy

Introduction

Social media platforms have significantly altered the way customers communicate and interact with each other, and with businesses. Platforms such as Facebook have grown rapidly; while it took 38 years for the radio to attract 50 million listeners, and 13 years for television to gain 50 million viewers, it took just 18 months for Facebook to reach 50 million participants (Nair 2011). In 2016, there were more than 1.65 billion monthly active users on Facebook, 1 billion monthly active users of WhatsApp, 500 million monthly active users of Instagram and 310 million monthly active users of Twitter (Statista 2016). The interactive properties of social media have transformed consumers from passive observers of content to active participants, who create vast quantities of user generated content through their conversations, interactions and behaviours online. In line with an increased focus on research exploring customer engagement (Brodie *et al.* 2013; Maslowska *et al.* 2015), particularly in the digital space (Hollebeek *et al.* 2014), practitioners and academics are looking for guidance on how customer engagement may be facilitated through social media. In this chapter, we explore how brands can facilitate engagement through the delivery of specific types of affective and rational social media messages.

Social media enables customers to interact with brands in various ways. Muntinga, Moorman and Smit (2011) show that consumers' 'online brand related activities' include creating, contributing and consuming online content. Customers engage online through positively valenced and active behaviours including leaving comments on content, sharing and 'liking' brand related content. Customer engagement can also be more passive, where fans read posts, view photos and watch videos, but do not actively contribute to the content (Dolan *et al.* 2016a). Engagement behaviour is also proposed to occur in a negatively valenced manner, where customers use social media forums to express their dissatisfaction and spread negative word of mouth (Dolan *et al.* 2016a). Although research like this shows the ways in which customers may engage through certain behaviours, it remains unknown how brands can deliver and design their online content, such as social media posts, to enhance engagement.

In this chapter, we expand on the work of Muntinga *et al.* (2011) and Dolan *et al.* (2016a, b) to empirically investigate the effects of social media content posted by brands on the social media engagement behaviours of consumers. We investigate how different types of content (affective versus rational) affect the intensity of a user's engagement behaviour. Engagement behaviour of low intensity is defined as consuming behaviour, of moderate intensity as contributing behaviour and of high intensity as creating behaviour. The three categories of engagement intensity are derived from Muntinga *et al.* (2011) and Dolan *et al.* (2016a). This chapter develops interesting results as to how these engagement behaviours are altered by the presence of various affective and rational message appeals. As such, we address one of the challenges in the delivery and design of social media content, and focus on a Marketing Science Institute key topic of interest; to understand how social media marketing activities create customer engagement (MSI 2014).

Literature review

Consumers are increasingly becoming more active participants on social media sites. They are increasingly able to interact with each other and with brands through real-time, two-way communication (Brodie *et al.* 2013). The interactive properties of social media serve as an ideal forum for product and brand-related advocacy (Chu and Kim 2011; Riegner 2007), customer-led content generation (Vivek *et al.* 2012) and customer-created product innovations (Hoyer *et al.* 2010; Sawhney *et al.* 2005). Therefore, there is a significant amount of social and network value provided to both users and organizations through social media. Social media have become a popular topic of academic enquiry, with scholars exploring the concept from varying perspectives, including the usage motivations of participants (Joinson 2008; Raacke and Bonds-Raacke 2008), social interactions, usage patterns (Golder *et al.* 2007; Hsu and Lin 2008; Lampe *et al.* 2006) and characteristics of users (Gjoka *et al.* 2008; Hargittai 2007).

Less academic attention has been given to the role of social media from a strategic marketing perspective. Practitioners have largely been at the forefront of efforts to advise businesses on the design of their social media content, with an inundation of industry blogs, websites and guides on the best practice for marketing within the social network sphere emerging in recent years (Steeves 2013). While the nature of social media influences the degree to which customers engage with the organization (Malthouse *et al.* 2013), little research has investigated how engagement is achieved. Although recent research has explored both the antecedents and consequences of customer engagement (Gambetti *et al.* 2012; Leckie *et al.* 2016;

van Doorn *et al.* 2010), studies that consider engagement with social media are only beginning to emerge (Malthouse *et al.* 2013).

Characterizing consumers' online brand related behaviour

Previous research has focussed on traditional categorizations of 'users' of online communities, distinguishing between users who create content such as 'posters', compared to those who are members of a community but do not post, referred to as 'lurkers' (Nonnecke and Preece 1999; Preece *et al.* 2004). This basic categorization of online users is limited in its general nature and fails to take into account the diverse number of possible roles available to users on dynamic platforms. Previous research categorized social media users who 'like' brands on Facebook into groups based on their brand loyalty, brand love, use of self-expressive brands and word of mouth (Wallace *et al.* 2014). While such investigations are practically useful, a lack of understanding remains in terms of understanding engagement intensity and actions, beyond the primary actions of 'liking' a brand on Facebook. In an attempt to define customer engagement intensity within social media, scholars have also characterized engagement behaviours on a continuum of low to high activity (Muntinga *et al.* 2011). Muntinga *et al.* (2011) propose three social usage types: *consuming* (low level of brand related activity), *contributing* (medium level) and *creating* (highest level).

Creating behaviour: According to Muntinga *et al.* (2011), 'creating' behaviour represents the ultimate level of online brand-related activeness. It denotes actively producing brand-related content that other social network members can consume and contribute to. Within social media platforms, creating users make unique, active contributions to social media content by disseminating their knowledge, resources and experiences (Brodie *et al.* 2013). This behaviour goes beyond relaying (e.g. sharing, liking) content created by the brand and reflects a user's contribution to the brand's social media site (Dolan *et al.* 2016b).

Contributing behaviour: The contributing type of online brand related behaviour is reflective of the middle level of activeness (Muntinga *et al.* 2011). Users contribute to existing content on social media platforms (Dolan *et al.* 2016b). Contributing sees users forward or contribute to existing content; however, they do not create any additional or new content in the form of writing a comment or post (Dolan *et al.* 2016b). Through functions such as 'sharing' content on Facebook, and 'retweeting' messages on Twitter, users contribute by forwarding brand content to members of their own network. Additionally, users contribute to content by indicating their preferences for specific social media content through selecting the 'Like' function on Facebook and Instagram, tagging friends and other users in comments, and functions such as the 'favourite' option on Twitter.

Consuming behaviour: Consumption behaviour is passive, whereby consumers exhibit a level of engagement but do not actively contribute to or create content (Dolan *et al.* 2016b). Consuming is defined as the passive consumption of brand related content through reading reviews, discussion and comments, viewing photos, watching videos and clicking on content and links. Consuming represents a minimum level of online brand related activeness (Muntinga *et al.* 2011). Through the consumption of content within social media platforms, individuals may extract individual value but their consumption will not impact on other users of the social media platform. Reading discussions (e.g. to find information) is a form of passive engagement, whereas posting comments is active engagement (Shang *et al.* 2006; Gummerus *et al.* 2012).

In this chapter, we explore how the three types of consumers (creating, contributing and consuming) in online brand related activities may be influenced by the type of message delivered by brands.

Strategically enhancing online engagement behaviour

In social media, a brand's overt goal is to attract an audience by providing value, or gratification, through its content. Content must therefore be designed in a way that creates value for individual consumers to build engagement (Malthouse *et al.* 2013; Dolan *et al.* 2016b). In 2017, social network advertising spending is expected to reach $36 billion worldwide, representing 16% of all digital advertising spending globally (eMarketer 2015). However, scholars have suggested that most of the investment into digital strategy may be largely wasted (Griffin 2013). Supporting research has shown poor online engagement rates, with an average of only 0.07% of Facebook fans interacting with a brand's post (Gayomali 2014). Marketing practitioners have identified that they have lack of awareness and knowledge regarding effective social media strategy, creating a significant challenge as practitioners navigate through this forum with little guidance or empirical understanding (Stelzner 2014). Within this chapter, we extend the work of Muntinga *et al.* (2011) and Dolan *et al.* (2016a, b) to predict how online engagement behaviours (creating, contributing and consuming behaviours) may be facilitated, mitigated or neutralized by the delivery of *affective or rational message appeals* within social media. While the nature of social media influences the degree to which customers engage with the organization (Malthouse *et al.* 2013), little research has investigated how engagement is achieved.

Rational message appeals

Rational messages appeal to facts and reasoning, whereas emotional messages appeal to the consumers' feelings (Hahn *et al.* 2016). In traditional media, researchers argue that informational properties of messages (e.g. rational message appeals), are more influential than affective/emotional appeals in generating positive responses among consumers (Holbrook 1978). Research has shown that consumers tend to prefer rational advertisements for utilitarian products, and affective/emotional advertisements for hedonic products (Drolet and Aaker 2002). However, Drolet *et al.* (2007) show that for certain customers (over sixty-five years of age), attitudes are more favourable toward affective (versus rational) ads, regardless of the product category, whereas, for younger consumers (age 18–25) affective ads are only favoured for hedonic products. Rationally-framed message appeals include factual information related to the product (McKay-Nesbitt *et al.* 2011). Comparatively, emotional or affective appeals can include positively framed appeals focussed on warm emotions associated with or related to the product (McKay-Nesbitt *et al.* 2011).

Rational message appeals in social media include information regarding details on price, availability, location and product names (Lee *et al.* 2013). Further, rational information may contain explanatory images referring to the brand's location, facilities and products. The rational content may also relate to brand contact details such as the provision of contact phone numbers, email addresses, links to a website and opening hours where applicable. While the importance of delivering rational content in the form of product related information through advertisements has been well recognized with respect to traditional media (Rubin 2002), the role of rational message appeals and content in the online domain has only recently received attention. Obtaining information is one of the most important reasons consumers use the Internet (Stafford *et al.* 2004), and a positive association exists between levels of informativeness and attitude towards websites (Chen *et al.* 2002). On social media, customers willingly select the brands they wish to follow and receive updates from, compared to traditional media in which advertisements are presented to viewers regardless of their levels of interest in the topic. It can therefore be argued that customers are more likely to seek information through their selected brand followings, and thus messages with a rational appeal may be more effective on social media, compared to traditional media. Recent studies have suggested a positive relationship between rational, informative content and engagement behaviour in a social media context (De Vries *et al.* 2012; Cvijikj and Michahelles 2013; Lee *et al.* 2013). However, these studies do not distinguish between levels of engagement intensity (e.g. creating, contributing and consuming), nor do they examine the effects of specific types of rational content.

Affective message appeals

In traditional media, Brown *et al.* (1998) argue that emotions can influence behaviour and determine greater advertising effectiveness compared to rational and informative appeals. Affective social media message appeals may include small talk, banter or attempts to appeal to a person's emotions. Further, affective content may not focus on the brand or product, but may be written in the form of a teaser, slogan or word play, which has been found to increase the number of likes, comments and shares made on Facebook posts (Cvijikj and Michahelles 2013). Affective message appeals such as the use of entertaining advertisements have also been found to lead to positive attitudes towards both the advertisements (Taylor *et al.* 2011) and the brand, and produce a desire to return to the websites (Raney and Janicke 2013). Further, affectively-framed advertisements can motivate users to consume, contribute to and create brand-related content online

(Muntinga *et al.* 2011). Social media content that attempts to appeal to a person's emotions has been empirically found to increase engagement behaviour in the form of likes and comments (Lee *et al.* 2013). However, it is unknown what types of affective appeal specifically have a greater impact on the various intensities of engagement.

While there has been significant attention paid to affective or emotional versus. rational advertising message appeals in traditional media (Williams and Drolet 2005; Drolet and Aaker 2002; Drolet *et al.* 2007), little attention has focussed on the role of these specific message appeals in influencing consumers' engagement in the online, social setting. Within this chapter, we assess how these two contrasting message appeals are used by brands within social media. We examine three dependent variables, representing the various intensity levels of consumers' online engagement behaviour.

Research design

This study utilized Facebook Insights data from active Facebook brand pages in the Australian wine industry. Facebook Insights is a tool accessible by administrators of Facebook brand pages that enables high-level monitoring of the activities that occur on that page. It allows administrators to download data concerning the performance of a post, such as the number of people the post reached, the number of people who clicked the post and the number of people who liked, commented on or shared the post. If the post is a video, Insights data also shows the total number of video views, and the length of these views (Facebook 2015). Facebook Insights provides access to the engagement metrics used in this study.

As access to Facebook page insights is restricted to page administrators, an introductory email was sent to fifty Australian wine brands outlining the study and requesting access to the required data. Twelve Australian wine brands were selected to participate in the study, and each provided data for a twelve-month period, beginning on 1 January 2013 and concluding on 31 December 2013. A range of brands were selected in order to ensure a representative sample, including consideration of the number of fans, region and/or location, ownership (family owned and corporate) and frequency of posting. This data enabled the researchers to access and explore the actual behavioural metrics of the engagement (creating, contributing and consuming) and match this data with the social media content posted by the brands. The independent variables were the affective and rational message appeals presented in Table 8.1. The dependent variables were the engagement behaviours of creating, contributing and consuming, derived through an examination of the engagement metrics available from Facebook Insights. The metrics for the dependent variables are presented in Table 8.1.

The researchers collected and analysed a total of 2,236 Facebook posts over a twelve-month period. To categorize social media content according its presence of affective and rational message appeals, we followed Neuendorf's (2002) approach to quantitative content analysis, which allows the researcher to objectively and systematically identify specified characteristics of messages (Carney 1972). Given the significant amount of data provided through tools such as Facebook Insights and NCapture, we used automated quantitative methods of text analysis. Specifically, we employed computer coding and text analysis to make inferences about social media content. This approach generated a full coding scheme and a custom dictionary for the text analysis of each type of social media content appeal (affective and rational). After developing the full coding scheme and custom dictionaries, we coded the content in a binary manner. Where a type of social media content was present (e.g. affective or rational appeal), it was coded as 1, while its absence was recorded as 0. In addition, each sub-category was coded as 1 or 0, which allowed for the level of content to be calculated. The individual rational and affective message elements are presented in Table 8.2.

Binary logistic regression was applied to empirically investigate the relationships between the types of content (affective versus rational) embedded within a social media post, and the effect on the dependent variables (creating, contributing and consuming engagement behaviours). Of the 2,236 posts, 82.6 per cent contained rational message appeals within the content, and 50.7 per cent contained affective message appeals within the content. The social media posts varied in the *amount* of affective or rational content present. To illustrate, whilst some posts had just one element of rational content, others had up to eleven different rational elements.

TABLE 8.1 Facebook Insights metrics for creating, contributing and consuming

Engagement Behaviour	Facebook Insights Metric (per post)
Creating	Number of comments made on post
Contributing	Number of posts that are 'liked' or 'shared'
Consuming	Clicks to play videos; Link clicks; Other clicks (photo, status); Photo view; Reading content (measured by no. of clicks to 'read more')

TABLE 8.2 Rational vs. affective message appeals coded

Rational Message Appeals Coded	Affective Message Appeals Coded
Product image	Discussion of local weather
Location image	Fun/entertaining fact
Website information/link	Scenic imagery
Product medal/award	Food and product images/discussion
Event information	Use of celebrity or influential person
Brand name information	Meme image (humour)
Product variety information	Animal image
Service related information	Animal mentioned/discussed
Product origin information	Relaxed and casual language used
Product description	Employee image used

Findings and discussion

The results show that various types of affective and rational message appeals within social media content have a strong and significant relationship with the online engagement behaviours of users. This section will present the results for creating behaviour, followed by contributing and consuming behaviour, including corresponding discussion of the effects of both rational and affective message appeals. Overall, five types of rational message appeals had an effect on creating behaviour, seven types of rational appeals had an effect on contributing behaviour in the form of shares, six types of rational message appeals had an effect on contributing behaviour in the form of likes and there were no types of rational appeals that effected consuming behaviour. Interestingly, the rational message appeals that affected contributing behaviour in the form of 'shares' were different than the appeals that caused the post to be 'liked'. In terms of affective message appeals, eight appeals had a significant effect on creating behaviour, while only two types of affective message appeals influenced contributing behaviour in the form of shares, and contributing behaviour in the form of likes. There was no evidence to suggest that affective message appeals facilitate consuming behaviour.

Creating behaviour

When social media users comment on statuses, videos and pictures posted by the brand, they exhibit creating behaviour. Through the creation of their comment, the user creates new content, which can facilitate the further engagement behaviour of other brand fans.

The results presented in Table 8.3 show that certain forms of rational content facilitate creating behaviour. Specifically, the presence of a product image, location image and details about a product award or medal, increase the odds of creating behaviour occurring. The results also show that the presence of some forms of rational content will reduce the likelihood of users exhibiting creating behaviours. This includes content in the form of a website link and details of an event. This could be explained by the fact that provision of such information would cause the user to navigate towards an external page (e.g. the website), rather than exhibiting engagement within the Facebook platform. Overall, the most effective type of rational content shown to facilitate creating behaviour is product images, which almost double the likelihood that a user will exhibit creating behaviour (i.e. write a comment). Photos and images have a higher degree of richness, or vividness, and have been known to be more effective in facilitating attention and engagement (Cvijikj and Michahelles 2013).

Creating behaviour can also be enhanced or mitigated by specific forms of affective content. Affective content that increases the odds of creating behaviour occurring includes: a scenic image, images of food and produce, details or images of a celebrity or social influencer, details about the weather, meme images, and animal images. The results in Table 8.3 show that when a brand posts affective

TABLE 8.3 Binary logistic regression results for social media content types and engagement behaviours

Type		Creating			Contributing (shares)			Contributing (likes)			Consuming	
		B		Exp(B)	B		Exp(B)	b		Exp(B)	b	Exp(B)
Rational Message Appeals	Product image	.690	***	1.99	.60	***	1.82	.55	*	1.74	-.419	.658
	Location image	.314	*	1.37	.183	***	1.201	.473		1.604	-.169	.845
	Website link	-.472	***	.62	-.165		.848	-.119		.888	1.122	3.070
	Product medal/award	.551	**	1.73	.66	***	1.94	2.47	*	11.77	16.067	NR
	Event details	-.824	***	.44	-.61	*	.545	-.505		.604	-.194	.284
	Brand name	.28		1.33	.350	**	1.42	.95		1.64	1.156	3.178
	Product variety	.171		1.18	.44	*	1.55	.95	*	2.58	.665	1.945
	Service details	.278		1.321	.46	*	1.59	1.90	*	6.69	.202	1.224
	Product origin	.163		1.177	.221		1.248	.73	*	2.07	1.382	3.984
	Wine description	.137		1.147	.192		1.212	1.12	*	3.07	16.825	NR
Affective Message Appeals	Weather	.397	*	1.487	.205		1.228	.972	*	2.643	1.381	3.980
	Fun fact	-1.24	*	.29	-.017		.983	-.868		.420	17.020	NR
	Scenic image	.485	*	1.625	0.12		1.012	.795	*	2.215	-.409	.665
	Food/produce image	.297	*	1.345	.462	*	1.587	.045		1.046	-.416	.660
	Celebrity/influencer	.966	*	2.628	.867		2.380	18.601		NR	17.087	NR
	Meme image	.640	*	1.897	.495		1.641	.309		1.362	17.010	NR
	Animal image	.497	*	1.644	.398		1.489	.535		1.707	.486	1.626
	Animal mentioned	.858		2.359	.858	*	2.359	18.66		NR	16.671	NR
	Slang language	-.443		.642	-.488		.614	-.937	*	.392	-.712	.491
	Employee image	.648	***	.912	.082		1.085	.464		1.590	-.291	.747

NR = Exp(B) not reported when > 10 and non-significant

content in the form of an image of an employee or staff member, the odds of a user exhibiting creating behaviour is almost doubled (Exp(B)=1.912). In other words, when social media content includes an image of an employee, fans are twice as likely to write a comment. This type of affective content is visually engaging, and also provides a personal representation of the brand through the image of the employee. Only one type of affective content was found to reduce creating behaviour: the provision of a fun fact, which reduced the odds of creating behaviour occurring by 71% (Exp(B) = .29).

Contributing behaviour

Contributing behaviour was measured in this study through two social media engagement functions: 'liking' a social media post, and 'sharing' a showing media post.

Table 8.3 demonstrates that rational appeals in the form of a product image increase the chances of contributing behaviour in the form of both likes and shares occurring. Similarly, including rational appeals in the form of product success such as an award or medal increases the odds of both liking and sharing occurring. Mentioning the product variety (in the case of this study, the product variety relates to the variety of wine, e.g. 'Shiraz') is a positive informational element in predicting both likes and shares. Describing the origin of the product almost doubles the likelihood that a user will 'like' the post, while describing the characteristics of the product triples the odds that the content will be 'liked' (Exp(B) = 3.07). This finding demonstrates that fans are interested in product specific information, and whilst they may not comment on or share the information, they are more likely to 'like' posts which possess this information.

While there were seven types of rational appeals that significantly predicted the occurrence of creating behaviour, only two types of affective message appeals predicted contributing behaviour in the form of shares. These were food and produce images, and the mention of an animal or pet. Affective message appeals in the form of a food or produce image increased the odds of the content being shared by 1.58 times, while the mention of an animal in affective message appeals increased the odds of the content being shared by 2.36 times. Affective message appeals regarding local weather conditions were 2.643 times more likely to be 'liked', and scenic images were 2.215 times more likely to be 'liked'. The use of casual and slang language, for example 'lol' or 'omg' within affective message appeals had a detrimental effect on contributing behaviour in the form of likes. The results show a negatively weighted beta of -.937, indicating that users are almost 60% less likely to 'like' a post which contains this form of content (Exp(B) = .392).

Consuming behaviour

Consuming behaviour involves online users consuming content (e.g. reading or viewing content) without any form of active reciprocation or contribution. This behaviour is an example of a passive online brand related activity. Consuming behaviour was measured though clicks to play videos, link clicks, other clicks (on a photo or status), enlarged photo views and reading content (number of clicks to 'read more'). One limitation to mention is the inability to measure the extent to which the fans consume the content created by other fans, such as a comment. The consuming behaviours measured are all directly related to the content delivered by the brand, rather than the content added by other fans and users. The results showed that there were no message appeals that had a significant effect on consuming behaviour. This is an interesting finding as it demonstrates that the actual content of social media message appeals are not a driving factor in a fan's decision to watch videos, click through photos, read comments or read posts. Further research is needed in order to understand exactly what motivates and causes brand fans to consume content online. Investigation of factors such as the time of the day may show interesting effects, with users being more likely to consume content when they are in a relaxed frame of mind, compared to scrolling through content whilst limited for time. The amount of content the fans are exposed to may also have implications for their lack of consumption, with a potential for informational overload occurring (Eppler and Mengis 2004).

Implications and conclusion

Malthouse *et al.* (2013) suggest that a brand's goal in social media strategy should be to attract an audience by providing value through social media content. The study presented in this chapter empirically demonstrates that brands are able to deliver varying types of both affective and rational message appeals within social media content in order to enhance fan engagement behaviour. We demonstrate an empirical relationship between social media content message appeals (rational and affective) and the online engagement behaviours proposed by Muntinga *et al.* (2011) and Dolan *et al.* (2016b). This demonstrates that content can be designed in a way that encourages individual consumers to exhibit a greater level of engagement (Malthouse *et al.* 2013).

The presence of rational appeals within social media posts was found to predict the occurrence of creating and contributing behaviours. This finding was consistent with previous literature which has stated that Internet users increase their usage patterns as a result of content gratification such as information seeking, knowledge and learning (Stafford *et al.* 2004). Similarly, the presence of affective message appeals within a social media post significantly predicted the occurrence of creating and contributing behaviour. This finding is consistent with Cvijikj and Michahelles (2013) who demonstrated that affective and entertaining content was a significant factor in increasing the number of likes, comments and shares made on social media posts. However, the effects of affective message appeals were not as strong as those observed for rational message appeals, demonstrating that there may be a benefit in brands focussing on informing their fans, rather than entertaining them.

Managers can benefit from our insights in multiple ways. First, we provide important implications regarding the strategic design and delivery of social media content and message appeals in order to facilitate creating and contributing online brand related behaviours. We show that both rational and affective message appeals can have a significant and positive effect on engagement behaviour in the form of 'creating' behaviour, which was measured as the likelihood of Facebook fans writing a comment. The most effective message appeal to increase the number of comments was the use of a celebrity or social influencer, which increased the odds of a fan writing a comment 2.6 times. The results also showed that contributing behaviour in the form of both likes and shares could be strategically enhanced through the use of rational and affective message appeals. The use of an affective message appeal that specifically includes discussion regarding an animal (e.g. a pet) was the most effective in terms of increasing the likelihood that the content would be shared. In terms of increasing the number of post 'likes', the rational message appeal of specifically mentioning and describing a product which has won an award had the strongest effect, with fans being almost twelve times more likely to 'like' the post. Interestingly, we did not find any significant relationships between the affective and rational message appeals and consuming behaviour. This indicates that while content can be strategically designed with various message appeals to enhance the number of comments, likes and shares, the message appeals do not appear to affect whether or not a fan will actively consume the content.

Although Muntinga *et al.* (2011) and Dolan *et al.* (2016a) propose that consumers vary in their online brand related activities or social media engagement behaviours, little is known about how brands *strategically deliver* online content to engage consumers in these ways. This chapter empirically investigated the effects of two types of social media content posted by brands on creating, contributing and consuming behaviours. Future research should consider the factors beyond affective and rational appeals that may be used by brands to facilitate engagement behaviours of a high intensity (e.g. creating). Future research should also investigate the consequences of creating, contributing and consuming behaviours, and the extent to which various types of users' online behaviours lead to outcomes such as future purchase intention and behaviour, brand loyalty, word-of mouth, and satisfaction, would add substantial value to the body of research concerning marketing strategy and social media.

References

Brodie, R. J., A. Ilic, B. Juric and L. Hollebeek. 2013. 'Consumer engagement in a virtual brand community: an exploratory analysis'. *Journal of Business Research*, 66: 105–114.

Brown, S. P., P. M. Homer and J. J. Inman. 1998. 'A meta-analysis of relationships between ad-evoked feelings and advertising responses'. *Journal of Marketing Research*, 114–126.

Carney, T. F. 1972. *Content analysis: A technique for systematic inference from communications*. New York: University of Manitoba Press.

Chen, Q., S. J. Clifford and W. D. Wells. 2002. 'Attitude toward the site II: new information'. *Journal of Advertising Research*, 42: 33–46.

Chu, S.-C. and Y. Kim. 2011. 'Determinants of consumer engagement in electronic word-of-mouth (eWOM) in social networking sites'. *International Journal of Advertising*, 30: 47–75.

Cvijikj, I. P. and F. Michahelles. 2013. 'Online engagement factors on Facebook brand pages'. *Social Network Analysis and Mining*, 3: 843–861.

De Vries, L., S. Gensler and P. S. Leeflang. 2012. 'Popularity of brand posts on brand fan pages: an investigation of the effects of social media marketing'. *Journal of Interactive Marketing*, 26: 83–91.

Dolan, R., J. Conduit and J. Fahy. 2016a. 'Social media engagement: a construct of positively and negatively valenced engagement behaviours'. In Brodie, R. J., L. Hollebeek and J. Conduit (eds), *Customer Engagement: Contemporary Issues and Challenges*. New York: Routledge.

Dolan, R., J. Conduit, J. Fahy and S. Goodman. 2016b. 'Social media engagement behaviour: a uses and gratifications perspective'. *Journal of Strategic Marketing*: 1–17.

Drolet, A. and J. Aaker. 2002. 'Off-target? Changing cognitive-based attitudes'. *Journal of Consumer Psychology*, 12: 59–68.

Drolet, A., P. Williams and L. Lau-Gesk. 2007. 'Age-related differences in responses to affective vs. rational ads for hedonic vs. utilitarian products'. *Marketing Letters*, 18: 211–221.

Emarketer. 2015. 'Social network ad spending to hit $23.68 billion worldwide in 2015' [online]. Available at http://www.emarketer.com/Article/Social-Network-Ad-Spending-Hit-2368-Billion-Worldwide-2015/1012357. Accessed 23 August 2015.

Eppler, M. J. and J. Mengis. 2004. 'The concept of information overload: a review of literature from organization science, accounting, marketing, MIS, and related disciplines'. *The Information Society*, 20: 325–344.

Facebook. 2015. 'Page post metrics' [online]. Available at https://www.facebook.com/help/336143376466063/. Accessed 14 September 2015.

Gambetti, R. C., G. Graffigna and S. Biraghi. 2012. 'The grounded theory approach to consumer-brand engagement'. *International Journal of Market Research*, 54: 659–687.

Gayomali, C. 2014. 'Brands are wasting time and money on Facebook and Twitter' [Online]. Available at http://www.fastcompany.com/3038801/brands-are-wasting-time-and-money-on-facebook-and-twitter-report-says. Accessed 3 April 2016.

Gjoka, M., M. Sirivianos, A. Markopoulou and X. Yang. 2008. 'Poking Facebook: characterization of osn applications'. Proceedings of the first workshop on online social networks. ACM: 31–36.

Golder, S. A., D. M. Wilkinson and B. A. Huberman. 2007. 'Rhythms of social interaction: messaging within a massive online network'. *Communities and Technologies 2007*. London: Springer.

Griffin, C. 2013. 'Social media: why it's a big fat waste of time and money'. Available at https://www.socialmediaexplorer.com/social-media-marketing/social-media-why-its-a-big-fat-waste-of-time-and-money/. Accessed 3 April 2016.

Gummerus, J., V. Liljander E. Weman and M. Pihlström. 2012. 'Customer engagement in a Facebook brand community'. *Management Research Review*, 35: 857–877.

Hahn, M. H., K. C. Lee and S. W. Chae. 2016. 'An eye-tracking approach to evaluating decision-makers' cognitive load and need-for-cognition in response with rational and emotional advertising stimuli'. International Conference on Human-Computer Interaction. London: Springer: 209–215.

Hargittai, E. 2007. 'Whose space? Differences among users and non-users of social network sites'. *Journal of Computer-Mediated Communication*, 13: 276–297.

Holbrook, M. B. 1978. 'Beyond attitude structure: toward the informational determinants of attitude'. *Journal of Marketing Research*: 15(4): 545–556.

Hollebeek, L. D., M. S. Glynn and R. J. Brodie. 2014. 'Consumer brand engagement in social media: conceptualization, scale development and validation'. *Journal of Interactive Marketing*, 28: 149–165.

Hoyer, W. D., R. Chandy, M. Dorotic, M. Krafft and S. S. Singh. 2010. 'Consumer cocreation in new product development'. *Journal of Service Research*, 13: 283–296.

Hsu, C.-L. and J. C.-C. Lin. 2008. 'Acceptance of blog usage: the roles of technology acceptance, social influence and knowledge sharing motivation'. *Information and Management*, 45: 65–74.

Joinson, A. N. 2008. 'Looking at, looking up or keeping up with people? Motives and use of Facebook'. Proceedings of the twenty-sixth annual SIGCHI conference on human factors in computing systems. Florence, Italy: ACM.

Lampe, C., N. Ellison and C. Steinfield. 2006. 'A face (book) in the crowd: social searching vs. social browsing'. Proceedings of the 2006 twentieth anniversary conference on computer supported cooperative work. Banff, Alberta, Canada: ACM: 167–170.

Leckie, C., M. W. Nyadzayo and L. W. Johnson. 2016. 'Antecedents of consumer brand engagement and brand loyalty'. *Journal of Marketing Management*, 32(5–6): 1–21.

Lee, D., K. Hosanagar and H. Nair. 2013. 'The effect of advertising content on consumer engagement: evidence from Facebook' [online]. Available at http://www.researchgate.net/publication/257409065.

Malthouse, E. C., M. Haenlein, B. Skiera, E. Wege and M. Zhang. 2013. 'Managing customer relationships in the social media era: introducing the social CRM house'. *Journal of Interactive Marketing*, 27: 270–280.

Maslowska, E., E. Malthouse and T. Collinger. 2015. 'The customer engagement ecosystem'. Available at SSRN 2694040.

Mckay-Nesbitt, J., R. V. Manchanda, M. C. Smith and B. A. Huhmann. 2011. 'Effects of age, need for cognition, and affective intensity on advertising effectiveness'. *Journal of Business Research*, 64: 12–17.

Msi. 2014. '2014–2016 Research priorities' [online]. Available at http://www.msi.org/uploads/files/MSI_RP14-16.pdf. Accessed 21 August 2014.

Muntinga, D. G., M. Moorman and E. G. Smit. 2011. 'Introducing COBRAs'. *International Journal of Advertising*, 30: 13–46.

Nair, M. 2011. 'Understanding and measuring the value of social media'. *Journal of Corporate Accounting & Finance*, 22: 45–51.

Neuendorf, K. A. 2002. *The Content Analysis Guidebook*. Thousand Oaks, CA: Sage Publications.

Nonnecke, B. and J. Preece. 1999. 'Shedding light on lurkers in online communities'. *Ethnographic Studies in Real and Virtual Environments: Inhabited Information Spaces and Connected Communities*, Edinburgh: 123–128.

Preece, J., B. Nonnecke and D. Andrews. 2004. 'The top five reasons for lurking: improving community experiences for everyone'. *Computers in Human Behavior*, 20: 201–223.

Raacke, J. and J. Bonds-Raacke. 2008. 'MySpace and Facebook: applying the uses and gratifications theory to exploring friend-networking sites'. *CyberPsychology & Behavior*, 11: 169–174.

Raney, A. and S. Janicke. 2013. 'How we enjoy and why we seek out morally complex characters in media entertainment'. In Tamborini, R. (ed.), *Media and the Moral Mind*. London: Routledge.

Riegner, C. 2007. 'Word of mouth on the Web: the impact of Web 2.0 on consumer purchase decisions'. *Journal of Advertising Research*, 47: 436–447.

Rubin, A. M. 2002. 'The uses-and-gratifications perspective of media effects'. In Jennings, B. (ed.) *Media Effects: Advances in Theory and Research*, second ed. Mahwah, NJ, US: Lawrence Erlbaum Associates Publishers.

Sawhney, M., G. Verona and E. Prandelli. 2005. 'Collaborating to create: the Internet as a platform for customer engagement in product innovation'. *Journal of Interactive Marketing*, 19: 4–17.

Shang, R.-A., Y.-C. Chen and H.-J. Liao. 2006. 'The value of participation in virtual consumer communities on brand loyalty'. *Internet Research*, 16: 398–418.

Social Media Marketing Industry Report.

Stafford, T. F., M. R. Stafford and L. L. Schkade. 2004. 'Determining uses and gratifications for the Internet'. *Decision Sciences*, 35: 259–288.

Statista. 2016. 'Statistics and market data on social media and user-generated content' [online]. Available at https://www.statista.com/markets/424/topic/540/social-media-user-generated-content/. Accessed 13 June 2016.

Steeves, N. 2013. 'Best practices: posting and analyzing effective Facebook content' [online]. Available at http://www.nimble.com/blog/posting-and-analyzing-on-facebook/. Accessed 4 September 2016.

Stelzner, M. 2014. 'How marketers are using social media to grow their businesses'. *Social Media Examiner*: 1–22. Accessed 2 June 2014.

Taylor, D. G., J. E. Lewin and D. Strutton. 2011. 'Friends, fans, and followers: do ads work on social networks?'. *Journal of Advertising Research*, 51: 258–275.

Van Doorn, J., K. N. Lemon, V. Mittal, S. Nass, D. Pick, P. Pirner and P. C. Verhoef. 2010. 'Customer engagement behavior: theoretical foundations and research directions'. *Journal of Service Research*, 13: 253–266.

Vivek, S., S. Beatty and R. Morgan. 2012. 'Customer engagement: exploring customer relationships beyond purchase'. *Journal of Marketing Theory and Practice*, 20: 122–146.

Wallace, E., I. Buil, L. De Chernatony and M. Hogan. 2014. 'Who likes you and why? A typology of Facebook fans'. *Journal Of Advertising Research*, 54(1): 92–109.

Williams, P. and A. Drolet. 2005. 'Age-related differences in responses to emotional advertisements'. *Journal of Consumer Research*, 32: 343–354.

9

SOCIAL MEDIA ENGAGEMENT AND RETURN ON ENGAGEMENT

Ritu Srivastava

Introduction

The term 'social media' refers to a bouquet of online services that facilitate the way communication and content sharing is happening today through collaborative networks of people, communities and organizations (Ludwig *et al.* 2013; Muniz and Schau 2011; Mangold and Faulds 2009; Kane *et al.* 2009). In the present world, companies cannot afford to neglect considering this media along with other traditional media, as the Internet has become the backbone of urban society. With the advent of Web 2.0 we have moved to an interactive social system that is available to most of us 24/7. Accessibility to gadgets such as personal computers, smart phones, webcams and digital recorders has given individuals the freedom to create and share content. Today is the day of the 'horizontal' communication revolution, where each one of us can communicate online with a huge number of people through a single click (Tuten and Solomon 2015: 4).

As elaborated by Zimmerman and Sahlin (2010: 10), social media include several services such as:

- **blogs**: websites designed to let you easily update or change content and which allow readers to post their own opinions or reactions
- **social networking services**: the origin of these services was to facilitate the exchange of personal information (messages, photos, videos, audio) to groups of friends and family. These included full networks such as Facebook and Myspace, professional networks such as LinkedIn, and microblogging sites such as Twitter
- **social media sharing services**: these media channels facilitate posting and commenting on videos, photos and podcasts
- **social bookmarking services**: social bookmarks are a publicly viewable list of sites that others have recommended, which are similar to private bookmarks

- **social news services**: peer-based recommendations on articles, where users often vote on the value of the postings
- **social geolocation and meeting services**: these services bring people together in real space rather than cyberspace; examples include Foursquare and Gowalla
- **community building services**: forums and message boards where content and comments are shared. Examples are Yahoo and Google groups, and Wikipedia

Along with these examples, there are also many service channels available to businesses to reach out and communicate with their customers. However, while companies understand the benefits of social media, it is a big challenge for them to design an effective social media strategy.

The benefits of social media

Social media as a new channel offers many benefits, but from a marketing perspective in particular it offers a much wider targeted reach as compared to traditional media (Kumar, Choi and Greene 2016). A marketing communications campaign exclusively based on viral ads can be much cheaper as there are no (or low) media costs involved, with only production costs incurred. Viewers are likely to share these ads or search online for additional related content (the brand's website, other ads, etc.). Viral advertising thus reduces the cost of advertising while increasing the branding outcome (Muniz and Schau 2011).

But you need to be cautious

While the benefits and the ease of starting with a social media strategy are a motivator for businesses, to adopt social media marketing companies need to take adequate care at the planning stage. Decathlon, a leading global sports goods retailer, entered China through the offline mode in 2009 and planned to experiment with the online mode as well, given the characteristics of the Chinese market[1] outlined in what follows.

The number of Chinese Internet users in 2010 was estimated to be 457 million (35 per cent of the population), an increase of 19 per cent compared with the previous year, which is more than 300,000 new users per day. Internet usage was intensive, with the average daily time spent on the Internet twice that in Europe and America, but this usage was varied, consisting of blogs, IM (instant messaging), social networks (235 million users, which comprised 18 per cent of the population) and e-commerce (more than 100 million online users, around 8 per cent of the population in 2009 according to Goldman-Sachs). These figures were very impressive, but when one considers them in relation to the entire population, they were far from being fully developed, and thus predicting anything was not possible. In addition, in China it was the big local social service providers who shared the market, occupying similar market positions to their American counterparts: Baidu was the Google equivalent; Sina Weibo (a mix of Facebook and Twitter) was the most popular Chinese social network; Tencent was another major social player which owned QQ (IM); Taobao was similar to eBay (70 per cent of e-commerce, 2 per cent of retail); Alipay was the equivalent of PayPal (more than 1.5 billion RMB of transactions/day); Tudou was YouTube; and, in March 2011, there were already more than 4,000 group purchasing sites comparable to Groupon. So the external environment characteristics offered potential but with its own set of challenges.

The younger generation was consumerist, hedonistic and confident of the future, feelings that are reinforced by their country's growth. They were also torn between the two opposing poles of westernization on one hand, and pride in being Chinese on the other. The Chinese are very extraverted and love to explain and share their opinions, posting, for example, many photographs of themselves online, and love clubs, privileges and social circles. Politics was discussed on the network using a coded language that evaded the filters of the censor. Contrary to received ideas, consumers did not necessarily want to buy fake brands, and the shopping malls were as much a place for a sociable stroll as they were destinations at which to make purchases.

E-commerce in China at that time was essentially a place for transactions between consumers. Ninety-two per cent of transactions were consumer to consumer, with almost as many sellers as buyers. More than 100 million people, each with a modest commercial space online, sold on Taobao.

At the outset of their move into China, Decathlon established a store on Taobao. Taobao allows companies to display their products and provides customer support by communicating with customers through an online messaging system. Taobao also provided payment processing for online sales. In return, it charged a service fee. The Decathlon store was opened in 2010 and sales increased but the limitations posed another challenge; when a prospective customer searched for a product, all related products, including competitor brands, were displayed. This reduced the rate of conversion and the prospect would move on to a competing brand as there was nothing to attract them to Decathlon. Decathlon realized this and changed their strategy to include multiple social media options, where the customer started talking to the brand and engaging with it. Thus, merely having an online presence or a social media presence leads businesses nowhere. Gone are the days when an online presence along with some customer interaction would satisfy the customer or the business interest. This holds true globally and adapting it to a local context poses an even more specific challenge as seen in the previous section.

Designing an effective social media strategy – understanding the basics of communication for engagement

When designing an effective social media strategy it is important for firms to appreciate that social media are a communications platform that works on

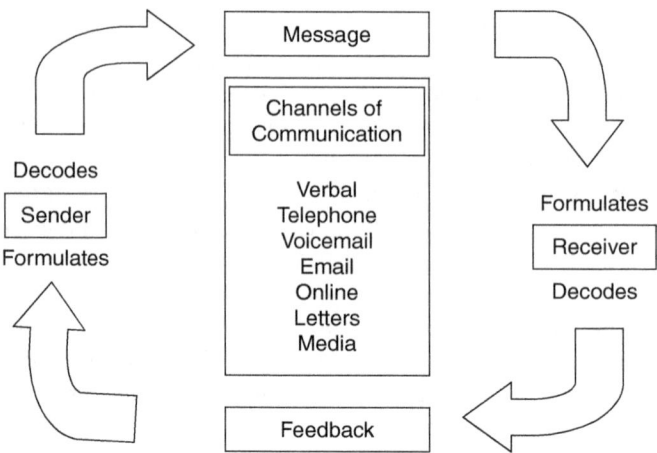

FIGURE 9.1 The communication cycle.

Adapted from Shanon and Weaver. 1949. *The Mathematical Theory of Communication*, University of Illinois Press: USA.

Web 2.0, therefore offering the benefits associated with Web 2.0: speed, connectivity, scalability and reach. However, being a communications platform, social media work on an underlying communication cycle with the interaction between the two parties becoming very strong and dynamic. Strategically, it becomes imperative to consider the communications cycle as given by Shanon and Weaver (1949).

For businesses to communicate with their customers they occupy the position of the sender and send the message to the customer group, which gets further transmitted or operates as a customer node and participates in the viral cycle at high speed. Communication happens across several customer-to-customer, sender/receiver loops, which form viral networks. Because of the speed and gregariousness of this activity, there is a chance for both the messages to travel many times positively and negatively, or for the messages not to travel at all. This is a very important point because firms do not want to have a social media strategy that does not perform, as in the Decathlon case. For the social media strategy to perform the message will have to go through the hierarchy of effects, as emphasized in response hierarchy models (Strong 1925; Lavidge and Steiner 1961; Rogers 1962; and McGuire; 1968). The customer interaction characteristics at each stage will be different and for customers to speak virally, businesses will have to make an effort to engage the customer throughout these stages (Kane *et al.* 2009)

Revisiting communication response hierarchy models

Figure 9.2 highlights the major communication response hierarchy models, which suggest that consumers often respond to messages in a hierarchical order

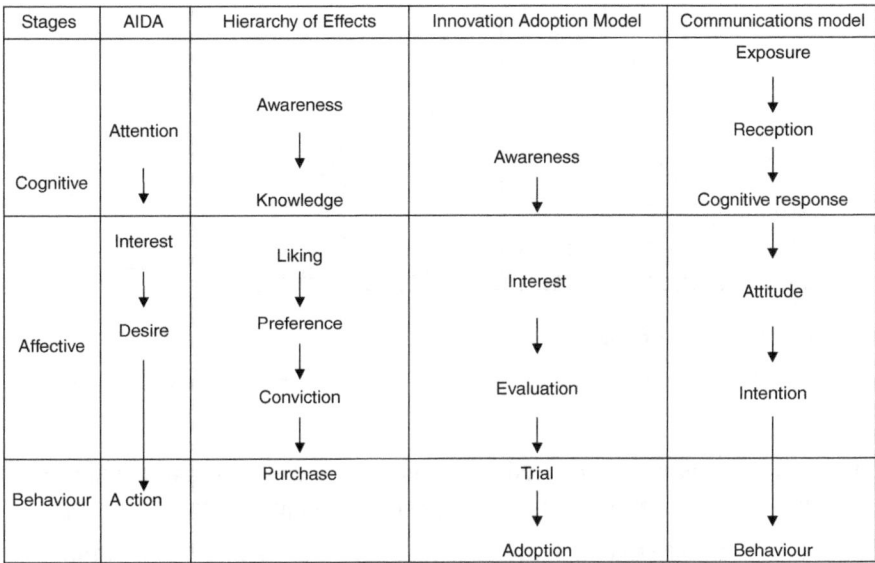

Stages	AIDA	Hierarchy of Effects	Innovation Adoption Model	Communications model
Cognitive	Attention ↓	Awareness ↓ Knowledge	Awareness ↓	Exposure ↓ Reception ↓ Cognitive response ↓
Affective	Interest ↓ Desire	Liking ↓ Preference ↓ Conviction ↓	Interest ↓ Evaluation ↓	Attitude ↓ Intention ↓
Behaviour	A ction ↓	Purchase	Trial ↓ Adoption	Behaviour

FIGURE 9.2   Response hierarchy models.

Adapted from Kotler, Keller, Koshy and Jha. 2013. 'Designing and managing integrated marketing communications', *Marketing Management: A South Asian Perspective*, 14e. Pearson Education: India.

of behaviour. These traditional models propose that a consumer typically moves through various stages of responses ranging from first becoming aware of a product to finally making a purchase. These responses can typically be divided into cognitive, affective and behavioural responses. For each stage of consumer readiness or response, communicators must perform specific actions. The models are described briefly as social media appends them as a hybrid (Mangold and Faulds 2009) in the hierarchy and the decision maker has to adjust his aperture through different perspectives across the stages.

Attention – Interest – Desire – Action (AIDA) model

Awareness: As proposed by Strong 1925, in the initial stage, most of the target audience is unaware of the product or the brand and hence the communicator's objective is to build awareness, maybe aiming just for name recognition with simple messages repeating the brand name or giving basic information about the product. This function is important in a new product category.

Interest: At this stage, consumers graduate from awareness about the product to interest in it. Marketers need to find out how consumers feel about their product.

Desire: It is not enough to just create interest in the product. Once the target audience is aware of, and interested in, the product, the function of advertising is to get them positively inclined towards buying it.

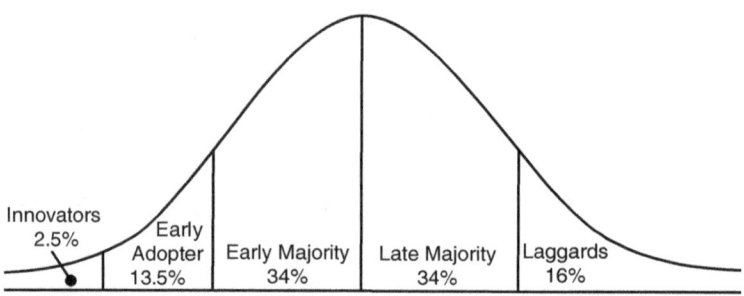

FIGURE 9.3   Diffusion of innovations.

Adapted from Rogers, Everett M. 1962. *Diffusion of innovations* (1st ed.). Free Press: New York.

Action: In most cases, the desired action is to lead consumers to making purchases, but in certain cases it can relate to generating inquiries, brand building etc.

The **hierarchy of effects model** developed by Lavidge and Steiner (1961) is one of the older linear models that states that advertising must shift people up a series of steps from cognitive processing to attitude change to purchase behaviour. Consumers do not switch from being impartial individuals to convinced purchasers in one single step and this holds true for social media also. The first stage of exposure and visibility is where many Indian firms were stuck until the first decade of 2000, when Internet penetration was 5 million, compared to 81 million in 2013.

The **innovation adoption** model developed by Rogers (1962) holds that individuals adopt products with different intensities. Based on the diffusion of innovation theory, it looks at customers as adopters of new innovations and classifies them as: innovators, first to adopt, early majority, late majority, and laggards, the last to adopt. It points out that not all customers will be convinced in one go and it makes more sense for firms to direct their promotional efforts at the innovators and early adopters first.

McGuires's **information-processing model** (1968, 1969), explains consumer response to a persuasive message by viewing the receiver of the message as an information processor and problem solver who goes through six stages, as shown in Figure 9.2. The model has been revised for thirteen stages.

As a communications manager, it will be very important from the company's perspective to assess the customer's adoption readiness as this will help the company to focus on specific market segments. This has to be studied in tandem with the industry and product life cycle and with an understanding of the different promotional needs and tools that can be used at each stage; for example, in the awareness stage, advertising and publicity are more cost effective than other media options. The nature of the product and its involvement with the customer will be the next most important variables. Once all of this background information is obtained, the first step could be to establish precise, smart and measurable objectives.

The DAGMAR approach for setting SMART social media objectives

Originally developed by Colley in 1961 for the advertising industry, the DAGMAR approach holds true for social media strategy as well. It takes a strategic communications approach to social media strategy and would want to work through the communications funnel. The differences would be in the percentages of the filter, which works within a many-to-many mode instead of one-to-many.

The first and most important task is to define what outcome is expected and how it should be measured. While the specific objectives will vary from brand to brand, they will most likely cover the following comprehensive issues:

i. Motivating some behaviour in the target audience, such as visits to the website, purchasing, advocacy etc.
ii. Influencing brand knowledge and attitudes specifically among those who are likely to spread the message to their own viral networks.
iii. Working media options within budgetary constraints.

When setting the objectives, they must be SMART, that is, they must be specific as to what is being expected as the outcome, must have measurable metrics, should be appropriate to the task and realistic. This can be done with regard to a defined time frame, for example, 'How much time did the customer invest in engaging with our socially published content?'

Engaging the customer

Today, customer engagement has become a more relevant concern (Schulze 2014; Kietzmann *et al.* 2011; Kaplan and Haenlein 2010) compared to a few years ago, when firms were more prominent at the visibility stage, that is, the attention and exposure phase at the lower stages, as in Figure 9.4 with respect to social media. To engage with the customer across various stages as outlined in the response hierarchy models, firms will have to follow certain ground rules:

1. Firms must be clear about their target audience (Verhoef *et al.* 2009; Straker and Wrigley 2016), its key characteristics in terms of demographics, but even more importantly in terms of behaviour and decision making processes. What motivates them?; what are their preferences, likes and dislikes that can be organized around values, lifestyles, activities and preferences?; how are their attitudes shaping up?; which role models do they follow?; what are their methods of self expression? These all become important pointers for content and activity design.
2. These behavioural characteristics provide a base for firms to design activities around, which can happen online when the customer is engaged (Barwise and Meehan 2010; Mangold and Faulds 2009). For example, for the re-launch of

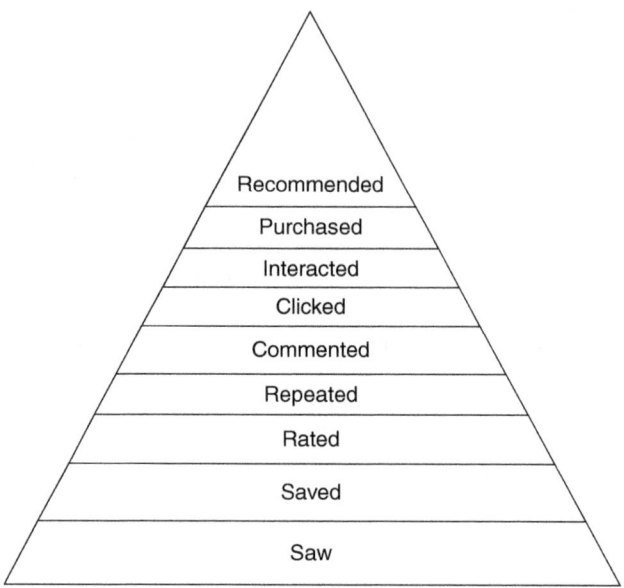

FIGURE 9.4 The communications funnel adapted to social media.

Adapted from Tuten L. T. and R. M. Solomon. 2015. *Social Media Metrics in Social Media Marketing*, 2e. Sage Publications India Pvt. Ltd.: New Delhi, India.

its brand Brisk, Lipton Pepsi carried out a social media campaign featuring animations that could relate better to its teen target audience.

3. At the point of choosing media options across the customer decision making stages, it is seen that traditional media such as television and print along with point of sale activities work better in terms of creating awareness and interest up until the trial stage; however, once the customer has tried the product, that is after trial and evaluation, the decision to repeat purchase and become loyal to the brand is strongly influenced by the image of the product and the customer often looks for content and conversations originating from brands on the Internet (Walther 1996; Robert and Dennis 2005).

4. At this stage, publishing engaging content is one of the critical tasks for engaging customers (Muniz and Schau 2011). Companies must invest in creating and publishing content that is relevant across different platforms, as the gadget friendly customer is quick to switch channels (Mangold and Faulds 2009). Content writers must be identified who can design creative content that can arouse target audience interest. These can be freelance writers, celebrity bloggers, celebrity endorsers, etc. Guidelines for the content must always be specified.

5. A metric to assess the effectiveness of engagement must also be developed or otherwise marketers may either be underspending or not optimally spending (Briggs 2012; Schultz 2011). These metrics are highlighted in the next section, as well as other metrics defined.

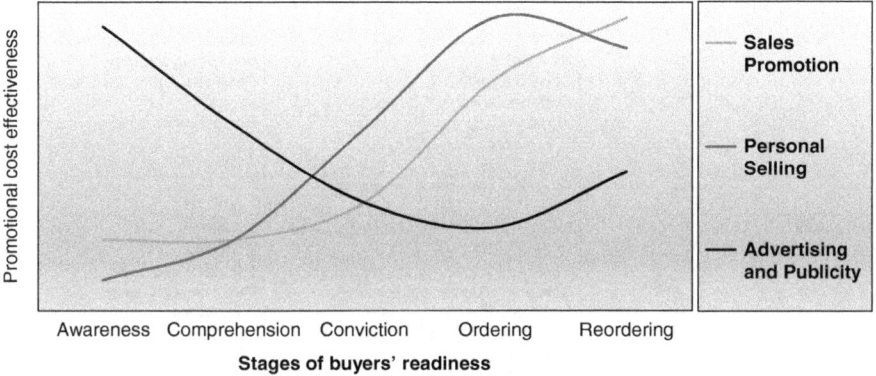

FIGURE 9.5 Customer decision stages and promotional tools.

Adapted from Kotler. 2003. 'Managing integrated marketing communications', *Marketing Management: A South Asian Perspective*, 11e. Pearson Education: India.

Measuring effectiveness: metrics

The choice of performance metric becomes critical as the metrics defined must match the outcomes expected (Fogel 2010), such as attitude shifts and behavioural responses from the target audience or efficiency and profitability measures resulting from cost savings and increased sales (Kitchen, Kim and Schultz 2008; Kliatchko 2008; McDonald 2008). While there are an overwhelming number of social media metrics available, putting them in a framework to manage the types of measure, as done by Solomon and Tuten, is helpful. The three types of metric include activity metrics, interaction metrics and return metrics. Activity metrics measure the actions an organization takes relative to social media. Interaction metrics focus on how the target market engages with social media activities, and return metrics focus on the outcomes that support the brand such as investment measures, cost reduction measures and so on.

Figure 9.6 indicates the kinds of metrics that can be used for each of these.

Return on investment

Return on investment (ROI) is one of the most common metrics used to evaluate the success of social media. It captures how effective a company is at using capital to generate profits. To determine ROI, we assign a financial value to resources and measure the financial outcomes. The ratio between the input and its outcomes gives us the ROI, which indicates how much income was generated from investments in certain activities. For social media, which is a communications based platform, this purely hard financial measure does not work. Instead, there are certain alternative approaches that calculate Social Media Return on Investment (SMROI) (Fisher 2009). While metrics measure the effects and success of activities, effectiveness is essentially considered through return metrics. However,

CATEGORY CHARACTERISTICS	QUANTITATIVE MEASURES	QUALITATIVE MEASURES
Activity Input	Number, Frequency and Recency of Blog Posts Updates/Posts Comments/Reply Comments White Papers Photo Posts Video Posts Activity across media channels	Creative messaging and positioning strategy Resonance/fit of campaign appeal Social media involvement
Interaction (responses)	Number, Frequency and Recency of Registrations Bookmarks/favourites/likes/ratings Comments/posts/mentions/logs Links/ trackbacks Downloads/installs/embeds Subscriptions Fans/followers/friends Share/forward/invite/refer Reviews/testimonials Traffic/visits/views/impressions Time spent on site Profile development UG content contributed Discount/deal redemption rate Echo effect/virality	Sentiment Engagement Influence effects Recommendations Buzz/virality
Performance (outcome)	Cost/prospects Lead conversion rate Average new revenue per customer Cost efficiencies across marketing functions Customer lifetime value Earned media values Shifts in average sales/site traffic/search engine ratings Share of voice Return on investment	Attitude toward the brand Brand loyalty Customer satisfaction Service quality perceptions

FIGURE 9.6   Social media metrics.

Adapted from Tuten L.T. and R. M. Solomon. 2015. *Social Media Metrics in Social Media Marketing*, 2e. Sage Publications India Pvt. Ltd.: New Delhi, India.

return on investment has also been criticized for its overemphasis of short-term returns over long-term brand building (Calkins and Rucker 2008).

Return on impressions

This model explains how many media impressions were generated by the social media tactics applied. An impression is simply an opportunity for the target audience to notice something. In the traditional method, advertising space was bought based on the number of impressions it could provide; while social media also provides impressions, media space is typically not purchased. The opportunity for exposure to the brand message might be delivered as a part of the virtual world event, on a social networking site, through product reviews and/or customer generated messages. Impressions are valuable according to this model because impressions lead to changes in awareness (a basic assumption made here), which follows the typical communication hierarchy, resulting in sales. Using the percentage of people reached who make a purchase; we can determine the return on impressions as gross revenue estimated minus the cost of the social media advertising programme, divided by the cost of the program.

Return on social media impact model

Using regression analysis, this model attempts to track coverage across media and in different markets against sales over time to analyze variables that may affect sales, including the mix of advertising and promotional tools used at each time and place. This approach offers the maximum potential for social media marketers as it can include lagged measurements that control for the order of events taking place online. Return on social media impact can show how sales are attributed to each element in the marketing mix and to tactics within the social media advertising strategy. Content generation and consumption are tracked and assigned algorithm scores to dictate the weight of relative influence. Sales are also tracked at the same intervals and then statistical analysis is used to determine how sales trends shifted according to the timing of the social media marketing.

Return on target influence

This model relies upon survey data to assess the effectiveness of social media marketing. Surveys assess whether participants were exposed to the social media tactics and what perceptions were formed because of this exposure. The change in the probability of purchase based on exposure is then calculated.

Return on earned media model

This approach uses a metric called advertising equivalency (AEV) value to equate publicity in news media outlets to its paid advertising equivalent. For social media advertising, an AEV would attempt to equate the following with paid advertising value: source authority, source prominence, depth of brand mention and recommendation.

While mentioning the approaches to measuring social media effectiveness, it becomes evident from the above section that costs form a very important component in evaluating effectiveness. How organizations view the cost function, as an expense or an investment, is also important. Costs are to be viewed against the value they give and therefore it is important to do a **cost benefit analysis**. What does it take to participate in a social media event and what is it worth? What is the value of a customer or a lead? What does it cost to maintain a blog? These are some of the questions that organizations need to answer to understand the costs of social media and their associated value. Costs would typically include opportunity cost, speed of control and the kind of message response.

The final step in measuring the effectiveness of social media is customer tracking. Data on the metrics are collected to compare and assess the effectiveness of the social media marketing strategy. The tracking stage will involve the following steps (as elaborated by Tuten and Solomon 2015):

i. identifying the tracking mechanisms
ii. establishing baseline comparisons
iii. creating activity timelines
iv. developing transaction data
v. measuring transaction precursors
vi. looking for patterns

An effective way to track customers is **listening and monitoring**. There are various ways of doing this, and companies may use individual social media vehicle-specific tools, as well such as Facebook Insights, Twitter Analytics etc. Tracking can be forward, coincident or reverse.

Forward tracking ensures that the tracking mechanisms are developed prior to launching the activity or campaign. It is the most precise approach because it enables the account team to track exactly the data desired. Coincident tracking is done concurrently throughout the campaign. It relies on residual data left at the point of interaction or sale and does not require a unique mechanism developed for the purpose. It is interaction or outcome oriented because tracking occurs only when people leave traces of their opinions or activity. Reverse tracking is done after the conclusion of an activity or campaign. It also uses residual data and may additionally use some primary data collection to assess the effects of the campaign. Baselines and measurement maps are two visual tools that allow marketers to compare its performance against specific dimensions or different types of tools used.

Gauging conversations: social media listening and monitoring

Social media listening and monitoring means to monitor conversations and content in social media channels by 'listening'. This listening works with the aid of software that systematically searches for particular keywords it finds in social spaces such as blogs, social networks and forums. By carefully choosing and searching the appropriate keywords and the relevant social communities, the researcher can gather insights into customer decision making, perceptions of the brand, perceptions of competitors and more. An automated monitoring service can be retained to crawl the web, collecting conversations according to established criteria for inclusion in a database. From this database, conversation volume, source and sentiment can be determined through a mix of quantitative and qualitative data.

Monitoring explains what was said, when, by whom and how many times. Thus, this process answers four basic questions:

1. How many times was the search item found?
2. When was the search item found?
3. Where was the search item found?
4. Who mentioned the search item?

The content of the data collected using monitoring serves many marketing purposes, such as using customer comments as testimonials and competitor information as competitive intelligence. Conversations among like-minded people provide information useful for targeting and positioning. If a firm can use data from multiple data sources and maintain a detailed database, many more insights can be gleaned as the data synthesize comments from thousands of people. In fact, data can be merged through multiple channels.

All this needs is a properly conceptualized social media marketing strategy, with a detailed plan taking in all of these steps. The steps in planning are essentially the same; the difference is in the way social media characteristics and consumer behaviour is understood and handled.

Conclusion

Effective social media engagement is an important business concern today. The key lies in understanding online customer behaviour as being part of a communication hierarchy, and designing online media content and activities, with a suitable assessment metric defined at each stage. Measurement using the metrics through a chosen tracking mechanism will help in assessing the progress of the social media strategy and the need to take corrective steps, as well as deciding on its cost effectiveness.

Note

1   http://www.butter-cake.com/2011/11/20/e-commerce-in-china-what-is-the-best-strategy-for-western-brands/

References

Barwise, P. and S. Meehan. 2010. 'The One Thing You Must Get Right When Building a Brand'. *Harvard Business Review*.

Briggs, R. 2012. *SIRFs-Up: Catching the next wave in marketing*. North Charleston, South Carolina: CreateSpace.

Calkins, T. and D. D. Rucker. 2008. *Don't overemphasize ROI as single measure of success. Advertising Age*: February.

Colley, R. 1961. *Defining advertising goals for measured advertising results*. New York: Association of National Advertisers.

Fisher, T. J. 2009. 'ROI in social media: A look at the arguments'. *Journal of Database Marketing & Customer Strategy Management*, 16:3: p. 189–195.

Fogel, S. 2010. 'Issues in measurement of word of mouth in social media marketing'. *International Journal of Integrated Marketing Communications*, 2:2: p. 54–60. Available at http://www.butter-cake.com/2011/11/20/e-commerce-in-china-what-is-the-best-strategy-for-western-brands/.

Kane, G. C., R. G. Fichman, J. Gallaugher and J. Glaser. 2009. 'Community relations 2.0'. *Harvard Business Review*, 87:11: p. 45–50.

Kaplan, A. M. and M. Haenlein. 2010. 'Users of the world, unite! The challenges and opportunities of social media'. *Business Horizon*, 53: p. 59–68.

Kietzmann, J. H. *et al.* 2011. 'Social media? Get serious! Understanding the functional building blocks of social media'. *Business Horizons*, 54: p. 241–251.

Kitchen, P. J., L. Kim and D. E. Schultz. 2008. 'Integrated marketing communications: practice leads theory'. *Journal of Advertising Research*, 48:4: p. 531–546

Kliatchko, J. 2008. 'Revisiting the IMC construct: a revised definition and four pillars'. *International Journal of Advertising*, 27:1: p. 133–160.

Kotler. P. 2003. 'Managing integrated marketing communications', *Marketing Management: A South Asian Perspective*, 11e, Pearson Education: India.

Kotler, P., K. L. Keller, A. Koshy and M. Jha. 2013. 'Designing and managing integrated marketing communications', *Marketing Management: A South Asian Perspective*, 14e, Pearson Education: India.

Kumar, V., J. B. Choi, and M. Greene. 2016. 'Synergistic effects of social media and traditional marketing on brand sales: capturing the time-varying effects'. *Journal of the Academy of Marketing Science*, June: p. 1–21.

Lavidge, R. J. and G. A. Steiner. 1961. 'A model for predictive measurements of advertising effectiveness'. *The Journal of Marketing*: p. 59–62.

Ludwig, S. *et al.* 2013. 'More than words: the influence of affective content and linguistic style matches in online reviews on conversion rates'. *Journal of Marketing*: 77:1: p. 87–103.

Mangold W. G. and D.J. Faulds. 2009. 'Social media: the new hybrid element of the promotion mix', *Business Horizons'* 52: p. 357–365.

McDonald, S. 2008. 'The long tail and its implications for media audience measurement'. *Journal of Advertising Research*, 48:3: p. 313–319.

McGuire, W. J. 1968. 'Personality and attitude change: an information processing theory'. In A. G. Greenwald, T. C. Brock and T. M. Ostrom (eds), *Psychological Foundations of Attitudes*. Academic Press: San Diego, CA, p. 171–196.

Muñiz, A. M. and H. J. Schau. 2011. 'How to inspire value-laden collaborative consumer-generated content'. *Business Horizons*, 543: p. 209–217.

Robert, L.P. and A. R. Dennis. 2005. 'Paradox of richness: a cognitive model of media choice'. *IEEE Transactions on Professional Communication*, 48:1: p. 10–21.

Rogers, Everett M. 1962. *Diffusion of Innovations* (1st ed.). Free Press: New York.

Schultz, D. E. 2011. 'IMC measurement: the challenges of an interactive marketplace'. *International Journal of Integrated Marketing Communications*, 3:1: p. 7–24.

Schulze, C., L. Schöler and B. Skiera. 2014 'Not all fun and games: viral marketing for utilitarian products', *Journal of Marketing* 78:1, p. 1–19.

Shannon, C.E. and W. Weaver. 1949. *The Mathematical Theory of Communication*. University of Illinois Press: Champaign, IL.

Straker, K and C. Wrigley. 2016. 'Emotionally engaging customers in the digital age: the case study of "Burberry love"', *Journal of Fashion Marketing and Management*, 20:3: p. 276–299.

Strong, E.K. 1925. *The Psychology of Selling*. McGraw-Hill: New York.

Tuten, L.T. and R. M. Solomon. 2015. *Social Media Marketing*, 2e. Sage Publications India Pvt. Ltd.: New Delhi, India.

Verhoef, P. C. *et al.* 2009. 'Customer experience creation: determinants, dynamics and management strategies', *Journal of Retailing* 85:1: p. 31–41.

Walther, J. B. 1996. 'Computer–mediated communication: impersonal, interpersonal, and hyperpersonal interaction'. *Communication Research*, 23: p. 3–43.

Zimmerman J. and D. Sahlin. 2010. *Social Media Marketing All in One*. Wiley India: New Delhi, India.

10

THE CONSUMER ENGAGEMENT/ RETURN ON SOCIAL MEDIA ENGAGEMENT INTERFACE

Development of a conceptual model

Birgit A. A. Solem and Linda D. Hellebeek

Introduction

Recent developments in information and communications technologies, including online brand communities (Muñiz and O'Guinn 2001; Habibi *et al.* 2014) and social media (e.g. Facebook, Twitter, YouTube; Kaplan and Haenlein 2010), are of significant relevance for firms to foster and develop consumer engagement (Sasser *et al.* 2014; Jahn and Kunz 2012). A key hallmark of social media lies in their interactive nature, which permits two-way communication and dialogue (Hoffman and Novak 2011; Schamari and Schaefers 2015; Maslowska *et al.* 2016); this reflects a level of conceptual correspondence with the higher-level theory of Service-Dominant (S-D) Logic (Vargo and Lusch 2008, 2016), which posits consumer behaviour to centre on interactive, co-creative experiences in networked service relationships (Vargo and Lusch 2016; Brodie *et al.* 2011).

Deploying web-based (including mobile) technologies, social media provide interactive engagement platforms (Breidbach *et al.* 2014), which enable one-on-one, one-to-many and many-to-many communications and consumer participation in communities and networks (e.g. by joining relevant communities; posting, liking, sharing and discussing relevant content in these communities; Baumöl *et al.* 2016; Baethge *et al.* 2016). Consumers can also use social media to help other consumers resolve product-related queries or issues, thus helping to reduce firms' service costs (Mathwick *et al.* 2008). Social media therefore provide ample opportunities for interactivity and value creation (Kietzman *et al.* 2011; Laroche *et al.* 2013; Hollebeek and Brodie 2016). Kaplan and Haenlein (2010) identify two major benefits of social media marketing, including: (i) ability to reach global audiences instantly and at relatively low cost; and (ii) capacity to influence consumer motivation and behaviour. On the other hand, social media have also been reported to reduce managerial control over brand-related communications and content, which used to be the exclusive domain of marketers, thereby creating a level of tension among marketing practitioners (Buhalis and Mamalakis 2015; Sasser *et al.* 2014).

In parallel, literature on consumer engagement (CE) has developed rapidly in the last five to seven years (e.g. Van Doorn *et al.* 2010; Cabiddu *et al.* 2014; Hollebeek *et al.* 2016c). CE has been viewed as an interactive experience comprising emotional, cognitive and behavioural dimensions (Brodie *et al.* 2011; Calder *et al.* 2009), which can be observed at distinct levels at different points in time. While we note the particular importance of consumers' *behavioural* engagement in social media (e.g. through comments, shares, click-through rates, etc.; Groeger *et al.* 2016), we also recognize the importance of consumers' underlying cognitive and emotional engagement, which motivates them towards executing particular social media behaviours (Solem and Pedersen 2016a; Ajzen and Fishbein 1973; De Vries *et al.* 2012), such as posting, or liking specific social media content.

Despite the growing managerial and research interest in social media and CE, insight into the dynamics of CE in social media environments remains limited to date. In particular, little is known about the ways in which CE drives social media performance (Hollebeek and Brodie 2016; Bitter and Grabner-Kräuter 2016). In this chapter, we investigate this gap by examining CE's contribution to return on social media investment (also termed 'return on social media engagement', or ROSME), which has received only very limited theoretical and empirical attention to date (Kumar 2013; Kumar *et al.* 2010). ROSME denotes the relationship between the level of profitability gained from, and the investments made in, engaging consumers with brands through social media marketing (Buhalis and Mamalakis 2015; Friedlob and Plewa 1996). With the rise of social commerce (i.e. use of social media as a sales channel) – thus providing greater opportunity for the direct monetization of CE (Stephen and Toubia 2010) – the development of in-depth understanding of firms' ROSME is of particular interest (Hollebeek and Brodie 2016).

In response to this observed research gap, this chapter is guided by the following research question: *What is the nature of the relationship between CE and ROSME (if any), and how can CE be used to optimize firms' ROSME outcomes?* To achieve this objective, we proceed by reviewing key literature on CE, social media and return on investment in the next section. Based on these analyses, we next develop a theoretical model of CE's contribution to ROSME. We argue that many firms are yet to fully understand and leverage CE in social media, thus leading to sub-optimal current ROSME outcomes. To optimize ROSME, a true consumer-centric approach is required (Shah *et al.* 2006), which better leverages social media's inherently social capabilities (Kaplan and Haenlein 2010; Culnan *et al.* 2010; Lusch and Vargo 2014) through fostering true CE with particular brands (Hollebeek *et al.* 2014; Hoffman and Fodor 2010; Calder *et al.* 2016). The chapter concludes with an overview of key theoretical and managerial implications arising from our observations.

Consumer engagement

The 'engagement' concept has been studied across a range of academic disciplines, including educational psychology (student engagement; Skinner and Belmont 1993), psychology (social engagement; Achterberg *et al.* 2003), sociology (civic engagement; Jennings and Stoker 2004), political science (political engagement; Galston 2001), computer systems (user engagement; O'Brien and Toms 2008, 2010), and organizational behaviour (employee engagement; Kahn 1990; Schaufeli *et al.* 2002). Engagement has gained interest in the marketing literature only in the last five to seven years (Gambetti and Graffigna 2010; Hollebeek 2011a, 2011b).

Engagement denotes the *interactivity* between a specific subject (e.g. a consumer) and an object (e.g. product, brand, media channels; Gambetti and Graffigna 2010; Hollebeek *et al.* 2016c; Van Doorn *et al.* 2010). Brodie *et al.* (2011) define CE as *interactive consumer experience*, which comprises focal cognitive, emotional and behavioural dimensions (Vivek *et al.* 2014). Building on the work of Brodie *et al.*, Hollebeek *et al.*'s (2014) measurement instrument proposes the following CE dimensions: (a) cognitive processing (i.e. the level of cognitive investment made by consumers in particular brand interactions); (b) affection (i.e. the level of positive affect invested by a consumer in a focal brand interaction); and (c) activation (i.e. the degree of energy, time and effort invested in focal brand interactions). Other CE scales include those developed by Calder *et al.* (2009), Vivek *et al.* (2014), Schivinski *et al.* (2016) and Baldus *et al.* (2015).

Some authors focus on the behavioural aspect of CE, which is key in consumers' social-media-based brand behaviours (Groeger *et al.* 2016), including social-media-based likes, shares, comments, posts etc. (Kaplan and Haenlein 2010). Our perspective aligns these views by defining social-media-based CE as:

> *Consumers' cognitive, emotional and behavioural investments in interactions with a particular brand on social media; with the individual's underlying (latent) cognitive and emotional engagement being manifested through one's social-media-based engagement behaviours.*

Our perspective aligns closely with the views of Hollebeek (2011a, 2011b), Hollebeek *et al.* (2014) and Brodie *et al.* (2011). We view CE as a multidimensional, context-dependent concept (Porter *et al.* 2011; Sashi 2012; Solem and Pedersen 2016b) and focus on consumers' directly observable engagement *behaviours* with particular brands (Verleye *et al.* 2014). In these interactions, consumers make particular cognitive (i.e. thought-based), emotional (i.e. affect-based) and behavioural (i.e. activity-based) *investments* that foster CE with particular brands (Hollebeek 2011a, 2011b; Hollebeek *et al.* 2014, 2016c). According to Brodie *et al.* (2011), CE is a highly context-dependent variable (Jahn and Kunz 2012; Mollen and Wilson 2010). In social media, CE's context-specific nature depends on the following factors: (a) individual factors (e.g. personality, need-for-cognition); (b) object-related factors (e.g. brand's perceived importance); (c) media-related factors (e.g. consumer perceptions of specific social media platforms); and (d) situational factors (e.g. mood). Consumers' online social media behaviours are also expected to be linked strongly to offline brand-related engagement behaviours (Hanna *et al.* 2011; Gummerus *et al.* 2012; Laroche *et al.* 2013; Solem and Pedersen 2016a).

The consumer engagement/social media interface

Social media are founded based on the premise of interactivity among, and proactive contributions of, users (Kaplan and Haenlein 2010). As stated, consumers' directly observable engagement *behaviours* are paramount in social media (e.g. likes, comments, shares etc.), which reflect individuals' underlying cognitive and emotional engagement (Hollebeek *et al.* 2014). Social media's interactive, experiential nature is ideal for engaging consumers (Sasser *et al.* 2014; Calder *et al.* 2016; Schultz 2016; Arnould and Thompson 2005).

To date, social-media-based CE research has tended to focus on CE *beyond* (i.e. outside of) exchange/purchase (Van Doorn *et al.* 2010; Solem and Pedersen 2016a). Examples of consumers' beyond-exchange engagement behaviours include positive/negative word-of-mouth (Bitter and Grabner-Kräuter 2016), consumer citizenship behaviours (Pervan and Bove 2011), blogging and helping other customers (Van Doorn *et al.* 2010; Groeger *et al.* 2016). Jaakkola and Alexander (2014: p. 9) identify four types of consumer engagement behaviours, including:

(i) augmenting behaviour: consumer contributions of resources (e.g. knowledge, skills, labour and time) that directly add to the focal firm's offering beyond that which is fundamental to the transaction (e.g. consumers sharing their brand-related knowledge on social media)

(ii) co-developing behaviour: consumer resource contributions to facilitate the firm's development of its offering (e.g. consumer contributions to new product development; Etgar 2008)

(iii) influencing behaviour: consumer resource contributions to affect other actors' perceptions, preferences or knowledge about the focal firm (e.g. through opinion leaders' social media posts)

(iv) mobilising behaviour: consumer resource contributions to motivate other stakeholders' actions towards the firm (e.g. by providing brand-related recommendations – which may also coincide with influencing behaviours).

We posit these engagement behaviours to be consumers' directly observable expressions of their underlying cognitive and emotional engagement. These engagement behaviours, in turn, are expected to contribute to higher consumer satisfaction (Gummerus *et al.* 2012), purchase intent (Naidoo and Hollebeek 2016) and loyalty (Gummesson 2008; Brodie *et al.* 2011; Solem 2016). To develop and retain loyal customers, firms need to understand how to best engage consumers with their brands on social media. In turn, this is expected to transfer to consumers' offline brand engagement (e.g. by generating enhanced brand loyalty; Gambetti and Graffigna 2010; Porter *et al.* 2011; Dessart *et al.* 2016). We thus expect that social media marketing can be used to engage customers and enhance future sales.

The increasing range of social media's direct monetizing capabilities

Social media provide firms with a range of opportunities for fostering CE (Hoffman and Novak 2011; Schamari and Schaefers 2015), not only by facilitating consumers' brand-related interactions and dialogue (Sasser *et al.* 2014), but also through increasingly enabling social commerce transactions (e.g. via Facebook and Pinterest; Baethge *et al.* 2016). Thus, while social media's monetizing capabilities were predominantly *indirect* before the advent of social commerce (e.g. through fostering brand-related dialogue, which may, *indirectly* or over time, influence consumers' brand-related purchase behaviour), these are rapidly becoming more *direct*; thereby rendering significant managerial importance for the effective execution of practitioners' brand-related social media campaigns (Baethge *et al.* 2016). An example of social media's increasing monetizing capabilities is 'buy buttons', which allow consumers to make purchases directly from social media platforms (e.g. Pinterest and Facebook).

Social media also enable more customized targeting of consumers, including by collecting and analysing consumers' demographic and purchase-history-related information, or by conducting location-based marketing (Cao 2015). For example, Starbucks leverages customer movement data by messaging personalized deals to engage customers (based on their purchase history), as they approach the store, particularly during the quiet hours of the day. In addition, Malthouse *et al.* (2013: p. 270) identify the growing importance of social CRM, which denotes firms' 'use of social media services, techniques and technology for customer relationship management purposes'.

Given social media's increasing range of direct monetizing capabilities, their role as engagement platforms connecting consumers and firms is growing. Breidbach *et al.* (2014: p. 594) define 'engagement platforms' as 'physical or virtual touch-points designed to provide structural support for the exchange and integration of resources, and thereby value co-creation between actors in a service system'. In this chapter, we focus on the particular actors of consumers and brands, as stated (Chandler and Lusch 2015; Hollebeek 2013, 2016). Given these social media trends, we observe an increasing academic and managerial need to better understand ROSME, which we explore in further depth in the next section.

Return on social media engagement

Return on investment (ROI) traditionally represents an accounting term (McNulty and Tharenou 2004). In its simplest form, ROI is defined as a financial ratio that expresses firm profitability in direct relation to investment (Flamholtz 1985; Franklin and Plewa 1996; Kaske *et al.* 2012). Schachner (1973) defines ROI as a profitability equation that may be used to calculate past performance (e.g. earnings), or expected earnings (e.g. anticipated profitability of an investment proposal). As a quantitative measure of financial accountability of proposed investments, ROI provides corporate management with a useful financial tool and performance indicator (Phillips 1997). ROI, correspondingly, has developed into a commonly used corporate profitability indicator (Friedlob and Plewa 1996). By determining ROI, managers are able to generate enhanced accountability of their actions, or proposals (Friedlob and Plewa 1996). While initial work has linked the use of social media to improved firm performance outcomes (e.g. heightened profitability; Coles 2014), relatively little remains known in this area. Given that social media are increasingly being used as buying (e.g. Facebook, Pinterest) and selling (e.g. eBay) platforms, managers require a solid understanding of the specific ways in which consumers' brand engagement on social media contributes to profitability and firm value creation (Rishika *et al.* 2013; Gummesson 2004).

Correspondingly, 'return on social media investment' (ROSMI; Hoffman and Fodor 2010; Lloret Romero 2011) measures a firm's profitability level gained from a particular social media marketing campaign, as reflected in the level and quality of consumers' brand-related behavioural engagement on social media, which have important underlying cognitive and emotional foundations (cf. Literature Review). Given the importance of CE in social media, ROSMI has been used interchangeably with the term 'return on social media engagement' (ROSME; Frick 2010), which we adopt in this chapter. Attaining sound managerial understanding of ROSME helps firms to better understand, and stay abreast of, social-media-based CE, thus contributing to value creation for firms (Doyle 2001).

Buhalis and Mamalakis (2015) report that calculating ROI in financial terms differs from a marketing (including social media) perspective of ROI. The authors thus argue for the development of unique performance metrics that reflect social media's distinctive, interactive nature (Baumöl *et al.* 2016; Frick 2010). Examples of unique social-media-based metrics include page visitors, unique visitors (i.e. where an individual's multiple site visits are counted as a single unique visitor), stickiness (i.e. the length of time an individual 'sticks' around on a site), pay-per-click advertising (i.e. an Internet advertising model to direct traffic to websites, where an advertiser pays a publisher (usually a website) when the ad is clicked) and conversions (i.e. the percentage of consumers visiting a social media site who are 'converted' by purchasing the product; Fisher 2009; Heathman 2012). Further, Rautio (2012) advocates the adoption of several (i.e. rather than a single) performance indicators to assess different aspects of social media, including CE, traffic measurement, customer service and reputation management. Buhalis and Mamalakis (2015) argue that CE (as measured by likes, comments, shares, posts etc.) represents a key non-financial metric of ROSME (Kumar 2013; Kumar *et al.* 2010; Bijmolt *et al.* 2010).

The CE/ROSME interface: a conceptual model

Hoffman and Fodor (2010) argue that effective social media use should start by turning the traditional ROI approach on its head. Specifically, the authors posit that, rather than solely emphasizing the firm's own marketing investments, and calculating the return on this investment in terms of consumer response, marketing managers should measure the social media investments *made by consumers*, thus concurring with our definition of CE and legitimizing the importance of CE as a key social media concept (Bitter and Grabner-Kräuter 2016; Dessart *et al.* 2016).

Based on our preceding analyses, CE provides a critical role as a driver not only of non-financial (e.g. consumer word-of-mouth), but also financial (e.g. by generating sales revenue), ROSME. With the rise of social commerce (Stephen and Toubia 2010), CE becomes more directly linked to social media's increasing range of monetizing capabilities, as addressed. ROSME denotes the relationship between the level of profitability gained from, and the investments made into, activities that foster CE in social media marketing (Buhalis and Mamalakis 2015), as shown in Figure 10.1.

The model shows that a firm's brand-related social media investments (e.g. investments in the development of shopping platforms, web applications, campaigns, etc.) are expected to positively affect cognitive and/or emotional CE. Correspondingly, we posit:

> H1: Social-media-based brand investments have a positive association with consumers' cognitive and emotional CE.

Whether the cognitive, or the emotional CE facet is dominant will depend on particular individual (e.g. personality), object-related (e.g. brand-based), medium-related (e.g. perceived social media site importance) and situational factors (e.g. mood; Hollebeek *et al.* 2014). Cognitive and emotional engagement, collectively, drive ensuing behavioural engagement (e.g. a consumer clicking the 'buy' button

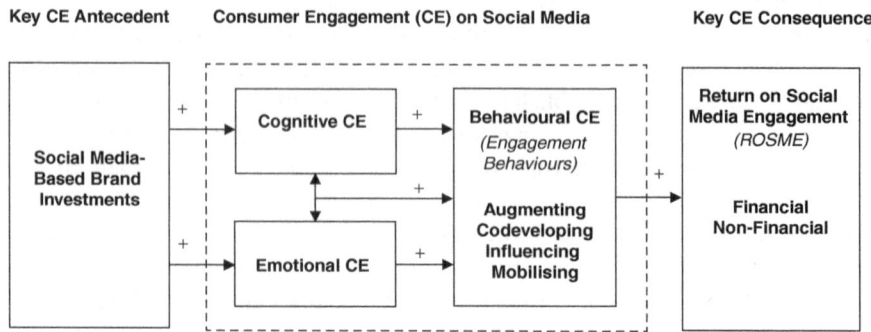

FIGURE 10.1 Conceptual model.

on Pinterest, Facebook etc.), as shown in the model (Ajzen and Fishbein 1973; Calder *et al.* 2009). We thus hypothesize:

> H2: Consumers' cognitive and emotional engagement have a positive association with the individual's ensuing behavioural engagement, which may include augmenting, co-developing, influencing and mobilizing behaviours.

The interplay of a consumer's behavioural engagement, in turn, is expected to have a positive impact on firms' ensuing ROSME, as shown in Figure 10.1. We posit:

> H3: Consumers' behavioural engagement (with its specific underlying cognitive and emotional engagement) has a positive association with the firm's ensuing financial and non-financial ROSME.

With consumers' increasing ability to make purchases via social media, we expect the gap between ROSME and traditional ROI to narrow through the growth of social commerce, which brings enhanced accountability of social media investments, and is also expected to foster enhanced CE (Hoffman and Fodor 2010). While our model helps to answer the first part of our stated research question, the second part (i.e. *'how can CE be used to optimize firms' ROSME outcomes?'*) still remains unanswered. To answer this question, we develop Table 10.1, which provides examples of specific consumer engagement behaviours and their expected effects on financial and non-financial ROSME. We note that while 'non-financial ROSME' does not have a direct financial impact on the firm it can, nonetheless, have an *indirect* effect (e.g. a consumer who helps another consumer resolve a brand-related query, which generates a sale several weeks later). For consistency with Buhalis and Mamalakis' (2015) terminology, we use the terms 'financial' and 'non-financial ROSME'.

Discussion and implications

Theoretical implications

A key theoretical contribution of this chapter lies in our exploration of the conceptual interface of CE and social media, which, while subject to recent interest, remains nebulous in the literature (Baumöl *et al.* 2016; Hollebeek *et al.* 2016a/b). The engagement concept's theoretical roots have been posited to reside in S-D Logic (Hollebeek *et al.* 2016c), which centres on interactive, co-creative interactions and exchanges between actors within broader networks and relational ecosystems (Vargo and Lusch 2004, 2008, 2016). While the theoretical linkage between S-D Logic and engagement has been recognized, future researchers may wish to empirically explore, and test, the nature of the CE/S-D Logic interface (for an in-depth theoretical review, refer to Hollebeek *et al.* 2016c).

TABLE 10.1 Expected effects of consumer engagement behaviours (CEBs) on ROSME

	Non-Financial ROSME	Financial ROSME
Augmenting behaviour	• Can be expressed through consumer citizenship behaviours (e.g. a consumer helping the brand by assisting other consumers resolve their brand-related queries); e.g. British Telecom Community Forum where customers are helping each other solve brand-related issues.	• Augmenting behaviour is expected to be predominantly non-financial in nature.
		• However, it can have an indirect financial effect (e.g. when a consumer who received brand-related help from another consumer purchases the brand in the future).
Co-developing behaviour	• Consumers' social sharing of their brand-related knowledge.	• In contrast to augmenting behaviours, co-developing behaviours are expected to have a stronger direct link to financial ROSME (e.g. by generating new product development (NPD) ideas relatively inexpensively; thus reducing the firm's NPD cost).
	• May stimulate enhanced levels of positive brand-related word-of-mouth (e.g. through consumers feeling that their voice is being heard by the firm, i.e. with respect, through their new product suggestions being implemented; e.g. McDonald's *Build Your Taste* campaign where consumers have the opportunity to design and order their favourite hamburger).	
Influencing behaviour	• By providing brand-related content, consumers may affect other consumers' brand-related perceptions (positively or negatively); e.g. brand communication offered by blogging customers, such as celebrity beauty or food bloggers, who may become opinion leaders among their loyal followers. Opinion leaders are of particular importance for firms when strategically building their brand(s).	• By shaping, refining or otherwise affecting opinion leaders' brand-related perceptions, firms are able to leverage their views to attract a larger following of consumers, which is expected to have a positive effect on future sales.
Mobilizing behaviour	• May exhibit a conceptual link with influencing behaviours; i.e. where consumers entice or propel other consumers towards the firm; e.g. sport athletics impact on consumers' relationship with sports brands.	• Similar to the cell directly above, a consumer's mobilizing behaviours can be used to expand the network of followers/customers of a brand. It is therefore important to appropriately reward opinion leaders or other consumers who act as brand ambassadors for the firm.

Reflecting firms' increasing use of social media as direct monetizing tools, we develop a conceptual model that proposes CE as a mediating concept in the relationship between a firm's brand-based social media investments, and ensuing non-financial and financial ROSME. We posit that leveraging CE is key to fostering ROSME, and thereby generating enhanced accountability of firm-based social media investments. Thus, through the analyses presented in this chapter, we provide enhanced understanding of the key role of CE in generating ROSME. Our model also acknowledges that while CE manifests through *observable* consumer behaviours displayed on social media, the concept also incorporates important underlying (latent) engagement cognitions and emotions that drive consumers' engagement behaviours (Hollebeek *et al.* 2014; Ajzen and Fishbein 1973). However, despite the theoretical insight gained in this chapter, we encourage the undertaking of future research (particularly large-scale, quantitative work) that tests and validates our proposed conceptual relationships (e.g. through the adoption of structural equations modelling or social media channel experiments).

This observation leads to the following limitation of this research, which gives rise to another, related future research avenue. Based on the tri-component perspective of attitudes, which comprises focal cognitive, emotional and behavioural aspects pertaining to a given object, a consumer's behaviour does not always match their particular cognitive and emotional perspectives relating to an object (e.g. despite a positive cognitive/emotional brand attitude, a consumer may not proceed to purchase the brand *per se*; Petty and Cacioppo 2012; Schiffman and Wisenblit 2015). Similarly, while cognitive and emotional CE may be positive, consumers' behavioural engagement related to the object may be negligible (neutral), or even negative (Bowden *et al.* 2015; Hollebeek and Chen 2014). Thus, future research that explores and tests the nature of positive versus negative CE and potential triggers that are conducive to engendering a transition (e.g. from positive to negative CE, or vice versa), is needed.

Second, a brand's social media activities are interdependent from the firm's activities in other media channels (both online and offline; Verhoef *et al.* 2007). A firm's brand-related social media investments and ensuing CE should thus be viewed as part of a balanced marketing communications portfolio, rather than in isolation. We thus recommend the undertaking of future research that investigates the effect of CE on ROSME and return on engagement through other media channels (e.g. physical retail stores, pop-up stores), thus resulting in a more comprehensive perspective. Third, our model assumes CE to represent a positively valenced concept, that is, with higher CE generating increasingly favourable ROSME for the firm (Hollebeek and Chen 2014). However, research is emerging that highlights the potentially negatively valenced nature of engagement, including the generation of negative brand-related word-of-mouth, brand equity dilution, lost sales revenue, consumer hostility towards particular brands etc. (Juric *et al.* 2016). Consequently, future research may wish to investigate the (damaging) effects of negatively valenced CE on ensuing ROSME outcomes.

In addition, CE may be ambivalent, or relatively neutral, in nature, thus reflecting limited levels of consumer motivation to make cognitive, emotional or behavioural investments in particular brand interactions (Schultz and Block 2011). Future research may, therefore, wish to investigate the effects of brand-related social media investments on neutral, or negatively valenced, engagement (e.g. managerial actions attempting to reverse negative CE) and the effect of neutral or negative CE on ensuing ROSME. The development of sound managerial practice to minimize or reduce the occurrence of any potential detrimental effects to their brands from negative CE is of paramount importance in today's increasingly net-worked environment (Hollebeek *et al.* 2016a/b/c). Finally, this research provides a strong impetus for future studies to investigate the specific approaches, tactics and strategies that are conducive to optimising CE and resultant ROSME outcomes.

Managerial implications

In this section, we highlight the importance of developing sound managerial accountability for firms' brand-related social media investments. Specifically, we advocate that to make accurate assessments in this area, firms need to consider *consumers'* cognitive, emotional and behavioural investments made into social-media-based brand interactions, thus reflecting a shift away from the traditional view of managerial control over brand-based communications and performance. Given the interactivity that social media and other Web 2.0 (and beyond) technologies provide, we draw attention to the need for managerial ceding of some level of their traditional control by putting consumers, and their brand-related engagement behaviours, in the driver's seat (Sasser *et al.* 2014).

While consumers' cognitive and emotional brand investments on social media are not directly observable, these manifest by virtue of particular engagement behaviours, which are of key managerial interest. Examples of consumer engagement behaviours include 'contributing' behaviours (e.g. liking, sharing or commenting) and 'creating' behaviours (e.g. posting organic brand-related content on one's Facebook page; Tsai and Men 2013), which reflect varying levels of inter-activity with, and investment in, the brand (Muntinga *et al.* 2011). Based on this information, marketers are able to segment consumers based on their behavioural engagement levels with the brand (Van Doorn *et al.* 2010). Further, the identification, targeting and leveraging of opinion leaders is also of paramount importance, as outlined in Table 10.1. Specifically, opinion leaders' posts, likes, shares and other brand-related social media activity has credence for their peers and others within their networks (Burt 1999; Schiffmann and Wisenblit 2015). Therefore, identifying, approaching and partnering with individuals viewed as opinion leaders by those in their networks is expected to be a fruitful strategy for furthering sales and ROSME.

Second, we advocate the incorporation of easy-to-use, easily accessible 'buy' buttons. We also invite managers to carefully consider consumers' perceived 'ideal' layout, look and feel of specific social media and social commerce platforms.

While social commerce platform design is beyond the scope of the present investigation, it remains a fruitful area for future research (Breidbach *et al.* 2014). Third, while we investigate key drivers of ROSME effectiveness, we have recognized that the majority of promotional and marketing communication campaigns occur by adopting some combination of traditional (e.g. newspapers, magazines) and new (e.g. event invitations through social media) media. Consequently, it is of key managerial interest to understand the ideal composition of promotional campaigns for particular brands (e.g. What percentage of promotional budget should be spent on new versus traditional media for my brand? Which types of new or traditional media should be used, and in what proportions?). We thus invite managers to carefully consider these issues so as to stimulate the attainment of optimal ROSME effectiveness and accountability through leveraging social media-based CE (Hollebeek *et al.* 2016b).

References

Achterberg, W., A. M. Pot, A. Kerkstra, M. Ooms, M. Muller and M. Ribbe. 2003. 'The effect of depression on social engagement in newly admitted Dutch nursing home residents', *The Gerontologist*, 43:2: p. 213–218.

Ajzen, I. and M. Fishbein. 1973, 'Attitudinal and normative variables as predictors of specific behavior', *Journal of Personality and Social Psychology*, 27:1: p. 41–57.

Arnould, E. J. and C. J. Thompson. 2005. 'Consumer culture theory CCT: twenty years of research', *Journal of Consumer Research*, 31:4: p. 868–882.

Baethge, C., J. Klier and M. Klier. 2016. 'Social commerce: State-of-the-art and future research directions', *Electronic Markets*. In Press, DOI:10.1007/s12525-016-0225-2.

Baldus, B. J., C. Voorhees and R. Calantone. 2015. 'Online brand community engagement: scale development and validation', *Journal of Business Research*, 68:5, p. 978–985.

Baumöl, U., L. Hollebeek and R. Jung. 2016. 'Dynamics of customer interaction on social media platforms', *Electronic Markets*. In Press, DOI:10.1007/s12525-016-0227-0.

Bijmolt, T. H., P. S. Leeflang, F. Block, M. Eisenbeiss, B. G. Hardie, A. Lemmens and P. Saffert. 2010. 'Analytics for customer engagement', *Journal of Service Research*, 13:3, p. 341–356.

Bitter, S. and S. Grabner-Kräuter. 2016. 'Consequence of customer engagement behavior: when negative Facebook posts have positive effects', *Electronic Markets*, 26:3, DOI:10.1007/s12525-016-0220-7.

Bowden, J., M. Gabbott and K. Naumann. 2015. 'Service relationships and the customer disengagement-engagement conundrum', *Journal of Marketing Management*, 31:7–8: p. 774–806.

Breidbach, C. F., R. Brodie and L. Hollebeek. 2014. 'Beyond virtuality: from engagement platforms to engagement escosystems', *Managing Service Quality*, 24:6, p. 592–611.

Brodie, R. J., L. D. Hollebeek, B. Juric and A. Ilic. 2011. 'Customer engagement: conceptual domain, fundamental propositions, and implications for research', *Journal of Service Research*, 14:3, p. 252–272.

Brodie, R. J., A. Ilic, B. Juric and L. Hollebeek. 2013. 'Consumer engagement in a virtual brand community: an exploratory analysis', *Journal of Business Research*, 66:1, p. 105–114.

Buhalis. D. and E. Mamalakis. 2015. 'Social media return on investment and performance evaluation in the hotel industry context', *Information and Communication Technologies in Tourism*, p. 241–253.

Burt, R. S. 1999. 'The social capital of opinion leaders', *Annals of the American Academy of Political and Social Science*, 566:1, p. 37–54.

Cabiddu, F., M. De Carlo and G. Piccoli. 2014. 'Social media affordances: enabling customer engagement', *Annals of Tourism Research*, 48:9, p. 175–192.

Calder, B. J., E. C. Malthouse and U. Schaedel. 2009. 'An experimental study of the relationship between online engagement and advertising effectiveness', *Journal of Interactive Marketing*, 23:4, p. 321–331.

Calder, B. J., E. C. Malthouse and E. Maslowska. 2016. 'Brand marketing, big data and social innovation as future research directions for engagement', *Journal of Marketing Management*, 32:5–6, p. 579–585.

Cao, G. 2015. 'Brief: engage Chinese consumers with interactive digital content: using digital intelligence tools to optimize customer engagement', Forrester Research. Available at https://www.forrester.com/report/Brief+Engage+Chinese+Consumers+W ith+Interactive+Digital+Content/-/ERES120849. Accessed 13 June 2016.

Chandler, J. D. and R. F. Lusch. 2015. 'Service systems: a broadened framework and research agenda on value propositions, engagement, and service experience', *Journal of Service Research*, 18:1, p. 6–22.

Coles, L. 2014. *Marketing with Social Media: 10 Easy Steps to Success for Business*. Melbourne: Wiley.

Culnan, M. J., P. J. McHugh and J. I. Zubillaga. 2010. 'How large US companies can use Twitter and other social media to gain business value', *MIS Quarterly Executive*, 9:4, p. 243–259.

Dessart, L., C. Veloutsou and A. Morgan-Thomas. 2016. 'Capturing consumer engagement: duality, dimensionality and measurement', *Journal of Marketing Management*, 32:5–6, p. 399–426.

De Vries, L., S. Gensler and P. S. H. Leeflang. 2012, 'Popularity of brand posts on brand fan pages: an investigation of the effects of social media marketing', *Journal of Interactive Marketing*, 26:2, p. 83–91.

Doyle, P. 2001. 'Shareholder-based brand strategies', *Journal of Brand Management*, 9:1, p. 20–30.

Etgar, M. 2008. 'A descriptive model of the consumer co–production process', *Journal of the Academy of Marketing Science*, 36:1, p. 97–108.

Fisher, T. 2009. 'ROI in social media: a look at the arguments', *Journal of Database Marketing & Customer Strategy Management*, 16:3, p. 189–195.

Flamholtz, E. 1985. *Human Resource Accounting: Advances in Concepts, Methods and Applications*, 2e. San Francisco: Jossey-Bass.

Franklin, J. and J. Plewa. 1996. *Understanding Return on Investment*, Canada: Wiley.

Frick, T. 2010. *Return on Engagement: Content, Strategy, and Design Techniques for Digital Marketing*, Burlington, MA: Elsevier.

Friedlob, G. T. and F. J. Plewa Jr. 1996. *Understanding Return on Investment*, John Wiley & Sons.

Galston, W. A. 2001. 'Political knowledge, political engagement, and civic education', *Annual Review of Political Science*, 4:1, p. 217–234.

Gambetti, R. and G. Graffigna. 2010. 'The concept of engagement: a systematic analysis of the ongoing marketing debate', *International Journal of Market Research*, 52:6, p. 801–826.

Groeger, L., L. Moroko and L. Hollebeek. 2016. 'Capturing value from non-paying consumers' engagement behaviours: field evidence and development of a theoretical model', *Journal of Strategic Marketing*, 24:3-4, p. 190–209.

Gummerus, J., V. Liljander, E. Weman and M. Pihlström. 2012. 'Customer engagement in a Facebook brand community', *Management Research Review*, 35:9, p. 857–877.

Gummesson, E. 2004. 'Return on relationships ROR: the value of relationship marketing and CRM in business-to-business contexts', *Journal of Business & Industrial Marketing*, 19:2, p. 136–148.

Gummesson, E. 2008. 'Extending the service-dominant logic: from customer centricity to balanced centricity', *Journal of the Academy of Marketing Science*, 36:1, p. 15–17.

Habibi, M. R., M. Laroche and M. O. Richard. 2014. 'The roles of brand community and community engagement in building brand trust on social media', *Computers in Human Behaviour*, 37, p. 152–161.

Hanna, R., A. Rohm and V. L. Crittenden. 2011. 'We're all connected: the power of the social media ecosystem', *Business Horizons*, 54, p. 265–273.

Heathman, B. 2012. 'Conversion marketing: the psychology of converting browsers into buyers'. In: *Conversion Marketing: The Online Marketing Economy*. Available at http://conversionmarketingbook.com/ConversionMktgChapter-1.pdf. Accessed 13 June 2016.

Hoffman, D.L. and M. Fodor. 2010. 'Can you measure the ROI of your social media marketing', *MIT Sloan Management Review*, 52:1, p. 41–49.

Hoffman, D. L. and T. P. Novak 2011. 'Marketing communication in a digital era', *Marketing Management*, 20:3, p. 36–43.

Hollebeek, L. D. 2011a. 'Demystifying customer brand engagement: exploring the loyalty nexus', *Journal of Marketing Management*, 27:7–8, p. 785–807.

Hollebeek, L. D. 2011b. 'Exploring customer brand engagement: definition and themes', *Journal of Strategic Marketing*, 19:7, p. 555–573.

Hollebeek, L. D. 2013. 'The customer engagement/value interface: an exploratory investigation', *Australasian Marketing Journal*, 21:1, p. 17–24.

Hollebeek, L. D. 2016. 'Customer engagement: a multi-stakeholder perspective'. In: Brodie, R. J., J. Conduit and L. D. Hollebeek (eds.). *Customer Engagement: Contemporary Issues and Challenges*. London: Routledge.

Hollebeek, L. D., J. Conduit, J. Sweeney, G. Soutar, I. O. Karpen, W. Jarvis and T. Chen. 2016b. 'Epilogue to the special issue and reflections on the future of engagement research', *Journal of Marketing Management*, 32:5–6, p. 586–594.

Hollebeek, L. D. and T. Chen. 2014. 'Exploring positively- versus negatively-valenced brand engagement: a conceptual model', *Journal of Product and Brand Management*, 23:1, p. 62–74.

Hollebeek, L. D., M. S. Glynn and R. J. Brodie. 2014. 'Consumer brand engagement in social media: conceptualization, scale development and validation', *Journal of Interactive Marketing*, 28:2, p. 149–165.

Hollebeek, L. D., E. Jaakkola and M. Alexander. 2016a. 'Beyond the dyadic: customer engagement in increasingly networked environments', *Journal of Service Management*. Forthcoming.

Hollebeek, L. D. and R. J. Brodie. 2016. 'Non-monetary social and network value: understanding the effects of non–paying customers in new media', *Journal of Strategic Marketing*, 24:3–4, p. 169–174.

Hollebeek, L. D., J. Conduit, J. Sweeney, G. Soutar, I. O. Karpen, W. Jarvis and T. Chen. 2016b. 'Epilogue to the special issue and reflections on the future of engagement research', *Journal of Marketing Management*, 32:5–6, p. 586–594.

Hollebeek, L. D., R. K. Srivastava and T. Chen. 2016c. 'S-D Logic-informed customer engagement: integrative framework, revised fundamental propositions, and application to CRM,' *Journal of the Academy of Marketing Science*, Online First.

Jennings, M.K and L. Stoker. 2004, 'Social trust and civic engagement across time and generations', *Acta Politica*, 394, p. 342–379.

Jaakkola, E. and M. Alexander. 2014. 'The role of customer engagement behavior in value co-creation: a service system perspective', *Journal of Service Research*, 17:3, p. 247–261.

Jahn, B. and W. Kunz. 2012. 'How to transform consumers into fans of your brand', *Journal of Service Management*, 23:3, p. 344–361.

Juric, B., G. Wilks and S. Smith. 2016. 'Negative customer brand engagement: an overview of conceptual and blog-based findings'. In: Brodie, R. J., L. D. Hollebeek, and J. Conduit (eds.), *Customer Engagement: Contemporary Issues and Challenges.* Singapore: Routledge, p. 272–286.

Kahn, W. A. 1990. 'Psychological conditions of personal engagement and disengagement at work', *Academy of Management Journal*, 33, p. 692–724.

Kaplan, A. M. and M. Haenlein. 2010. 'Users of the world, unite! The challenges and opportunities of social media', *Business Horizons*, 53:1, p. 59–68.

Kaske, F., M. Kügler and S. Smolnik. 2012. 'Return on investment in social media – does the hype pay off? Towards an assessment of the profitability of social media in organizations'. In *System Science* (HICSS), 2012, 45th Hawaii International Conference on (p. 3898–3907) IEEE.

Kietzman, J. H., K. Hermkens, I. P. McCarthy and B. S. Silvestre. 2011. 'Social media? Get serious! Understanding the functional building blocks of social media', *Business Horizons*, 54:3, p. 241–251.

Kumar, V. 2013. *Profitable customer engagement: concept, metrics, and strategies*, New Delhi: Sage Publications.

Kumar, V., L. Aksoy, B. Donkers, R. Venkatesan, T. Wiesel and S. Tillmanns. 2010. 'Undervalued or overvalued customers: capturing total customer engagement value', *Journal of Service Research*, 13:3, p. 297–310.

Laroche, M., M. R. Habibi and M. O. Richard. 2013. 'To be or not to be in social media: how brand loyalty is affected by social media?', *International Journal of Information Management*, 33:1, p. 76–82.

Lloret Romero, N. 2011. 'ROI. Measuring the social media return on investment in a library', *The Bottom Line*, 24:2, p. 145–151.

Lusch, R. F. and S. L. Vargo. 2014. *Service-Dominant Logic.* Cambridge: Cambridge University Press.

Malthouse, E. C., M. Haenlein, B. Skiera, E. Wege and M. Zhang. 2013. 'Managing customer relationships in the social media era: introducing the social CRM house', *Journal of Interactive Marketing*, 27:4, p. 270–280.

Mathwick, C., C. Wiertz and K. De Ruyter. 2008. 'Social capital production in a virtual p3 community', *Journal of Consumer Research*, 34:6, p. 832–849.

Maslowska, E., E. G. Smit and B. van den Putte. 2016. 'It is all in the name: a study of consumers' responses to personalized communication', *Journal of Interactive Advertising*, 16:1, p. 74–85.

McNulty, Y. M. and P. Tharenou. 2004. 'Expatriate return on investment: a definition and antecedents', *International Studies of Management & Organization*, 34:3, p. 68–95.

Mollen, A. and H. Wilson. 2010. 'Engagement, telepresence, and interactivity in online consumer experience: reconciling scholastic and managerial perspectives', *Journal of Business Research*, 63:9–10, p. 919–925.

Muñiz, A. M., Jr., and T. C. O'Guinn. 2001. 'Brand community', *Journal of Consumer Research*, 27:4, p. 412–432.

Muntinga, D.G., M. Moorman and E. G. Smit. 2011. 'Introducing COBR as exploring motivations for brand-related social media use,' *International Journal of Advertising*, 30:1, p. 13–46.

Naidoo, V. and L. D. Hollebeek. 2016. 'Higher education brand alliances: investigating consumers' dual-degree purchase intentions', *Journal of Business Research*, 69:8, p. 3113–3121.

O'Brien, H. L. and E. G. Toms. 2008. 'What is user engagement? A conceptual framework for defining user engagement with technology', *Journal of the American Society for Information Science and Technology*, 59:6, p. 938–955.

O'Brien, H. L. and E. G. Toms. 2010. 'The development and evaluation of a survey to measure user engagement', *Journal of the American Society for Information Science and Technology*, 61:1, p. 50–69.

Pervan, S. J. and L. L. Bove. 2011. 'The engagement of customers beyond their expected roles', *Journal of Strategic Marketing*, 19:7, p. 551–554.

Petty, R. and J. T. Cacioppo. 2012. *Communication and persuasion: central and peripheral routes to attitude change*, New York: Springer Verlag.

Phillips, J. J. 1997. *Measuring return on investment*, Volume 2, Englewood Cliffs, NJ: American Society for Training and Development.

Porter, C. E., N. Donthu, W. H. MacElroy and D. Wydra. 2011. 'How to foster and sustain engagement in virtual communities', *California Management Review*, 53:4, p. 80–110.

Rishika, R., A. Kumar, R. Janakiraman and R. Bezawada. 2013. 'The effect of customers' social media participation on customer visit frequency and profitability: an empirical investigation', *Information Systems Research*, p. 108–127.

Rautio, A. 2012. 'Social media ROI as part of marketing strategy work – observations of digital', Aalto University School of Business Master's Thesis.

Sashi, C. M. 2012. 'Customer engagement, buyer-seller relationships, and social media', *Management Decision*, 50:2, p. 253–272.

Sasser, S., M. Kilgour and L. D. Hollebeek. 2014. 'Marketing in an interactive world: the evolving nature of communication processes using social media', in Lertwachera, K. and A. Ayanso (eds.), *Harnessing the Power of Social Media and Web Analytics: Techniques, Tools, and Applications*. New York: IGI Global, p. 29–52.

Schachner, L. 1973. 'Return on investment – its values, determination and uses', *The CPA Journal*, 43, p. 277.

Schamari, J. and T. Schaefers. 2015. 'Leaving the home turf: how brands can use webcare on consumer-generated platforms to increase positive consumer engagement', *Journal of Interactive Marketing*, 30, p. 20–33.

Schaufeli, W. B., M. Salanova, V. González-Romá and A. B. Bakker. 2002. 'The measurement of engagement and burnout: a two sample confirmatory factor analytic approach', *Journal of Happiness Studies*, 3:1, p. 71–92.

Shah, D., R. T. Rust, A. Parasuraman, R. Staelin and G. S. Day. 2006. 'The path to customer centricity', *Journal of Service Research*, 9:2, p. 113–124.

Schiffman, L. G. and J. L. Wisenbilt. 2015. *Consumer Behavior* (11e), London: Pearson: Global Edition.

Schivinski, B., G. Christodoulides and D. Dabrowski. 2016. 'Measuring consumers' engagement with brand-related social-media content: development and validation of a scale that identifies levels of social-media engagement with brands,' *Journal of Advertising Research*, 56:1, p. 64–80.

Schultz, C. 2016. 'Insights from consumer interactions on a social networking site: findings from six apparel retail brands', *Electronic Markets*, 26:3, DOI:10.1007/s12525-015-0209-7.

Schultz, D. E. and M. P. Block. 2011. 'Understanding customer brand engagement in today's interactive marketplace,' *Micro and Macro-Marketing*, p. 227–244, DOI:10.1431/35137.

Skinner, E. A. and M. J. Belmont. 1993. 'Motivation in the classroom: reciprocal effects of teacher behavior and student engagement across the school year', *Journal of Educational Psychology*, 85:4, p. 571.

Solem, B. A. A. 2016. 'Influences of customer participation and customer brand engagement on brand loyalty', *Journal of Consumer Marketing*, 33:5. Forthcoming.

Solem, B. A. A. and P. E. Pedersen. 2016. 'The effects of regulatory fit on customer brand engagement: an experimental study of service brand activities in social media', *Journal of Marketing Management*, 32:5–6, p. 445–468.

Solem, B. A. A. and P. E. Pedersen. 2016. 'The role of customer brand engagement in social media: conceptualization, measurement, antecedents and outcomes', *International Journal of Internet Marketing and Advertising*, (in press).

Stephen, A. T. and O. Toubia. 2010. 'Deriving value from social commerce networks', *Journal of Marketing Research*, 47:2, p. 215–228.

Tsai, W. H. S. and L. R. Men. 2013. 'Motivations and antecedents of consumer engagement with brand pages on social networking sites', *Journal of Interactive Advertising*, 13:2, p. 76–87.

Van Doorn, J., K. N. Lemon, V. Mittal, S. Nass, D. Pick, P. Pirner and P. C. Verhoef. 2010. 'Customer engagement behaviour: theoretical foundations and research directions', *Journal of Service Research*, 13:3, p. 253–266.

Vargo, S. L. and R. F. Lusch. 2004. 'Evolving to a new dominant logic for marketing', *Journal of Marketing*, 68:1, p. 1–17.

Vargo, S. L. and R. F. Lusch. 2008. 'Service-Dominant Logic: continuing the evolution', *Journal of the Academy of Marketing Science*, 36:1, p. 1–10.

Vargo, S. L. and R. F. Lusch. 2016. 'Institutions and axioms: an extension and update of Service-Dominant Logic', *Journal of the Academy of Marketing Science*, 44:1, p. 5–23.

Verhoef, P. C., S. A. Neslin and B. Vroomen. 2007. 'Multichannel customer management: understanding the research-shopper phenomenon', *International Journal of Research in Marketing*, 24:2, p. 129–148.

Verleye, K., P. Gemmel and D. Rangarajan. 2014. 'Managing engagement behaviors in a network of customers and stakeholders: evidence from the nursing home sector', *Journal of Service Research*, 17:1, p. 68–84.

Vivek, S. D., S. Beatty, V. Dalela and R. Morgan. 2014. 'A generalized multidimensional scale for measuring customer engagement', *Journal of Marketing Theory and Practice*, 22:4, p. 401–420.

11

AN UNEXPECTED JOURNEY

The influence of social media on consumer decision-making

Wolgang Weitzl and Clemens Hutzinger

Introduction

Today, marketers can choose from an extensive arsenal of online marketing instruments, including paid search engine marketing, display marketing and email to reach current and potential customers (Raman *et al.* 2012). Numerous companies use more than one of these instruments simultaneously and, together with the radical improvements in digital technologies, the way consumers can interact with brands along their online customer journey has changed dramatically. Earlier marketing practitioners and scholars were tempted to draw on a very narrow definition of an *online customer journey* (Lee 2010) or *path to purchase* (e.g. Xu *et al.* 2014), including all touchpoints of any individual customer with a brand over all online marketing channels, prior to a potential purchase decision (e.g. Anderl *et al.* 2016). This traditional perspective essentially guided marketers' attention to a process that is terminated by an act of purchase, but also to a focus on the role of *owned* or *paid for* touchpoints (e.g. corporate website) in contributing towards stimulating a purchase. However, the recent evolution of the 'empowered customer' has transformed the rules of marketing and induced new mechanisms that have made many of the assumptions of the traditional view on consumer decision-making obsolete.

In this chapter, we challenge this old-fashioned perspective and advance a more contemporary view on consumer journeys in a social media world. Marketers should recognize that in the digital age, marketing touch points (i.e. all the experiences the consumer has when he/she 'touches' any part of the brand) have changed in number, nature and role. A new set of online marketing channels that include *owned*, *paid*, but also *earned*, touch points – and especially *social media* – provide new opportunities to interact with and influence consumers. Consumers are increasingly using social media to source information for their purchasing decisions, while turning away from the classic marketing touchpoints, like TV advertising (Mangold and Faulds 2009). We have been witnessing this tendency for many years. Social media platforms offer an opportunity for consumers to interact with other shoppers – a need that is important across all phases of the consumer-brand experience. As a consequence, companies are no longer the sole source of brand communication and meaning (e.g. Moe and Schweidel 2012). In addition, consumers regard user-generated social media content as a more trustworthy and useful source of information than the traditional instruments of marketing communication that are perceived as biased by corporate interests in order to steer consumer behaviour (Foux 2006). This creates an environment that is not without risk for companies (Moe and Schweidel 2012). There is considerable evidence that posted product ratings and product reviews become increasingly negative as the social media environments mature (Godes and Silva 2012). Research findings show that more than 90 per cent of all consumers read product comments by others online before making a purchase decision, and that user-generated content influences 67 per cent of all purchases of consumer goods. On average, a consumer reads at least four consumer comments before buying a product (Kee 2008). Importantly, however, these comments play a key role in purchase decisions themselves (Godes and Silva 2012). Consequently, social media content creates empowered and knowledgeable consumers who are more led by the opinions of other customers than by advertising messages.

Nonetheless, social media also furnishes marketers with a new touchpoint to convey their own messages to consumers at various points in time during the consumer decision-making process. An excellent example of successful social media usage is *Starbucks*. The company has managed to receive 37.32 million Facebook 'likes' as well as 6.56 million Twitter followers. Thus the company can reach a tremendous amount of current and potential customers with their very eye-catching posts that have a good balance between fun, recommendations and subtle sales messages. This and other success stories motivate managers to invest heavily in social media in order to inform and engage customers, who contribute to positive word-of-mouth dissemination (Vries *et al.* 2012). Therefore, when investigating the role of social media in consumer decision-making, it is essential to differentiate between *marketer-generated* (MGC) and *user-generated* (UGC) social media communication and further examine the effect of these two types of social media content separately. The source effects (i.e. consumer reactions to different perceptions of MGC versus UGC) of social media content have become a topic of growing importance (Godes and Mayzlin 2009).

For marketing practitioners, it is common practice to devote a significant proportion of the financial resources (and particularly social media budgets) to the consideration and purchase stages. However, this neglects other important follow-up stages, when consumers enter the experience phase and engage in brand co-creation, and are often even more susceptible to influence. In research literature, for instance, one can find support that the influence of touchpoints on consumers is particularly present in the after-purchase stage, when decisions on brand loyalty or switching are typically made. Social media has turned out to be particularly effective in this stage and is increasingly acquiring a dominant role for the consumer-brand relationship (e.g. Powers *et al.* 2012). Therefore, we want to address the differential role of MGC and UGC in social media, as well as the reasons that make one or the other more important for consumer decision-making.

Hence, this chapter will include a discussion of (1) the traditional funnel approach to purchasing, (2) a contemporary approach for classifying the pre- and post-purchase decision stages of digitalized, engaged consumers, and (3) the factors that steer consumer active and passive engagement towards MGC and UGC during decision-making. The concluding discussion section targets several implications based on earlier research insights and brand success stories.

The traditional funnel approach

Marketing scholars and practitioners generally agree that a purchase decision is a multistage process (Roberts and Lattin 1997). This view dates back to Lewis (1903), who proposed the *purchase funnel* as a marketing model that illustrates the purchase process in several stages. The model has been modified multiple times over recent years. However, the basic conceptual framework and stages that build the consumer journey remain the same (Bruyn and Lilien 2008). It is generally agreed that, in the initial phase, consumers are aware of only a limited number of alternative brands (i.e. the awareness set), which are deemed to satisfy their consumption goals. Only a subset of the awareness set, the often so-called 'consideration set', is actively considered for a specific purchase. This means that, according to the funnel approach, in a typical purchase decision, consumers start at the wide end of the funnel with many brands in their consideration set before they narrow them down to the final choice (Shocker *et al.* 1991). Hence, the consideration set should be regarded as dynamic, as consumers can remove (but also add) brands until they arrive at an ultimate decision.

During the sequential selection process, consumers collect and apply information that helps them to filter out inappropriate brands. As the selection criteria change, so do consumers' information needs during the purchase-decision process (Payne *et al.* 1988). For example, after identifying a broad set of alternative brands, a consumer typically seeks more external information on the brand's website in order to get a basic idea of the market's offerings. After that, he/she evaluates the most promising options in depth by investigating others' consumption experiences on review websites such as Epinions or Yelp, before making a purchase decision (Häubl and Trifts 2000). After a short consumer-seller interaction which culminates in the purchase of the item, the buyer's relationship with the brand typically ends, with no further interactions between the two parties. Such a perspective characterizes consumers as relatively passive and unengaged information-seekers who are not interested in contributing to their own brand experiences or sharing it with others.

Given this dominant view, companies have traditionally put substantial emphasis on the identification and selection of paid-media push marketing, used at well-defined stages of the purchase decision to create awareness, enhance consideration and ultimately inspire purchase. Recent academic literature still builds on the validity of the funnel approach by studying the role of online touchpoints for the pre-purchase stages of relatively uninvolved consumers (e.g. Xu *et al.* 2014).

The engagement circle approach

Nowadays, however, academic (e.g. Hollebeek *et al.* 2014) as well as managerial literature (e.g. Edelman 2010) provides evidence that consumer patterns have dramatically changed and that the decision journey has become much more complex than it was initially considered to be. While some conceptual differences exist, recent contributors generally agree that a consumer's journey should now be regarded as an iterative process that typically doesn't end with a consumer's conversion (i.e. single time purchase). Instead, consumers enter a highly sensitive and important phase after the purchase, which impacts his/her (but also others') relationship with the focal brand. For instance, in the model proposed by McKinsey (Court *et al.* 2009), the consumer journey is conceptualized as a purchasing loop. Here, one of the model's key assertions is that instead of systematically narrowing their choices, today's consumers take a much more circular and less reductive journey with three general stages: (i) *pre-purchase stages* including consumer brand awareness, consideration and evaluation; (ii) *purchase stage*; and (iii) the *post-purchase stage*, which is characterized by intensive brand-consumer experiences, retention and advocacy. It is widely agreed among marketing professionals and scholars that the latter phase should be regarded as ultimately the most important part of the consumer journey as the consumer re-evaluates his/her attitudes towards the brand by personally experiencing it, makes the decision to re-purchase the brand based on these experiences and informs others about his/her brand decisions. Given the recognition of the multifaceted behaviours related to brand purchases, this comprehensive sequence of actions is considered to be more capable of predicting future consumer behaviour. Additionally, modern versions of the purchase funnel model account in particular for the influence of social media before and after the consumer has decided to purchase a particular product or brand. Examples for this introduction to the classic Elmo Lewis' model are the models of McKinsey, which emphasize the idea that consumers typically take a journey of four stages (i.e. (i) consider, (ii) evaluate, (iii) buy, and (iv) enjoy, advocate and bond), as well as the model proposed by Forrester. The latter especially highlights the great impact of user-generated content on the consumer's final purchasing and after-purchasing decision. Specifically, the model proposes that consumers follow a sequence of discovering, exploring, buying, using, asking and engaging with the brand and that specific social media platforms have a differentiated role across this circle.

The process that includes all the interactions of any individual customer with a brand, over all online marketing channels during a purchase episode, can be defined as the *customer engagement circle* or *full online customer journey*. We have chosen to include the term 'engagement' to express the various voluntary and characterizing involvement behaviours that consumers typically show during modern decision processes that typically involve interactive participation in social media settings. In literature, consumer engagement is defined as "behaviors that go beyond simple transactions, and may be specifically defined as a customer's behavioral manifestations that have a brand focus, beyond purchase, resulting from motivational drivers" (van Doorn *et al.* 2010, p. 254). The concept, therefore, includes all kinds of actions which occur before *and* after a particular purchase (Libai 2011), and integrates a great number of transactional and non-transactional behaviours during the whole consumer journey. Such behaviours typically fall on a continuum ranging from low- ('passive engagement') to high-intensity ('active engagement') levels. A consumer is passively engaged, for example, when consuming information or asking questions on a Facebook brand 'fan' page in order to identify the most appropriate brand. However, he/she might become actively engaged when writing referrals, engaging in word-of-mouth activities or actively supporting other customers. Today, such behaviours are regularly shown offline, but particularly on social media when consumers share their opinions, feelings and thoughts with friends, family and fellow shoppers, collaborate with other consumers, provide after-sales service (e.g. helping other customers with the use of a product), and assist the company to improve their products and services. Therefore, consumers have often become co-creators of online content (i.e. UGC) and brand experiences.

As outlined earlier, purchase decisions are considered to result from a multi-stage decision process (Shocker *et al.* 1991). In this chapter, we adopt the widely acknowledged stages of: awareness, information search, evaluation, purchase decision and post-purchase experience. Consumers' information needs also change during these stages (Jang *et al.* 2012). Consequently, their appreciation of MGC and UGC varies across these stages accordingly. Given this, we now discuss the roles of the different social media communication types (e.g. Facebook brand pages) and the factors that determine their differential influence.

Pre-purchase stages

In the first stage, the *awareness stage*, consumers are usually aware of only a subset of all available brands in the market (Shocker *et al.* 1991). All brands that are outside a consumer's awareness set have no chance of being considered for purchase. Hence, the main goal of marketers is to stimulate needs and raise awareness of their brands. One way to achieve this is by publishing MGC, for example, by posting messages on social media (e.g. Fournier and Avery 2011). The theoretical background for the relationship between MGC and consumer awareness (and attitudes) is provided by Schema Theory (Eysenck 1984), which claims that consumers individually compare communication stimuli with their knowledge of comparable communication activities. Consequently, the perception of the degree of fit influences the mental processing of the stimulus, and the formation of attitude in the recipient. Hence, communication stimuli cause positive effects in the consumer as the recipient, such that their perception of the communication positively influences their *awareness* level and attitude towards the brand. Therefore, MGC positively influences consumer associations, as long as the message creates a satisfactory consumer reaction towards the brand in question, compared to a similar non-branded product (Yoo *et al.* 2000).

Research shows that brand communication, in general, increases the probability that a brand is incorporated into a consumer's consideration set, simplifies brand choice and thus assists in the process of brand decision-making (Yoo *et al.* 2000). As MGC is likely to be perceived by individuals as a kind of advertising, the same applies for social media content generated by the company. Some studies already provide some insight that MGC arouses brand awareness and brand perception directly (e.g. Coulter *et al.* 2012). Additionally, if MGC is perceived as valuable, it also increases fan page engagement and usage intensity (Verma *et al.* 2012), which also finally leads to brand awareness.

Another way to create awareness is by *electronic word-of-mouth* (eWOM), which is brand-related UGC (e.g. Hinz *et al.* 2011). Online conversations between potential customers play a very important role in the early phases of the decision journey (Divol *et al.* 2012). More specifically, studies tell us that consumer awareness regarding a company, its brands or products increases as more UGC is created (Dhar and Chang 2009) and disseminated (Duan *et al.* 2008). The more UGC postings are available on a brand's social media page, the higher its social interaction value, which causes an increase in the engagement of its users (Verma *et al.* 2012), which consequently affects brand awareness. In addition, the access to eWOM often leads to an increase in the consumers' initial choice set, before it is narrowed. This is supported by Mark Granovetter's (1973) work, which claims that new insights (e.g. product ideas) often come from persons with whom the individual shares only weak ties, a situation which can be regularly witnessed on social media, where many information recipients do not know the contributors in person.

After consumers have become aware of a brand that appears attractive to them, they may become interested in obtaining more information (Bruyn and Lilien 2008) (i.e. *information search*). Consumers typically collect information from internal sources (e.g. own experiences) and external sources (e.g. ads, customer reviews). Hence, the next challenge for marketers is to stimulate consumer interest by providing additional information that later assists the consumer to evaluate the brand. MGC can offer consumers additional cues that may help them to judge whether the brand is likely to satisfy their underlying consumption goals (Goh *et al.* 2013). This is achieved by delivering attribute-related information about the product, which is particularly relevant for consumers striving to purchase 'search goods'. MGC can also convey information that is not directly related to the brand's characteristics, but which can help to reduce perceived purchase risks and influence consumer expectations (e.g. information about the purchase process). However, consumer trust in MGC is generally low (Escalas 2007), as marketers always have an incentive to present their brand in a positive light. Consequently, marketers should strive to regain consumer trust by offering value-added content via social media that not only educates consumers about the core benefits of the brand, but also about the augmented product (i.e. the non-physical part of the product) and the relevance of the brand in a greater consumption or lifestyle context. This suggests that the brand understands and satisfies consumption needs that go beyond even the current knowledge of the potential customer. Such an approach potentially helps to overcome typical information source obstacles.

In contrast, UGC is generally perceived as much more credible and trustworthy than MGC (e.g. Moon *et al.* 2010). Hence, consumers are increasingly relying on seemingly unbiased UGC, rather than MGC, when searching for information (Moon *et al.* 2010) and assistance in the purchasing decision (e.g. Dellarocas 2003). Goh *et al.* (2013) show, in the context of online social networks, that the information richness of UGC has a larger impact on purchasing decisions than classical MGC, which does not meet the consumers' true needs before selecting a specific brand. Consumers typically try to reduce perceived purchase risk by searching for information beyond brand descriptions on the attribute basis provided by marketers. Hence, reading fellow shoppers' opinions about, and subjective experiences with, the brand helps consumers to determine the extent to which the identified brand matches their preferences, expectations and consumption goals. This is particularly true for experience goods and lifestyle products. Dimoka *et al.* (2012) demonstrate that positive UGC reduces significantly the perceived risk associated with a purchase. Negative UGC, however, results in the reverse effect (e.g. Dellarocas 2003) and often impacts consumer attitudes and behaviours to a greater extent than positive UGC.

During the *evaluation stage*, the consumer already knows the brand and evaluates it. Such an evaluation frequently happens with respect to other similar brands the consumer knows. At this stage, consumers regularly enter a phase of heightened engagement, as they actively investigate the brand in comparison with its competitors by asking for opinions and formulating questions in online communities. There is ample evidence that social media has an important role for brand evaluations (e.g. Coulter *et al.* 2012). Here, UGC, in particular, seems to be very influential, because it triggers consumer-to-consumer interactions. In addition, it is not uncommon for consumers to express their preference towards a specific brand online. This behaviour is regularly driven by heightened consumer involvement (in the brand, product or product category), which has been found to create greater external search behaviours, greater depth of mental processing and more elaboration. Active sharing of future purchasing plans is also often triggered by the consumers' search for social recognition and status.

Purchase stage

In the purchase stage, consumers ultimately make their decision to purchase a brand or not. This decision mainly depends on the brand's perceived attractiveness

(Hauser and Wernerfelt 1990) and on the perceived risk which the consumer associates with the purchase (Cunningham *et al.* 2005). Clearly, the marketer's reasons for actively managing social networking sites are to influence consumer perceptions of brands, disseminate information, foster brand-consumer relationships and ultimately increase sales. MGC supports the latter goal by increasing the consumer's purchase willingness, due to its informational value (Goh *et al.* 2013), but also its persuasiveness (e.g. Russo and Chaxel 2010). MGC has an important role when it comes to reducing situational factors that may hinder the purchase. However, in general, consumers are more attracted by UGC (Dellarocas 2003). Among the different perceivable UGC characteristics, research has found some evidence that particularly volume (Dhar and Chang 2009) and valence (i.e. positive versus negative eWOM) (Chintagunta *et al.* 2010) can strongly affect a consumer's purchase decision. Positive UGC has repeatedly been reported to increase sales (e.g. Zhu and Zhang 2010). This finding has also been supported in the context of online social networks (Sonnier *et al.* 2011). In addition, UGC valence has a larger impact on sales than MGC valence (Goh *et al.* 2013), highlighting its dominant role. Concerning the relative impact of positive versus negative UGC, the research findings are not conclusive. While some studies conclude with an opposite finding (e.g. Sonnier *et al.* 2011), most previous research shows that negative UGC can influence purchase decisions to a greater extent than positive or neutral UGC (e.g. Lee *et al.* 2009). This tendency has been referred to as the 'negativity effect'. It is claimed that, when individuals form impressions of an object, they are more affected by negative characteristics than positive ones (Lee and Koo 2015). Prospect theory gives a possible explanation of this pattern, as it implies that losses generally loom larger than gains. Negative reviews make consumers more aware of a brand's consumption risks and hence of the potential losses that a consumer has to accept by purchasing it. Unfavourable comments about a brand reduce the positive outcomes or gains that a consumer hopes to receive from the brand. This said, consumers sometimes also become actively engaged by explicitly conveying their decision to buy on social media or making comments referring to the transaction involved when actually buying the brand.

Post-purchase stage

With changing consumption patterns, it has become the rule that consumers typically do not terminate their relationship with the brand after purchase, but remain extensively engaged with it (Baldus *et al.* 2015). In the *post-purchase stage*, consumers enter a phase when they are trying the product, sharing their personal experience with others by criticizing, recommending or simply communicating perceptions to others, and then finishing the journey by re-buying, upgrading, replacing or choosing a competitor (which means re-starting a new customer journey with another company). Social media is one of the key marketing touchpoints after the purchase, when consumers get involved in a deeper connection with the brand as they interact with products, brands and their communities.

Prior research has shown that 60 per cent of consumers conduct online research about the product *after* its purchase (Court *et al.* 2009) – the majority visiting social media channels. Here, UGC in particular is deemed useful to compare the consumer's own experiences with those of others. This behaviour is particularly driven by the desire to affirm their own earlier purchase decisions.

A considerable number of consumers, however, become more active, as they have the motivation to inform others about their personal opinions and feelings relating to their own consumption experiences. Past research on UGC has shown that consumers contribute to the process of content creation for reasons including self-promotion, intrinsic enjoyment and the desire to change public perception (Berthon *et al.* 2008). In their often-cited study, Hennig-Thurau and his colleagues (2004) identify eight motives that drive eWOM contributors, including the desires to help the company or fellow consumers by informing them about a brand's true nature, and to vent negative feelings. Consequently, UGC expressions can be manifold. While *brand advocates* wish to promote publicly the products they have bought, *brand haters* or *trolls* pursue the goal of harming the company, or at least warning others of bad experiences through their negative comments. Such online complaints have feedback effects on the complainants themselves (e.g. reinforcement of past decisions and steering future behaviours), but most importantly on the observers. The negative effects that the adverse comments of dissatisfied consumers have on bystanders who are in the pre-purchase stage have been repeatedly demonstrated in past research (e.g. Chakravarty *et al.* 2010) and include a wide range of detrimental effects, such as unfavourable brand evaluations and brand switching.

Literature suggests that among the most important factors affecting post-purchase engagement are attitudinal variables emphasizing the relationship between the consumer and the brand itself. These variables include, but are not limited to, customer satisfaction, brand commitment, identification, trust and brand performance (e.g. Matos and Rossi 2008). A variety of personality characteristics (e.g. personal traits, predispositions) have been found to affect the level of consumer engagement. For instance, some individuals have a high desire to be positively recognized by others (i.e. self-enhancement). These individuals have been shown to engage in higher eWOM behaviours (e.g. Hennig-Thurau *et al.* 2004). It is also possible that these consumers help others, blog more and generally engage more often in activities that co-promote the brand with which the consumer is highly involved (van Doorn *et al.* 2010).

Discussion

This chapter underlines and exemplifies the significant influence of social media on all stages of the consumer decision-making process. Specifically, the chapter reviews the importance of MGC and UGC along the consumer engagement circle. It concludes that, given the increasing engagement of consumers and their desire to communicate with others about the brand, UGC has a dominant role during the whole process. This applies in particular during the post-purchase stage when consumers passively engage in UGC by reading others' comments for making consumption comparisons. However, this also applies when they actively contribute to UGC by sharing their personal opinions and feelings about the brand with others. Does this mean that investing in MGC is a waste of resources? No, not necessarily. Consumer insights on MGC suggest that this form of communication is most effective in the early stages, especially when brand awareness matters. However, it should be clear that consumer education by MGC is a very demanding task. Consumers not only strive for attribute-level product information but more importantly they are increasingly looking for high quality content that both informs and entertains. A company that does an extraordinary job in this regard is Red Bull. The social media outlets of this brand are characterized by an in-depth knowledge of the identity of their customers and the capacity to communicate the brand meaning in a relevant, interesting and unique way. Such an approach puts the steering wheel back into the hands of the marketer. However, Red Bull's content marketing strategy, with its emphasis on editorial brand stories, photos and videos, overburdens most other companies. Here, authentic and creative storytelling which fosters a close and bilateral relationship between the brand and its users could be a potential solution. It is important for companies to be present on social media as this presence enables them to build relationships with their customers that cannot be built anywhere else in such a way. However, marketers have to understand the true nature of social media as a communication tool that predominantly enables interactions between individuals in a private context. Social media platforms like Facebook bring various benefits. This is particularly true when it comes to pacifying the minds of dissatisfied consumers after the purchase. Online complaint handling has been shown to produce positive outcomes for the brand. This is supported by academic research (e.g. Willemsen *et al.*, 2013) as well as practice. With adequate service recovery, companies can reconnect with its dissatisfied consumers who have experienced a failure during service delivery, but they can also connect with new customers by demonstrating their sensitivity, customer orientation and dedication to solve their customers' problems in their interest. Consequently, marketers should consider handling complaints in the public online arena as a valuable asset in their marketing strategy. A company that is able to integrate their brand ambassadors in this crucial phase of the consumer-brand relationship (e.g. by introducing vivid brand forums or communities) is highly likely to overcome even severe product crises.

References

Anderl, E., J. H. Schumann and W. Kunz. 2016. 'Helping firms reduce complexity in multichannel online data: a new taxonomy-based approach for customer journeys', *Journal of Retailing*, 92:2, p. 185–203.

Baldus, B. J., C. Voorhees and R. Calantone. 2015, 'Online brand community engagement: scale development and validation', *Journal of Business Research*, 68:5, p. 978–985.

Berthon, P., L. Pitt and C. Campbell. 2008. 'Ad lib: when customers create the ad', *California Management Review*, 50:4, p. 6–30.

Bruyn, A. de and G. L. Lilien. 2008. 'A multi-stage model of word-of-mouth influence through viral marketing', *International Journal of Research in Marketing*, 25:3, p. 151–163.

Chakravarty, A., Y. Liu and T. Mazumdar. 2010. 'The differential effects of online word-of-mouth and critics' reviews on pre-release movie evaluation', *Journal of Interactive Marketing*, 24:3, p. 185–197.

Chintagunta, P. K., S. Gopinath and S. Venkataraman. 2010. 'The effects of online user reviews on movie box office performance: accounting for sequential rollout and aggregation across local markets', *Marketing Science*, 29:5, p. 944–957.

Coulter, K. S., M. Bruhn, V. Schoenmueller and D. B. Schäfer 2012. 'Are social media replacing traditional media in terms of brand equity creation?', *Management Research Review*, 35:9, p. 770–790.

Court, D., D. Elzinga, S. Mulder and O. J. Vetvik. 2009. 'The consumer decision journey', *McKinsey Quarterly*, 3, p. 96–107.

Cunningham, L. F., J. H. Gerlach, M. D. Harper and C. E. Young. 2005. 'Perceived risk and the consumer buying process: internet airline reservations', *International Journal of Service Industry Management*, 16:4, p. 357–372.

Dellarocas, C. 2003. 'The digitization of word of mouth: promise and challenges of online feedback mechanisms', *Management Science*, 49:10, p. 1407–1424.

Dhar, V. and E. A. Chang. 2009. 'Does chatter matter? The impact of user-generated content on music sales', *Journal of Interactive Marketing*, 23:4, p. 300–307.

Dimoka, A., Y. Hong and P. A. Pavlou. 2012. 'On product uncertainty in online markets: theory and evidence', *MIS Quarterly*, 36:2, p. 395–426.

Divol, R., D. Edelman and H. Sarrazin. 2012. 'Demystifying social media', *McKinsey Quarterly*, 2:12, p. 66–77.

Duan, W., B. Gu and A. Whinston. 2008. 'The dynamics of online word-of-mouth and product sales – an empirical investigation of the movie industry', *Journal of Retailing*, 84:2, p. 233–242.

Edelman, D. C. 2010. 'Branding in the digital age', *Harvard Business Review*, December, p. 2–8.

Escalas, J. E. 2007. 'Self-referencing and persuasion: narrative transportation versus analytical elaboration', *Journal of Consumer Research*, 4:33, p. 421–429.

Eysenck, M. W. 1984. *A Handbook of Cognitive Psychology*. Lawrence Erlbaum: London, UK.

Fournier, S. and J. Avery. 2011. 'The uninvited brand', *Business Horizons*, 54:3, p. 193–207.

Foux, G. 2006. 'Consumer-generated media: get your customers involved', *Brand Strategy*, 202, p. 38–39.

Godes, D. and D. Mayzlin. 2009. 'Firm-created word-of-mouth communication: evidence from a field test', *Marketing Science*, 28:4, p. 721–739.

Godes, D. and J. C. Silva. 2012. 'Sequential and temporal dynamics of online opinion', *Marketing Science*, 31:3, p. 448–473.

Goh, K.-Y., C.-S. Heng and Z. Lin. 2013. 'Social media brand community and consumer behaviour: quantifying the relative impact of user- and marketer-generated content', *Information Systems Research*, 24:1, p. 88–107.

Granovetter, M. 1973. 'The strength of weak ties', *American Journal of Sociology*, 78:6, p. 1360–1380.

Häubl, G. and V. Trifts. 2000. 'Consumer decision making in online shopping environments: the effects of interactive decision aids', *Marketing Science*, 19:1, p. 4–21.

Hauser, J. R. and B. Wernerfelt. 1990. 'An evaluation cost model of consideration sets', *Journal of Consumer Research*, 16:4, p. 393.

Hennig-Thurau, T., K. P. Gwinner, G. Walsh and D. D. Gremler. 2004. 'Electronic word-of-mouth via consumer-opinion platforms: what motivates consumers to articulate themselves on the Internet?', *Journal of Interactive Marketing*, 18:1, p. 38–52.

Hinz, O., B. Skiera, C. Barrot and J. U. Becker. 2011. 'Seeding strategies for viral marketing: an empirical comparison', *Journal of Marketing*, 75:6, p. 55–71.

Hollebeek, L. D., M. S. Glynn and R. J. Brodie. 2014. 'Consumer brand engagement in social media: conceptualization, scale development and validation', *Journal of Interactive Marketing*, 28:2, p. 149–165.

Jang, S., A. Prasad and B. T. Ratchford. 2012. 'How consumers use product reviews in the purchase decision process', *Marketing Letters*, 23:3, p. 825–838.

Kee, R. 2008. 'The sufficiency of product and variable costs for production-related decisions when economies of scope are present', *International Journal of Production Economics*, 114:2, p. 682–696.

Lee, G. 2010. 'Death of "last click wins": media attribution and the expanding use of media data', *Journal of Direct, Data and Digital Marketing Practice*, 12:1, p. 16–26.

Lee, K.-T. and D.-M. Koo. 2015. 'Evaluating right versus just evaluating online consumer reviews', *Computers in Human Behaviour*, 45, p. 316–327.

Lee, M., S. Rodgers and M. Kim. 2009. 'Effects of valence and extremity of eWOM on attitude toward the brand and website', *Journal of Current Issues & Research in Advertising*, 31:2, p. 1–11.

Lewis, E. 1903. 'Advertising department: catch-line and argument', *The Book-Keeper*, 15, p. 124–128.

Libai, B. 2011. 'Comment: the perils of focusing on highly engaged customers', *Journal of Service Research*, 14:3, p. 275–276.

Mangold, W. G. and D. J. Faulds. 2009. 'Social media: the new hybrid element of the promotion mix', *Business Horizons*, 52:4, p. 357–365.

Matos, C. A. de and C. A. V. Rossi. 2008. 'Word-of-mouth communications in marketing: a meta-analytic review of the antecedents and moderators', *Journal of the Academy of Marketing Science*, 36:4, p. 578–596.

Moe, W. W. and D. A. Schweidel. 2012. 'Online product opinions: incidence, evaluation, and evolution', *Marketing Science*, 31:3, p. 372–386.

Moon, S., P. K. Bergey and D. Iacobucci. 2010. 'Dynamic effects among movie ratings, movie revenues, and viewer satisfaction', *Journal of Marketing*, 74:1, p. 108–121.

Payne, J. W., J. R. Bettman and E. J. Johnson. 1988. 'Adaptive strategy selection in decision making', *Journal of Experimental Psychology: Learning, Memory, and Cognition*, 14:3, p. 534–552.

Powers, T., D. Advincula, M. S. Austin, S. Graiko and J. Snyder. 2012. 'Digital and social media in the purchase decision process', *Journal of Advertising Research*, 52:4, p. 479–489.

Raman, K., M. K. Mantrala, S. Sridhar and Y. Tang. 2012. 'Optimal resource allocation with time-varying marketing effectiveness, margins and costs', *Journal of Interactive Marketing*, 26:1, p. 43–52.

Roberts, J. H. and J. M. Lattin. 1997. 'Consideration: review of research and prospects for future insights', *Journal of Marketing Research*, 34:3, p. 406.

Russo, J. E. and A.-S. Chaxel. 2010. 'How persuasive messages can influence behaviour without awareness', *Journal of Consumer Psychology*, 20:3, p. 338–342.

Shocker, A. D., M. Ben-Akiva, B. Boccara and P. Nedungadi. 1991. 'Consideration set influences on consumer decision-making and choice: issues, models, and suggestions', *Marketing Letters*, 2:3, p. 181–197.

Sonnier, G. P., McAlister, L. and Rutz, O. J. 2011, 'A dynamic model of the effect of online communications on firm sales', *Marketing Science*, 30:4, 702–716.

van Doorn, J., K. N. Lemon, V. Mittal, S. Nass, D. Pick, P. Pirner and P. C. Verhoef. 2010. 'Customer engagement behaviour: theoretical foundations and research directions', *Journal of Service Research*, 13:3, p. 253–266.

Verma, R., B. Jahn and W. Kunz. 2012, 'How to transform consumers into fans of your brand', *Journal of Service Management*, 23:3, p. 344–361.

Vries, L. de, S. Gensler and P. S. Leeflang. 2012. 'Popularity of brand posts on brand fan pages: an investigation of the effects of social media marketing', *Journal of Interactive Marketing*, 26:2, p. 83–91.

Willemsen, L., P. C. Neijens and F. A. Bronner. 2013. 'Webcare as customer relationship and reputation management? Motives for negative electronic word of mouth and their effect on webcare receptiveness', *Advances in Advertising Research*, pp. 55–69.

Xu, L., J. A. Duan and A. Whinston. 2014. 'Path to purchase: a mutually exciting point process model for online advertising and conversion', *Management Science*, 60:6, p. 1392–1412.

Yoo, B., N. Donthu and S. Lee. 2000. 'An examination of selected marketing mix elements and brand equity', *Journal of the Academy of Marketing Science*, 28:2, p. 195–211.

Zhu, F. and X. Zhang. 2010. 'Impact of online consumer reviews on sales: the moderating role of product and consumer characteristics', *Journal of Marketing*, 74:2, p. 133–148.

12

NETWORK BASED CHOICE FORMATION

A review in the context of online communities

Shameek Sinha and Sreyaa Guha

Introduction

Over the past two decades, marketing practitioners have witnessed a sweeping change in the way consumers participate and interact on online social media platforms that influences their subsequent product evaluations and purchase decisions towards favourable, unfavourable or neutral courses. Online communities have made information conveniently accessible to decision-making consumers without any distortion or loss due to intervention of intermediaries. Consumers are exposed to direct or indirect feedback from members of diverse networks, where the available information includes other consumers' evaluations based on their usage experiences over time and in some cases responses from the firms themselves. Such networks facilitate connection between consumers as well as between consumers and firms. Amazon and eBay, the e-commerce pioneers, who have been allowing product reviews since 1997, report having 40 per cent of their customers say that online reviews are mandatory information for them when buying any electronic product (Nielsen, Global Online Shopping Report 2010). In this context, an investigation of the global trends within and across countries leads us to some interesting insights. According to a survey by Statista. com (2015), the share of online shoppers who are influenced by reading social media reviews,comments and feedback for any product in general, is significantly high for countries like Malaysia, India and China (about 69 per cent, 66 per cent and 63 per cent respectively; see this chapter's Appendix I). It is evident, therefore, that online review platforms have gained substantial popularity among consumers and that is why they have become a matter of increasing focus for the firms who want to understand the network formation structures in online communities, especially in a dynamic environment where consumers are heterogeneous.

Why do consumers join online communities?

Before forming choices and arriving at purchase decisions, consumers explore how the majority of like-minded consumers within a certain community are reviewing the product, especially when they themselves possess incomplete knowledge about the product type or class. They try to understand whether the perceptions of others are positive, negative or neutral towards the product in question. They use these cues to shape their own choices. However, prior research has found that the effect of reviews, both positive and negative, is somewhat uncertain. Studies by Huang and Chen (2006) reveals that there is a herding effect in online product choices and that consumers use the choices and evaluations of others as cues for making their own choices. But they find that herding effects are reduced significantly by negative comments from others. In contrast, Sridhar and Srinivasan (2012) show that, based on product failure or product recovery, positive reviews and negative reviews by other consumers can surprisingly act as an aggravating or upsetting factor respectively. Studies by AlpacaDirect.com show that even with bad reviews, sales increased 23 per cent for their products that had reviews enabled. According to *MIT Technology Review* Editor Christopher Mims (2011), bad reviews also help customers know the worst scenario they can expect and serve as risk-mitigators. Some studies have also found that, of the participants who read reviews, 83.65 per cent compare positive and negative reviews with each other (Lackermair *et al.* 2013).

What happens when consumers interact with each other within a community?

Consumers choose to participate in social media communities based on their perceived utility of being a member (either as an observer or as a contributor) in the community. This helps them form perceptions and make decisions (Fishburn 1970) based on the induced interactions within the community. Brock and Durlauf (2001) developed a utility based model to describe choice formation in a community. According to this model, in a community with a finite number of agents, each agent tries to maximize their utility for a given action (opinion or choice) according to the following equation:

$$V(\omega_i) = u(\omega_i) + S(\omega_i, \mu_i^e(\omega_{-i})) + \varepsilon(\omega_i)$$

The individual utility $V(\omega_i)$ of each agent can be written as an aggregate of a private utility component $u(\omega_i)$, a social utility component $S(\omega_i, \mu_i^e(\omega_{-i}))$ and of course, some unobserved random utility component $\varepsilon(\omega_i)$. The private utility associated with a particular opinion or actual choice is essentially related to the individual's personal utility devoid of any effect of the choices made by others in the community. The social utility component accounts for the effect of the social interactions that the individual engages in with others in the community. Here, it is important to define what we mean by a social interaction. In a community, when an individual agent observes the other agents expressing their opinions and choices, it can be called a social interaction, even if that individual agent does not directly engage in a dialogue or conversation. Therefore, the choice that an individual agent makes has a utility or pay-off attached to it which is directly dependant on the choices of others in the community. The random utility component in the model is independent for each agent (i.e. random utility of one agent does not depend on that of any other agent) and identically distributed (i.e. has the same probability distribution for all agents). Now, the social utility component is a function of the personal choice of the individual agent (ω_i) and the conditional probability measure $\left(\mu_i^e(\omega_{-i})\right)$ that the individual agent places on the choices of the others. By conditional probability measure we mean the assertion, prediction or evidence that the individual agent will make a certain choice, given all the agents have already made their own choices. This conditional probability depends on the subjective expected value from individual agent i's perspective of individual agent j's choice. What this means is, individual agent i has an expected value for individual agent j's choice and similarly for all other individual agents' choices and draws an expected mean value of choices of all other individual agents in the community apart from her.

To understand this concept better, let us imagine that a consumer is contemplating the purchase of a newly released book for which she is not only forming her own opinion but also reading reviews and comments on a Facebook community. The private utility associated with the choice of buying or not buying the book is determined by reading the synopsis and author evaluations, which exist within her knowledge domain. If she finds the genre and storyline of the book interesting (uninteresting) and has liked (not liked) previous works by the same author, the chances are she will make the choice of buying (not buying) the book, irrespective of others' reviews and purchase decisions. The social utility component of the purchase decision is structured as the consumer reads other consumers' reviews. She decides which reviews she prefers to read and take into consideration in order to form an opinion.

Now, individual agents within the community usually make their choices without coordinating with each other (non-cooperative decision making from a game-theoretic point of view) and the model assumes that all individual agents have rational expectations of others' choices. This means that when an individual assumes an expected choice action of any other individual in the community, her expectation is self-consistent or she expects others' choices to be same as hers on average. Under this assumption, there exists at least one expected mean choice level which could go up to three mean choice levels depending on the value of the private utility and the rate of change of change in social utility of an individual. When the difference in private utilities between choosing and not choosing is zero for an individual, then there can be herding behaviour towards favourable, unfavourable and undecided choice actions depending on the strength and directionality of the rate of change of change in social utility. When the difference in private utilities between choosing and not choosing is not zero but less than that of the rate of change of change in social utility, then there can also be herding behaviour towards favourable, unfavourable and undecided choice actions. However, if the difference in private utilities between choosing and not choosing is not zero but more than that of rate of change of change in social utility, then the choice is entirely dependent on the said difference in the private utilities between two types of choice actions. Therefore, the choice is favourable if the private utility for choosing the product is higher than that of not choosing it and unfavourable if the private utility of not choosing the product is higher than that of choosing it.

Again, let us understand this equilibrium concept by revisiting the example. The consumer who is reading the reviews of a newly released book might be indifferent with regard to choosing or not choosing the book before looking at the preferences of the others in the community. In that case, depending on her intensity of reading the reviews or actively participating in the review process and the mean preferences of all other members of the community, she can form a favourable or an unfavourable opinion or remain undecided about the book. And since the same is true for all consumers, under this equilibrium some consumers will prefer the book, some will not and others will, still, remain undecided about it. But if the consumer is not indifferent with regard to choosing or not choosing the book, that is, she either already prefers it or does not prefer it before reading others' reviews, then there are two possibilities. First, her personal preference is weaker than the effect of others' reviews on her, in which case she can still be guided towards preferring, not preferring or remaining undecided. Second, her personal preference is stronger than the effect of others' reviews on her, in which case she goes by her personal preference.

However, according to the model, it is sustainable that most members either prefer the product or do not prefer it but it is not sustainable that most members remain undecided about it. We still cannot say that any individual is strictly better off through finally choosing a product or not choosing it. This is because, as we mentioned earlier, the utility derived from preferring or not preferring a product has a random component in it. Extreme realization of the random component will cause some individuals to prefer and some to not prefer it.

In a nutshell, this model provides us with an economic explanation of how consumer choices are formed based on private and social utilities associated with a binary choice in a social community.

What happens when consumers are faced with a set of choice options instead of binary choices?

Let us consider an example. Say there is a philanthropic organization that is raising money to help victims of a natural disaster. These fundraising activities usually provide the potential donors with multiple different donation options and corresponding amounts. The forums or discussion threads associated with such philanthropic activity contain comments from other donors who have made contributions to the same charity or other similar causes. Each potential donor usually goes through these threads before donating, to understand the efficiency of the non-profit charity and the cause, which creates the social interaction opportunity.

Brock and Durlauf (2003) have modelled the consequences of such interactions when consumers are faced with multiple choices. They found that the equilibria of choices follows a similar pattern as under binary choice but with a few differences. First, when consumers are faced with a set of choices, the greater the number of consumers whose behaviour is determined by the random utility component, the lesser are the chances of social utility affecting the multiplicity of self-consistent equilibria. This is because, since more consumers are guided by the randomness in their decision, to have a rational expectation of others' choices is a difficult assumption to impose on the model. An extension to this discussion would be to consider the situation that there is a possibility of accruing negative social utility with the unchosen but available choices, that is, a donor who is willing to donate $50 can derive negative utility from interactions with donors who wish to, or have, donated $90. Second, in this model, in contrast with the model of binary choice, there could be variables that are relevant for two choices but irrelevant for other choices, but certainly not irrelevant for whether those possibilities are chosen. Third, social interactions analysed using the multinomial logit model do not depend on the random utilities of individuals but rather are based on the underlying logic of these variables incorporated into the model.

What are the various ways in which a social network can be formed?

Although in large online communities a social network is formed in a way where all individuals interact with each other, there are other forms of network formation which need mention as well. The different network formations are generated based on the various spatial structures of social interactions that can take place

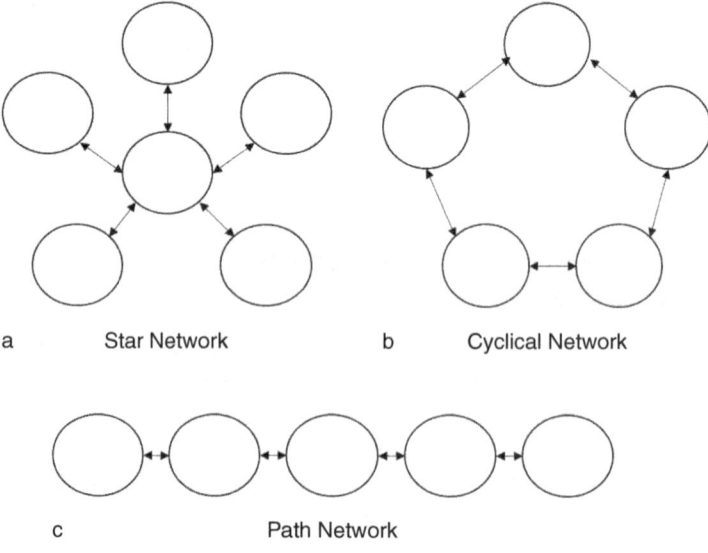

a   Star Network   b   Cyclical Network

c   Path Network

FIGURE 12.1 Types of network.

between or amongst individuals within a community. The most common types of such interactions are star interaction, cyclical or wheel interaction and path interaction (see Figure 12.1). Based on the study by Brock and Durlauf (2001), Ioannides (2006) describes the equilibrium choice outcomes under each of these interactions given that the individuals or members of the social network take their choice actions based on expectations of their neighbours' decisions.

A 'star network' is formed when an individual i is at the centre of the star and all other individuals are interacting only with that individual. In such a network, individual i is the only neighbour of all other individuals and all other individuals are i's neighbours.Individual i possesses rational expectations of choices for all her neighbours and all her neighbours possess common expectations of individual i's decision. When individual i and her neighbours are optimistic about each other's preferences, then the equilibrium is towards positive preference. When individual i and her neighbours are pessimistic about each other's preferences, then the equilibrium is towards negative preference. When the preferences are different, then the equilibrium can move towards either positive or negative preferences. In a 'cyclical or wheel network' the individuals are in a wheel form of social interaction, that is, each individual has two neighbours. In such a network the equilibrium is similar to that discussed above in the Brock and Durlauf model. The 'path network' has start and end individuals. In this formation, equilibria of preference can be multiple or unique as well. However, since there are start and end agents here and there is no cyclical symmetry as in the case before, we might need to have a boundary condition that the end individuals or the start individuals are constrained to be in a particular state, otherwise the entire network unravels. As described by Ioannides using the classic example from Schelling (1978):

> If everybody needs 100 Watts to read by and a neighbour's bulb is equivalent to half one's own, and everybody has a 60-Watt bulb, everybody can read as long as he and both his neighbours have their lights on. Arranged in a circle, everybody will keep his lights on if everybody else does (and nobody will if his neighbours do not); arranged in a line, the people at the ends cannot read anyway and turn their lights off, and the whole thing unravels.
>
> *(p. 214)*

So far the models we have discussed have explored the possibilities of unique or multiple choice equilibria based on regular interactions or interactions based on spatial locations of the individuals in a social network. The treatments discussed for each of these models have been done under the assumption that the interactions are static or such that the interaction outcomes can be thought of as pertaining to a single period of interaction. However, in the real world of online social networks, this is not the case. Consumers often revisit the communities to look for new reviews, better reviews and even sometimes reviews from experts. Every time consumers revisit these communities, there is change in the preference formation. In other words, the process of preference formation is dynamic and it is imperative to model it in a dynamic choice formation environment to get as close as possible to the real world behaviour of an online community, where adaptation and learning are crucial.

How are choices formed under dynamic social interactions?

In order to understand how dynamic social interactions work, we can think of social interactions as a strategic dynamic game of choices. In such a game, the individuals observe, at any random period of time, the game being played by the other individuals and then adopt a new strategy or choice action in response to this game based on the same utility model we have been discussing so far. When all individuals choose to respond in this fashion, an overall dynamic framework emerges. Blume and Durlauf (2003) develop a model to capture this dynamic choice formation structure. The model can be imagined to work as if each individual is given a Poisson alarm clock. Whenever the clock rings, the individual updates her preference. Her preference is formed, as before, on the expectation of other individuals' choices. The same happens for all individuals and hence at each instance, any individual updates the aggregate of choices based on the other individuals' changes. Every time an individual changes the preference, the aggregate of preferences of all individuals changes state. Therefore, this can be called the birth or death of a state. The birth or death rates of a state or mean preference depend on the probability of transition from one state to another. Mathematically, the rates are the time derivatives of the transition probabilities. When the number of individuals in a community is significant, this change for each individual more or less averages out for a shorter time horizon. However, for long time horizons, large aberrations will occur and the pattern or sample path can diverge from the mean field approximation. In addition, when the number of members is large, the herding is most often towards the stable states of favourable and unfavourable and never at the undecided point. Here, another important finding, which is based on the population games literature, is that if the direction of undecidedness goes towards the negative side, in the absence of any personal preference (devoid of social interactions) the favourable state becomes risk dominant equilibrium out of the three equilibria states. As choice becomes less noisy, most consumers choose favourably. This is an improvement over the Brock and Durlauf (2001) model where, as mentioned earlier, there was no way to determine if any choice is strictly better than the others.

What should firms do?

Even though the frameworks discussed above provide a guideline to managers on the formation of endogenous dynamic communities, it is relatively difficult to understand choices since the behavioural, cultural and idiosyncratic aspects, still, remain considerably unexplored. Therefore, it is neither feasible nor appropriate to suggest a unified framework that can serve as a guidebook for managers to manage the consumer choice formation process in social networks. However, it is possible to suggest actionable points that can be considered by managers which will advance them in their endeavour to acquire and retain consumers. Here, one thing which deserves mention is that active management of online forums, particularly reviews, might have a differential impact depending on product characteristics (Feng Zhu, Xiaoquan (Michael) Zhang 2010). For example, whether the product is less or more popular, whether it is a product which has higher propensity to be bought online or offline and so on, could act as factors that could drive the choice formation process with higher or lower intensities and in different directions (favourable, unfavourable and undecided) as well.

Having said that, we recommend the following general actions for managers, using which they can manage interactions in online communities in order to shape and control the choice patterns emerging out of network interactions.

(a) Validating existing models – Firms are privy to huge databases of consumers on the social networks run by them for their products. They can proactively run the empirical equivalent versions of these models on the available data in order to better understand the dynamics and derive insights on how they can use the information on dynamics to shape the preferences towards desirable directions. By validating these models, the firms can gain considerable insights into consumer characteristics and idiosyncrasies related to evaluation of reviews and product preference formation. This can help them to decide on the signalling mechanisms that they might need to adopt.

(b) Signalling – In a situation where a firm wants to change consumer perceptions to facilitate stronger multiplier effects while simultaneously exercising a higher degree of control, it has to devise certain appropriate signalling mechanisms. These signals of a firm's quality changes consumer perceptions of firm provided information and, depending on the truthfulness of the signals, it can potentially be beneficial to consumers by avoiding moral hazards and adverse selection issues. Thus, they can not only indirectly allow firms to signal their true quality, but also simultaneously prevent free-riding. Unfortunately, incentives for firms to report their quality accurately are debatable in many scenarios because of the costs associated with control and therefore signalling by firms often turns out to be socially undesirable even though they are beneficial from the individual consumer's perspective.

(c) Incentivizing – Once the firms can successfully gauge the characteristics of the consumers who are interested in their product, they can start to incentivize favourable reviews by paying or by using other marketing tools like discounts and offers. However, there is no reason to believe that incentivizing always produce favourable reactions from consumers, as for some consumers it might indicate a firm's attempt to make up for poor product quality and that is why understanding consumer characteristics through model validation can give a better measurement of degree of consumers' personal preference (devoid of social interactions) and clear directions towards strategies to handle them.

These actions can make a change in sales plausible. As mentioned earlier, a more precise and executable guideline needs to be drawn after a close examination of several other factors (e.g. product characteristics). However, firms successfully using these existing models to strategize on their marketing moves can derive substantial benefit from the social interactions amongst consumers and turn social media into a powerful and effective marketing tool.

References

Blume, L. and S. Durlauf. 2003. 'Equilibrium concepts for social interaction models'. *International Game Theory Review*, 5(03), p. 193–209.

Brock, W. A. and S. N. Durlauf. 2001. 'Discrete choice with social interactions'. *The Review of Economic Studies*, 68(2), p. 235–260.

Brock, W. and S. N. Durlauf. 2003. 'Multinomial choice with social interactions'. *Working Paper*.

Fishburn, P. C. 1970. *Utility Theory for Decision Making* (No. RAC-R-105). Research Analysis Corp. McLean, VA.

Huang, J. H. and Y. F. Chen. 2006. 'Herding in online product choice'. *Psychology & Marketing*, 23(5), p. 413–428.

Ioannides, Y. M. 2006. 'Topologies of social interactions'. *Economic Theory*, 28(3), p. 559–584.

Lackermair, G.,D. Kailer and K. Kanmaz. 2013. 'Importance of online product reviews from a consumer's perspective'. *Advances in Economics and Business*, 1(1), p. 1–5.

Schelling, F. W. J. 1978. *System of Transcendental Idealism (1800)*. Charlottesville: University Press of Virginia, p. 58.

Sridhar, S. and R. Srinivasan. 2012. 'Social influence effects in online product ratings'. *Journal of Marketing*, 76(5), p. 70–88.

Zhu, F. and X. Zhang. 2010. 'Impact of online consumer reviews on sales: the moderating role of product and consumer characteristics'. *Journal of Marketing*, 74(2), p. 133–148.

Online sources

1. http://www.nielsen.com/us/en/insights/news/2010/global-online-shopping-report. html Accessed 23 March 2017.
2. https://www.statista.com/statistics/297006/internet-users-expert-opinions-before-purchase/ Accessed 23 March 2017.
3. https://www.sellwithwp.com/importance-of-product-reviews-ecommerce-site/ Accessed 23 March 2017.
4. http://money.cnn.com/2009/09/28/smallbusiness/retail_democracy.fsb/index.htm Accessed 23 March 2017.
5. https://www.technologyreview.com/s/425488/how-negative-reviews-increase-sales-online/ Accessed 23 March 2017.

APPENDIX I

Global online shoppers who are influenced by reading social media reviews, comments and feedback as of September 2015

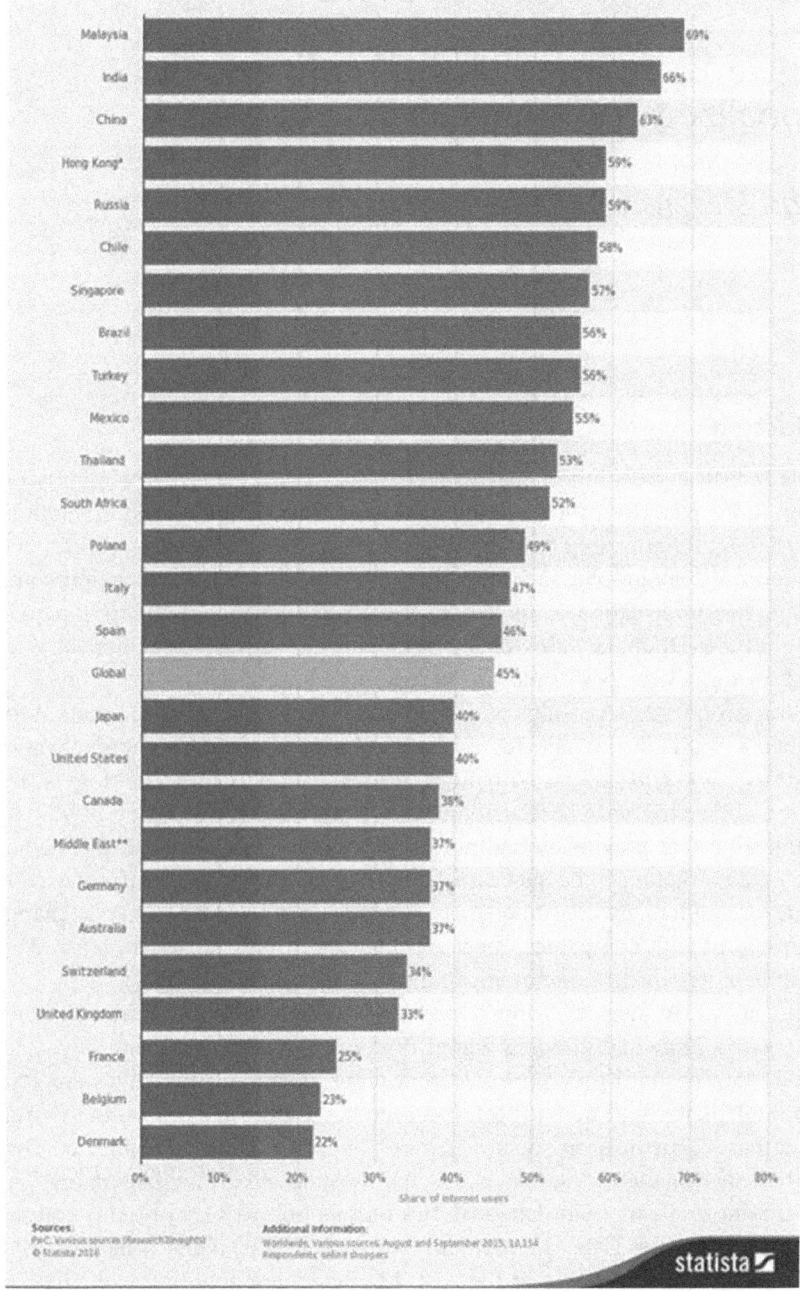

13

CREEPY AND INTRUSIVE

A consumer's perspective of online personalized communications

Arlonda Stevens and Casey Newmeyer

Introduction

Since the Industrial Revolution, marketing has progressed through several phases. However, in the past twenty-five years, marketers have been engaged in relationship marketing. Relationship marketing strives to understand customer likes, dislikes, interests, demographic information, and online and offline behaviours and then, using this information, aims to deliver the right message to the right person at the right time (Double Click Website 2011), thus increasing customer satisfaction and, in turn, firm performance (Morgan and Hunt 1994). This process of developing stronger relationships with customers has provided the foundation for social media marketing, which focuses on real-time connection and exchanges between firms and consumers. With the widespread adoption of technology, companies are connected with the customer 24/7, allowing for real-time, two-way communication that previously had not been possible (Trainor *et al.* 2014). For social media marketing to be successful, an ongoing exchange of information is required. Although many consumers may recognize that they are indeed exchanging information with companies, most are unaware of how these firms use their information to personalize communications (Morgan and Hunt 1994).

Every day, consumers knowingly and unknowingly provide marketers with data to create a large and growing digital footprint. From the moment they wake up in the morning until they go to sleep at night, details of their lives are captured through their phone activity, Internet searches, online and bricks-and-mortar retail purchases, postings on social networks, and other devices connected with the Internet such as their cars, televisions, thermostats and even refrigerators. The ability to mine and carry out data analytics on this information presents companies with opportunities to learn, infer and create knowledge about consumers that would not have been available in the past. Marketers are able to use the data in a consumer's digital footprint, along with information gathered offline, to craft online and offline personalized communications and other marketing activities. Companies hope that personalized marketing campaigns will increase customer satisfaction and loyalty rates, thus enabling them to build strong customer relationships (Chellappa and Sin 2005). However, consumers often view these types of firm activities negatively, and their satisfaction decreases (Stevens 2016). Although there are definite advantages for consumers, such as receiving relevant ads tailored to their interests, coupons for frequently purchased items and other loyalty reward programme perks, many consumers are becoming increasingly concerned about the collection, use and sharing of their personal information. Some consumers have even described these marketing tactics as intrusions of privacy and *creepy*. Take, for example, the case of Target, described in more detail in Figure 13.1. In 2012, a marketing analytics manager for the company was tasked with finding criteria to predict whether a Target customer was pregnant, and if so, when the baby was due (Hill 2012). Target then used this information to send coupons for baby-related items to specific consumers who had a high probability of pregnancy, and in one case, it sent coupons to a teenage girl. Universally, customers, traditional news outlets and social network websites described this example as creepy (Hill 2012). Target is not alone in conducting marketing campaigns that are perceived as creepy. One consumer recalls receiving an email about items viewed online, but not put in the 'cart'. The company later sent an email thanking

---

HOW DOES TARGET KNOW THAT YOU ARE PREGNANT

For Target to gather purchase information, compare it to buying habits of women on their baby registry, calculate the probability of pregnancy and then send coupons to women they suspect to be pregnant without that information being supplied to them by the individual, led consumers to feel surprised, uncomfortable. Perhaps, the creepiest of all is the Target example where through their predictive analytics efforts they were able to develop a pregnancy predictor score based on the buying habits of women and with nearly 80% accuracy could determine if a woman was pregnant. Without consumer's knowledge, Target assigns every consumer a Guest ID number, which is tied to his or her credit card, name, or email address. All buying history and available demographic information is stored for future analysis. One analyst began comparing the buying habits of women with women who were on or had been on Target's baby registries in the past. After reviewing and analyzing buying history, Target noticed that women on the Registry started buying certain baby-related or pregnancy health items at certain intervals of their pregnancy. This data was then compared to other women and similarities were found, from which Target then concluded that the woman was pregnant. With this knowledge, they were then able to send coupons for baby-related items. Target did not disclose what they were doing and this only came to light when a dad questioned a Target store manager as to why coupons for baby-related items were being sent to his teenage daughter. Had the father not come forward, this practice may not have been disclosed. However, after the father spoke to his daughter, he was informed that she was indeed pregnant and Target had it right!

FIGURE 13.1 Target knows when a woman is pregnant.

the consumer for stopping by and asking that they come back and take a second look at the items they were viewing. The email also contained a picture of the item that was viewed. The consumer indicated that the idea of the company using the viewing history to send an email was unsettling (Jennings 2015). Defining privacy as the right to determine how much of an individual's personal information is disclosed and to whom, how it should be maintained (Westin 1968), and how it should be disseminated, is applicable in the context of marketing, the Internet and digital information. However, describing what makes a personalized communication *creepy* is not as discernible. 'Creepy' is difficult to define and often is described as 'I know it when I see it' (Stewart 1964, 197). Unfortunately, consumers and marketers may each hold different definitions of creepy, while believing that their unique definitions are universally understood.

In this chapter, we define creepiness and discuss how privacy and perceived creepiness differ. Then, we explain why creepiness matters and provide recommendations to minimize the negative effect of perceived creepiness on customer satisfaction and, ultimately, to improve firm performance.

Privacy and perceived creepiness: similar *but* different

At the outset, one may presume that privacy intrusion and feelings of perceived creepiness are one and the same. However, a recent study on consumers' experience with personalized communication and online advertising revealed that not all ads that were privacy intrusive were considered creepy (Stevens 2016). To fully understand the subtle differences between perceived creepiness and privacy intrusiveness, one needs to have a basic understanding of what privacy is and what many consumers view as a violation of, or intrusion into, their privacy.

Privacy is multi-faceted in that it crosses multiple disciplines, including law, technology, marketing, economics and information systems; each discipline defines privacy slightly differently through their own interpretive lens, thus making privacy difficult to classify. Across disciplines, four tenets are typically used to discuss privacy: non-intrusion, seclusion, limitation and control (Tavani 2007).

Non-intrusion and seclusion

With roots in medieval Scottish history and based on theories and research in law, non-intrusion and seclusion theories of privacy provide much of the foundational understanding of privacy and explain a person's right to autonomy. A law article written by Samuel Warren and Louis Brandeis suggests that people have a right to privacy (Warren and Brandeis 1890) and freedom from observation and disturbance by others. Basically, every person has the right to be left alone (Kramer 1989); this includes being left alone by other individuals, the government, organizations and so on. As such, in the context of marketing, consumers should not be forced to endure unwanted solicitations (see, for example, services like the National Do Not Call Registry). However, in order to take advantage of online apps and other social media, the consumer must accept the terms and conditions relating to data collection, use and sharing. In the context of social media marketing this comes into play with the privacy statements that are provided. Yet, oftentimes the notices are not readily accessible, or are lengthy, not easy to understand and not user-friendly (Jensen and Potts 2004). Further, one study (Milne and Culnan 2004) showed consumers do not read privacy policies, which leads to the perception that companies are not being transparent. Among other things, the privacy notice informs consumers how their information will be shared with 'affiliated partners' and other third parties and how they can opt out of marketing communications. In some instances, consumers are able to opt out of marketing communications both before agreeing to the privacy statement and after, by unsubscribing. However, consumers are not able to opt out of online behavioural marketing and still feel that the barrage of junk email and spam is intrusive.

Limitation and control

Many social scientists and privacy theorists have included control as an element in the definition of privacy (Goodwin 1991). Limitation and control theories of privacy have a basic premise that one has privacy if one can control information about oneself (Westin 1968) and how much of said information is shared with others. The privacy theories regarding limitation and control are perhaps the most applicable to the growing discipline of information or data privacy and to understanding perceived creepiness. In the context of marketing, the Internet and digital communication, Westin's (1968) definition of privacy can be applied to social media as users having the right to determine how much of their personal information is disclosed, with whom it is shared, how it should be maintained and in what context it can be disseminated.

According to Culnan (1993), control over how personal data is collected and used is another determinant that affects people's attitudes towards, and perspectives on, information privacy. Goodwin (1991) contends that two dimensions of control can define privacy: (1) control of unwanted solicitation or personal intrusion into the consumer's environment; and (2) control over information about the consumer. Both factors are applicable to personalized communication or ads encountered on the Internet as most often consumers' privacy concerns in electronic transactions stem from their loss of control over personal information (Metzger 2007) and may also have an impact on the degree to which consumers deem a personalized communication or ad as creepy. Within the context of marketing and personalized communications, privacy exists when a consumer can limit access to, and control the flow of, information about them. Conversely, privacy is invaded when control is lost (Culnan 1993). A data breach is a prime example of loss of control over personal information. For example, in December 2014, 80 million health insurance records were accessed via a data breach at Anthem Health Insurance. In 2014, more than 70 million financial accounts were accessed at JPMorgan Chase. In these cases, personal information was shared with a third party that did not have permission to view the information and consumers had no control over how their personal information was used or maintained. Data brokers who collect personal information and sell it to various companies are entities that are also beyond consumers' control, because consumers do not know what information is being collected by the brokers or to whom it is being disseminated.

What is creepy?

As the previous discussion indicates, defining perceived creepiness is more ambiguous than defining privacy as both existing theories and a unified definition are missing. Some consumers view paid advertisements that use search engine cookies to customize content as creepy. Some organizations (e.g. Amazon. com) provide items that consumers may be interested in buying or recommend books based on their current book selection; Facebook recommends people who users may or may not know (Downes 2012); Facebook also knows what users are watching, as Figure 13.2 depicts. Social media activity classified as creepy usually develops in the form of an unexpected or surprising use of personal information as

FIGURE 13.2 Facebook is watching what you're watching.

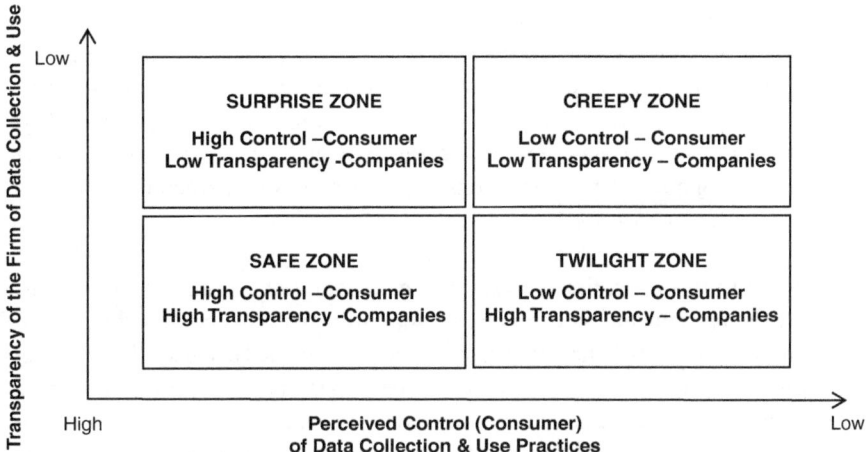

FIGURE 13.3 The Creepy Quadrant.

shown in the examples above. Although there is an element of control in perceptions of creepiness, as shown in the Creepy Quadrant of Figure 13.3, creepiness
centres on the feelings and emotions associated with consumers' personal information being used in a way they did not expect.

With Target, consumers described feeling creepy because Target knew so much
about them and their buying habits without them knowing that this information
was being tracked or monitored. In another case, Girls Around Me, a popular dat-
ing application, used location-based mobile services (e.g. Foursquare) to allow
users to scan profiles of women in an area who had checked in using a mobile
location service. If a woman of interest was identified, the user could then connect
with her on Facebook and gain access to her user profile. Soon, there was public
outcry and claims that this application took 'creepy to a new level' (Bilton 2012).
It is important to note that though these examples are considered extremely creepy,
nothing illegal occurred. At no time did Target have access to any information
beyond purchase behaviour and demographic information, which the firm legally
owns. With the Girls Around Me app, the information used was not restricted by
privacy settings and was generally public information. In both cases, the outcry
was due to the surprising use of seemingly innocuous information without the
data holder's knowledge or permission; in essence, consumers had no control over
the collection, use and sharing of their information. Research (Stevens 2016) has
shown that perceived creepiness is an emotional reaction to an experience, interaction, technology or unsolicited communication in which personal information has
been collected with or without a person's knowledge, unknowingly shared, or used
in an unexpected or surprising manner. Such surprise or shock then evokes negative feelings towards the source of the unexpected data use. Consumer perceptions
of creepiness increase when a firm is not transparent about its data collection, use
and sharing practices.

Research suggests that the relationship between transparency and control helps determine the degree of perceived creepiness. The Creepy Quadrant in Figure 13.3 is a visual depiction of the impact of transparency and control on consumers' level of perceived creepiness (Stevens 2016). Each of the four zones – surprise, creepy, safe and twilight – represents how the presence or lack of transparency and the presence or lack of control can affect consumers' perception of creepiness; the two extremes are creepy and safe.

- *Surprise*: In this case, the firm is not transparent, but consumers are in control. Although consumers can control what information is collected and even opt out, at some point, they are surprised about how the firm uses the personal information they willingly shared to generate personalized communications. For example, consumers can control what information they post on social networking websites like Facebook or LinkedIn giving them some measure of control over what data are collected. However, firms are not transparent about how they will use the collected information to deliver personalized communications.
- *Creepy:* This zone is characterized by no transparency by the firm and no control by the consumer. The Target and Girls Around Me examples clearly fall into this category.
- *Safe:* This zone is the area in which firms are transparent and disclose how they collect data, how they use data to create personalized messages, and with whom they share data; consumers have control over how their data are collected and have the ability to opt out of data collection or sharing practices by the firms. Consumers are fully aware of what is going on with their data. In this category, the personalized message is thought to be cool, smart and relevant. Coupons received with a receipt at the grocery store fall into the safe zone category.
- *Twilight:* In this area, the firm is transparent, but the consumer has no control. Consumers are aware that the firm is collecting, using and sharing their personal information and also know that the data may be used in an unexpected or surprising way but have no way of controlling the situation. For example, some sites indicate that they use cookies (historical website visit information) and ask consumers to acknowledge this declaration by checking a box or accepting the acknowledgement. Consumers have some control because they can either check or not check the box; however, if they accept the acknowledgement and continue using the website, they know that their information and activity will be tracked and may be used to deliver personalized messages, but they have no control over how, when or where this will occur.

Intrusions of privacy can vary depending on the context in which privacy is viewed. In summary, people's privacy in the context of marketing or online personalized communications is intruded upon when information that they intend to be confidential, such as medical history or financial information, is shared with a broader audience. Whereas, perceived creepiness is the effect that occurs when companies use personal information, while not always maintained as confidential, in a way that is unexpected and beyond the original purpose.

Creepy matters

In many instances, consumers benefit from personalized communications because they receive relevant messaging tailored to their preferences, product recommendations, reward points, loyalty rewards and other discounts for products they frequently use. These benefits often result in increased levels of customer satisfaction because customers feel that they are gaining more than they are losing from companies using their personal information to build a more personalized customer experience for them. In turn, companies benefit by strengthening their relationship with customers. However, marketing efforts that are viewed as creepy have the opposite effect and actually decrease customer satisfaction.

Customer satisfaction is a measure of expectations of purchase, consumption and post-purchase feelings and can affect repeat sales and brand loyalty. Measuring customer satisfaction provides insights to help companies improve and manage their business, as changes in customer satisfaction can have an impact on firm performance. Therefore, companies should carefully monitor any factors that may increase or decrease satisfaction. Although most marketers are aware of the positive impact of personalized communications on customer satisfaction, many tend to be less aware of the possibility of a negative impact. In a study of consumers' reactions to personalized communications, online communications that consumers perceived as creepy led to a decrease in their level of satisfaction with the company involved (Stevens 2016). Because customer satisfaction is a key measurement of firm performance, avoiding creepy communications clearly matters. In the case of Target, the firm experienced a backlash from consumers who were uncomfortable and dissatisfied with its marketing tactics, and this backlash had the broader effect of tarnishing the brand. In an effort to enhance the brand and improve overall satisfaction with the company, Target incorporated baby coupons into mailings that also included coupons for other items. With the Girls Around Me app, the backlash from consumers led to its removal from app stores, and the companies involved provided statements of apology for the fiasco. To avoid suffering the consequences and downstream impacts of decreased levels of customer satisfaction, marketing managers must have an awareness and understanding of the impact of personalized ads on consumers. Failing to understand the perspective of consumers means running the risk of being blindsided by decreasing customer satisfaction because of personalized communications perceived as creepy.

Mitigating perceptions of creepiness

Perceived creepiness is subjective; what one person perceives as creepy may be acceptable to another. In addition, what may be generally perceived as creepy at one point in time may eventually become the norm as people become accustomed to it. Such is the case with caller ID. This innovative landline telephone feature was rolled out in the early 1990s, and it bothered many people (Shaman 1990). Yet, after more than twenty years, caller ID has gained broad acceptance as the norm, and many people now will not answer the phone from an unknown caller or unfamiliar number. Thus, what is perceived as creepy continues to change, especially with rapid advances in technology and the varied ways personal information is collected, used and shared. Technology tends to advance more rapidly than norms are developed. Given this backdrop, companies may surmise that it is difficult to mitigate perceived creepiness, as it can be a moving target; however, this is not necessarily the case. Although marketers cannot always ascertain how individual consumers will respond to personalized ads, they can take steps to minimize or lessen the degree to which consumers perceive an ad as creepy or privacy intrusive. The creepiness of digital communication can be managed in three ways: (1) by being transparent and giving consumers control over the collection, use and sharing of their personal information; (2) by maintaining contextual integrity over the content and messages being sent; and (3) by engaging in trustworthy behaviours.

Transparency and control

As the Creepy Quadrant in Figure 13.3 shows, the juxtaposition of transparency and control can affect the degree to which something is perceived as creepy. To minimize perceived creepiness, marketers can be transparent with their customers about how they collect, use and share consumer information. At the core of firm transparency is openness and honesty about the firm's intention to collect, use and share this information. In the context of marketing communications, firms must provide clear and accurate details on how they will use and potentially share a consumer's information. Firms typically believe that privacy statements included on websites and at the point of transaction are enough; however, consumers and policy makers are beginning to question whether providing a privacy statement that is inconspicuous and difficult to interpret is enough transparency. Social media users often overlook phrases such as 'terms and conditions' and 'accept to continue'. For example, if Target had disclosed that it categorized buyers and tracked shopping habits to provide relevant coupons, perhaps the teenage girl's father would not have been so outraged that she received baby-related coupons.

Another aspect of the Creepy Quadrant involves consumers' ability to control how their information is managed. Consumers who are allowed to opt out or correct inaccurate information, can control the flow of information, and thus perceptions of creepiness can be minimized. If the teenager in the Target case had had the ability to opt out from her buying habits being tracked or from receiving marketing communications altogether, she would not have received coupons at all.

Context

In addition to being transparent and allowing consumers to control their personal information, marketers must provide messages that are 'in context' and do not violate the norms for information flow, thus maintaining a sense of contextual integrity (Nissenbaum 2004). For example, if a woman opens a baby shower registry at a given store, she will likely not perceive receiving coupons for baby-related items as creepy. Societal norms are important in determining how various types of information are collected, used and shared and, as mentioned previously, help people assess when a personalized communication has crossed the line from being relevant to creepy. Typically, messages 'out of context' are more likely to be perceived as creepy. Many consumers have come to accept coupons received from their preferred grocery store, or online retailers making suggestions based on previous searches, as normal. These tactics are now commonplace and within the context of acceptable uses of personal information. In contrast, airline companies (Hume 2012) or hotels (Lindberg n.d.) that Google their customers to learn more about them to deliver what they believe are more personalized experiences may also be perceived as creepy. Many of these tactics fall under the guise of online behavioural advertising or identity-based advertising, in which one's online identity or behaviours are the basis for personalized messages. As these examples indicate, when societal or social norms are violated and companies use personal information for a secondary purpose to what was originally intended, or when information is inferred from online behaviours, the message can be perceived as out of context and creepy. In a fictitious scenario, study (Stevens 2016) participants who were asked to imagine that they had recently purchased a trip to Italy found email communications about a wine tour acceptable but emails from a local Italian restaurant welcoming them home from their vacation as creepy. Thus, marketers should avoid creating messages that are out of context to minimize perceived creepiness in personalized communications and advertisements.

Trust

Last, to minimize perceived creepiness, companies can engage in trustworthy behaviours not only by being transparent but also by establishing a relationship with customers and engaging them on a human level by displaying such characteristics as high integrity, honesty and fairness (Morgan and Hunt 1994). To do so, companies can observe customer preferences around the collection, use and sharing of their data and ensure they are satisfied with previous interactions (Johnson and Grayson 2005). In order for companies to deepen the relationship with consumers and employ relationship marketing, trust is a central element that must be in place between the consumer and the company (Berry and Parasuraman 1992), which is particularly true when buying goods and services online (Shankar *et al.* 2002).

Conclusion

Understanding and measuring consumer perceptions of creepiness in online communications is imperative for all firms engaging in relationship marketing. Understanding how consumers perceive messages would help marketers communicate relevant information that facilitates relationship building and enhances customer satisfaction. In many cases, current marketing communications are doing the opposite, leading to the perceptions of privacy intrusion and creepiness. In addition, marketers should understand that messages that evoke negative feelings could affect the level of trust and ultimately a consumer's satisfaction with an organization.

References

Bilton, N. 2012. 'Girls Around Me: an app takes creepy to a new level'. *The New York Times*. Available at http://bits.blogs.nytimes.com/2012/03/30/girls-around-me-ios-app-takes-creepy-to-a-new-level/?_r=0. Accessed 07 July 2016.

Berry, L. L. and A. Parasuraman. 1992. 'Marketing services: competing through quality'. *Journal of Marketing*, 56:2, p.132. Available at http://www.jstor.org/stable/1252050?origin=crossref. Accessed 01 July 2016.

Chellappa, R. K. and R. G. Sin. 2005. 'Personalization versus privacy: an empirical examination of the online consumer's dilemma'. *Information Technology and Management*, 6:2–3, p.181–202.

Culnan, M. J. 1993. '"How did they get my name?": an exploratory investigation of consumer attitudes toward secondary information use'. *MIS Quarterly*, 17:3, p. 341–363. Available at http://search.ebscohost.com/login.aspx?direct=true&db=buh&AN=9404050726&site=ehost-live. Accessed 01 July 2016.

DoubleClick by Google. 2014. 'Kellogg viewability increase case study - DoubleClick'. [online] Available at: https://www.doubleclickbygoogle.com/articles/kellogg-dishes-offline-sales-programmatic-buying/. Accessed 01 July 2016.

Downes, L. 2012. 'Customer intelligence, privacy, and the "Creepy Factor"'. *Harvard Business Reveiw*. Available at http://blogs.hbr.org/2012/08/customer-intelligence-privacy/. Accessed 01 July 2016.

Goodwin, C. 1991. 'Privacy: recognition of a consumer right'. *Journal of Public Policy & Marketing*. Available at http://www.jstor.org/stable/10.2307/30000257. Accessed 21 November 2013.

Hill, K. 2012. 'How target figured out a teen girl was pregnant before her father did'. *Forbes*. Available at http://www.forbes.com/sites/kashmirhill/2012/02/16/how-target-figured-out-a-teen-girl-was-pregnant-before-her-father-did/. Accessed 01 July 2016.

Hume, T. C. 2012. *BA Googles passengers: Friendlier flights or invasion of privacy? - CNN.com*. [online] CNN. Available at: http://www.cnn.com/2012/08/22/travel/ba-google-image-passengers/. Accessed 01 July 2016.

Jennings, J. 2015. *Is It Smart Digital Marketing – Or Is It Creepy? | ClickZ*. [online] Clickz.com. Available at: https://www.clickz.com/is-it-smart-digital-marketing-or-is-it-creepy/25686/. Accessed 01 July 2016.

Jensen, C. and C. Potts. 2004. 'Privacy policies as decision-making tools: an evaluation of online privacy notices'. In *Proceedings of the SIGCHI conference on Human factors in computing systems*. p. 471–478. Available at http://portal.acm.org/citation.cfm?id=985752

Johnson, D. and K. Grayson. 2005. 'Cognitive and affective trust in service relationships'. *Journal of Business Research*, 58:4, p. 500–507.

Kramer, I. 1989. 'Birth of privacy law: a century since Warren and Brandeis', *The Catholic University Law Review.* Available at http://heinonlinebackup.com/hol-cgi-bin/get_pdf. cgi?handle=hein.journals/cathu39&section=28. Accessed 19 November 2013.

Lindberg, P. J. 2016. What Your Hotel Knows About You. *Travel + Leisure* [online] Available at: http://www.travelandleisure.com/articles/what-your-hotel-knows-about-you. Accessed 01 July 2016.

Metzger, M. J. 2007. 'Communication privacy management in electronic commerce'. *Journal of Computer-Mediated Communication*, 12, p. 335–361.

Milne, G. R. and M. J. Culnan. 2004. 'Strategies for reducing online privacy risks: why consumers read (or don't read) online privacy notices'. *Journal of Interactive Marketing*, 18:3, p. 15–29.

Morgan, R. and S. Hunt. 1994. 'The commitment-trust theory of relationship marketing'. *The Journal of Marketing.* Available at http://www.jstor.org/stable/1252308. Accessed 26 March 26 2016.

Nissenbaum, H. 2004. 'Privacy as contextual integrity'. *Washington Law Review*, 79, p.101–139. Available at http://heinonlinebackup.com/hol-cgi-bin/get_pdf.cgi?handle=hein. journals/washlr79&section=16. Accessed 01 July 2016.

Shaman, J.M. 1990. 'Caller ID Poses Invasion of Privacy'. *Chicago Tribune.* [online] Available at: http://articles.chicagotribune.com/1990-05-18/news/9002090934_1_ caller-id-phone-numbers. Accessed 01 July 2016.

Shankar, V., Urban, G. and Sultan, F. 2002. 'Online trust: a stakeholder perspective, concepts, implications, and future directions'. *The Journal of Strategic Information Systems*, 11(3–4), pp.325–344. Available at http://www.sciencedirect.com/science/ article/pii/S0963868702000227. Accessed 01 July 2016.

Stevens, A. 2016. *Antecedents and Outcomes of Perceived Creepiness in Online Personalized Communication.* Cleveland, OH: Case Western Reserve University.

Stewart, P. 1964. 'Jacobellis v Ohio'. *US Rep*, 378, p. 184.

Tavani, H. T. 2007. 'Philosophical theories of privacy: implications for an adequate online privacy policy'. *Metaphilosophy*, 38:1, p. 1–22. Available at http://doi.wiley.com/ 10.1111/j.1467-9973.2006.00474.x. Accessed 19 November 2013.

Trainor, K. J. *et al.* 2014. 'Social media technology usage and customer relationship performance: a capabilities-based examination of social CRM'. *Journal of Business Research*, 67:6, p. 1201–1208.

Warren, S. D. and L. D. Brandeis. 1890. 'The right to privacy'. *Harvard Law Review*, 4, p. 193–220. Available at http://www.jstor.org/stable/10.2307/1321160. Accessed 19 November 2013.

Westin, A. 1968. 'Privacy and freedom'. *Washington and Lee Law Review.* Available at http://scholarlycommons.law.wlu.edu/cgi/viewcontent.cgi?article=3659&context=wl ulr. Accessed 19 November 2013.

14

SOCIAL MEDIA MEASUREMENT AND MONITORING

Mudra Mukesh and Anand Rao

The social media landscape

The importance of social media has been increasing exponentially in recent times and has warranted many discussions about the importance of social media marketing and apportioning marketing budgets for this. A recently conducted survey of about 3,000 marketers by Salesforce to discuss the 'state of marketing in 2015 and in the future' (Salesforce 2015), revealed that 66 per cent of marketers have a dedicated social media team, and 64 per cent feel that they are a critical enabler for their business. Social media are also considered an element of the promotional mix and an important integrated marketing communication (IMC) tool (Mangold and Faulds 2009). They have also been pegged as one of the key areas where spending is expected to increase in the coming years. However, none of these discussions can come to fruition unless the right approach and tools are considered to monitor and measure the developments in social media marketing.

Organizations are engaging in a whole gamut of activities when it comes to social media such as content generation, content publishing, content distribution, social media advertising and social media customer service. In addition, they are also defining specific strategies for different social media channels such as Facebook, Instagram, Twitter, Snapchat and so on. With such an increasingly complex social media landscape, the pertinent question that all brands and social media managers are seeking to understand is, how can they keep track of where this effort is headed? Measuring the effectiveness of these efforts is essential to calibrating future efforts, and even for apportioning funds accordingly. One of the recommendations that came forward from the report 'State of Marketing 2015' (Salesforce 2015) was that organizations should engage in social listening to make sure that they are covering all bases when it comes to monitoring their brands or topics relevant to their brands. If someone is talking about the brand somewhere, the organization should know about it.

A treasure trove of data

Social media sites such as Twitter, Facebook, Instagram, Pinterest, LinkedIn and Snapchat are a treasure trove of data. Consumers constantly engage with brands, as do film and television celebrities, politicians, sportspersons, musicians, company employees and even your neighbour with a peculiar sense of humour.

But before proceeding further, we need to establish the scope of customer engagement particularly in the context of social and digital marketing. The term 'customer engagement' has gained widespread practitioner and academic attention particularly with the transition to more social channels. Traditionally customer engagement has been proven to enhance sales (Neff 2007), competitive advantage (Sedley 2006) and innovation (Sawhney, Verona and Prandelli 2005). But what exactly *is* customer engagement?

Hollebeek (2011) defines customer brand engagement as follows:

> The level of an individual customer's motivational, brand-related and context-dependent state of mind characterized by specific levels of cognitive, emotional and behavioral activity in brand interaction.

The following caveats can be noted about engagement:

- Engagement is characterized by a two way interaction between a consumer and a product/brand (Bowden 2009).
- Engagement yields 'customer repeat patronage, retention and loyalty' (Verhoef, Reinartz and Krafft 2010).
- 'Online customer engagement' is characterized by 'active sustained cognitive processing', 'instrumental value' and 'experiential value' (Mollen and Wilson 2010).

Organizations and brands need to monitor and measure the voice of the customer across various structured and unstructured messages, key words, hashtags, communities and be well equipped to address complaints with the resources necessary to respond to crisis situations. That sounds like a lot of work for social media managers; however in order to plan better, most organizations have guidelines to make the process smooth.

The objective of this chapter is to highlight the role that social media measurement and monitoring processes can play in influencing business outcomes based on consumer behaviour analysis.

Importance of social media measurement and monitoring

Consumers today have more devices and control at their fingertips, and are not afraid to explore and use the various technologies available to them. And with the presentation of new connected and wearable devices and communication channels, it has become even more important to continuously monitor consumer behaviour across relevant channel touchpoints in order to serve the consumer better with relevant offerings at the right time. In the era of Snapchat and Facebook, which largely started out as millennial fads, why is it important to talk about Social Monitoring and Measurement (SMM)? The answer to this question lies in understanding how monitoring and measurement of social media help organizations. Below we illustrate the benefits of the 4 E's of the SMM process.

1. *Engages* **Consumers**: Consumers talk about brands on social media using a myriad of hashtags, keywords, geolocation details, tags and content types such as photos, videos etc. In order to understand what is being said, organizations must actively listen and monitor online conversations about the organization itself or a particular brand, product category or campaign. Successful SMM processes yield actions that not only engage consumers but also enable organizations to manoeuvre towards consumer-first strategies.
2. *Enhances* **Focus**: SMM processes help organizations to maintain an enhanced focus on their marketing strategy and operations objectives within the social media sphere. Spelling out the important business objectives and how they can be measured recalibrates the focus of the organization on the issues that are important.
3. *Educates* **Performance**: Successful SMM processes enable organizations to continuously learn how to perform better *vis-à-vis* competitors. It also facilitates the reporting of relevant findings to any stakeholders within the organization.
4. *Enables* **Return on Investment (ROI) Discussion**: SMM process enables the linking of returns to the cost incurred on social media marketing efforts either at a strategic and organizational level or at the marketing campaign and operational level. This enables organizations to decide if and how investment should be made across the social media value chain.

The social media measurement and monitoring (SMM) process

The social media measurement and monitoring process is carried out to measure and monitor social media activities so an organization can achieve its goals.

First, the process begins with a social media audit to assess how efficiently and effectively the brand's existing social media efforts are performing, as well as evaluating where the consumers are engaging and communicating.

Second, mapping of objectives is carried out to understand the direction of the brand with regard to its efforts on social media and what it aims to achieve. Based on the different objectives various organizations may have, different strategies may have to be adopted. For instance, objective mapping could include deciding whether the goal of the brand is to seek feedback from consumers, provide customer service or increase brand awareness.

Third, brands would need to draw out key performance indicators (KPIs) for each objective, and that would be the foundation in determining what is to be

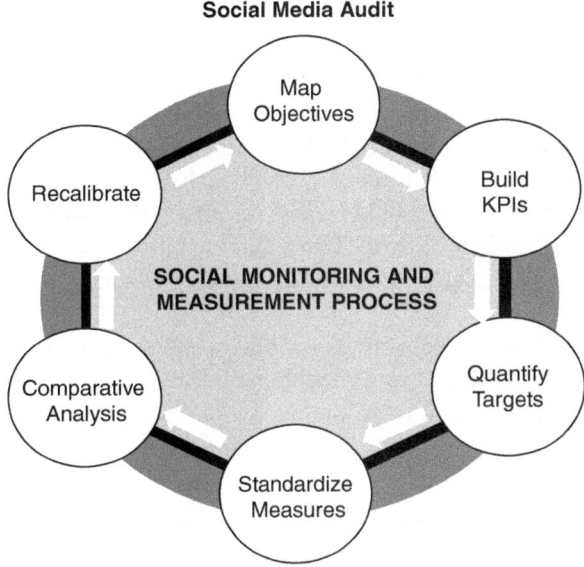

Social Media Audit

FIGURE 14.1   The social measurement and monitoring process (SMM process).

measured. An example of a KPI is *fan growth rate* (see Table 14.7) which tracks the growth of fans on a social media channel over a period of time.

Fourth, brands would have to set out quantifiable targets, and depending on the objective and the KPI these could range from a simple number of followers on Twitter to the number of comments on a post on Facebook. Further, brands could look to the market leader or its competitor to identify the target it wants to establish.

Fifth, the company would choose various measurement tools and chalk out approaches to measure the indicators they have established. These tools range from sentiment analysis and content analysis to automated tools and software that enable measurement and analysis.

Sixth, would be to perform a comparative analysis – to see how the actual indicators stack up against the targets, and then *finally*, recalibrate the social media strategy accordingly. Figure 14.1 gives a representation of the process.

The next sections discuss each of these steps in greater detail.

Social media audit

A social media audit involves performing a reconnaissance of the brand's social media landscape. Brands may already be engaged in various social media activities such as a brand page on Facebook, an Instagram account and a Twitter handle. Before the SMM process is to commence it is essential to understand the brand's exposure in terms of the platforms they are active on and how those initiatives are working for them. However, a mere presence on a platform is not the only parameter that needs assessment. It is also essential to understand what type of engagement is carried out on each platform, how regularly the platform is monitored and whether the brand's consumers regularly engage in the platform under consideration. The level of engagement can be varied across platforms – for instance on Twitter the brand may just be retweeting praise sent to it by consumers, but on Facebook a brand could be posting original content such as pictures from events and contests. A social media audit should be able to capture the status quo of social media activities being performed by the brand across platforms and also gauge the effectiveness across each platform. Table 14.1 provides a social media audit template.

While the template provided is just an example of how a social media audit can be performed, the template can also be amended to include other fields – for instance, the most popular content posted (with the most likes) or the format of

TABLE 14.1 Social media audit template

Social Media Platform	Presence	Frequency of Use	Engagement Level	Number of Followers	% Change
Facebook					
Instagram					
Twitter					
Snapchat					
YouTube					
LinkedIn					
Pinterest					
Google +					
Tumbler					
Other					

Parameter Key	
Presence	Yes
	No
Frequency of Use	Not Monitored
	Infrequent: Monitored every once in a while
	Daily: Monitored at least once a day but not hourly
	Hourly: Monitored at least once an hour but not around the clock
	24/7: Monitored around the clock ('live monitoring')
Engagement *(From content/marketer's perspective)*	No engagement: presence only
	Low engagement: monitoring only
	Medium engagement: monitoring and content reposting
	High engagement: content, conversation and customer service
Number of Followers	Numeric input (the number of current followers/fans of the company/brand page/account)
% Change	Records the increase/decrease in number of followers either from last month or last year

the most popular content (video, audio or image). Additionally, the frequency tab could be used to record the frequency with which the brand posts content rather monitors content.

BRANDS ON TWITTER

The most followed brand on Twitter is Chanel. Surprised? It has 12.2 million followers. This is followed by Samsung Mobile with 11.9 million followers and Starbucks with 11.7 million followers (Socialbakers 2016). However, Samsung ruled the roost only six months before. Chanel mostly tweets original content, usually pictures, and does not retweet any content. There are negligible to no conversations with followers. Moreover, there is evidence to show that Chanel posts at least one piece of content every day, sometimes more. What may have catapulted Chanel from the third spot six months ago to the top spot as far as Twitter followers go, ahead of Samsung Mobile?

Can you perform a social media audit for your favorite brand using the template provided? What do you think are the strengths and weaknesses of the brand's social media strategy?

Map objectives

After the social media audit is performed, the next step would be to enter the SMM process loop. The loop starts with mapping of objectives. In terms of social media, there can be several objectives for brands that may need attention. They may want to address one or many objectives at the same time; however that remains the discretion of the organization based on its overall marketing strategy, the social media audit performed and any developments in the market.

Mapping objectives for social media can be driven by:

1. *Need to learn from consumers*: Brands thrive on knowing their consumers and offering products and services they want. In order to do that brands can seek feedback and ideas from consumers to fine-tune their value propositions. This would also enable them to reduce cost, increase revenues, and amplify their reach and engagement.
2. *Potential expansion into new markets*: When brands want to acquire new markets they may have to develop objectives that enable them to increase their reach and acquire new customers. A tactical objective to increase reach would be to increase brand awareness.
3. *Push to increase sales*: Brands must grow and this is governed by more and more consumers buying their products and services. If the need is to increase

sales, brands may decide to formulate a social media objective of creating engagement with its e-commerce platform.

4. *Enhance customer satisfaction and increase loyalty*: Cost of acquisition of a new customer is higher than simply retaining an existing customer. Therefore, it is financially advisable for brands to keep their customers satisfied and happy, as then they are bound to be loyal (Heskett *et al.* 2008). From a strategic view point, the brand should aim to increase engagement with consumers. Providing mechanisms for customer service and redressing complaints could be an objective that helps in this direction.

5. *Brand equity*: Social media engagement can increase brand equity (Kim and Ko 2012). Brands should create engaging content to improve brand equity.

Depending on the business driver, sample tactical objectives can be drafted. For example, an airline may want to enhance customer satisfaction through engagement. To achieve this, they may want to reduce hold times on telephones and provide greater customer service. They may have alternative options for consumers to reach them such as via Twitter, Facebook or email, but if people don't see how the airline engages on these platforms and what their response rates and times are, they may not be prompted to use these mediums and prefer to call instead. Thus bringing traffic from call centres to social media could be a big challenge for a brand. If done right, it can help keep costs down and enhance customer satisfaction. Promoting enhanced responsiveness on social channels could be one way airlines could get more people to seek customer service through Twitter or Facebook. At the time of writing, KLM, Royal Dutch Airlines (@KLM), has announced on its Twitter profile page that its average response time is eighty-eight minutes and this is updated every five minutes.

> What is the KLM average response time now as mentioned on its Twitter profile now? How does this compare with other airlines' response times?

National Geographic (@natgeo) is the most followed brand on Instagram. It has more than 50 million followers (Instagram 2016). National Geographic posts

TABLE 14.2 Social media objectives and drivers

Business Driver	Strategic Objective	Tactical Objective
Market and Consumer Insights	Engagement & Influence, Reach, Revenue	Service feedback, Product feedback
New Markets	Reach	Brand awareness
Sales	Revenue	Engagement and website
Customer Satisfaction, Loyalty	Engagement & Influence	Customer service, promotions
Brand equity	Engagement & Influence	Develop engaging content

more than one stunning photo and sometimes several photos a day. However, one must be cognizant of the fact that the people are engaging with the content by commenting, liking or sharing it. For a brand like National Geographic it would be important to understand engagement, which may be a more relevant objective than brand awareness. As the National Geographic Instagram account already has a huge following, the real test would lie in knowing how people are engaging with the content posted by National Geographic over how many new followers it acquired over a period of time.

Build KPIs

The pace at which communication has shifted from traditional closed communication media, such as call centre services and email conversations, to a much more publicly visible and highly reactive medium, such as social media conversations, has positioned the social media community as one of the key critical communities in brand success. As a social media community manager, it has become even more important to regularly monitor existing and evolving social media networks to understand the customers, listen in to the trends, review campaign performance and track competitors. However, with so much information available online, as well as offline, it is often difficult to make sense of the statistics and indicators across all channels. In many cases, having clear performance metrics, goals and KPIs will help brands determine how to effectively and efficiently react to a given situation.

Performance metrics

We will broadly classify the performance metrics into *three* groups, namely:

- reach to increase awareness,
- influence and engagement to generate leads and nurture relations, and,
- raising revenues to focus on sales growth.

Reach

Reach helps focus on the probable size of the user base, based on the number of unique impressions, followers, shares, comments and likes. Brands can execute campaigns that can enable them to reach their target audiences in three ways – via organic reach, paid reach and viral reach.

- **Organic reach:** Anything unpaid or that which grows naturally is organic. For example, users viewing or engaging with content or messages which are distributed by the brands naturally and without any paid sponsorship. Let's say, Andy and Anne are active users of Twitter and Facebook respectively. Andy's Twitter feed and Anne's Facebook wall both show a video posted by the brand. Whether Andy and Anne engage with this video content or not, if the content appears in their respective channel feeds, then the brand's organic reach goes up by two. Brands can further filter this number by gender, channel, geography and so on, to accurately measure the organic reach.

- **Paid reach:** Any sponsorship or payment involved in promoting content or messages is paid reach. For example, users viewing or engaging with content or messages that are distributed by brands via paid networks. Let's say, if brand A buys a sponsored tweet on Twitter or a sponsored post on Facebook, then the tweet or the post appears in the user's feed. The paid networks allow brands to specify their target demographic, region, gender and so on, which facilitates targeted marketing.
- **Viral reach:** Viral reach is achieved when posts are visible in a user's feed from the people, brand, ambassadors or celebrities that the user may have followed/liked, commented on or re-shared. Let's say, Andy is friends with Anne. Andy likes the campaign status message of brand A which is publicly visible on Facebook. This status is then also visible to Anne, which Anne may be likely to comment on, re-share or like. This comprises viral reach.

Influence and engagement

While reach helps gauge the opportunity size, influence and engagement measure the exposure potential of campaign content or messages. The influence and engagement performance metric is important to measure the amplification potential of campaign content and the corresponding behaviour of the brands' audiences towards the campaign over time. This in turn helps brands to measure the customer acquisition and/or sales conversion potential.

Figure 14.2 below depicts the degree of separation between the brand and its audiences i.e. fans/followers, and the influence that a brand can capitalize on. A brand on a social media channel must actively listen and continuously engage with its audience to evaluate what is resonating with its immediate fans/followers,

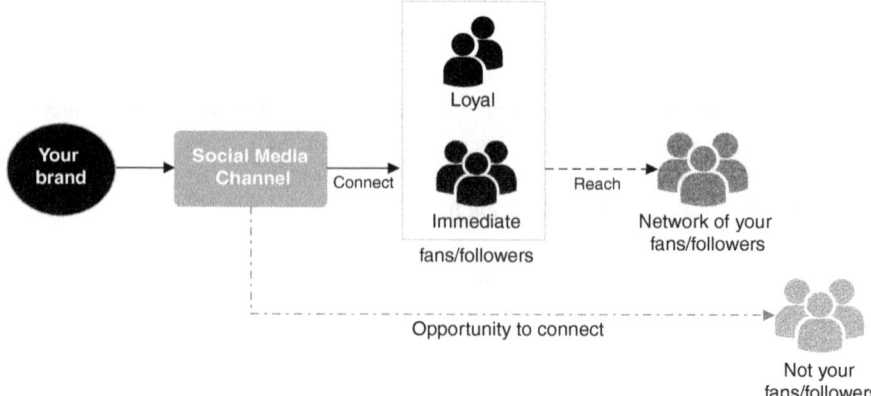

FIGURE 14.2 Influence a brand can capitalize on.

and their engagement and influencing potential to reach wider audiences. Such degrees of influence and engagement are likely to provide formidable insights that will further help fine-tune content creativity and creation, as well as the overall campaign messaging.

Raising Revenues

Revenue focused metrics are critical and justify the effort, budget and resources put towards the social media marketing programme. But it is commonly believed that the complexities involved in measuring social media revenue metrics make the measurement criteria a challenge, especially when the campaign initiatives are spread across multiple social media channels and touchpoints. No KPI is complete without appraising the revenue objectives, and brands can overcome challenges and complexities as long as the metrics and KPIs are clearly tied to the overall business goals, clearly articulated and aligned with relevant stakeholders.

When building KPIs to measure the reach of a brand, the following questions must be asked:

Q1: What social media channels is the brand using for its campaigns?

Q2: How are consumers/customers reaching the brand?

Building KPIs

Setting clear KPIs will enable brands to report the progress and performance of one or more campaigns across a number of social networks to senior management, and help evaluate the areas to engage, improve, invest or even withdraw.

For example, consider the *fan growth rate* KPI. *Fan growth rate* allows brands to track fans/followers growing over time. *Fan growth rate* is useful when

TABLE 14.3 Organizing the performance metric, purpose and KPIs

Performance Metric	Reach	Influence & Engagement	Raise Revenues
Tactical Objective	Increase awareness	Generate leads and nurture relations	Sales growth
KPIs	• Fan growth rate • Content reach • … • … • … • … • …	• Sentiment indicator • Share of conversations vs. competitors • Amplification rate • Applause rate • … • …	• Social Media Return on Investment • Sales from social media leads • … • …

'…' denotes more KPIs, custom KPIs relevant to the brand.

appraising how quickly the brand is growing. Such a KPI helps estimate the influence potential the brand can capitalize on by reaching out to its fans/followers and possibly engaging with them. However, note that one must not just rely on one KPI to determine the success of a campaign, but instead must focus on all goal relevant and correlated KPIs. Quality of fan/follower or likely leads can be used in conjunction with the *fan growth rate* KPI under consideration to build relevant and meaningful insights.

With a number of metrics offered by various social media networks, it is often difficult to determine which KPIs are relevant and align with the business objectives. When developing KPIs, understanding and evaluating what is relevant for the brand is essential. For example, asking questions such as the following will help outline clear KPIs:

- What are the objectives to be achieved from social media marketing?
- What social media channels should be considered for campaign management?
- How are the consumers reaching the brand?
- Which KPIs are in use and how efficiently will they measure success?
- Are KPIs to be evaluated in silos or correlated with other KPIs?

Quantify targets

Once the KPIs are defined, they must be linked to the strategic business metrics and goals. KPIs must be measurable in order to benchmark the growth objectives to deliver; and concrete in order to assess the necessary budget and resources required to execute the operations.

For example, if a brand is looking to increase number of followers (*fan growth rate*) across a breadth of social media platforms such as Twitter, Facebook, Instagram and Snapchat, but fails to do so on a given platform, say Twitter, then the campaign is not completely lost. The brand needs to now measure the overall percentage increase in the number of fans/followers across various social media

TABLE 14.4 Exercise template – defining a KPI using the following template, build a KPI to measure an objective

KPI	*<Name of the KPI>*
Performance Metric	*<Business metric under consideration>*
Tactical Objective	*<Purpose of this metric>*
Definition	*<Define the KPI>*
Description	*<Describe the KPI, highlight correlation or dependency, if any>*
Target	*<Outline tangible, measurable goal for KPI under consideration>*
Calculation	*<Provide an equation on how this KPI will be computed>*
Example	*<Provide an example to support the basis of the calculation>*
Comparative	*<Evaluate all the possible benchmarking parameters for the KPI>*
Visualization	*<Outline the graphic representation techniques for reporting>*

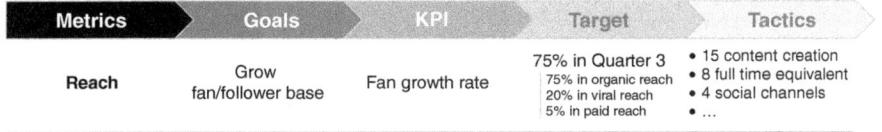

Metrics	Goals	KPI	Target	Tactics
Reach	Grow fan/follower base	Fan growth rate	75% in Quarter 3 75% in organic reach 20% in viral reach 5% in paid reach	• 15 content creation • 8 full time equivalent • 4 social channels • ...

FIGURE 14.3 Example – developing social KPIs from metrics to tactics.

channels, including Twitter as a first. It can also focus instead on measuring the increase in audience, who may have seen the brand's content organically, or via sponsored posts, even though they may not be fans or followers of the brand.

Such a measurement provides great insight into evaluating the investment in tools, resources and social media channels necessary for future campaigns. However, it should be noted that *fan growth rate* is not an accurate indication of the quality of the fan/follower base. A better tool for assessing the quality of the fan/followers could be sales leads (see Table 14.11) or monitoring network influencers. For instance Kylie Jenner, who has 76.2 million followers (as of October 2016) on Instagram, is considered an influencer in the domain of beauty and fashion. A leading fashion brand may find that a *mention* of their product or brand by a notable network influencer like Kylie Jenner can help their reach increase exponentially.

Quantifying social media objectives is always challenging, and hence when developing targets, determining the practical and measurable goals relevant to the brand is critical. For example, asking questions such as the following will help outline clear measurable KPIs:

- What should the business aim to achieve with the KPI?
- What measures are the competitors within the industry adopting?
- What budget, resources and technology are available to meet this target?
- Is the target realistic and does it take into account all factors to reach the goal?
- Does the target have milestones or deadlines and is it measured regularly?

For example; if the brand has decided to focus on the performance metric of *Reach*, in order to enhance brand awareness and drafted a KPI of *fan growth rate*, how does it decide what would constitute a reasonable *fan growth rate* percentage? Some approaches to quantifying targets include:

- *Market leader*: A brand could decide to fix a target based on the *fan growth rate* of the market leader on a select social media channel.
- *Competitor*: A brand could also fix its target based on the *fan growth rate* of its closest competitor.
- *Event driven decision*: A potential development in the business environment could also guide the target quantification. For example, if a brand is sponsoring an event, then during the airing of the event it may quantify its target for *fan growth rate* as higher than usual due to the increased visibility during that period.

TABLE 14.5 Various computations to determine fan/follower growth

Legends: 🔺 High 🔺 Medium 🔺 Low

Fan/Follower	Jan	Feb	Mar
Total	25459	🔺 37345	🔺 38000
Percentages		🔺 46.68%	🔺 1.75%
Count		🔺 11886	🔺 655
Ratios		🔺 1.46	🔺 1.02
Average		🔺 33601	

Standardize measures

The 'I' in the KPI refers to the indicator, which is nothing but statistics and arithmetic values associated with an activity. The arithmetic values give a scorecard about the performance of the activity at a given point in time or over a certain period, and help benchmark the performance against an indicator.

While indicators are usually easy to quantify and calculate, brands may still need to create a custom scale of measurements, and also decide upon the best computation methods to report findings, such as percentages, counts, totals, averages or ratios.

For example, if the brand is measuring the *fan growth rate* for a specific channel, say Instagram, over a quarter, then it can either measure the percentage increase or decrease in the number of fans between the start of the quarter and the end of the quarter. However, if a brand wants to measure the quality increase or decrease in the number of fans, then many factors could potentially be introduced into the calculation such as number of authorized Instagram accounts, audiences acquired through loyal fans/followers, leads to sales conversions etc.

Quantifying social media objectives is always challenging, and hence when developing KPIs, it is good practice to determine the practical and measurable goals relevant to the brand. For example, asking questions such as the following will help outline clear measurable KPIs:

- Is the KPI objective well understood?
- Can the KPI be easily measured?
- Are all the factors and assumptions needed to compute the KPI considered?
- Is the KPI simple and easy to explain?
- Does the measurement depend on other KPIs?

Comparative analysis

Comparative analysis is about comparing apples to apples of two or more alternatives, such as campaigns, content, content type, message, brand ambassador, sub-brands and so on. In social media terms, for example, the change in *fan growth*

TABLE 14.6 Comparative analysis of fan growth for January

United Kingdom

Name	Fans	Fan Growth
Company A	25459	+0.76%
Company B	63875	+1.52%
Company C	11245	- 0.65%

rate, say, may be presented over a period of time and benchmarked against one or more competitors to evaluate the overall standing of the brand reach with respect to the social media or company goals. Comparative analysis fully estimates the completeness of measuring the success of the KPI as well as the brand within (sub-brands, if any) and outside (competitors) of the brand ecosystem.

In the example highlighted in Table 14.6, for the month of January, Company A has grown positively, lagging in the race with Company B, but leading in the race with Company C.

Performing a comparative analysis over time, across regions, demographics and social media channels, as well as benchmarking against family of brands, competitors or campaigns will enable brands to effectively and efficiently compute and measure the success of the initiative.

The level of detail needed to engineer comparative analysis must be based on the resources available and the importance of the KPI. For example, asking questions such as the following will help outline clear comparative analysis for a given KPI:

- Why does the brand need comparative analysis?
- Are there enough parallels to perform meaningful analysis?
- Is the limitation to analysing and comparing various data points understood?
- How frequently must the comparative analysis be executed?
- What is the level of detail to evaluate the comparison on?

From performance metric to calculation: tabulation of various performance metrics with KPI and calculations

Recalibrate

Based on the findings during the measurement and comparative analysis stage a brand may decide to recalibrate its approach. The need for recalibration could arise due to:

- *Non-achievement of the targets*: If a brand is unable to achieve its targets it would need to investigate the reasons for falling short. Was the non-achievement due to the target being set at an overzealous level or did they fall short in their efforts?

- *Changes in the environment*: A change in the external environment or internal environment of the brand can also force a recalibration of the SMM process. If the brand expects a cut in the social media marketing budget, it may have to forgo certain resources and dial down its targets.
- *Misguided KPI*: A brand may have erroneously decided to focus on a KPI that may not have been relevant to the business. For instance, a brand looking to increase brand awareness and increase brand engagement may have decided to focus on sales from *social media leads* rather than *applause rate average* (see Table 14.9). While the first KPI is linked to revenue, the second is more about influence and engagement. The brand may want to focus on the *applause rate average* to tap into influence and engagement.

TABLE 14.7 Fan growth rate

Fan growth rate	
Performance Metric	Reach
Tactical Objective	Increase brand awareness
Definition	The ability to track your fans/followers growing over a period of time.
Description	Fan growth rate allows brands to track fans/followers growing over time. Fan growth rate is useful when appraising how quickly the brand is growing. Such a KPI will help estimate the influence potential the brand can capitalize on by reaching out to its fans/followers and possibly engaging with them. Brands must not just rely on one KPI to determine the success of a campaign, but instead all relevant and correlated KPIs such as engagement KPIs or content consumption KPIs must be used in conjunction with a specific KPI to build relevant insights.
Target	*Based on analysis (see Section 3.4)*
Calculation	Total fan growth rate % = [(Present data – Past data) / (Past data)]*100
Example	Say, Followers on [Social Media Network] on 1 July = 100,000 Followers on [Social Media Network] on 30 July = 165,000 Followers on [Social Media Network] on 30 September = 175,000 Fan Growth Rate % = [(165,000-100,000)/100000] *100 = 65% over 30-day period = [(175,000-100,000)/100,000] *100 = 75% over a quarter In this case, the brand observed only 6.06% increase in fan/follower base between July and September.
Comparative	The fan growth rate can be drilled down by region, country, county/state and city across one or more social media channels. Further, the relative share of fans/followers can be determined by drilling into specific brand(s) and products or services within the brand(s). Also, the fan growth rate can be measured against the competitor's brand.
Visualization	Pie chart

TABLE 14.8 Share of conversations vs. competitors

Share of Conversations vs. Competitors

Performance Metric	Influence & Engagement
Tactical Objective	Brand engagement
Definition	The ability to deduce the number of mentions in an online conversation for the brand against that of the competitor's brand within a given market and channel.
Description	The share of conversations tracks actual conversations, and any mentions, about the brand(s). If the brand is not already being spoken about, then you can identify the right conversations to participate in. The share of conversations and the sentiment indicator together will provide great insights that enable the brand to react quickly to a negative scenario or act to engage in a positive one. The closer you are to the conversations, the better the position you are in to influence the consumer or the influencer, and the higher is the value gained from their conversations.
Calculation	Share of conversations vs. competitors % = (Number of mentions for [brand name A] / Total number of mentions for [brand name B, C, D...])*100
Target	*Based on Analysis (see Section 3.4)*
Example	Say, Mentions for Brand A = 10 Mentions for Brand B = 20 Mentions for Brand C = 40 Mentions for Brand D = 30 Total Mentions = 100 Share of conversations vs. competitors = 10/100 = 10%
Comparative	The sentiments can be drilled down by region, country, county/ state and city across one or more social media channels for a specific brand, product or service.
Visualization	Pie chart is one of the best visual representation to project share of conversation vs. competitor.

Sentiment visualization

With so much content being created and shared on social networks, brands need to constantly listen in to relevant conversations, words and themes to be informed about sentiment around their products, brands and the organization itself. The listening has to be in accordance with privacy and security laws regulated in the region, and calibrated according to the goal. If the goal is awareness then one way of measuring it would be to see how many people are using the name of the brand in conversations across social and to what extent the conversation is positive or negative. This is where sentiment analysis or opinion mining would fit in. Usually, considering the number of data points, sentiment analysis is performed by written programmes. To perform it manually for 500 million tweets sent out every day

TABLE 14.9 Applause rate average

Applause Rate Average	
Performance Metric	Influence & Engagement
Tactical Objective	Increase brand reach
Definition	The frequency at which the social media audience react to your content and/or message and like it.
Description	Every time a content or message is liked, loved, pinned, given a thumbs up or +1, then your message has been applauded. In other words, it implies how many likes/favorites on average your post has received.
	Applause rate is positive when > 1, negative when < 1, neutral when = 1.
Calculation	Applause Rate = No. of Likes / (No. of Posts * No. of fans/followers)
Target	*Based on Analysis (see Section 3.4)*
Example	Say, for a given post,
	Likes on Facebook = 500
	Hearts on Twitter = 500
	Total Likes = 1000
	Assuming 500 fans, Applause Rate Avg. = 1,000 / (1 * 500) = 2
	Assuming 5,000 fans, Applause Rate Avg. = 1,000 / (1 * 5,000) = 0.2
Comparative	The sentiments can be drilled down by region, country, county/state and city across one or more social media channels for a specific brand, product or service. Further, the amplification rate can have relative measures which allow the accurate comparison between several accounts that have different numbers of followers and when you wish to compare against competitors. You may also calculate the overall amplification for your campaign by considering an average of all the messages posted during the campaign.
Visualization	Histogram bar is one of the best visual representations to project the applause rate over a period of time.

would be humanly impossible. There is a range of tools available to track sentiment online.

The tweet sentiment visualization (Tweet Sentiment Visualization 2016) developed by Healey and Ramaswamy at NCSU is one such free website. Type in a keyword and you are presented with a graph plotting the tweet text across ranges of sentiments such as unpleasant to pleasant, active to subdued (on the X and Y axis respectively), and among other sentiments as well such as depressed, excited, nervous and calm. The graph can also show each data point used to craft the sentiment analysis; in the case of Healey and Ramaswamy 2016, clicking on each circle shows you the corresponding tweet. A keyword search for the hugely popular augmented reality game 'Pokémon Go' developed by Niantic yields a vast amount of positive data points (see Figure 14.4).

However, machine driven sentiment analysis can sometimes lead to misleading results, considering it is difficult for an algorithm to account for cultural linguistic

TABLE 14.10 Social media return on investment (ROI)

Social Media Return on Investments (ROI)	
Performance Metric	Raising revenues
Tactical Objective	Return on investment
Definition	The ability to measure the returns on your overall social media goals
Description	While outlining the social media ROI, it is important to introspect, how you define the social media ROI. It is a very powerful KPI with an objective to measure sales. It is important that you consider your CAPEX and OPEX spend, as well as any promotional costs, across channels. These become your total investment which needs to be measured against the number of conversions via social media that resulted in sales. It is the value you derive from one or more social media channels based on the campaign targets. A positive ROI is considered better and more efficient than a negative ROI.
Calculation	ROI = [(Revenue generated by Social Media – Total Social Media Expenses) / (Total Social Media Expenses)] * 100
Target	*Based on Analysis (See Section 3.4)*
Example	Say, Revenues from multiple social channels = US$ 500,000 Total CAPEX and OPEX invested in social media = US$ 200,000 Then, ROI = [(500,000-200,000)/200,000] * 100 = 150%
Comparative	Use the KPI to measure ROI across one or more campaigns, across one or more geographies, demographics and social media channels. Further, use the social ROI against the overall sales generated to determine the percentage of revenue share from social media.
Visualization	100% stacked bar is one of the best visual representations to project the social media ROI. You may also look into pie charts.

nuances, such as sarcasm and double entendre. This often leads to confusion in classification. For a tweet that says 'This cupcake is wickedly sinful' to be perceived as negative by the algorithm would be very wrong and give an incorrect indication to the brand about the sentiment surrounding it. Alternatively, for two statements with similar words but different meanings such as 'I want the new iPhone SO bad' versus 'The new iPhone is so bad', sentiment analysis coding would classify them in the same way – negatively, as the automated code cannot read between the lines in terms of the context.

To take another example, a music production house tracking the sentiment for a new song gets a sentiment bordering on the negative: could it be due to the presence of tweets such as 'This song is sick!'? Perhaps this is something to think about before relying completely on algorithm-driven sentiment analysis.

There are some tools which organizations can use, but it really depends on the sophistication of the algorithm. Better yet, organizations can get experts to perform a sentiment analysis on a small sample of text manually.

TABLE 14.11 Sales from social media leads

Sales from Social Media Leads	
Performance Metric	Influence & Engagement
Tactical Objective	Sales
Definition	The ability to measure the sales on average order value or customer lifetime value on qualified converted leads
Description	Sales measurement enables the evaluation of the sales derived from a lead across one or more channels and can be calculated either on average order value or forecasted at customer lifetime value. A tangible sales target will enable brands to measure the business guidance around a specific campaign or channel or the overall social media ecosystem.
Calculation	Sales from Social Media Lead (Average Order Value) = [(No. of qualified social media leads identified) * (% lead-to-customer conversion rate) * average order value)] Sales from New Social Media Lead (Customer Lifetime Value) = [(No. of qualified online social leads identified) * (% lead-to-customer conversion rate) * customer lifetime value)]
Target	*Based on Analysis (see Section 3.4)*
Example	Say, No. of qualified social media leads = 1,000 % lead-to-customer conversion rate = 10% Average order value (AOV) = US $ 120 Customer Lifetime Value (CLV) = US $ 2,000 Sales from Social Lead (AOV) = [1,000 * 10% * 120] = US$ 12,000 Sales from New Social Lead (CLV) = [1,000 * 10% * 2,000] = US$ 200,000
Comparative	Use the KPI to measure the sales lead across geographies, demographics and social channels
Visualization	X Y scatters with smooth curves and markers is one of the best visual representations to project the social media ROI.

Data visualization

Data visualization is the process of collecting data and exhibiting them in a graphical format, which allows complex information to be conveyed in an easy-to-interpret format and story.

> *"A picture is worth a thousand words"*
>
> *– English idiom*

The ever-evolving nature of social media means that there are new social media networks, technologies and interaction features emerging every year. More networks mean more customers engaging across various channels, and eventually more data to process and interpret. Brands can either choose to manually process

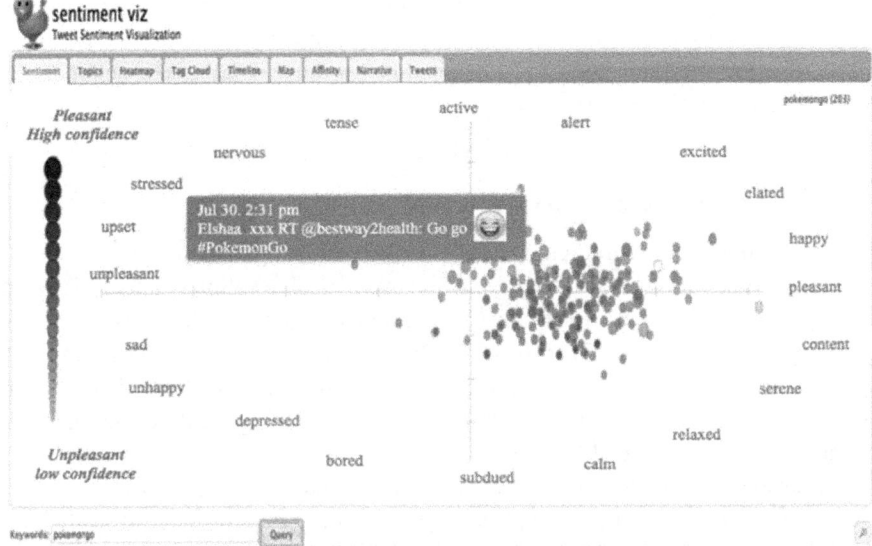

FIGURE 14.4 Tweet sentiment visualization for key word 'PokémonGo' showing a high confidence/pleasant and alert/active tweet.

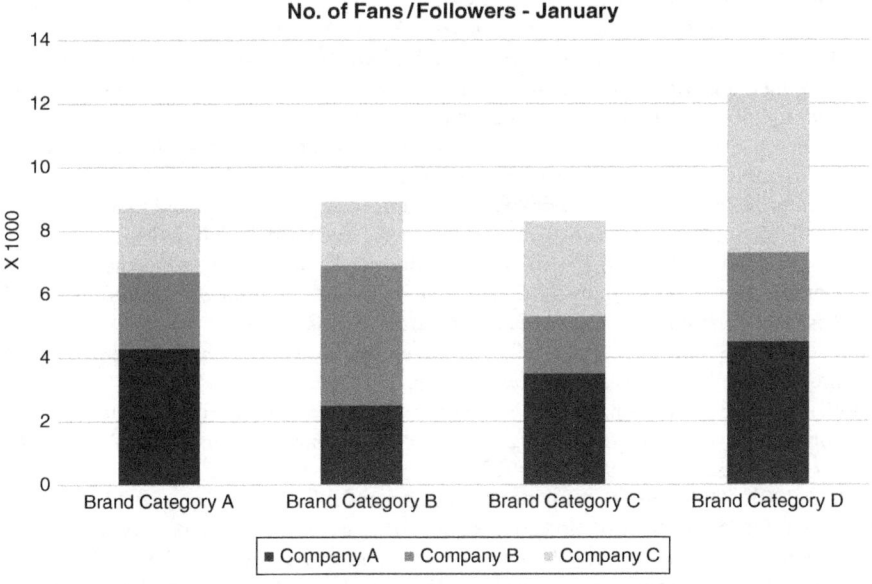

FIGURE 14.5 Bar chart – number of fans/followers for different brands against competitor for a given period.

the data and ingest the results within the brand ecosystem, or automate the data gathering and ingestion process. This can be achieved by using the public application programme interface (API) exposed by various social media channels for easy-to-measure parameters.

Conclusion: don't get obsessed with numbers

Isn't social media measurement and monitoring enthusing? Brands may have multiple digital touchpoints and journeys which may involve solidifying brand awareness, generating leads, acquiring new customers, retaining existing customers and growing revenues. It is indeed possible that certain deadlines, targets and goals may not be achieved. With a plethora of data and insights, social media managers must be able to assess how to navigate from social media to recalibrating the KPIs in the SMM process (see Figure 14.1).

Regardless of the consumer journey mapped out, it is important that brands maintain a clear goal-driven approach, which is aligned with the overall business goals in order to evaluate the social media marketing efforts. Ultimately, it is important to be realistic and measure wisely!

References

Bowden, J. L.-H. 2009. 'The process of customer engagement: a conceptual framework', *Journal of Marketing Theory and Practice*, 17:1, p. 63–74.

Heskett, J. L., T. O. Jones, G. W. Loveman, J. W. Earl Sasser and L. A. Schlesinger. 2008. 'Putting the service-profit chain to work', *Harvard Business Review*. Available at https://hbr.org/2008/07/putting-the-service-profit-chain-to-work. Accessed 29 July 2016.

Hollebeek, L. D. 2011. 'Demystifying customer brand engagement: exploring the loyalty nexus', *Journal of Marketing Management*, 27:7–8, p. 785–807.

Instagram. 2016. National Geographic (@natgeo). Instagram photos and videos [online]. Available at https://www.instagram.com/natgeo/. Accessed 29 July 2016.

Kim, A. J. and E. Ko. 2012. 'Do social media marketing activities enhance customer equity? An empirical study of luxury fashion brand', *Journal of Business Research, Fashion Marketing and Consumption of Luxury Brands*, 65:10, p. 1480–1486.

Mangold, W. G. and D. J. Faulds. 2009. 'Social media: the new hybrid element of the promotion mix', *Business Horizons*, 52:4, p. 357–365.

Mollen, A. and H. Wilson. 2010. 'Engagement, telepresence and interactivity in online consumer experience: reconciling scholastic and managerial perspectives', *Journal of Business Research*, 63:9, p. 919–925.

Neff, J. 2007. 'OMD proves the power of engagement', *Advertising Age*, 78:27, p. 3–4.

Salesforce (2015) The State of Marketing Report 2015. Available from: https://www.salesforce.com/form/marketingcloud/2015-state-of-marketing.jsp. Accessed 28 May 2016.

Sawhney, M., G. Verona and E. Prandelli. 2005. 'Collaborating to create: the Internet as a platform for customer engagement in product innovation', *Journal of Interactive Marketing*, 19:4, p. 4–17.

Sedley, R. 2006. 'Annual online user/customer engagement survey 2006'. Available at http://surveys.e-consultancy.com/app/survey/response.jsp. Accessed 13 January 2016.

Tweet Sentiment Visualization. 2016. Tweet Sentiment Visualization App [online]. Available at https://www.csc.ncsu.edu/faculty/healey/tweet_viz/tweet_app/. Accessed 30 July 2016.

Verhoef, P. C., W. J. Reinartz and M. Krafft. 2010. 'Customer engagement as a new perspective in customer management', *Journal of Service Research*, 13:3, p. 247–252.

15

ATTITUDES TOWARDS BRANDS AND ADVERTISEMENTS

Qualitative and thematic analysis of social media data

Emmanuel Mogaji and Temitope Farinloye

Introduction

Social media have been described as a platform for discussing ideas, communicating experiences and exchanging knowledge. They have changed the way individuals interact, providing a huge amount of data and rich market insight as customers and brands engage and build relationships. This public declaration is of great concern for any organization as it transfers the power to shape brand images from the hands of advertisers to the words of consumers' online connections.

This chapter sets an agenda proposing the possibilities of qualitatively analysing user-generated content on social media platforms to provide insight into attitudes towards advertisements and their brands. Unlike participants being interviewed in a focus group, filling in questionnaires, or neuroscience providing insight into how the mind perceives advertisements, which typically requires expensive, bulky equipment and lab-type settings that limit and influence the experience, this is readily available public data which can be thematically analysed to add to existing knowledge.

Presenting the idea, publicly declared responses to the advertisements of UK banks on Facebook were analysed in order to gain insight into their perceptions and attitudes towards the advertisements and their brands. An outline of how to perform an analysis of user-generated content was provided to buttress the research method. Challenges and limitations of this research method were also considered.

Social media and brand communication

The power of social media cannot be underestimated; they have revolutionized personal and organizational communications and interactions worldwide (Ngai *et al.* 2015). However, as far as the terminology is concerned, Kaplan and Haenlein

(2009) note that the term 'social media' is commonly used interchangeably with social computing, social networking, Web 2.0 and virtual social worlds. Ngai *et al*. (2015) acknowledge the many definitions of these terms, but summarize these by 'dividing the compound term "social media" into its two components, "social" and "media." The "social" part refers to the activities carried out among people, whereas "media" refers to Internet-enabled tools and technologies used to carry out such activities' (p. 771).

Malita (2011), however, provides a more suitable definition, by considering social media as the 'tools that facilitate the socialization of content [...] social media services encourage collaboration, interaction, and communication through discussion, feedback, voting, comments, and sharing of information from all interested parties' (p. 748). This further supports the co-creating of brand meaning, which is enhanced by the interaction on social media that this current chapter intends to explore.

Mangold and Faulds (2009) consider social media an obvious choice as a marketing tool and view them as an integral part of the integrated marketing communication strategies of firms. Hence, social media can be considered as a new component in marketing promotional material. Ngai *et al*. (2015) also acknowledge that their use in marketing has increased rapidly in recent years and they have received increasing attention from academia, as well as various industries.

Kaplan and Haenlein (2010) provide six classifications according to the level of social presence/media richness (low, medium and high) and self-presentation/self-disclosure (low and high) that can be observed on social media. The six classifications include: blogs, social networking sites (e.g. Facebook), virtual social worlds (e.g. Second Life), collaborative projects (e.g. Wikipedia), content communities (e.g. YouTube) and virtual game worlds (e.g. World of Warcraft).

This interaction between brand and social media users is the main focus of this study. Social networking sites (SNS) such as Facebook, Twitter and Google+, and content communities such as YouTube and Instagram, which allow the creation and exchange of user-generated content, are considered suitable for this research method. It is envisaged that not all social media users will already be customers of the brand; some users will want to engage with the brand in anticipation of making a purchase. Irrespective of the intention, social media provide a central location for online social engagement and a strategic means for building and maintaining a strong brand presence online (Wallace, Wilson and Miloch 2011).

As Tsai and Men (2013) note, academic research struggles to keep pace with the rapid growth of social media networks; the possibility of customers' comments on social media providing insights into their attitudes to the brand and advertisements has not been explored. This highlights a gap that this chapter hopes to fill. The study focuses on examining the possibility that self-reports from consumers (through their social media comments) can be used to explore the attitude to advertisement and brand construct. It draws attention to a social function that allows customers to interact with brands and allows brands to have a better understanding of how their consumers engage with their advertisement and, importantly, the attitude-towards-the-ad theory that suggests that a positive attitude towards the advertisement in turn has a positive effect on purchase intention (PI) (Bruner and Kumar 2000).

Analysing the user-generated qualitative data

This section provides an outline of how to perform an analysis of self-reported comments on social media to gain qualitative insight into advertisements and brands. To begin, it is important to identify the context and idea behind the analysis. Why would you want to carry out analysis on social media content? Perhaps a brand has just launched an advertisement and would like to know what people think of it or a Brand Manager observed 'thumbs down' (dislikes) on their YouTube video and wants to know why people disliked it. Analysing the comments provides an insight. Users on social media might find it easier to click a like or dislike button to show their attitude, but it takes effort and a certain degree of interest to actually type constructive comments and such feedback should be cherished. This highlights further benefits in user-generated data that suggest why it is imperative to take note of these comments.

Identifying the content

The content for analysis could be a brand logo or a slogan but, for this study, UK bank television advertisements have been selected to illustrate the possibilities of analysing user-generated content on social media to gain insight into attitudes towards the advertisements and their brands. Specifically, in the light of the global financial crisis and the negative attitude towards bank brands (Kottasz and Bennett 2014), the study explores user-generated comments on UK bank advertisements (see Mogaji (2016) and Mogaji, Farinloye and Aririguzoh (2016) for a full study).

Selecting the media

Bank advertisements can be distributed through different media – newspapers, billboards or social media to name a few. However, for the purpose of this study, Facebook was selected to illustrate the possibilities of analysing user-generated content on social media to gain insight into attitudes towards the advertisement and the brand. It is important to also note that possibilities abound on alternative social media – tweets from Twitter, comments on YouTube and Instagram – which can also be thematically analysed. In addition, with Facebook being the biggest social media network, this research process can actually be transferrable.

Extracting the data

Since UK bank advertisements and Facebook were selected as content and media sources respectively for this analysis, the next stage was to extract the data. The user-generated qualitative data in this research exercise were the comments and replies made by Facebook users relating to bank advertisements. The data collection process involved viewing the comments, as well as clicking 'see more' and replies. These comments could either be extracted manually (i.e. copied) or extracted using NCapture, a web browser extension on NVivo (Version 10) – see Bazeley and Jackson (2013) for Qualitative Data Analysis with NVivo – or using an Application Programming Interface (API) developed specially for that social media site. The extraction method, however, depends on the volume of data. For example, hundreds of comments for a student project on Facebook can be copied and pasted into a word processing software programme for further analysis, whereas a larger project for a business might need an API.

Analysing the data

Analysing the extracted data requires various steps in order to deduce a meaningful conclusion. It is important to repeatedly read over the data to get a feel for it, remove inappropriate text and have a better understanding of the data, in order to identify labels and elements that would be of theoretical significance and of particular importance, as this focuses on the identification of patterns that are interpreted in terms of themes (Aronson 1995). Braun and Clarke (2006, p. 81) noted: 'Thematic analysis can be an essentialist or realist method, which reports experiences, meaning and the reality of participants, or it can be a constructionist method, which examines the way in which events, realities, meaning, experiences and so on are the effects of a range of discourse operating within society'.

Different methods abound for thematic analysis – Interpretative Phenomenological Analysis explores personal meaning and lived experiences, exploring in detail how individuals make sense of their personal and social world (Smith and Osborn 2015). Template analysis involves analysing data from a textual format, creating codes and categories of interrelating importance that can be interpreted by the researcher to 'uncover the real beliefs, attitudes, values and so on of the participants in their research' (King 1998, p. 119). Another method is the Grounded Theory, which follows a three-part process coding of data: (1) open coding – breaking down, comparing, conceptualizing, and categorizing data; (2) axial coding – reassembling data into groupings or families; and (3) selective coding – developing core themes and relating them to other identified themes (Strauss and Corbin 1994, 1998).

This chapter adopted the Grounded Theory for the data analysis (see Smith 2015 for a practical guide to qualitative research methods). The extracted comments were coded, following a three-part process in order to understand consumers' attitudes towards the bank's brand image and the advertisement. As part of the open coding, all extracted comments were read several times, with everything carefully examined; no comments were ignored and tentative labels were coded. This was followed by axial coding where the relationship between the open codes were established, making connections and researching these codes in more detail.

The analysis was completed with selective coding where the core variables were integrated and refined, which included all the central activities of consumer attitudes towards the brand and the advertisement.

Reporting the results

In reporting the thematic analysis, one or two key themes emerged, with sub-themes as well, in order to provide empirical details on the phenomenon being observed. As with the study on attitude towards UK bank advertisements (Mogaji 2016), two key findings emerged: firstly, consumers are able to publicly express their attitudes towards the brand and advertisement; and secondly, creative features of the advertisement, such as the background music and the black horse, evoked a response towards the advertisement from the viewers (see https://www.youtube.com/watch?v=UlZ46oXe1Xo). Additionally, the study on attitudes towards UK bank brands highlights the key factor of reliability, which is supported by seven other sub-factors.

Shenton (2004) suggests that steps must be taken in order to help ensure as far as possible that the findings from the research are the result of the experiences and ideas of the informants, rather than the characteristics and preferences of the researcher. Detailed methodological descriptions to enable the readers to determine how far the data and constructs emerging from it may be accepted, should also be provided. This includes: guiding the reader through the inquiry process; providing a detailed account of the methods, procedures and decision points involved in carrying out the study (Merriam and Tisdell 2015), which allows any observer to trace the course of the research step-by-step via the decisions made and procedures described; and also using quotes from the comments to buttress the emerged themes.

Challenges

This section of the chapter builds on the works of Zimmer (2010) and Convery and Cox (2012), highlighting: a set of ethical challenges that must be addressed before embarking on future research in qualitative analysis of social media, including the nature of consent, privacy and anonymity on social network sites; providing strategies; and overcoming the challenges.

Demography

To better understand the results and interpret the findings of research, information about the demography of the participants is important. However, in the context of social media research for attitudes towards a brand and its advertisement, this is considered a challenge, as personally identifiable data is not collected. For example, it might not be possible to know the age, gender or race of those who have left comments on a social media post as this data is not collected. However, the general demography of the social media can be used to get an insight into the demography of the participants. In addition, the brand location can provide further insight into the demography of the participants. For example, Mogaji (2016) explored Lloyds Bank advertisements in the UK. The demography of monthly active users (MAUs) of Facebook, as well as the context of the UK, was considered as the majority of the respondents are more likely to be in the UK. Therefore, for a brand based in a South American country, most of the comments will be from users within that country who use the brand and are willing to engage with it.

Whose data?

LeBoeuf (2016) noted that the amount of data generated is increasing every day, every minute and every second, as users are continuously utilizing the Internet more and more each day; this offers many opportunities for communication and media providers to experience the benefits of increased data. The challenge here, however, is who owns this data – the users, the brands or the social media network?

Facebook acknowledges that its users own all of the content and information they post on its network. According to Twitter (2016), users retain their rights to any content they submit, post or display on or through their services. Instagram likewise does not claim ownership of any content that is posted on or through their service (Instagram 2017). Instead, the users grant these social media networks a non-exclusive, fully paid and royalty-free, transferrable, sub-licensable, world-wide licence to use the content that they post on or through the service.

Extracting these data can also become complicated with the knowledge that brands also have the right to use the comments generated by their customers on their pages. According to the social media terms of use of Lloyds Bank and Halifax Bank in the UK, for example, the customers grant the brands a worldwide, non-exclusive, royalty-free licence to freely use, copy, edit, alter, reproduce, pub-lish, display and/or distribute such material for any and all commercial and non-commercial purposes in any media or through any distribution method.

Paragraph 4a of Lloyds Bank's social media terms of use notes that their social media channels are public and any contribution users make will be available for anyone to see (Lloyds Bank 2016). Paragraph 9 of Halifax Bank's social media terms of use similarly states, 'We will assume that any material you transmit or post to our social media channels is not confidential. We will have the right to freely use, edit, alter, reproduce, publish and/or distribute such material for any and all commercial and non-commercial purposes, including the publication of such content on our own website and on third party websites' (Halifax 2016).

In the understanding of the ownership of online comments, especially when posted on brand pages, they can be considered to be publicly available for public use – like word of mouth and other comments or reviews online. These can no longer be treated as a private conversation between the brand and the users and that is why in most cases brands will encourage users to use direct/private mail to send confidential information. Therefore, in overcoming this challenge regarding ownership, it can be concluded that the transfer of exclusive rights to social media networks and brands makes this data readily available for analysis, albeit after permission from the brands.

Accessing the data

It is expected that students, academic researchers and brand managers will be able to analyse qualitative social media data to gain insight into brand knowledge and attitudes towards advertisements. However, accessing this data is also considered a challenge. As noted by the incident reported by Zimmer (2010), Facebook data was extracted through profile pages of research assistants, highlighting a peculiarity inherent to using in-network RAs to access Facebook profile data, as each of the RAs may have had a different level of default access based on individual students' privacy settings.

If a researcher is collecting data from a brand's page, privacy settings may be of concern. However, based on the focus of this idea – analysing users – generated comments on a brand's social media pages, researchers can still access the publicly available comments to carry out their research without necessarily creating a profile; the intention is not to join in the conversation, but more like an observer.

Consent

The idea of what constitutes 'consent' within the context of social media research needs to be addressed, especially in light of this contextual understanding of norms of information flow within specific spheres (Zimmer 2010). Eysenbach and Till (2001, p. 1,104) argue that to determine whether informed consent is required, it is first necessary to decide whether or not communication is private or public. Convery and Cox (2012) also note that what constitutes 'public' and 'private' spaces, with corresponding implications for whether or not informed consent is required, is one of the central issues with Internet-mediated research, and literature concerning the use of informed consent in private spaces is not clear.

The British Psychological Society's (2009) *Code of Ethics and Conduct* suggests that, unless informed consent has been obtained, research based upon observations of public behaviour should be restricted to those situations in which persons being studied would reasonably expect to be observed by strangers (p. 25). This shares a close resemblance to comments posted on the brand's page on social media networks, which can be seen and read by strangers, including researchers, suggesting there are practical limitations and implications for procedures around valid consent.

Though it might be theoretically possible to reach out to everyone for consent, the technicalities don't make this encouraging (e.g. based on the huge number of comments generated by hundreds of users). This was also corroborated by Convery and Cox (2012), who suggested that it would be time-consuming and cumbersome to reach out to each person whose posts have been used. In addition, not every participant would be reachable through messages on social media, simply because the researcher might not be in their network, meaning they may not be able to send them a message to request their permission. However, as has been previously discussed, brands now own the right to comments and the best option would be to contact the brand in order to get informed consent to use comments for analysis. Convery and Cox (2012) also conclude that the Internet is usually considered a public place and therefore informed consent may not always be required as public behaviour does not necessarily require informed consent.

Ethics

The final challenge, however, summarizes all the previous challenges into the ethics of social media research: How ethical can it be? What other considerations need to be taken? Can this be treated as research with human subjects? Various research bodies have tried to provide answers to these questions, but the ever-changing face of social media research has always posed a challenge. One of these faces is Ethical Decision-Making and Internet Research provided by the Association of Internet Researchers, which is an academic association dedicated to the advancement of the cross-disciplinary field of Internet studies (Markham and Buchanan 2012). The British Psychological Society has also provided Ethics Guidelines for Internet-Mediated Research (British Psychological Society 2013), acknowledging that advancements in Internet-mediated research (IMR) may have introduced 'additional, and sometimes non-obvious, complexities around adherence to ethics principles' (p.3) as the boundaries between social media research and other designs can be blurred where research includes elements of both face-to-face observation/interaction and remote data collection.

As expected from qualitative research, the responders' anonymity is considered crucial. However, on social media, this often poses a challenge as it is possible for the brand, the researcher and even the general public to know who made the comments being studied. Remaining anonymous online has become increasingly difficult (Davisson and Booth 2016). Dan Kaminsky, chief scientist at New York-based security vendor, White Ops, has also argued that absolute anonymity online is not a particularly achievable thing. Comments can still be anonymized as much as possible by using initials in the reporting of the result and in the case the actual comment needs to be embedded in the report. It is advisable to blur the profile picture and also the names of commenters, probably leaving visible the first letter.

Smith et al. (1996, p. 172) noted that privacy violations can occur when, 'extensive amounts of personally identifiable data are being collected and stored in databases'. In this case, the data gathered are user-generated comments on a brand's social media posts and these data do not give the researcher the ability to discern gender, age, ethnicity or other physically-observable characteristics. Therefore, as long as the objectives of the research are strictly adhered to, the privacy of the participants is violated.

Conclusion

This chapter acknowledges that social media are changing the manner in which brands and consumers relate to one another. Customers are co-creating value and meaning with brands, generating data which can be qualitatively analysed to further enhance our understanding of attitudes towards brands and their advertisements.

It is important to note that this user-generated data is not only restricted to Facebook, but also comments on YouTube videos, Instagram posts and tweets on Twitter – in fact, all possible avenues for brands to engage with consumers.

The possibilities of analysing user-generated comments on brand content on social media in order to understand consumers' responses and attitudes towards the brand and its advertisements have been represented, with case studies of a UK bank Facebook post. It is believed that this proposed technique will allow researchers and practitioners to have a greater insight into consumers' attitudes towards brand advertisements, to capture the public display of attitude towards their brand and to provide managers with important insights that can guide the development and execution of their advertising campaigns.

Significant theoretical and marketing practice implications for students, academics, advertisers, brand managers and social media marketing practitioners are presented within this chapter. However, ethical issues surrounding the research method discussed must be considered, such as limitations in understanding the demography, getting informed consent and developing sufficient strategies for data anonymization. It has, however, been argued that these ethical considerations may not pose so great a challenge, provided that the main objective of the research is to analyse data already available in the public domain and not to search further, invading the privacy of users by digging deep into their personal information.

The thematic analysis of a user-generated brand is not connected to profiling individuals. It is anticipated that this approach will solely be based on what the user has expressed about the brand and its advertisement at a particular time, with no need to intrude into their profile to further gain insight into who they are.

References

Aronson, J. 1995. 'A pragmatic view of thematic analysis'. *The Qualitative Report*, 2(1), p. 1–3.

Bazeley, P. and K. Jackson. 2013. *Qualitative data analysis with NVivo*. 2nd edn. London: Sage.

Braun, V. and V. Clarke. 2006. 'Using thematic analysis in psychology'. *Qualitative Research in Psychology*, 3(2), p. 77–101.

British psychological society. 2013. *Code of Ethics and Conduct. Guidance published by the Ethics Committee of the British Psychological Society.* Leicester, UK: British Psychological Society.

British psychological society. 2009. *Code of Ethics and Conduct. Guidance published by the Ethics Committee of the British Psychological Society.* Leicester, UK: British Psychological Society.

Bruner, G. C. and A. Kumar. 2000. 'Web commercials and advertising hierarchy-of-effects. *Journal of Advertising Research*, 40:1–2, p. 35–42.

Convery, I. and D Cox. 2012. 'A review of research ethics in internet-based research'. *Practitioner Research in Higher Education*, 6:1, p. 50–57.

Convery, I. and D. Cox. 2012. 'A review of research ethics in internet-based research'. *Practitioner Research in Higher Education*, 6:1, p. 50–57.

Davisson, A. and P. Booth. 2016. *Controversies in Digital Ethics*. Bloomsbury Publishing: USA.

Eysenbach, G. and J. E. Till. 2001. 'Ethical issues in qualitative research on internet communities'. *BMJ (Clinical research ed.)*, 323:7,321, p. 1,103–1,105.

Facebook. January 30, 2015, 2015-last update, Statement of Rights and Responsibilities. Available at https://www.facebook.com/terms. Accessed 18 June 2016.

Halifax. 2016-last update, Social media terms of use. Available at http://www.halifax.co.uk/securityandprivacy/privacy/social–media–privacy/?pagetabs=1&LB=474583775. Accessed 18 June 2016.

Instagram.com. 2017. 'Terms of Use – Instagram'. Available at https://www.instagram.com/about/legal/terms/before-january-19-2013/. Accessed 15 March 2017.

Kaplan, A. M. and M. Haenlein. 2010. 'Users of the world, unite! The challenges and opportunities of social media'. *Business Horizons*, 53:1, p. 59–68.

Kaplan, A. M. and M. Haenlein. 2009. 'The fairyland of Second Life: virtual social worlds and how to use them'. *Business Horizons*, 52:6, p. 563–572.

King, N. 1998. 'Template analysis'. In Symon, G. and C. Cassell (eds.) *Qualitative Methods and Analysis in Organizational Research: A Practical Guide*. London: Sage, p. 118–134.

Kottasz, R. and R. Bennett. 2014. 'Managing the reputation of the banking industry after the global financial crisis: implications of public anger, processing depth and retroactive memory interference for public recall of events'. *Journal of Marketing Communications*, 22:3, pp. 284–306.

Kwak, D. H., Y. K. Kim and M. H. Zimmerman. 2010. 'User-versus mainstream-media-generated content: media source, message valence, and team identification and sport consumers' response'. *International Journal of Sport Communication*, 3:4, p. 402–421.

Leboeuf, K. 2016. 'Overcoming challenges to make big data profitable'. Available at http://www.excelacom.com/resources/blog/overcoming-challenges-to-make-big-data-profitable. Accessed 15 March 2017.

Lloyds Bank. 2016-last update, Social media terms of use. Available at https://www.lloydsbank.com/privacy/social-media-terms-of-use.asp [April 22, 2017].

Malita, L. 2011. 'Social media time management tools and tips'. *Procedia Computer Science*, 3, p. 747–753.

Mangold, W. G. and Faulds, D. J. 2009. 'Social media: the new hybrid element of the promotion mix'. *Business Horizons*, 52:4, p. 357–365.

Markham, A., E. Buchanan and AoIR Ethics Working Committee. 2012. 'Ethical decision-making and Internet research: version 2.0'. *Recommendations from the AoIR Ethics Working Committee. Final Draft, Association of Internet Researchers.*

McCorkindale, T. 2010. 'Can you see the writing on my wall? A content analysis of the Fortune 50's Facebook social networking sites'. *Public Relations Journal*, 4:3, p. 1–13.

Merriam, S. B. and E. J. Tisdell. 2015. *Qualitative Research: A Guide to Design and Implementation*. San Francisco, CA: John Wiley & Sons.

Mogaji, E. 2016. 'This advert makes me cry: disclosure of emotional response to advertisement on Facebook'. *Cogent Business & Management*, 3:1, doi: 1177906.

Mogaji, E., T. Farinloye, and S. Aririguzoh. 2016. 'Factors shaping attitudes towards UK bank brands: an exploratory analysis of social media data'. *Cogent Business & Management*, 3:1, doi.1223389.

Ngai, E. W., S. S. Tao and K. K. Moon. 2015. 'Social media research: theories, constructs, and conceptual frameworks'. *International Journal of Information Management*, 35:1, p. 33–44.

Shenton, A. K. 2004. 'Strategies for ensuring trustworthiness in qualitative research projects'. *Education for Information*, 22(2), p. 63–75.

Smith, H. J., S. J. Milberg and S. J. Burke. 1996. 'Information privacy: measuring individuals' concerns about organizational practices'. *MIS Quarterly*, p. 167–196.

Smith, J. A. (ed.). 2015. *Qualitative Psychology: A Practical Guide to Research Methods*. London: Sage.

Smith, J. A. and M. Osborn. 2015. 'Interpretative phenomenological analysis'. In Smith, J. A. (ed.) *Qualitative Psychology: A Practical Guide to Research Methods*. London: Sage, p. 25–52.

Strauss, A. and J. Corbin. 1998. *Basics of Qualitative Research: Procedures and Techniques for Developing Grounded Theory*. Thousand Oaks, CA: Sage.

Strauss, A. and J. Corbin. 1994. 'Grounded theory methodology'. *Handbook of Qualitative Research*. London: Sage, pp. 273–285.

Tsai, W. S. and L. R. Men. 2013. 'Motivations and antecedents of consumer engagement with brand pages on social networking sites'. *Journal of Interactive Advertising*, 13:2, p. 76–87.

Wallace, L., J. Wilson and K. Miloch. 2011. 'Sporting Facebook: a content analysis of NCAA organizational sport pages and Big 12 conference athletic department pages'. *International Journal of Sport Communication*, 4(4), p. 422–444.

Zimmer, M. 2010. '"But the data is already public": on the ethics of research in Facebook'. *Ethics and Information Technology*, 12(4), p. 313–325.

16

STRATEGIZING SOCIAL MEDIA PRESENCE

Francesca Pucciarelli

Introduction: everyone is going social media!

The rapid rise and nearly universal adoption of social media have fundamentally altered the ways in which people interact with each other, with media, and ultimately with brands. Originally designed as platforms where individuals could carry out conversations and share information, social media websites were quick to adopt commercial features, and have rapidly become the twenty-first century's most dominant marketplace (Holt 2016), encompassing 2 billion users around the world (Simply Measured 2016). This (r)evolution of social media has created a range of possibilities and challenges for organizations.

In general, as evidenced by the vast number of business pages on Facebook (more than 50 million; Chaykowski 2015), most firms have understood by now that the question is not whether to cultivate a social media presence, but rather, how to do so most effectively. If correctly understood and used, social media can be valuable venues for branding of for-profit and non-for-profit organizations. For example, in 2014 the viral success of the ALS Ice Bucket Challenge – where individuals shared videos in which they poured buckets of ice water on themselves – helped to raise over $100 million for ALS research, 3,500 per cent more than the funds raised in the previous year (Diamond 2014). Moreover, a number of social media practices are replacing traditional methods of reaching and assisting consumers, customer service included (Heller and Parasnis 2011).

Yet, at the same time, the proliferation of social media has made the Internet a crowded place, in which users are inundated with information – sometimes even substituting the role of company marketing and public relations teams (Holt 2016) – and it is becoming increasingly difficult for firms to get noticed (Charlesworth 2014). Thus, whereas some businesses are already deploying a solid strategic approach to social media, others are still struggling to find their path.

This chapter aims to guide marketing professionals as they attempt to determine how to leverage the opportunity offered by social media. I first provide a brief overview of the current social media landscape from a marketer's perspective, highlighting some of the major social media and their particular strengths. Next, I provide an actionable five-step road map that a firm can implement to extract value from its social media presence. I conclude by briefly looking forward to the opportunities and challenges that lie ahead.

The social media landscape in 2016

New social media platforms and features are continuously emerging, such that a platform that seems exciting or worthy of an investment today might be irrelevant tomorrow (Kaplan and Haenlein 2010). Nevertheless, the most popular and populated social networks have not changed in years, giants such as Facebook and Twitter, and more recent additions such as Snapchat and Tumblr.

Facebook remains the goliath of social media platforms, with over 1.6 billion monthly active users, and accounting for one in every six minutes spent online, and one in every five minutes spent on mobile (Walters 2016). Other platforms have their own unique strengths that marketers should be aware of: for example, users on Instagram are more likely than users on other platforms to interact with the brands they follow, and Twitter has the highest average number of posts per brand per week (Elliott 2015); Snapchat is highly popular among young people (the app is used by 60 per cent of smartphone users under the age of 34; Walters 2016); LinkedIn and Google+ remain mainstays with very high penetration, while Pinterest and Tumblr have attracted marketers' attention thanks to their considerable growth over the last number of years (ComScore 2015).

Beyond these well-known social networks, there is a diverse, ever-changing universe of social media channels serving different scopes (Kietzmann *et al.* 2011), ranging from Blogger, which serves conversational purposes, to Periscope, which enables live streaming video sharing, and more. Thus, marketing professionals must constantly monitor the evolution of the social media landscape, and adapt their presence and strategies accordingly.

Strategizing social media presence: an actionable five-step road map

Given that consumers discuss brands and products on social media, thereby shaping their own opinions and those of others, it might seem obvious that brands should be present on social media channels to leverage such opportunities. However, not every firm is successful in this. Accordingly, this section provides a five-step approach for developing a strategic social media presence that delivers business value (see Figure 16.1).

These steps include: (i) SET strategic objectives; (ii) CHOOSE a platform (or small set of platforms) to focus on; (iii) LAUNCH content, listen to reactions, learn

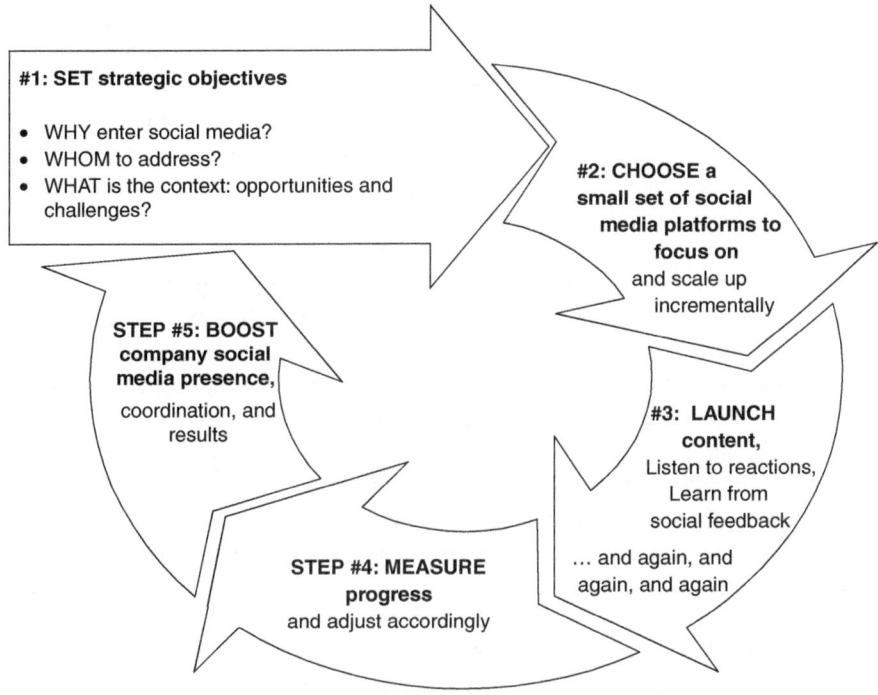

#1: SET strategic objectives

- WHY enter social media?
- WHOM to address?
- WHAT is the context: opportunities and challenges?

#2: CHOOSE a small set of social media platforms to focus on and scale up incrementally

STEP #5: BOOST company social media presence, coordination, and results

#3: LAUNCH content, Listen to reactions, Learn from social feedback

... and again, and again, and again

STEP #4: MEASURE progress and adjust accordingly

FIGURE 16.1 Social media road map.

from feedback, and repeat; (iv) MEASURE value created through social media strategy; and (v) BOOST social media presence to enhance results over time.

Step #1: SET social media objectives

Generally speaking, strategy is about defining guidelines to pursue an established objective, i.e. 'where you would like to be and how to get there' (Sola and Couturier 2013). Clearly, in the social media context, strategy development entails leveraging social possibilities. In particular, marketers should begin to develop their strategies by addressing three seemingly simple but actually tricky questions:

1. WHY enter social media?
2. WHOM should we address?
3. WHAT is the context?

Answering question one means defining what the firm is trying to achieve by entering social media. Firms may have diverse motivations for participating, including: building brand awareness or engagement; stimulating consumers to perform a specific action (e.g. making a purchase); or gaining insights into consumer behaviour. At this stage in the strategy development process, it is advisable to 'keep it simple' and focus on a limited number of goals. Such simplicity can enable marketers to better isolate the most effective social media 'recipe', the 'how to', or the tactics to deploy towards the selected objectives and the appropriate metrics to use to evaluate progress, discussed in what follows (Stoke 2013). Conversely, too many objectives reflect a lack of focus and may even be equivalent to having no objectives at all. It is also important to remember that while strategic objectives should remain fixed, tactics can – and should – change over time, to adapt to emerging opportunities (Wilson *et al.* 2011).

Addressing question two – the whom – means acknowledging that brands join social networks in order to build long-lasting relationships with their customers, a process that entails learning who these customers are: What are they like? What are they exposed to? What do they enjoy? Whom do they interact with? Achieving an understanding of one's customer base is crucial to enabling a firm to position branded stimuli in the right places, and beneficial for increasing user engagement (Edelman 2010), or even encouraging followers to transition from merely 'liking' a brand to actively spreading word of mouth about it.

Finally, responding to question three – understanding the context and the opportunities available – means dedicating time to business intelligence, and investigating whether there are any industry 'must haves', or social media trends that the firm must follow. One widely-adopted practice in this regard is to observe key competitors' social media presences to determine where and how rivals are active and to devise an appropriate competitive response (Kietzmann *et al.* 2011). For example, the extent to which key competitors are active in a specific network should influence executives as they attempt to determine how much effort to invest in cultivating a presence in that network. In particular, firms should bear in mind that choosing not to participate in some platforms creates opportunities for competitors to do so.

Answering these three strategic questions should enable managers to identify clear, overarching strategic objectives and to begin to devise an appropriate plan for pursuing them, as well as a preliminary short list of suitable platforms that they might consider focusing on.

Step #2: CHOOSE the right platform to get started on, but start small

As suggested above, the process of setting strategic objectives should enable managers to come up with a short list of social media platforms where they might consider focusing their efforts. In the second step, managers should assess the opportunities offered by each platform and thereby determine how to prioritize their various options. A fundamental premise here is that, with so many actors striving for online mass attention, companies seeking to emerge in social media must understand that building a valuable presence in any given social media channel takes skill and hard work, and that it does not happen overnight.

After assessing the availability of internal resources, managers should subject each platform on the short list to an accurate cost-benefit analysis. A helpful exercise in this regard is to outline the pros and cons of starting with one specific platform rather than another. Various considerations should enter the

BOX 16.1 THEORY IN PRACTICE:

Examples of considerations in selecting a social media channel

Benefits	• A firm seeking to establish itself as an **expert in a specific field** might opt for blogs (an in-house blog, or guest posts on established blogs), or micro-blogging activities on Twitter; • A firm seeking to **hire new members** might focus on professional networks such as LinkedIn, and broaden the visibility of job offers on Twitter or Facebook.
Audience	• A firm that wishes to **appeal to multiple age groups** might prefer more mature social media channels such as Facebook; • A firm focusing on **young people** might focus more on Snapchat.
Resources/ content	• A firm that plans to share video content might focus more on YouTube or Vimeo; • A firm that plans to issue frequent news updates might focus more on Twitter or Facebook.

platform selection process, including: benefits offered and their compatibility with the firm's strategic objectives; characteristics of the target audience; and firm resources and capacity to deploy them on social media, i.e. in terms of the type and format of content to be produced (see Box 16.1 for an example). Managers should also take into account the fact that different platforms serve different purposes, and, accordingly, their user bases access them at different times of day, and with different expectations (Kaplan and Haenlein 2010).

After prioritizing the various networks on the short list, the manager should carry out a final cross-check, by comparing the list with the set of platforms on which the firm's key competitors are active. It is useful to focus both on platforms where competitors are absent and where they are present, to have a benchmark for one's own social media activities and results, and to determine whether it makes sense to stay off the platforms or whether it is time to enter them.

In general, it is advisable to start small and to focus on a limited set of social media channels that really have the potential to enable the firm to reach its objectives and audience. Further, firms should take the time to write down their social media strategies and prepare to scale them up by devising a set of guidelines that can be applied to any form of social media (Kaplan and Haenlein 2010).

Step #3: LAUNCH, listen and learn

Once the firm has mapped out the social media channels where it wishes to focus its attention, it is time to begin to populate those channels. Readers are probably familiar with the adage 'content is king'. Step #3 is about creating that content: crafting valuable posts that target communities, while making the firm's voice stand out in the crowd and get clicked-through, commented on and shared.

The extent to which a firm gets noticed will be a function of the time and resources it invests in its social media content. Marketers should start by focusing on making people aware that the firm exists and encouraging them to simply 'like' or follow the company's page. The next step is to reinforce that relationship, by *launching* potentially valuable content, *listening* to online reactions to that content and *learning* from that feedback to develop the next wave of content. Then, the 'launch, listen, learn' cycle is repeated.

Generally speaking, developing great content to *launch* means figuring out how to grab the audience's attention. Stoke (2013) proposes four means of achieving this: (i) enlightening the community with useful information about a brand or a product category; (ii) teaching something new; (iii) evoking an emotion; or (iv) providing entertainment ('social media' contains the word 'social' for a reason). In all cases, a firm might seek to inspire social media conversations about the brand, instead of promoting the brand directly – for example, providing 'how to' advice on topics related to the firm's offer, rather than promoting the offer itself, and letting the community discuss it. Moreover, a brand should strive to make its 'voice' unique and recognizable.

A pilot test of the quality of the editorial plan designed is advisable (Lardi and Fuchs 2013), for example by individuating a list of helpful community members – because of their influence or high frequency of interaction with the brand – and inviting them into a Facebook group to preview and pre-discuss the firm's content strategy.

Feedback is a precious ally, and social listening is fundamental in ensuring social media success. Listening is about activating an online radar to observe, digest, learn and, when needed, react to the community's actions and reactions (Charlesworth 2014).

Listening starts by monitoring reactions to deployed social media initiatives, to validate audience's preferences (social networks' embedded insights are very helpful in this regard), and goes much further too, including both consumer-to-business direct questions posed on owned channels, as well as firm-related spontaneous consumer-to-consumer exchanges (Harrysson *et al.* 2012). Moreover, listening to user-generated content about competition can provide useful insights, increasing knowledge about consumer sentiment towards brands and products, and establishing the company's online reputation. Various service sites offer tools for online monitoring (see, for example, Social Mention or Hootsuite), navigating through a variety of networks (e.g. Simply Measured scans eighty sites) and returning a number of ready-to-use metrics (e.g. mention strength and reach, sentiment etc.).

Last but not least, firms should *learn* from users' conversations and use the information they gain to enhance their social media strategies – or even their business strategies.

Even negative feedback can turn into an opportunity, by acting as an early warning sign of the company's weaknesses in products, operations or customer service (Baer 2016). Given that relatively few companies actually address their customers' queries, a firm that shows it is willing to listen and assist can positively affect consumers' engagement and can even turn critics into new fans. Conversely, ignoring negative feedback could give a negative signal about the company's responsiveness, and even put the brand's reputation at risk. Comcast, for example, reversed negative buzz and even won back engagement by setting up a @ComcastCare Twitter profile (in the early days of Twitter), with four magic words as its signature – 'How can we help?'.

Step #4: MEASURE, analyse and adjust

While most executives understand the power of social media and want their companies to participate, many are simultaneously reluctant or unable to think strategically about social media, or to allocate funding to such activities (Kietzmann *et al.* 2011). This disparity might stem from the fact that it is still difficult to measure the value generated by social media in terms of the firm's bottom line. In other words, marketers nowadays are squeezed between the mantra that firms 'must be on social media', and the challenge of using traditional analysis approaches and metrics to justify the allocation of resources to social media (Fisher 2009). Thus, to evaluate the performance of its social media strategy, a firm must determine a set of metrics that will enable it to monitor its progress towards its objectives and to adjust the road map accordingly.

For example, an indicator such as the number of followers provides a valid proxy of a brand's social popularity; however, this metric is of limited use in informing strategic decisions. Another metric of interest is user engagement; however, as engagement can manifest in a variety of ways, it is important to develop metrics of engagement that correspond to the company's objectives and the tactics deployed to achieve these. For example, if the company's objective is to raise awareness, then impressions, clicks and click-through rate are valuable indicators of success. If the objective is to increase word of mouth, then the company might measure referrals and repeat purchases. Finally, to assess the impact of social media strategy on sales, leads and conversions should be measured.

Yet, even if a company has decided to focus on certain metrics of engagement, it may still find it difficult to establish a connection between those metrics and the firm's bottom line. Indeed, evaluating the return on investment (ROI) of social media programmes remains a critical challenge: in a recent survey of marketers (Simply Measured 2016), 61.1 per cent of respondents identified measurement of ROI as the top challenge in social media marketing, and only 9.4 per cent stated that they were able to quantify the revenue driven by their firms' social media presence. Hoffman and Fodor (2010) believe that marketers are approaching ROI the wrong way; they suggest that, instead of the traditional approach of focusing on companies' investments in marketing, firms should turn ROI 'on its head' and monitor their customers' investments in their social relationships with the brand. This approach may reveal the likelihood of long-term payoff, and enable marketers to make smarter and more consumer-driven decisions.

Step #5: Boost presence and results

Once a firm has determined that its deployed social media strategy is moving in the right direction, the last step in the proposed road map is to amplify the firm's social media presence and reach. In practice, firms typically adopt three approaches to doing this.

The first is to engage in an authentic dialogue with the online community, by showing the human side of the brand. This approach entails using social media as a giant megaphone to enable real people's voices to be heard – both inside and outside the company – and to enable them to become active contributors to the firm's social media pages. In other words, the firm should give value to all supporters of the brand – employees, customers, followers, partners and influencers – and let them give life to the brand with their fresh and authentic stories. After all, 90 per cent of us trust peer recommendations, whereas only 14 per cent trust branded communication (Nielsen 2015); thus, supporters' genuine voices and passion are far more powerful than direct attempts by the brand to communicate its own strengths. A useful approach here is to balance branded messages with those of supporters. More generally, allowing advocates of the brand to make their voices heard can serve to continue to boost these individuals' engagement and desire to spread word of mouth on behalf of the brand.

A second means of expanding a firm's reach in a social media setting is to encourage social sharing, that is, asking community members to spread branded content throughout their social networks. The more a brand's content is shared, the greater the potential for a snowball effect, in which the message is passed on to people who do not yet follow (or even know) the brand (Stoke 2013). A good practice in this sense is to identify top influencers in the field, as these individuals account

TABLE 16.1 Social media DOs and DON'Ts

Dos	DON'Ts
DO always focus on audience first!	DON'T isolate social media *(fully integrate it into the overall strategy)*
Have a few smart objectives and key indicators to assess progress	DON'T always speak about 'yourself' *(inspire and pass the voice to the community)*
Launch, listen, learn *(and again, and again)*	DON'T ignore negative posts *(turn critiques into opportunities)*
Add value in a unique and human way	DON'T get distracted by latest news *(focus on strategic social media)*
Write down social media strategy and spread it around the whole company	DON'T take it too seriously *(be social, entertainment is key)*

for a disproportionate share of the total social influence generated: 5 per cent of recommenders account for about 45 per cent of social activity (Bughin 2015).

Finally, the third path to boosting social visibility involves adding some paid influence (e.g. paying to 'boost' posts) into the marketing mix. Sponsored content is an important complement to both organic community-management efforts in terms of generating awareness and engagement, and earned influence. Moreover, thanks to their user profiling capabilities, social media platforms typically provide firms with the capacity to target specific user demographics and interests.

Table 16.1 provides a summary of social media DOs and DON'Ts to foster strategic thinking regarding a firm's social media presence.

A look forward

As this chapter has shown, the rise of social media has created numerous marketing opportunities for brands, enabling them to interact with and engage their customers in more genuine and participative ways. However, to fully exploit these opportunities, marketers must develop effective social media strategies. The chapter has provided a road map that can assist marketers in this endeavour, with the ultimate goals of informing customers, engaging them and extracting value from them. By executing each step of this road map carefully, while simultaneously remaining flexible and open to new developments in the social media landscape, firms can give themselves the potential to seize upon a vast array of possibilities: learning about and adapting to new content formats (e.g. mobile and video); transferring traditional services to the social space (e.g. customer service and care); or even transforming the entire organization into a social entity, in which all members and departments communicate with and obtain insights from the outside world.

References

Baer, J. 2016. *Hug Your Haters: How to Embrace Complaints and Keep Your Customers.* New York: Portfolio/Penguin.

Bughin, J. 2015. 'Getting a sharper picture of social media's influence'. *McKinsey Quarterly*, 3, 8–11.

Charlesworth, A. 2014. *Digital Marketing: A Practical Approach* (second edition). London: Routledge.

Chaykowski, K. 2015. 'Number of Facebook business pages climbs to 50 million with new messaging tools'. Available at: https://www.forbes.com/sites/kathleen chaykowski/2015/12/08/facebook-business-pages-climb-to-50-million-with-new-messaging-tools/#100440f66991. [Accessed 10 June 2016].

ComScore 2015. 'US digital future in focus 2015'. Available at https://www.comscore. com/Insights/Presentations-and-Whitepapers/2015/2015-US-Digital-Future-in-Focus [Accessed 3 June 2016].

Diamond, D. 2014. 'The ALS Ice Bucket Challenge has raised $100 million—and counting'. *Forbes*, 29 August. Available at: https://www.forbes.com/sites/dandiamond/2014/08/29/the-als-ice-bucket-challenge-has-raised-100m-but-its-finally-cooling-off/#7a8e9bb25cfb [Accessed 15 April 2016].

Edelman, D. C. 2010. 'Branding in the digital age: you're spending your money in all the wrong places'. *Harvard Business Review*, 88:12, p. 62–69.

Elliott, N. 2015. 'How does your brand stack up on Facebook, Twitter, and Instagram?' Available at http://blogs.forrester.com/nate_elliott/15-09-15-how_does_your_brand_stack_up_on_facebook_twitter_and_instagram [Accessed 10 June 2016].

Fisher, T. J. 2009. 'ROI in social media: a look at the arguments'. *Journal of Database Marketing & Customer Strategy Management*, 16:3, p. 189–195.

Heller Baird, C., and G. Parasnis. 2011. 'From social media to social customer relationship management'. *Strategy & Leadership*, 39:5, p. 30–37.

Harrysson, M., E. Metayer, and H. Sarrazin. 2012. 'How "social intelligence" can guide decisions'. *McKinsey Quarterly*, 4, p. 81–89.

Hoffman, D. L. and M. Fodor. 2010. 'Can you measure the ROI of your social media marketing?' *MIT Sloan Management Review*, 52:1, p. 41–49.

Holt, D. 2016. 'How digital has changed branding'. *Harvard Business Review*, 94:5, p. 18.

Kaplan, A. M. and M. Haenlein. 2010. 'Users of the world, unite! The challenges and opportunities of social media'. *Business Horizons*, 53:1, p. 59–68.

Kietzmann, J. H., K. Hermkens, I. P. McCarthy, and B. S. Silvestre. 2011. 'Social media? Get serious! Understanding the functional building blocks of social media'. *Business Horizons*, 54:3, p. 241–251.

Lardi, K. and R. Fuchs. 2013. *Social Media Strategy*. Zurich: vdf Hochschulverlag AG.

Nielsen. 2015. 'Global trust in advertising report: September 2015'. Available at https://www.nielsen.com/content/dam/nielsenglobal/apac/docs/reports/2015/nielsen-global-trust-in-advertising-report-september-2015.pdf [Accessed 24 September 2015].

Simply Measured. 2016. 'The state of social marketing 2016'. Simply Measured (2016). The state of social marketing 2016. Downloadable at http://simplymeasured.com/blog/introducing-the-2016-state-of-social-marketing-report/#sm.0000ti5qzy1atcf4fs0bun4wj8w9o [Accessed 1 July 2016].

Sola, D. and J. Couturier. 2013. *How to Think Strategically: Your Roadmap to Innovation and Results*. London: Pearson UK.

Stoke, R. 2013. *eMarketing: The Essential Guide to Marketing in a Digital World* (fifth edition). Cape Town: Quirk eMarketing.

Walters, K. 2016. '125+ essential social media statistics every marketer should know in 2016'. Available at https://blog.hootsuite.com/social-media-statistics-for-social-media-managers/ [Accessed 27 July 2016].

Wilson, H. J., P. J. Guinan, S. Parise, and B. D. Weinberg. 2011. 'What's your social media strategy?'. *Harvard Business Review*, 89:7/8, p. 23–25.

17

SALIENT ROLE AND CENTRALITY OF TRUST IN SOCIAL MEDIA MARKETING

Anil Bhat and Nirankush Datta

Introduction

By offering almost free or low-budget marketing options, online social media have emerged as the great leveller for the David and Goliath in the modern marketing space, fast replacing the earlier era of print or electronic marketing media. While Fortune 500 companies are using social media marketing to a great extent (refer to Barnes *et al.* 2015 for more details), the smaller rivals are not lagging far behind. The sheer volume of consumer base actively crowding social media daily makes this new form of marketing a coveted one, which no marketer can afford to ignore, for reaching out to new customers, communicating with existing ones or even pleasing disgruntled consumers by providing delightful service.

Until now, most organizations have been using social media marketing as an extension of their conventional marketing activities to increase exposure to their brands, enhance traffic to their websites, develop a loyal fan base, provide insights into the marketplace, generate leads, improve search engine rankings, grow business partnerships, improve sales and reduce marketing expenditure (Stelzner 2015). Thus, their brand pages would primarily redirect consumers to company websites, offer sneak peeks of the latest products, distribute discount coupons, or offer customers an insight into the work environment of their preferred brands. But the major social media sites, like Facebook, Twitter, Pinterest, Instagram and so on, have already started rolling out direct sales options from within their social networks (Lorenze 2014; Sorokina 2015). In these circumstances, companies need to go back to the basics of social media marketing to reap the full benefit of these powerful media. The rise of social media marketing was predominantly aided by the availability of trustworthy recommendations from general consumers. Hence, in the next few years, the battle in the social media space will be won by those organizations that earn consumers' trust and turn them into loyal evangelists. Therefore, a thorough understanding of influencing factors of trust in social media marketing and their expected outcome gains vital importance for modern marketers and researchers alike.

This chapter points to the importance of trust in a business scenario, followed by deliberation on probable avenues of investigation into the antecedents of trust in the context of social media marketing and their effect on certain outcomes. Borrowing heavily from earlier research works in various disciplines, like marketing, information systems, sociology and psychology, among others, and previous studies in online marketing, this chapter endeavours to introduce the reader to some theoretical concepts that deserve attention for enhancing the effectiveness of social media marketing in general, and trust in the context of online social media marketing in particular. Thus, it provides direction for research avenues as well as a rough guidance to social media marketing managers to evaluate their efforts with the help of a predefined matrix.

Importance of trust

Trust is of vital importance for interpersonal and commercial relationships (Morgan and Hunt 1994), that is, wherever risk, uncertainty or interdependence occurs. It is important for both virtual teams and e-Commerce spaces (Ba *et al.* 2003; Hoffman *et al.* 1999; Jarvenpaa *et al.* 2000) affecting individual consumers (Schurr and Ozanne, 1985), as well as for industrial buyers.

Increased transaction complexity in computer mediated communication leads to the higher importance of trust (Mishra 1996). Lack of consumer trust may significantly reduce the potentialof Internet marketing to consumers (Ganguly *et al.* 2010). Thus, trust is considered a critical factor in stimulating purchases over the Internet (Gefen and Straub 2004; Kim *et al.* 2004; Klein and Quelch 2015; Lim *et al.* 2006; Pavlou and Fygenson 2006).

Proper utilization of different kinds of social media applications may enhance the feeling of social presence by supporting two-way interactions between online shoppers (Karimov and Brengman 2011) and helping to increase consumer trust in organizations, especially in retailers. On the other hand, the relatively unregulated freedom of expression offered by social media sites to general consumers may not always be positive. It has been observed that negative word of mouth has a greater effect than its positive counterpart (Park and Lee 2009; Solomon 2006), potentially jeopardizing a company's effort to gain consumer trust. Hence, a thorough understanding of the factors affecting formation of trust in the context of social media marketing is extremely important.

In spite of its immense importance, empirical research on trust in the context of social media marketing is very limited, as it is a comparatively new form of marketing and many researchers perceive it as a slightly different form of traditional e-Commerce (Dutta and Bhat 2016a). It needs to be borne in mind that 'Social Media Marketing ... provides meaning and connection between brands and consumers and offers a personal channel and currency for user-centered networking and social interaction' (Chi 2011, p. 46). Thus, though it thrives on electronic communication, social media marketing differs from traditional e-Commerce by virtue of the superior power given to the general consumer. Moreover, transparent intercommunication between sellers and buyers, as well as design restrictions placed on the pages maintained by sellers on these social media sites, adds to the differentiating characteristics of social media marketing. Because of these characteristics, the effectiveness of social media marketing calls for further in-depth research. Undoubtedly, research on trust in the context of social media marketing should be based on earlier works, but it should also include an amalgamation of diversified fields of study, namely marketing, information systems, psychology and sociology among others, for a richer understanding.

Antecedents of trust

Based on studies by various authors (Barney and Hansen 1994; Doney and Cannon 1997; McKnight *et al.* 2002a; Walczuch *et al.* 2001), antecedents of trust can be categorized into four classes (Dutta and Bhat 2016b; Dutta and Bhat 2014): (a) cognition-based (e.g. privacy, security, system reliability, information quality etc.); (b) affect-based (e.g. reputation, third party seals, referrals, recommendations, buyers' feedback, word-of-mouth etc.); (c) experience-based (e.g. familiarity, Internet experience, e-Commerce experience etc.); and (d) personality-oriented (e.g. disposition to trust, shopping style, etc.) (Figure 17.1).

Trust can be studied from four different levels (Kelton *et al.* 2008): (i) individual (personality trait); (ii) interpersonal (trust placed on one entity by another); (iii) relational (mutual trust between two entities); and (iv) societal/system (trust in a community). This is quite similar to the framework put forward by McKnight and Chervany (2002), who suggest three high levels of trust, namely (i) dispositional trust, (ii) institutional trust and (iii) interpersonal trust (Figure 17.1).

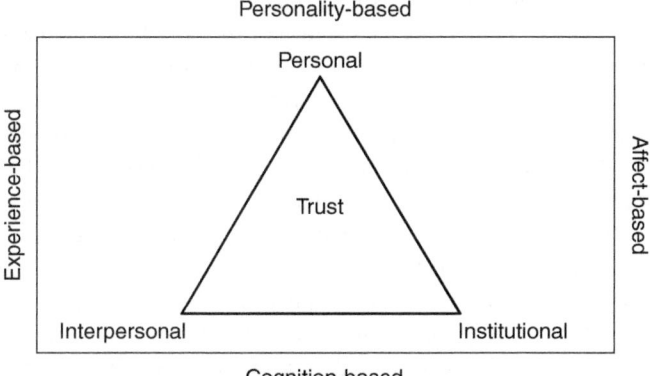

FIGURE 17.1 Perspectives of study of trust.

Various facets of these different levels of trust can have different effects on their outcomes. For example, interpersonal trust is characterized by integrity, ability and benevolence (Gefen and Straub 2004; McKnight *et al.* 1998). Integrity primarily affects intentions to engage in a purchase, while ability basically affects intentions to inquire about the product without actually purchasing it (Gefen and Heart 2006). On the other hand, benevolence has a stronger effect on price premiums than ability and integrity (credibility) (Pavlou and Dimoka 2006). Similarly, propensity to trust or dispositional trust acts as the foundation which affects more case-specific trust situations (Merritt and Ilgen 2008), influencing consumers' trust in Internet shopping (Cheung and Lee 2001; Lee and Turban 2001).

Institutional trust refers to the mechanism in which the technology provider is trusted (e.g. Facebook or Twitter) for providing proper structural assurance to facilitate trust in the trustee who is utilizing it as the online platform (Dutta and Bhat 2016c). Structural assurance arises from the perceived existence of guarantees and regulations, as well as technical and legal resources, due to an appropriate structure for promoting successful interaction in a particular environment (Shapiro 1987; Zucker 1986). This may influence a vital factor known as situational normality, which is generally considered another dimension of institution-based trust indicating a person's expectation of a successful outcome in lieu of taking a risk in a particular environment (Baier 1986). Although structural assurance is more pronounced in e-Commerce, it is still in a nascent stage in social media marketing. This can be attributed to the evolving nature of this new form of marketing whereby the rules and regulations governing its usage are changed regularly. Moreover, direct purchase from various sellers using a social media marketing platform is quite a new phenomenon to consumers. Thus, their perception of it is also rather weak. While this logic may seem to reduce the importance of structural assurance in a consideration of the antecedents of trust in social media marketing, it should in fact be of vital importance to the developers of various social media marketing platforms as well as to marketers, who are responsible for choosing the appropriate platform for their marketing efforts.

Deriving from these earlier models, antecedents of trust in social media marketing can also be studied based on their sources. This seems more logical, easier to comprehend, analyze and implement from a practitioner's point of view. The sources of antecedents of trust can be arrived at from the very definition of social media marketing, also called social commerce or s-Commerce by different authors (Zhang and Benyoucef 2016), which refers to the 'exchange-related activities that occur in, or are influenced by, an individual's social network in computer-mediated social environments, where the activities correspond to the need recognition, pre-purchase, purchase, and post-purchase stages of a focal exchange' (Yadav *et al.* 2013, p. 312). Thus, this definition clearly points to four vital sources to be considered: (a) seller or online store; (b) individual's social network; (c) computer mediated social environment; and (d) individual personality traits. These four sources can be referred to as perceived store characteristics, perceived structural characteristics of social media, perceived design characteristics of social media and individual characteristics. Antecedents of trust arising from these different sources may affect both interpersonal trust and institutional trust, whereas propensity to trust is one of the important components of individual characteristics.

The later parts of this chapter briefly discuss some of the factors influencing these sources of antecedents of trust in social media marketing. Social network sites have gained the most importance and popularity among various kinds of social media. Hence, the concepts related to social media are often explained with reference to social network sites.

Store characteristics

While organizations or online stores established prior to the emergence of social media marketing generally have their customers arriving at their social media pages from their websites, it may be a bidirectional flow for new business entities, with more consumers visiting websites of online stores from their social media pages. These consumers or prospective customers may form ideas about various store characteristics from the social media page itself. Some of these perceived store characteristics are brand knowledge, reputation, store size and transaction risks. These perceived store characteristics in social media marketing are very important for the sellers, as they have the maximum control on these. Thus, stores should attempt to improve their associated brand knowledge and enhance their reputation, while trying to reduce perceived risk of transaction.

Brand knowledge is reflected by brand awareness and brand image (Keller 1993). Awareness is a necessary condition, although not sufficient, to evoke trust. It can influence perception of risk and trusting belief associated with the online store or brand (Lowry *et al.* 2008; Yoon 2002). By enhancing brand knowledge through effective use of social media marketing, online stores may increase trust in them. Its importance is underscored by the fact that increased exposure is the most sought after benefit of social media marketing as perceived by marketers (Stelzner 2015).

Managing reputation in the present era of social media marketing is considered among the most difficult tasks for executives. Using social media, consumers can communicate quickly, creating viral messages that have the potential to make or break the fortune of an organization. Thus, executives need to protect their online reputation through consistent relationship-enhancing behaviour, as this is significantly related to online trust (Yoon 2002), acting as an antecedent of it (McKnight *et al.* 2002b).

Reduced perception of risk increases trustworthiness (Ganesan 1994), thus acting as a mechanism to increase trust (Dieberger *et al.* 2000; Resnick *et al.* 2000; Resnick and Varian 1997). Although perceived risk may not affect intention, it can influence attitude towards shopping on the Internet (Jarvenpaa and Todd 1997). Consumer fear of marketing through social media has been found to play a statistically significant role in the formation of attitudes towards marketing with social media (Akar and Topçu 2011).

Earlier research has also established that perceived size of the store plays an important role in evoking trust (Doney and Cannon 1997; Jarvenpaa *et al*. 2000), since a large store indicates large investment, greater expertise, availability of a support system (Hsu 2008), control over the suppliers and ability to overcome unexpected events at their own expense, thereby achieving trust from its earlier customers (Pavlou 2003; Koufaris and Hampton-Sosa 2004). Declarations about the variety of product categories, the number of products in each category, the number of customers who might have already purchased from the store and the number of people talking about the store on social media provide cues about the size of the store.

Organizations, especially online stores, utilizing social media marketing may highlight various cues to enhance perception regarding these characteristics and thereby attempt to increase their trustworthiness.

Structural characteristics of social media

Trust can be analyzed from a social networking approach, assuming that individual actors are embedded within a network of relationships (Jones *et al* 1997). Social Identity Theory (Tajfel 1978) indicates that individuals derive their identity by differentiating the group to which they belong from others (Sohn 2009). The sense of community and belongingness exhibited by different social media is characterized by different kinds and levels of structural attributes, which are influenced by the participants, complexity and relations among the participants, as well as content, direction, strength of their relations, composition derived from their social attributes (Garton *et al*. 1997), network topology and informal social circles (Burt 1995). On the other hand, Social Exchange Theory (Blau 1964) reveals that people participate in social interactions expecting social rewards such as approval, status and respect (Wasko and Faraj 2005). Therefore, interpersonal trust in a social network community may be attributed to the closeness and familiarity developed among its members resulting from these social interactions (Ng 2013). As various virtual communities are often inspired, founded or maintained by marketers to drive their social media marketing strategy, the composition and nature of these communities may influence trust among their participants.

Depending on amount of time, emotional intensity, intimacy (mutual confiding) and reciprocity, people experience different strengths of relationship or tie (Granovetter 1973). Common Ground Theory (Clark 1992) suggests that shared understanding and tailor-made response make the communication process easier among people with strong ties. Successful exchange of useful information by people sharing strong ties subsequently results in formation of trust among them (Adam and Rončević 2003; Burke and Kraut 2013; Panovich *et al*. 2012). On the other hand, by placing weak ties within a social context of friends and facilitating the verification of their identity (Donath 2007), social network sites add trust to weak ties (Donath 2007). This tie strength is also positively associated with electronic word-of-mouth (e-WOM) behaviour (Chu and Kim 2011). Strong ties are

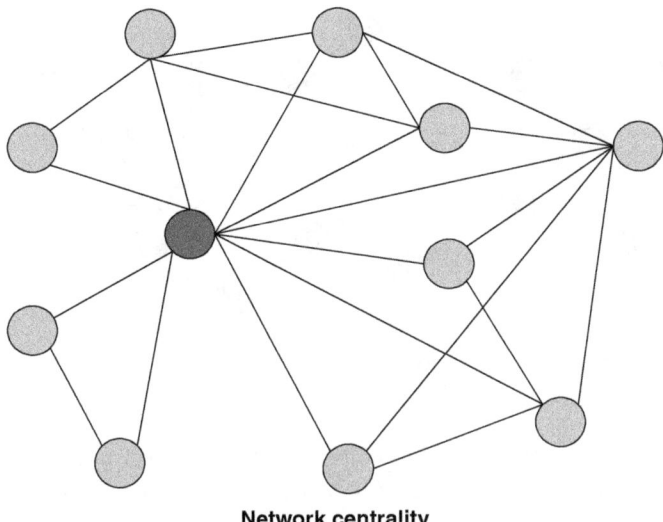

Network centrality

FIGURE 17.2   Network centrality.

influential in the consumer's decision making process (Brown and Reingen 1987), while weak ties too display an important bridging function in dissemination of word-of-mouth (WOM) (Rogers 2003).

Individuals occupying a central position play an important role in the dissemination of information and in influencing others (Chau and Xu 2007), thereby acting as opinion leaders (Figure 17.2). The size of an individual's friend list, their ranking in the network, the number and frequency of their posts and the responses generated in response to those posts, are all indicative of their centrality in the network (Chengqi *et al.* 2010). Access to more information makes such an individual more involved with others, resulting in that person having more influence in the trust building process in the network.

A dense network increases the degree of trust (Sparrowe *et al.* 2001) and facilitates the flow of information (Rowley 1997) (Figure 17.3). Stronger connections between individuals in a network reinforce the social norm through mutual influence. This minimizes uncertainties and creates a sense of belonging, resulting in likely enhancement of trust (Chua and Morris 2006). Network density positively affects interpersonal trust (Coleman 1988; Millar and Choi 2009; Wong and Boh 2010) and has a significant effect on an individual's intention to pass along e-WOM (Sohn 2009).

Collective Mind Theory indicates that cognition of structure emerging from the collective meaning of a group helps in the coordination of activities (Weick and Roberts 1993). Again, the Theory of Planned Behavior (Fishbein and Ajzen 1975) holds that behaviour is a multiplicative function of expectations of what others consider to be socially desirable and the motivation to comply with these expectations. Thus, it helps to conceptualize the effects of group cohesiveness on

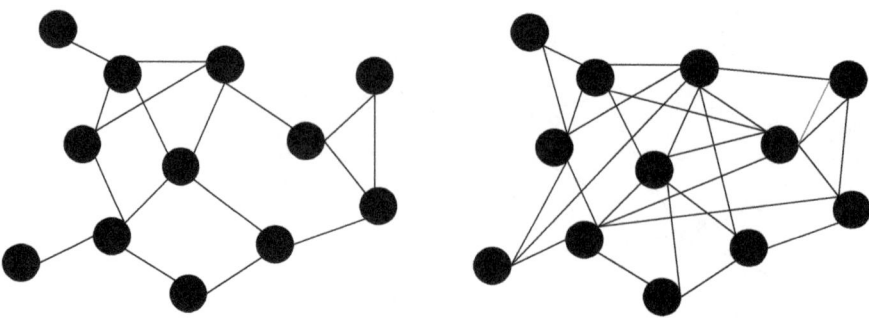

FIGURE 17.3 Network density (left: low density, right: high density).

group members. Teams, especially with high cohesiveness, can exert powerful influence on individuals to conform (Baron *et al*. 1996), putting personal feelings, attitudes and beliefs aside to act in a socially appropriate manner. Therefore, being embedded in a cohesive network accelerates the creation of trust with the help of accumulation of positive experiences (Granovetter 1992).

Exchange of information most frequently occurs among those who share certain common attributes attached externally, like socio-demographics (e.g. age, sex, race/ethnicity, education), or states embedded internally, like psychological (e.g. intelligence, attitude, aspiration), behavioural and interpersonal characteristics (Rogers 2003; Rogers and Bhowmik 1970). This state of homophily among individuals subjects them towards a greater level of interpersonal trust than is expected among dissimilar individuals (Ruef *et al*. 2003) by enhancing perceived credibility. Homophily can result in increased emotional and cognitive trust by enhancing affective and cognitive involvement to the network (Shin *et al*. 2011).

Social capital, a concept closely related to but different from tie strength, is the investment in personal relationships or social structure to facilitate individual or collective gains (Glanville and Bienenstock 2009). Online social interaction has been found to be positively related to purpose-oriented bridging social capital enhancing relatively thinner generalized trust, rather than thick localized trust gained from bonding social capital with emphasis on emotional charge (Best and Krueger 2006; Briggs 2003; Ellison *et al*. 2007; Pigg and Crank 2004). Researchers found that bridging social capital is positively related to perceptions of information usefulness on Facebook (Gray *et al*. 2013; Lampe *et al*. 2012). Trust builds along with usefulness of information shared in a community.

FirCry.com – a primarily online retailer of baby products in India – has reaped the benefits of these attributes by bringing together the mothers of newborn babies through their Facebook page and their blogs, where mothers can engage in conversation among themselves. Because of the shared characteristics of being a mother to a newborn baby, the contributions of each person are highly valued among the group members. The conversations, which often revolve around day-to-day issues faced by parents, especially the mothers, result in highly valued social capital for the members. This entire process facilitates the formation of trust not only in the members, but also in the store that provides such a platform, thereby increasing the probability of spreading e-WOM and encouraging more purchases (Dutta and Bhat 2016d).

Leading beauty product brand Dove discovered homophily in the concern about physical appearance among its consumers, 80 per cent of whom generally encounter negative comments on social media that critique their looks. Moreover, the women themselves critique their look the most on social media sites. On several occasions, Dove teamed up with social networking sites, like Twitter, or used their pages on other social media sites (e.g. Facebook or YouTube) to encourage women to start conversations. This goes beyond simple selling of their products and helps the formation of a cohesive community. The result is enhanced trust in the brand which is seen as being on social media not only to sell its products, but also to care for its customers. These advertisement campaigns were marked by the addition of thousands of followers and the huge spread of e-WOM.

Undoubtedly, maintaining a proper balance of the attributes discussed in this section requires a lot of effort by the social media marketing manager. Marketers should identify and utilize people in a central position in their network with the aim of building a cohesive and dense social network structure having the right mix of homophily and tie strength for generation of social capital. The right mix is dependent on the expected outcome of the social media marketing strategy. But the common focus of any marketer should be to drive conversation among the participants of their virtual community, rather than using the community space solely as another place to disseminate blatant marketing information.

Social media design characteristics

Different social media platforms offer different design characteristics. Kaplan and Heinlein (2010) classified social media into six different categories based on social presence/media richness and self-presentation/self-disclosure level. From the perspective of studying antecedents of trust in social media marketing, characteristics related to errors, security, privacy, navigation, community features and availability of advice gain importance. Social media marketers need to evaluate these design characteristics as important antecedents of trust because they influence users to join such sites. A lack of the required level of these characteristics reduces trust in the social media site and diverts users to other platforms, rendering marketing effort on those sites ineffective.

Moreover, Trust Transference Theory (Campbell 1958; Stewart 2003) suggests that trust in the social media sites may also have an impact on trust in the organizations using those sites. This may eventually become an important factor predicting purchase intention from the online stores/brands (Everard and Galletta 2006; Gurung et al. 2008) and intention to spread e-WOM about them (Chu and Kim 2011; de Matos and Rossi 2008).

Users of social media expect right, relevant and updated information devoid of any error. A social media platform that consistently offers these attributes is perceived to be more trustworthy because of its apparent ability to satisfy one's information needs properly. For example, Twitter has established itself as the medium offering the most relevant and up to date information in situations of crisis. However, security breaches affecting user privacy may have reduced the trust placed in it by users. Concern for security is one of the primary factors affecting trust in a website (Rios and Riquelme 2010) and perception of good security increases consumer trust (Kim *et al.* 2008). As social media sites have started offering purchase of apps, games and products directly through them, perceived security may emerge as a vital factor leading to trust in the social media site.

An increasing number of security breaches has become a cause of concern for users and resulted in the emergence of privacy as a key driver of online trust (Hoffman *et al.* 1999). Thus, customers look for assurance that identifiable personal information collected from their electronic transactions is protected from indecent and/or unauthorized disclosure (Ratnasingham 1998) by adopting and implementing privacy policy, notice, disclosure and choice/consent of website visitors (Bart *et al.* 2005).

Navigation, layout, presentation, possible sequence of clicks and so on, may affect the perception of ease of use for members of social media, reflecting their ability to provide the required information conveniently. This also leads to increased trust (Bart *et al.* 2005; Belanger *et al.* 2002) in the social media site.

Although the basic requirement of any social media site is to offer community features to its users, different sites offer inherent design variations affecting the freedom offered to their members to interact with others to get their opinion, advice and feedback regarding issues of common interest in a supportive environment. For example, communication on Twitter is more public in nature, while Facebook provides the option of different types of communities with different levels of privacy settings (public, closed and secret). These features may increase trustworthiness and influence a user's individual evaluations, aspirations or behaviour (Pentina *et al.* 2008). Besides these, availability of spontaneous advice from a large number of users to resolve different issues may increase trust in the social media site. By providing automated advice to join communities of interest, take part in different events and consider products of relevance, social media sites may enhance users' trust in them with a heightened sense of their ability to solve the problems and issues they are facing (Bart *et al.* 2005).

Personal characteristics

Personal characteristics probably constitute the most important antecedents of trust. Since the propensity to trust varies across individuals, the same organization using social media marketing may evoke different levels of trust in different persons who otherwise perceive similar structural characteristics in the particular social media site. Personality, experience and culture constitute three major factors influencing personal characteristics (Schoorman *et al.* 2007). Hofstede's (1980) theory on cultural dimension provides a good basis for predicting how different cultures shape dispositional trust. For example, task-oriented cultures may result in higher initial trust towards strangers, unlike relationship-oriented cultures.

Other demographic factors may also significantly affect trust in the context of social media marketing. Trust may have different influences across gender (Awad and Ragowsky 2008). Researchers have claimed that men trust more than women in various contexts (Alesina and La Ferrara 2002; Buchan *et al.* 2008; Glaeser *et al.* 2000). Riedl *et al.* (2010) found that brain areas that encode trustworthiness differ between men and women.

Similarly, technical expertise, prior online shopping experience and one's perceived enjoyment of shopping online may also influence trust in a social media marketing context, by affecting attitude towards risks involved in shopping online.

Implications for businesses

High e-trust is more likely to germinate into positive word-of-mouth in online retailing (Cater and Zabkar 2009; Mukherjee and Nath 2007). A 2014 report by Ernst & Young found that success of social media marketing strategy is largely measured by engagement and social reach (Ernst & Young 2014). On the other hand, another report claimed that 29 per cent of social media marketers insist on driving conversion by attempting to reach more consumers and increasing sales volume with the help of their marketing efforts (Shively 2015). Thus, outcomes of trust in social media marketing may be mainly studied from the point of view of intention to purchase and intention to spread word of mouth, mostly of an electronic nature.

From a theoretical perspective, formation of attitude may be included in this list of outcomes. Trust facilitates higher usage of information with heightened perceived credibility (Nahapiet and Ghoshal 1998). As members of social media sites exchange information amongst themselves, they form a trusting attitude towards each other.

Lin (2006) suggests that perceived trust is one of the components of attitudes responsible for participation in virtual communities. Earlier research work established trust as related to attitude towards a website (Donthu 2001). Perceived as a belief, trust can indirectly mediate behaviours through attitudes towards the website (Chen and Dibb 2010). Thus consistent with both the Theory of Planned Behavior (Ajzen 1985) and the Theory of Reasoned Action (Fishbein and Ajzen 1975), which both advocate that beliefs influence attitudes, subsequently affecting behavioural intentions, trust may influence intention to purchase and intention to spread e-WOM through formation of attitude (Figure 17.4).

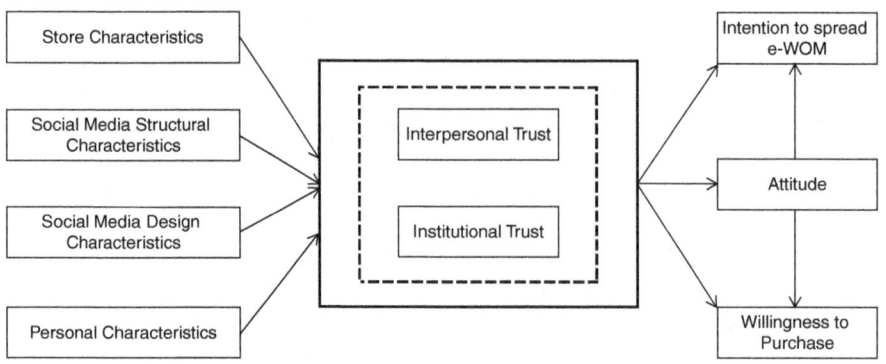

FIGURE 17.4 Proposed model of trust in social media marketing.

Conclusion

Trust plays a vital role in the context of social media marketing. This evolving form of marketing, based on the Theory of Six Degrees of Separation (Milgram 1967), gains popularity from the assumption that there are not more than six steps separating any two individuals in the world. Thus, people tend to transfer trust to even unknown people or business entities on social media sites, as they feel a sense of connectivity in the small world of the Internet. Trust can become so influential in social media marketing that consumers may even bypass attitude formation before making a purchase decision (Dutta and Bhat 2016e). This feeling of trust generated by various activities in social media marketing has helped many small businesses like Herschel Supply Co., Emerson Salon, The Social Man and others to achieve success in a very short period.

Social media have the potential to rapidly emerge as the most successful and effective marketing platform, provided consumers feel a sense of trust in business entities using them. Prudent social media marketing managers may attempt to build a matrix based on the recommended antecedents described in this chapter to analyze their status in a trustworthiness index at a certain time and hence plan to improve on it. This would require careful inspection of their social media marketing page, interaction and observation of members of their virtual communities on various social media sites, as well as interaction between consumers outside the virtual communities. Various marketing analytics and social network analysis tools available in the market may help in this regard. But contrary to popular belief, this would require high manual intervention, time and money. The brief discussion of some antecedents of trust described in this chapter through a systematic categorization of source should provide direction for future research and help marketers organize their strategy in an effective manner.

Questions

1. Why is trust in the context of social media marketing more important than in traditional e-Commerce?
2. If you were the social media marketing manager of an online retail store, how would you manage the store characteristics to facilitate formation of trust in it?
3. Describe how structural characteristics of a virtual community can play a vital role for a newly launched product. In addition, explain how structural characteristics may influence general perception of a brand in case of a product failure.
4. How important is it to analyse the personal characteristics of members of a virtual community to influence the formation of trust in social media marketing? How can you identify the personal characteristics of members of a virtual community that you are managing?
5. What other factors can influence formation of trust in the context of social media marketing?

References

Adam, F. and B. Rončević. 2003. 'Social capital: recent debates and research trends ', *Social Science Information*, 42:2, p. 155–183.

Akar, E. and B. Topçu. 2011. 'An examination of the factors influencing consumers' attitudes toward social media marketing', *Journal of Internet Commerce*, 10:1, p. 35–67.

Alesina, A. and E. La Ferrara. 2002. 'Who trusts others?', *Journal of Public Economics*, 85:2, p. 207–234.

Awad, N. F. F. and A. Ragowsky. 2006. 'Establishing trust in electronic commerce through online word of mouth: an examination across genders', *Journal of Management Information Systems*, 24:4, p. 101–121.

Ba, S., A. B. Whinston and H. Zhang. 2003. 'Building trust in online auction markets through an economic incentive mechanism', *Decision Support Systems*, 35:3, p. 273–286.

Baier, A. 1986. 'Trust and antitrust', *Ethics*, 96:2, p. 231–260.

Barney, J. B. and M. H. Hansen. 1994. 'Trustworthiness as a source of competitive advantage', *Strategic Management Journal*, 15, p. 175–190.

Baron, R. S., J. A. Vandello and B. Brunsman. 1996. 'The forgotten variable in conformity research: impact of task importance on social influence', *Journal of Personality and Social Psychology*, 71:5, p. 915–927.

Bart, Y., V. Shankar, F. Sultan and G. L. Urban. 2005. 'Are the drivers and role of online trust the same for all web sites and consumers? A large-scale exploratory empirical study', *Journal of Marketing*, 69:4, p. 133–152.

Belanger, F., J. S. Hiller and W. J. Smith. 2002. 'Trustworthiness in electronic commerce: the role of privacy, security, and site attributes', *Journal of Strategic Information Systems*, 11:3–4, p. 245–270.

Best, S. J. and B. S. Krueger. 2006. 'Online interactions and social capital: distinguishing between new and existing ties', *Social Science Computer Review*, 24:4, p. 395–410.

Blau, P. M. 1964. *Exchange and Power in Social Life*. New Brunswick: Wiley, Transaction Publishers.

Briggs, X. de S. 2003. 'Types of social capital'. In Christensen, K. and D. Levinson (eds.), *The Encyclopedia of Community: From the Village to the Virtual World*. Thousand Oaks, CA: Sage Publications, p. 1277–1283.

Brown, J. J. and P. H. Reingen. 1987. 'Social ties and word-of-mouth referral behavior', *Journal of Consumer Research*, 14:3, p. 350–362.

Buchan, N. R., R. T. A. Croson and S. Solnick. 2008. 'Trust and gender: an examination of behavior and beliefs in the Investment Game', *Journal of Economic Behavior and Organization*, 68, doi:10.1016/j.jebo.2007.10.006.

Burke, M. and R. Kraut. 2013. 'Using Facebook after losing a job: differential benefits of strong and weak ties', *Proceedings of the 2013 Conference on Computer Supported Cooperative Work*, p. 1419–1430.

Burt, R. S. 1995. 'Structural holes: the social structure of competition', *Industrial and Corporate Change*. Cambridge, MA: Harvard University Press.

Campbell, D. T. 1958. 'Common fate, similarity, and other indices of the status of aggregates of persons as social entities', *Behavioral Science*, 3:3, p. 14–25.

Cater, B. and V. Zabkar. 2009. 'Antecedents and consequences of commitment in marketing research services: the client's perspective', *Industrial Marketing Management*, 38:7, p. 785–797.

Chau, M. and J. Xu. 2007. 'Mining communities and their relationships in blogs: a study of online hate groups', *International Journal of Human Computer Studies*, 65:1, p. 57–70.

Chen, J. and S. Dibb. 2010. 'Consumer trust in the online retail context: exploring the antecedents and consequences', *Psychology and Marketing*, 27:4, p. 323–346.

Chengqi, G., J. P. Shim and R. Otondo. 2010. 'Social network services in China: an integrated model of centrality, trust, and technology acceptance', *Journal of Global Information Technology Management*, 13, p. 76–99.

Cheung, C. M. K. and M. K. O Lee. 2001. 'Trust in Internet shopping: instrument development and validation through classical and modern approaches', *Journal of Global Information Management*, 9:3, p. 23–35.

Chi, H. 2011. 'Interactive digital advertising vs. virtual brand community', *Journal of Interactive Advertising*, 12:1, p. 44–61.

Chu, S.-C. and Y. Kim. 2011. 'Determinants of consumer engagement in electronic word-of-mouth (eWOM) in social networking sites', *International Journal of Advertising*, 30:1, p. 47.

Chua, R. Y. J. and M. Morris. 2006. 'Dynamics of trust in guanxi network', in Chen, Y.-R. (ed.), Volume 9: *National Culture and Groups: Research on Managing Groups and Teams*, JAI Press, p. 95–113.

Clark, H. H. 1992. 'Arenas of language use', *Arenas of Language Use*, 18:6, p. xviii, 419.

Coleman, J. S. 1988. 'Social capital in the creation of human capital', *American Journal of Sociology*, 94, S95–S120.

Dieberger, A., P. Dourish, K. Höök, P. Resnick and A. Wexelblat. 2000. 'Social navigation: techniques for building more usable systems', *Interactions*, 7:6, p. 36–45.

Donath, J. 2007. 'Signals in social supernets', *Journal of Computer-Mediated Communication*, 13:1, p. 231–251.

Doney, P. M. and J. P. Cannon. 1997. 'An examination of the nature of trust in buyer-seller relationships', *Journal of Marketing*, 61, p. 35–51.

Donthu, N. 2001. 'Does your website measure up?', *Marketing Management*, 10:4, p. 29–32.

Dutta, N. and A. Bhat. 2014. 'Exploration of factors affecting initial trust in online social networks', *International Conference on Social Media for Business*, Raipur, p. 1–7.

Dutta, N. and A. Bhat. 2016a. 'Exploring the effect of store characteristics and interpersonal trust on purchase intention in the context of online social media marketing', *Journal of Internet Commerce*, 15:3, p. 239–273.

Dutta, N. and A. Bhat. 2016b. 'Exploration of factors affecting initial trust in online social network', in Sahay, V. and S. Prashar (eds.), *Social Media for Business*, first edition. New Delhi: Excel India Publishers, p. 137–144.

Dutta, N. and A. Bhat. 2016c. 'Effect of social media characteristics on intention to purchase and pass along electronic word of mouth', *2016 Summer AMA Conference*, American Marketing Association, p. 1–20.

Dutta, N. and A. Bhat. 2016d. 'FirstCry.com: fighting to lead the giant online baby care products market', *International Journal of Case Studies in Management*, 14:3, p. 1–20.

Dutta, N. and A. Bhat. 2016e. 'Effect of trust and perceived usefulness of recommendation on online purchase intention', *Online Information Review*, Under review.

Ellison, N. B., C. Steinfield and C. Lampe. 2007. 'The benefits of facebook friends: social capital and college students' use of online social network sites', *Journal of Computer Mediated Communication*, 12:4, p. 1–24.

Ernst & Young. 2014. *Social Media Marketing: India Trends Study 2014*. Kolkata, India: Ernst & Young, LLP.

Everard, A. and D. F. Galletta. 2006. 'How presentation flaws affect perceived site quality, trust, and intention to purchase from an online store', *Journal of Management Information Systems*, 22:3, p. 56–95.

Fishbein, M. and I. Ajzen. 1975. 'Belief, attitude, intention, and behavior: an introduction to theory and research', *Philosophy Rhetoric*, 10, doi:10.1002/cncr.26402.

Ganesan, S. 1994. 'Determinants of long-term orientation in buyer-seller relationships', *Journal of Marketing*, 58:2, p. 1–19.

Ganguly, B., S. B. Dash, D. Cyr and M. Head. 2010. 'The effects of website design on purchase intention in online shopping: the mediating role of trust and the moderating role of culture', *International Journal of Electronic Business*, 8:4/5, p. 302–330.

Garton, L., C. Haythornthwaite and B. Wellman. 1997. 'Studying on-line social networks', *Journal of Computer-Mediated Communication*, Blackwell Publishing Ltd., 3:1, p. 75–105.

Gefen, D. and T. H. Heart. 2006. 'On the need to include national culture as a central issue in e-Commerce trust beliefs', *Journal of Global Information Management*, 14:4, p. 1–30.

Gefen, D. and D. W. Straub. 2004. 'Consumer trust in B2C e-Commerce and the importance of social presence: experiments in e-Products and e-Services', *Omega*, 32:6, p. 407–424.

Glaeser, E. L., D. I. Laibson, J. A. Scheinkman and C. L. Soutter 2000. 'Measuring trust', *Quarterly Journal of Economics*, August, p. 811–846.

Glanville, J. L. and E. J. Bienenstock. 2009. 'A typology for understanding the connections among different forms of social capital', *American Behavioral Scientist*, 52:11, p. 1507–1530.

Granovetter, M. 1992, 'Problems of explanation in economic sociology', *Networks and Organizations: Structure, Form and Action*, p. 25–56.

Granovetter, M. S. 1973. 'The strength of weak ties', *American Journal of Sociology*, 78:6, p. 1360–1380.

Gray, R., N. B. Ellison, J. Vitak and C. Lampe. 2013. 'Who wants to know?: question-asking and answering practices among facebook users', *Proceedings of the 2013 Conference on Computer Supported Cooperative Work*, p. 1213–1224.

Gurung, A., X. Luo and M. K. Raja. 2008. 'An empirical investigation on customer's privacy perceptions, trust and security awareness in e-Commerce environment', *Journal of Information Privacy and Security*, 4:1, p. 42–64.

Hoffman, D. L., T. P. Novak and M. Peralta. 1999. 'Building consumer trust online', *Communications of the ACM*, 42:4, p. 80–85.

Hofstede, G. H. 1980. *Culture's Consequences: International Differences in Work-related Values*, Newbury Park, CA: Sage Publications.

Hsu, C. J. 2008. 'Dominant factors for online trust', *Proceedings of the 2008 International Conference on Cyberworlds, CW 2008*, p. 165–172.

Jarvenpaa, S. L. and P. A. Todd. 1997. 'Is there a future for retailing on the internet?'. In Peterson, R. S. (ed.), *Electronic Marketing and the Consumer*, Thousand Oaks, CA: Sage Publications, p. 139–156.

Jarvenpaa, S. L., N. Tractinsky and M. Vitale. 2000. 'Consumer trust in an internet store', *Information Technology and Management*, 1, p. 45–71.

Kaplan, A. M. and M. Haenlein. 2010. 'Users of the world, unite! The challenges and opportunities of social media', *Business Horizons*, 53, p. 59–68.

Karimov, F. P. and M. Brengman. 2011. 'Adoption of social media by online retailers', *International Journal of E-Entrepreneurship and Innovation*, 2:1, p. 26–45.

Keller, K. L. 1993, 'Conceptualizing, measuring, and managing customer-based brand equity', *Journal of Marketing*, 57:1, p. 1–22.

Kelton, K., K. R. Fleischmann and W. A. Wallace. 2008. 'Trust in digital information', *Journal of the American Society for Information Science and Technology*, 59:3, p. 363–374.

Kim, D. J., D. L. Ferrin and H. R. Rao. 2008. 'A trust-based consumer decision-making model in electronic commerce: the role of trust, perceived risk, and their antecedents', *Decision Support Systems*, 44:2, p. 544–564.

Kim, H. W., Y. Xu and J. Koh. 2004. 'A comparison of online trust building factors between potential customers and repeat customers', *Journal of the Association for Information Systems*, 5:10, p. 392–420.

Klein, L. R. and J. A. Quelch. 2015. 'The Internet and international marketing', *Sloan Management Review*, 37:3, p. 60.

Koufaris, M. and W. Hampton-Sosa. 2004. 'The development of initial trust in an online company by new customers', *Information & Management*, 41:3, p. 377–397.

Lampe, C., J. Vitak, R. Gray and N. Ellison. 2012. 'Perceptions of Facebook's value as an information source', *Proceedings of the SIGCHI Conference on Human Factors in Computing Systems*, p. 3195–3204.

Lee, M. K. O. and E. Turban. 2001. 'A trust model for consumer internet shopping', *International Journal of Electronic Commerce*, 6, p. 75–91.

Lim, K., C. Sia, M. Lee and I. Benbasat. 2006. 'Do I trust you online, and if so, will I buy? An empirical study of two trust-building strategies', *Journal of Management Information Systems*, 23:2, p. 233–266.

Lin, H.-F. 2006. 'Understanding behavioral intention to participate in virtual communities', *Cyberpsychology & behavior: the impact of the Internet, multimedia and virtual reality on behavior and society*, 9:5, p. 540–547.

Lorenze, T. 2014. 'Now we can shop via Twitter! Social media platform's new "buy" button allows users to make a purchase direct from a tweet', *Daily Mail*. Available at http://www.dailymail.co.uk/femail/article-2748028/Now-shop-Twitter-Social-media-platform-s-new-buy-button-allows-users-make-purchase-direct-tweet.html. Accessed 26 June 2016.

Lowry, P. B., A. Vance, G. Moody, B. Beckman and A. Read. 2008. 'Explaining and predicting the impact of branding alliances and web site quality on initial consumer trust of e-commerce web sites', *Journal of Management Information Systems*, 24:4, p. 199–224.

de Matos, C. A. and C. A. V. Rossi. 2008. 'Word-of-mouth communications in marketing: a meta-analytic review of the antecedents and moderators', *Journal of the Academy of Marketing Science*, 36:4, p. 578–596.

Mcknight, D. H. and N. L. Chervany. 2002. 'What trust means in e-Commerce customer relationships : an interdisciplinary conceptual typology', *International Journal of Electronic Commerce*, 6:2, p. 35–59.

McKnight, D. H., V. Choudhury and C. Kacmar. 2002a. 'Developing and validating trust measures for e-commerce: an integrative typology', *Information Systems Research*, 13:3, p. 334–359.

McKnight, D. H., V. Choudhury and C. Kacmar. 2002b. 'The impact of initial consumer trust on intentions to transact with a web site: a trust building model', *The Journal of Strategic Information Systems*, 11, p. 297–323.

McKnight, D. H., L. L. Cummings and N. L. Chervany. 1998. 'Initial trust formation in new organizational relationships', *Academy of Management Review*, 23, p. 473–490.

Merritt, S. M. and D. R. Ilgen. 2008. 'Not all trust is created equal: dispositional and history-based trust in human-automation interactions', *Human Factors*, 50:2, p. 194–210.

Milgram, S. 1967. 'The small-world problem', *Psychology Today*, 1:1, p. 61–67.

Millar, C. C. J. M. and C. J. Choi. 2009. 'Networks, social norms and knowledge sub-networks', *Journal of Business Ethics*, 90: SUPPL. 4, p. 565–574.

Mishra, A. K. 1996. 'Organizational responses to crisis: The centrality of trust', *Trust in Organizations: Frontiers of Theory and Research*, 261, p. 261–287.

Morgan, R. M. and S. D. Hunt. 1994. 'The commitment-trust theory of relationship marketing', *Journal of Marketing*, 58, p. 20–38.

Mukherjee, A. and P. Nath. 2007. 'Role of electronic trust in online retailing: A re-examination of the commitment-trust theory', *European Journal of Marketing*, 41, doi:10.1108/03090560710773390.

Nahapiet, J. and S. Ghoshal. 1998. 'Social capital, intellectual capital, and the organizational advantage', *Academy of Management Review*, 23, p. 242–266.

Ng, C. S. P. 2013. 'Intention to purchase on social commerce websites across cultures: A cross-regional study', *Information and Management*, 50:8, p. 609–620.

Panovich, K., R. C. Miller and D. R. Karger. 2012. 'Tie strength in question & answer on social network sites', *CSCW '12*, Seattle, WA, p. 1–10.

Park, C. and T. M. Lee. 2009. 'Information direction, website reputation and eWOM effect: A moderating role of product type', *Journal of Business Research*, 62:1, p. 61–67.

Pavlou, P. A. 2003. 'Consumer acceptance of electronic commerce: integrating trust and risk with the technology acceptance model', *International Journal of Electronic Commerce*, 7:3, p. 101–134.

Pavlou, P. A. and A. Dimoka. 2006. 'The nature and role of feedback text comments in online marketplaces: implications for trust building, price premiums and seller differentiation', *Information Systems Research*, 17:4, p. 392–414.

Pavlou, P. A. and M. Fygenson. 2006. 'Understanding and predicting electronic commerce adoption: an extension of the theory of planned behavior', *MIS Quarterly*, 30:1, p. 115–143.

Pentina, I., V. R. Prybutok and X. Zhang. 2008. 'The role of virtual communities as shopping reference groups', *Journal of Electronic Commerce Research*, 9:2, p. 114–136.

Pigg, K. E. and L. D. Crank. 2004. 'Building community social capital: the potential and promise of information and communications technologies', *The Journal of Community Informatics*, 1:1, p. 58–73.

Ratnasingham, P. 1998. 'The importance of trust in electronic commerce', *Internet Research*, 8:4, p. 313–321.

Resnick, P. and H. R. Varian. 1997 'Recommender systems', *Communications of the ACM*, 40:3, p. 56–58.

Resnick, P., R. Zeckhauser, E. Friedman and K. Kuwabara. 2000. 'Reputation systems', *Communications of the ACM*, 43:12, p. 45–48.

Riedl, R., M. Hubert and P. Kenning. 2010. 'Are there neural gender differences in online trust? An fMRI study on the perceived trustworthiness of eBay offers', *MIS Quarterly*, 34:2, p. 397–428.

Rios, R. E. and H. E. Riquelme. 2010. 'Sources of brand equity for online companies', *Journal of Research in Interactive Marketing*, 4:3, p. 214–240.

Rogers, E. M. 2003. *Diffusion of Innovations, 5th Ed.* New York: Simon and Schuster.

Rogers, E. M. and D. K. Bhowmik. 1970. 'Homophily-heterophily: relational concepts for communication research', *Public Opinion Quarterly*, 34:4, p. 523–538.

Rowley, T. J. 1997. 'Moving beyond dyadic ties: a network theory of stakeholder influences', *Academy of Management Review*, 22:4, p. 887–910.

Ruef, M., H. E. Aldrich and N. M. Carter. 2003. 'The structure of founding teams: homophily, strong ties, and isolation among U.S. entrepreneurs', *American Sociological Review*, 68, p. 195–222.

Schoorman, F. D., R. C. Mayer and J. H. Davis. 2007. 'An integrative model of organizational trust: past, present, and future', *Academy of Management Review*, 32, p. 344–354.

Schurr, P. H. and J. L. Ozanne. 1985. 'Influences on exchange processes: buyers' preconceptions of a seller's trustworthiness and bargaining toughness', *Journal of Consumer Research*, 11:4, p. 939.

Shapiro, S. P. 1987. 'The social control of impersonal trust', *The American Journal of Sociology*, 93:3, p. 623–658.

Shin, J., M. Park and Y. Ju. 2011. 'The effect of the online social network structure characteristics on network involvement and consumer purchasing intention: focus on Korean social promotion sites', *The 11th International DSI and the 16th APDSI Joint Meeting*, p. 1–8.

Shively, K. 2015. *The State of Social Marketing: 2015 Report*, doi:10.1007/SpringerReference_75636.

Sohn, D. 2009. 'Disentangling the effects of social network density on electronic word-of-mouth (eWOM) intention', *Journal of Computer-Mediated Communication*, 14:2, p. 352–367.

Solomon, M. R. 2006. *Consumer Behavior: Buying, Having, and Being*. Harlow, Essex: Pearson Prentice Hall.

Sorokina, O. 2015. 'What Instagram & Pinterest's buy buttons mean for your business', *Hootsuite*. Available at https://blog.hootsuite.com/instagram-and-pinterest-get-buy-buttons-what-this-means-for-your-business/. Accessed 26 June 2016.

Sparrowe, R. T., R. C. Liden, S. J. Wayne and M. L. Kraimer. 2001. 'Social networks and the performance of individuals and groups', *Academy of Management Journal*, 44:2, p. 316–325.

Stelzner, M. 2015. '2015 social media marketing industry report: how marketers are using social media to grow their businesses', *Social Media Examiner*, May, p. 1–53.

Stewart, K. J. 2003. 'Trust transfer on the world wide web', *Organization Science*, 14:1, p. 5–17.

Tajfel, H. 1978. 'Differentiation between social groups: studies in the social psychology of intergroup relations', *European Monographs in Social Psychology*, 14.

Walczuch, R., J. Seelen and H. Lundgren. 2001. 'Psychological determinants for consumer trust in e-retailing', *Eighth Research Symposium on Emerging Electronic Markets (RSEEM 01)*, Maastricht, Netherlands, 2001, p. 1–21.

Wasko, M. and S. Faraj. 2005. 'Should I share? Examining social and knowledge capital contribution in electronic networks of practice?', *MIS Quarterly*, 29:1, p. 35–57.

Weick, K. and K. Roberts. 1993. 'Collective mind in organizations: heedful interrelating on flight decks', *Administrative Science Quarterly*, 38:3, p. 357–381.

Wong, S. and Boh, W. 2010, 'Leveraging the Ties of Others to Build a Reputation For Trustworthiness among Peers', *Academy of Management Journal*, 53:1, p. 129–148.

Yoon, S.-J. 2002. 'The antecedents and consequences of trust in online-purchase decisions', *Journal of Interactive Marketing*, 16:2, p. 47–63.

Zhang, K. Z. and M. Benyoucef. 2016. 'Consumer behavior in social commerce: a literature review', *Decision Support Systems*, Elsevier B.V., 86, p. 95–108.

Zucker, L. G. 1986. 'Production of trust: institutional sources of economic structure, 1840-1920', *Research in Organizational Behavior*, 8:1, p. 53–111.

18

TRUST RELATIONSHIPS IN SOCIAL NETWORKS

A typology of strategies for communication between companies and their consumers

Zandra Balbinot and Sandrine Prom Tep

Introduction

The emergence of social networks (or social media) is a phenomenon affecting both our personal lives and the lives of businesses on a daily basis. In this era of Web 2.0, our behaviour as consumers and the way businesses communicate with the latter has changed dramatically. Thanks to these social networking technology platforms, the most radical change has been in the area of bidirectional communications. The arrival of popular platforms such as Facebook and Twitter has created a new trend in communications between businesses and individuals, providing individuals with a voice accompanied with considerable power (Bernoff and Li 2011). Contact with businesses, whether for informational purposes or while making a purchase, is increasingly conducted remotely via digital channels, and this tends to make interactions less 'human' (i.e. rarely face-to-face). This phenomenon is called 'computer-mediated communication' (Hoffman and Novak 1996). As a result, consumers and businesses no longer make contact directly, but rather through the experience of media controlled environments operating as self-service technologies (SSTs) (Kimes 2015; Majra, Saxena, Jha and Jagannathan 2016). As intermediaries in consumer-to-business (C2B) and consumer-to-consumer (C2C) interactions, social media become important tools in building and strengthening trust relationships between consumers and businesses; this results from the increased frequency of interactions (known as interactivity) that they facilitate, thanks to their ability to enable dialogue with the user (Gensler, Völckner, Liu-Thompkins and Wiertz 2013).

Managers have understood that social media should be part of business strategy. However, simply ensuring a social presence is not enough; companies need to optimize the use of this presence. It has become essential for companies to review and possibly modify their communication strategies in order to tune their consumer relationship management to the essential reality of interactivity in a digital context. Developing consumer trust in a virtual environment is a key success factor for companies (Jim Wu, Shen and Chang 2015). Given significant participation in social networks, they can take advantage of this special virtual place to communicate about brands, create buzz, develop virtual communities and fan groups, win new customers, build brand images, make promotions, and above all, strengthen relationships with their consumers. According to the Global Social Media Trends from the European Publishers Council, in 2015, there were 2.078 billion active accounts on social media on the planet, representing 29 per cent of the world population, actively connected via social media (Global Social Media Trends 2015). According to eMarketer.com (2016), in 2016, one third of the population will have used a social network, representing 2.34 billion users worldwide. This reinforces the importance of identifying communication strategies that enable the company to develop a relationship of trust with consumers and benefit from the use of social media as a competitive lever. Consequently, a study addressing the type of communication strategies a company should use to develop a relationship of trust with consumers through social media is of great assistance to managers hoping to obtain more positive results from their virtual community.

To provide companies with some guidance on this issue, we propose a typology of communication strategies. This chapter seeks to fill the void of information regarding the practical aspects of using social media. Our typology is oriented towards managers and their choice of communication strategies. Contrary to the most common focus of market research, on a specific sector or type of content (Kozinets 2014), this chapter provides a relational typology crossed between the company and the customer-consumer. We believe the use of a systematized typology will ensure success in the use of bidirectional social media for consumer-business relationships – C2BR (Gensler, Völckner, Liu-Thompkins and Wiertz 2013). Taking into account both the consumer and the organization, these strategies identify the crucial stages in managing a social medium and developing consumer trust in a company. It is a first attempt in the literature to build a theoretical paper that puts together different theories and translates them into a managerial language, presenting a useful typology for managers that want to optimize the use of social media communication strategies in their businesses.

Consumer-to-business relationships on the web

To understand online consumer-business relationships (C2BR), we must first examine the concept of trust and its extension in the online context in order to highlight differences to trust in a traditional situation.

Foundations of trust

As Sheppard and Sherman (1998) put it: 'Some form of trust is inherent in all relationships' and 'trust entails the assumption of risks' (p. 422). In their article, the authors contend that trust is not a singular construct and can be conceptualized according to four distinct forms, ranging from shallow dependence/interdependence to deep dependence/interdependence. Relational form is the type of interdependence, and relational depth is a structural feature of a relationship. These relationships serve as the structural building blocks of all relationships, and trust varies as a function of the nature and depth of the interdependence in a given relationship. Trust also means accepting the risks associated with the corresponding level of interdependence. Understood by involved parties at a cultural level, 'mechanisms for trust management exist at individual, relational and institutional levels in our society' (p. 422).

Hence, from the social psychologists' perspective, the vantage point adopted is the truster's one, be it a person or an entity that is engaged in the trusting behaviour. From that perspective, the consumer engaging in a relationship with a brand through social media is the truster engaged in a unidirectional shallow dependency, in comparison for instance, with the deep dependency that one parent can experience in hiring a babysitter to watch over their child. In both cases, the risk of unreliability exists (the concern that the other will not behave as expected), as well as the risk of indiscretion (the concern that sensitive information will be shared). However, the risks entailed in the two cases are not comparable in vulnerability for the truster, which defines the level of dependency depth. The second case entails critical consequences (a child's safety), while the first does not involve potential life threats, and is concerned more with poor service or practical inconvenience arising from incompetence or privacy failures. Hence, in all relationships, 'risk arises from one party transferring responsibility to another, thus creating a dependency upon that other' and 'trust is the acceptance of the risks associated' (Sheppard and Sherman 1998, p. 424–425).

Reliability is at the heart of service quality (Parasuraman, Zeithmal and Berry 1985), as well as being central to electronic service quality (Parasuraman, Zeithma and Malhotra 2005). In technology-based self-service options for consumers, the digital context forces them to rely solely on the interactive system quality to convey trust as a proxy to the trust invested in a brand relationship (Dahbolkar 1996), be it a telephone banking system (Curran and Meuter 2005), a website offering in a virtual marketplace (Santos 2003) or social media (Imrie 2013). Hence, in the electronic context to which social media pertain, the two main differences between online trust and traditional trust are: the physical absence of the other party, and the exposure of the consumer to risk and increased vulnerability.

Physical absence of the other party

First, the most important feature in the electronic environment is the physical absence of the other party (or vendor in an e-commerce context); from a consumer perspective this transforms the relationship. The human-to-human relationship becomes one between a human and a machine. In the e-Commerce context, Chouk (2005) argues that this relationship change can affect consumer trust whenever the consumer might be led to express the need for physical contact with the other party at any given time. This need can be expressed across three dimensions: a functional/utility dimension (the need to obtain information directly from the vendor); a relational/social dimension (the need to be in direct contact with the other party); and a reassurance dimension (the need for advice directly from the other party). Of these dimensions, reassurance is the most important because consumers tend to want to rely on the expertise and competence of vendors in making choices (Chouk 2005). Its importance is highlighted by Urban Sultan and Qualls (1999) in their studies, providing evidence that the presence of 'virtual salespeople' had a positive impact on consumer trust. Trust is also considered a key dimension in the electronic service quality construct (Wu, Shen and Chang 2015).

Risk and increased vulnerability

The issue of risk and vulnerability concerns situations where the virtual environment puts consumers in a position of dependency *vis-à-vis* the vendor. Indeed, dematerialization of the transaction puts the consumer in an unfamiliar situation. To illustrate, when purchasing online the consumer must generally pay for the transaction in advance, but his/her certainty of obtaining the product, and of the product meeting expectations, has been weakened since there has been no contact with either the vendor or the product. The consumer must rely on the vendor's good faith. 'The consumer loses her/his traditional frame of reference and may question the reliability and integrity of the vendor interface' (Rouby 2013). Building trust in such an environment is difficult (Koufaris 2002). Many barriers stand in the way of establishing online trust such as security, confidentiality of information and the protection of privacy on the web (Hoffman and Novak 1996).

Dimensions in online trust

Online trust is defined as 'a belief that allows consumers to accept their vulnerability with regard to an Internet merchant' (Pavlou 2003), or as 'a consumer's willingness to rely on the seller to undertake certain actions even if they make him/her vulnerable' (Jarvenpaa, Tractinsky and Saarinen 1999). This vulnerability is due to the very essence of Self-Service Technologies (SST), the interface of which allows consumers to obtain service despite the absence of human contact (Kimes and Collier 2015).

The variables most frequently used to establish online trust are the site, merchant, consumer and context (Chen and Dhillon 2003; Chouk 2005; Kim, Song, Braynov and Rao 2005). Each variable and its components is discussed below.

Site-related variables

(a) **Perceived site quality**: The concept of quality can refer to the ease of navigation and the up-to-dateness, or indeed relevance, of the available information

(Fung and Lee 1999). The quality of information is assessed on accuracy, ease of understanding, usefulness, relevance and up-to-dateness (Liang and Chen 2009).

(b) **Security and privacy**: In the Internet environment, and especially in the context of electronic transactions, security is of high importance (Chouk 2005). Internet transactions represent a risk to consumers in that unauthorized third parties (hackers) can be tempted to use their private information (bank details) for fraudulent purposes. Some traders use advanced encryption technologies such as 'Secure Socket Layer' (SSL) or 'Secure Electronic Transactions' (SET) to ward off any violation of confidentiality (Corbitt, Thanasankit and Yi 2003; Chouk 2005; Suh and Han 2003; Yoon 2002). However, even though security control is a prerequisite, which tends to reassure consumers, it still remains insufficient. In fact, security only has an asymmetrical effect on confidence. By this we mean that an unsecured site elicits mistrust on the part of the consumer, while a website boasting secure technology will have only a minor impact on trust (Shankar, Smith and Rangaswamy 2003, Llosa 1997). Five mechanisms can ensure consumer protection on the Internet: authentication, non-repudiation, confidentiality, protection of privacy, and information integrity (Suh and Han 2003).

Vendor-related variables

(a) **Perceived vendor reputation**: A vendor's reputation is an important determinant in research on trust online as well as in a traditional setting (Jarvenpaa and Tractinsky 1999; McKnight, Choudhury and Kacmar 2002; Yoon 2002). Reputation is capital that companies should protect since it provides assurance to consumers.

(b) **Satisfaction with past experience of the vendor**: Satisfaction following previous interactions with the company is a factor in explaining trust (Pavlou 2003).

Consumer-related variables

(a) **Propensity to trust**: Propensity to trust is considered a natural personality trait that remains stable with an individual, and therefore varies from one person to another depending on the situation. Individuals are generally classified as 'trusting' (which assumes from the outset that others can be trusted) or 'mistrustful' (Gefen 2000; McKnight, Choudhury and Kacmar 2002; Stewart 2003).

(b) **Familiarity with the site**: Familiarity or habits, which are based on past events, can assist people in predicting future behaviours. They reduce uncertainty, simplify relationships between the parties and promote the establishment of trust (Bhattacherjee 2002; Corbitt, Thanasankit and Yi 2003; Gefen 2000).

Contextual variables

(a) **Perceived risk**: Perceived risk as seen above, can be defined as the consumer's forecast of possible losses when presented with choices to be evaluated

(Aqueveque 2006), or uncertainty about the negative consequences that could arise following a purchase decision (Bauer 1960). In the virtual environment, that is, the Internet, the concept of risk is much higher when it comes to e-Commerce (Yousafzai, Pallister and Foxall 2003). The authors were able to distinguish different types of risk; Pavlou (2003) identifies behavioural risks (merchant opportunism) and environmental risks (hacking, fraud, etc.), while Kim, Song, Braynov and Rao (2005) distinguish financial risks (product complexity, significant amounts to invest etc.).

Communication strategies and their relationship to the development of online trust

Our proposal marries concept with practice by proposing steps for companies wishing to develop trust relationships with consumers through social media in order to get closer to those customers and users they are interested in. To develop a typology of social media management, we rely on the five key concepts of Social CRM (Customer Relationship Management) described by Monnot (2012), supplemented by online trust and business quality variables. This typology is divided into static and dynamic criteria, for the purpose of drawing in users at different stages in their adoption of social media, according to a techno-persuasive approach in which the interface gradually engages the consumer and modifies behaviour (Fogg 2009; Némery, Brangier and Kopp 2011).

Based on our review of the literature, these elements include those basically essential for a company wishing to develop online trust. It is important to include these variables in the order presented by these strategies, following an operational logic. These elements could therefore be used to put together social networks for the company, to incorporate them into the existing online strategy, or simply to serve as control tools to check if they are present and properly installed to foster the development of trust relationships. Table 18.1 shows the types of communication strategies that we detail below.

Secure employee engagement with the company: To develop its social networks, it is imperative that employees feel involved since they are the company's primary vehicle for communication with Internet users. Developing a positive atmosphere around social networks, and recruiting young people who are active on them, ensures optimal employee investment when implementing the strategy (Ang 2011).

Select social networks matching the company's objectives: The strategy should specify social networks that it will use according to the message to be communicated, and the individuals to be reached. This enables the firm to be sure of reaching the desired goal, optimizing its online presence, and also secures the visibility and presentation of its messages.

Create and develop an online community: The company must build a strong community around its brand and take into account the heterogeneous composition of its members. This is the second lever to increase the visibility that social

TABLE 18.1 Typology of strategies for communication between companies and their consumers

Communication Strategies			Consumer Behaviour	Expected Benefits
STATIC STRATEGY	**STATIC STRATEGY** (business)	Employee engagement	Engagement	Respond to consumer expectations
		Network selection	Consumer Perception	Active presence on social networks / Visibility
DYNAMIC STRATEGY	**UNIDIRECTIONAL STRATEGY** (business)	Reactivity	Perception of the seller in the relationship	Quickly resolve disputes by increasing client satisfaction
		Transparency	Information sharing	Stand out from the competition / Company reputation / Company visibility
		Coherence	Perceived satisfaction	Consumers liable to trust in lived experiences / Transfer offline trust to online trust
	BIDIRECTIONAL STRATEGY (business-consumer)	Create your community	Information sharing	Visibility / Approach customers and strengthen links with them
		Management of published content	Perceived quality of the website	Foster a favourable consumer attitude towards the company page/site / Inspire confidence
		Reciprocity	Information sharing	Share privileged information

networks already provide; the community enables users to get closer to each other, and strengthens the firm's ties with customers.

Manage content publications: The company must publish content regularly at a level which does not constitute an abusive presence for its users, and yet is adequate to prevent users losing interest. Ensuring impeccable design and presentation of its publications stimulates users to develop a positive attitude towards the site, and encourages online trust.

Reciprocate: Online consumers are mines of information through their interactions with the company and with other members of the community. In the context of social networks the followers share information, and the company should respond similarly.

Be reactive: Reactivity is the ability to propose a change in response to an external action. To achieve this, the company must be actively listening to its Internet users, and be able to analyse their posted comments to find an appropriate response as quickly as possible.

Be transparent: To build trust in its social network, the company must demonstrate a certain degree of openness in transmitting information, such as any means to support the reliability of participants in interactive exchanges. Transparency can differentiate the company from its competitors, enhance its reputation and increase its visibility.

Be consistent: Consistency across actions on its social networks and its other communication channels will create a synergy between the company's online and offline activities (Monnot 2012). Interactions with consumers promote good experiences that develop trust (Meyer and Schawager 2007).

Challenges in operationalizing communication strategies

The real challenge in operationalizing these communication strategies lies at the managerial level. Applying the PDCA – Plan-Do-Check-Act – quality control approach (Deming 1982) procedural steps, managers will encounter the following constraints.

PLANning the communication strategies has its challenges. Managers will have to integrate different variables that compose the static and dynamic strategies in order to have a complete social media communication strategy (Mangold and Faulds 2009). At the planning stage, the most important issue is getting the company's employees committed to the project. They will be the 'doers', the 'checkers' and above all the interface between the company and the consumers.

DOing or operationalizing the strategy implies the creation and development of an online community, where a bond with consumers must be established (Hede and Kellett 2012). This bond comes from the type and quality of publications and their contents, which will define consumer interest and loyalty. To guarantee the strategy will be successful, reciprocity and reactiveness, as well as transparency, will be essential throughout the whole process. This is where content and employee actions will earn and keep consumers' trust and interest.

Due to the speed of social media, the content of publications can become obsolete very quickly. As a result, regular periodic checking is needed. In our context, CHECK refers to the measuring of activities, which is not always easy to accomplish beyond the social media platform's analytical tools. On social media, the ROI shows whether the plan was successful; however, in order to execute a sustainable strategy, managers should measure the level of consumer commitment and loyalty (e.g. number of fans or followers, interactions such as posts and reposts) which is most consistent with the social media context (Hoffman and Fodor 2010).

Finally, to ACT upon social media platforms communications, community managers, via their employees, should be in charge of feeding the social media platforms, ensuring interactions with consumers to secure UGC creation (User-Generated Content) (Kaplan and Haenlein 2010) and analysing the content through data extraction and semantic analysis (Rieder 2013).

Potential findings and limits

Although this is a theoretical paper, empirical tests are underway. First, social media use itself needs to be tested. Research on Facebook is being conducted in order to test the external validity of this type of social media. Initial results indicate that it is difficult to generalize the results from a sample to a population using just one type of social media. Each of the types has a different audience. This indicates one of the limits of this instrument. In fact, all the types of social media used in the company's communication strategies need to be tested. The overall performance shows the suitability of the company's communication strategies choice.

Conclusion

A review of the literature reveals that consumer trust can be developed and influenced in various ways. Variables such as familiarity or past experiences, for example, play a role in the development of an online trust relationship. However, social networks present their own specificities, which oblige companies to adjust to certain norms expected by Internet users. We present here a typology of communication strategies, which ensures success in using social networks for a business-to-consumer relationship (B2CR). Associated with each other, they list the essential stages in managing a social network, which are crucial for a company to develop the trust of its consumers. It would be interesting in the future to conduct an empirical study to test the proposed typology. Current trends show that more and more managers have understood that social networks must become a part of their business strategy. It needs to be stressed, from the start, that their use should be optimized beyond the simple fact of having them in place. This theoretical typology shows that grouping strategies for developing trust through social networks offers a good operational guide for businesses wishing to install these new interactive channels online. More empirical tests need to be done.

References

Ang, L. 2011. 'Community relationship management and social media'. *Journal of Database Marketing and Customer Strategy Management*, 18:1, p. 31–38.

Aqueveque, E. 2006. 'Extrinsic cues and perceived risk: the influence of consumption situation'. *Journal of Consumer Marketing*, 23:5, p. 237–247.

Bauer, R. A. 1960. 'Consumer behaviour as risk taking'. In R. S. Hancock (ed.), 'Dynamic marketing for a changing world', *Proceedings of the 43rd Conference of the American Marketing Association*, p. 389–398.

Bhattacherjee, A. 2002. 'Individual trust in online firms: scale development and initial test'. *Journal of Management Information Systems*, 19:l, p. 211–241.

Bernoff, L. and C. Li. 2008. 'Harnessing the power of the Oh-So-Social Web'. *MIT Sloan Management Review*, 49:3, p. 17.

Chen, S. C. and G. S. Dhillon. 2003. 'Interpreting dimensions of consumer trust in e-commerce,' *Information Technology and Management*, 4, p. 303–313.

Chouk I. 2005. *Déterminants de la confiance du consommateur vis-à-vis d'un marchand Internet et non familier: Une approche par le rôle de tiers*. PhD. Université Paris IX Dauphine.

Corbitt, B. J., T. Thanasankit and H. Yi. 2003. 'Trust and e-Commerce: a study of consumer perceptions'. *Electronic Commerce Research and Applications*, 2:3, p. 203–215.

Curran, J. M. and M. L. Meuter. 2005. 'Self-service technology adoption: comparing three technologies'. *Journal of Services Marketing*, 19:2, p. 103–113.

Dahbolkar, P. A. 1996. 'Consumer evaluations of new technology-based self-service options: an investigation of alternative models of service quality'. *International Journal of Research in Marketing*, 13:1, p. 29–51.

Deming, W. E. 1982. *Quality Productivity and Competitive Position*. Cambridge, Mass.: MIT Press, p. 373.

eMarketer.com. 2016. Worldwide Social Networks Users: eMarketer's Estimates for 2016. [online] Available at https://www.emarketer.com/corporate/coverage#/results/1298?look. Accessed 18 October 2016.

Fogg, B. J. 2009. 'A behaviour model for persuasive design'. In Persuasive '09. [online]. California: Claremont Graduate University, p. 26–29. Available at http://bjfogg.com/fbm_files/page4_1.pdf. Accessed 18 April 2015.

Fung, R. K. K. and M. K. O. Lee. 1999. 'EC-trust (trust in electronic commerce): exploring the antecedent factors'. In W. D. Haseman and D. L. Nazareth (eds.), *Proceedings of the Fifth Americas Conference on Information Systems*, p. 517–519.

Gefen, D. 2000. 'E-Commerce: The role of familiarity and trust'. *The International Journal of Management Science*, 28:6, p. 725–737.

Gensler, S., F. Völckner, Y. Liu-Thompkins and C. Wiertz. 2013. 'Managing brands in the social media environment'. *Journal of Interactive Marketing*, 27:4, p. 242–256.

Global Social Media Trends. 2015. The EPC Global Media Trends Book – Series. Volume 2. [pdf] UK: European Publishers Council. Available at http://epceurope.eu/wp–content/uploads/2015/09/epc–trends–social–media.pdf. Accessed 10 February 2015.

Hede, A-M. and P. Kellett. 2012. 'Building online brand communities: exploring the benefits, challenges and risks in the Australian event sector'. *Journal of Vacation Marketing*, 18:3, p. 239–250.

Hoffman, D. L. and M. Fodor. 2010. 'Can you measure the ROI of your social media marketing?' *MIT Sloan Management Review*, 52:1, p. 41–49.

Hoffman D. L. and T. P. Novak. 1996. 'Marketing in hypermedia computer-mediated environments: conceptual foundations'. *Journal of Marketing*, 60:3, p. 50–68.

Imrie, B. C. 2013. 'The influence of social capital on service quality evaluation'. *Management Decision*, 51:4, p. 871–889.

Jarvenpaa, S. L., N. Tractinsky and L. Saarinen. 1999. 'Consumer trust in an Internet store: a cross-cultural validation'. [online] *Journal of Computer-Mediated Communication*, 5:2, p. 0. Available at http://onlinelibrary.wiley.com/doi/10.1111/j.1083-6101.1999.tb00337.x/full. Accessed 15 April 2016.

Kaplan A. M. and M. Haenlein. 2010. 'Users of the world, unite! The challenges and opportunities of social media'. *Business Horizons*, 53:1, p. 59–68.

Kim, D. J., Y. I. Song, S. B. Braynov and H. R. Rao. 2005. 'A multidimensional trust formation model in B2C ecommerce: A conceptual framework and content analyses of academia/practitioner perspective'. *Decision Support Systems*, 40:2, p. 143–165.

Kimes, S. E. and J. E. Collier. 2015. 'How customers view self-service technologies'. *MIT Sloan Management Review*, 57:1, p. 24–26.

Koufaris, M. 2002. 'Applying the technology acceptance model and flow theory to online consumer behavior', *Information Systems Research*, 13:2, p. 205–223.

Kozinets, R. V. 2014. 'Social brand engagement: a new idea', *GfK Marketing Intelligence Review*, 6:2, p. 8–15.

Liang, C.-J. and H.-J. Chen. 2009. 'A study of the impacts of Website quality on customer relationship performance'. *Total Quality Management* and *Business Excellence*, 20:9, p. 971–988.

Llosa S. 1997. 'L'analyse de la contribution des éléments du service à la satisfaction: Un modèle tétraclasse'. *Décisions Marketing*, 10, p. 81–88.

Majra, H., R. Saxena, S. Jha and S. Jagannathan. 2016. 'Structuring technology applications for enhanced customer experience: evidence from India Air travellers'. *Global Business Review*, 17:2, p. 351–374.

Mangold, W. G. and D. J. Faulds. 2009. 'Social media: the new hybrid element of the promotion mix'. *Business Horizons*, 52:4, p. 357–365.

McKnight H. D., V. Choudhury and C. Kacmar. 2002. 'The impact of initial consumer trust on intentions to transact with a web site: a trust building model'. *Strategic Information Systems*, 11:3–4, p. 297–323.

Meyer, C. and A. Schwager. 2007. 'Understanding customer experience'. *Harvard Business Review*, 85:2, p. 116–126.

Monnot J. 2012. '*Social CRM: L'impact des réseaux sociaux dans la stratégie relation client des entreprises*'. Master's. ISEG Marketing and Communication School. Available at http://fr.slideshare.net/julieMonnot/social-crm-limpact-des-rseaux-sociaux-dans-la-stratgie-relation-client-des-entreprises?related=1. Accessed 7 December 2014.

Némery, A., E. Brangier and S. Kopp. 2011. 'First validation of persuasive criteria for designing and evaluating the social influence of user interfaces: justification of a guideline'. In A. Marcus (ed.), *Design, User Experience, and Usability: Theory, Methods, Tools and Practice*. Berlin: Springer, p. 616–624.

Parasuraman, A., V. A. Zeithaml and L. L. Berry. 1985. 'A conceptual model of service quality and its implications for future research', *Journal of Marketing*, 49:4, p. 41–50.

Parasuraman, A., V. A. Zeithaml and A. Mlahotra. 2005. 'E-S-QUAL A multiple-item scale for assessing electronic service quality'. *Journal of Service Research*, 7:3, p. 1–21.

Pavlou, P. A. 2003. 'Consumer acceptance of electronic commerce: integrating trust and risk with the technology acceptance model'. *International Journal of Electronic Commerce*, 7:3, p. 101–134.

Rieder, B. 2013. 'Studying Facebook via data extraction: the Netvizz application'. In *WebSci'13*, New York: ACM, p. 346–355.

Rouby, G. 2013. 'La confiance à l'ère du numérique: l'enjeu du téléchargement illégal pour l'industrie cinématographique comme paradigme de la relation individus-entreprises' (Master's Thesis). HEC, Montreal, Canada.

Santos, J. 2003. 'E-service quality: a model of virtual service quality dimensions', *Managing Service Quality: An International Journal*, 13:3, p. 233–246

Shankar, V., A. K. Smith and A. Rangaswamy. 2003. 'Customer satisfaction and loyalty in online and offline environments'. *International Journal of Research in Marketing*, 20:2, p. 153–175.

Sheppard, B. H. and D. M. Sherman. 1998. 'The grammars of trust: a model and general implications'. *Academy of Management Review*, 23:3, p. 422–437.

Stewart, K. J. 2003. 'Trust transfer on the World Wide Web'. *Organization Science*, 14:1, p. 5–17.

Suh, B., and I. Han. 2003. 'The impact of customer trust and perception of security control on the acceptance of electronic commerce'. *International Journal of Electronic Commerce*, 7:3, p. 135–161.

Urban, G. L., F. Sultan and W. Qualls. 1998. 'Trust based marketing on the Internet', Cambridge, MA, MIT.

Wu Y.-C. J., J.-P. Shen and C.-L. Chang. 2015. 'Electronic service quality of Facebook social commerce and collaborative learning'. *Computers in Human Behaviour*, 51(Part B), p. 1395–1402.

Yoon, S. J. 2002. 'The antecedents and consequences of trust in online-purchase decisions'. *Journal of Interactive Marketing*, 16:2, p. 47–63.

Yousafzai, S. Y., J. G. Pallister and G. R. Foxall. 2003. 'A proposal model of e-trust for electronic banking'. *Technovation*, 23:11, p. 847–860.

19

LIKE-INFLUENCER FRAMEWORK

A study of factors influencing click of 'Like' option by users on Facebook

Rashmi Sharma

Introduction

The Like option on Facebook was activated on 9 February 2009 and introduced on 21 April 2010 so that users could express their endorsements of status updates, photos, newsfeeds, products/services, fan pages and so on. Marketers have come to realize that when a user clicks on 'Like', not only does he/she endorse the object in question, but they also add a whole new meaning to electronic word-of-mouth (eWOM) marketing. eWOM is known to be one of the most effective tools in marketing (Haque *et al.* 2013) and ultimately results in brand engagement. Kotler and Keller (2012) understood clearly for many years that one of the main influencers that impacts consumer choices and purchasing intent was friends and family. Since the Facebook network comprises friends and family, the potential outreach and influence of this social network is highly relevant to brand recall and future purchasing intent. However, current research lacks empirical evidence as to whether a friend's endorsement in the form of clicking the Like option on Facebook influences purchasing decisions of the Facebook user.

These now all-pervasive socio-technical networks have brought about new technological and conceptual challenges for marketing research. There is extensive research being undertaken to evaluate the intensity of relations linking users and how these relations facilitate communication and the spread of WOM (Pasquale *et al.* 2014). The social sciences framework 'Strength of Weak Ties' proposed by Mark Granovetter (1983) has been extended to online social networks suggesting interaction data can be used to predict the strength of ties. In this context, how strong and weak ties affect the information diffusion process has been studied (Pasquale *et al.* 2014; Wallace *et al.* 2014, Luaren *et al.* 2015). There are enormous studies that have illustrated that interpersonal relationships are different across genders due to the difference in gender schema and self-presentation.

Females on Facebook provide more social support than males do as the former place a high priority on interpersonal communication, giving and receiving more social support than males (Luaren *et al*. 2015). Facebook has stated that people who click the Facebook Like option are more engaged, active and connected than the average Facebook user (Facebook 2010). This suggests another dimension to examine in relation to the Like option as an influencer i.e. how personality traits affect the use of the Like option by Facebook users to endorse a post presenting an opinion about a product/service. For example, people who are high on extroversion, agreeableness and openness are associated with higher information disclosure on Facebook.

The factors that can affect the clicking of the Like option on Facebook to endorse a post regarding a product/service/brand have not been considered in these studies. The implications from the studies so far highlight the need to consider strength of ties, gender and personality traits as factors that affect a Facebook user when he/she clicks the Like option. Therefore, the study was conducted to assess the role of the Like option on Facebook as an influencer i.e. how the Like option clicked by a Facebook friend or family member for a certain post which may pertain to a product or service influences the purchasing decision of the reader of that post. On the other hand, it is vital to know the reasons/factors behind the actions of a Facebook user when he/she clicks the Like option for a certain post on a particular product or service. Is it gender, personality traits or strength of social ties that governs the mind of the Facebook user when he/she clicks on the Like option? The study of factors affecting the clicking of Like and, finally, a framework was developed to identify the Like option on Facebook as an influencer and the factors affecting the clicking of the Like button.

Literature review of sentiment analysis, personality types, gender, strength of social ties

The sentiment analysis process helps marketers to collect data on customer's sentiments to gain insights about the customer's feelings and perceptions. Marketers have recognized the influence of social communities on consumer behaviour (Gruen *et al*. 2006; Park *et al*. 2007). Using the document and sentence level analysis technique, a framework has been proposed to identify and analyse positive and negative sentiments present on Twitter and Facebook and an algorithm has been prepared to measure the intensity and influence of these positive and negative sentiments (Sharma *et al*. 2014).

Since Facebook is the largest and most popular social networking site to date (Shih 2011), it becomes imperative to identify the factors that influence how users perceive and process the advertising messages that are endorsed using the Like option by friends within the Facebook network, and whether these likes affect future purchasing decisions.

Hof (2011) suggested that Facebook users view a friend's recommendation as more credible than recommendations by marketers. Goodrich (2011) suggested that consumer awareness of a brand promotes attention which leads to increased brand recall, while another study suggested that there is a significant correlation between brand trust and motivation (Ha *et al.* 2004). As online social networks (OSNs) have become increasingly interconnected, testing the famous social sciences framework 'Strength of Weak Ties' proposed by Mark Granovetter becomes challenging on platforms like Facebook. As per Granovetter, 'The strength of a tie is a (probably linear) combination of the amount of time, the emotional intensity, the intimacy (mutual co-findings) and the reciprocal services that characterize the tie.' Recent research has focused on the effects of tie-strength and gender difference on social support for online friendships. Users share their purchasing experiences with their social circles on Social Networking Sites (SNS). Frequently, instead of writing direct responses, the Like option is clicked as a source of feedback and emotional support (Tufekci *et al.* 2008; Newman *et al.* 2011). Previous studies have illustrated that interpersonal relationships are different between males and females due to the difference in gender-schema, identity and self-presentation (Coulsonet *et al.* 2005; Manago *et al.* 2008; Reevy *et al.* 2001). Thus, females are more likely to seek and receive emotional support than males.

Facebook has stated that people who click the Facebook Like option are more engaged, active and connected than the average Facebook user (Facebook 2010). The Like option, therefore, offers a way for marketers/organizations to attract fans well connected on their social networks, enhancing the breadth of the brand message (Nelson *et al.* 2012). On social networks, Facebook likes are advocated as a proxy measure of WOM (Hoffman *et al.* 2010). Facebook users may also be connected to others who share the same values, a phenomenon that is more prevalent among younger generations or newer friend connections (Bramoulle *et al.* 2012). Some researchers have explored brand fans' attitudes with regard to their opinion leadership and/or opinion seeking (Wallace *et al.* 2014). If users have low self-esteem, their ideal and actual selves are not congruent and they may become fans of status enhancing brands (Malar *et al.* 2011). Positive self-presentation leads to relationship formation, which would enhance self-esteem further (Gonazales *et al.* 2011). Facebook's popularity has also generated discussions on the individual level effects of social networking. Third Party Effect (TPE) has been applied to perceptions of the effects of traditional media. However, SNSs allow personalization and user-generated content. In this context, very recently the TPE has been applied to SNSs. Zhang (2009) found that undergraduates believed Facebook to have a greater effect on others than on themselves. TPE, within the domain of Facebook use, occurs for respondents' perceptions of influence on personal relationships, future employment and privacy such that they view themselves as significantly less influenced than their closest friends, younger people, friends in their Facebook network and Facebook users in general (Paradise *et al.* 2012). Self-presentation is the process of managing the impression one conveys to others and has three functions: to influence others, to enhance the construction of self-identity and to promote positive emotions (Leary *et al.* 1990). Personality traits and personality structure have been viewed as the objects of social perception.

Some researchers went so far as to suggest that personality structure only exists as an illusion in the heads of the perceivers (Andrade *et al.* 1965; Shweder *et al.* 1975). The Big Five Model is useful for the analysis of 'how people perceive people and what words they use in formulating such perceptions' (Denissen *et al.* 2008). Several studies based on the Big Five Model (Acar *et al.* 2008; Correa *et al.* 2010; Amichai *et al.* 2010; Ross *et al.* 2009; Wilson *et al.*, 2010) reveal that people high in extraversion, agreeableness and openness are associated with higher information disclosure on Facebook; therefore, users who are more open to experience are most likely to be associated with using a social networking site to seek out novel experiences. A positive relationship exists between a person's level of agreeableness and the tendency to share things about oneself on Facebook.

Extensive literature review has revealed that there is little emphasis on the Like option as an influencer on Facebook users' purchasing decisions. Moreover, there is no integrative framework to assess the factors that makes a user click on the Like option on Facebook.

Research methodology

The title of this study is 'Like-influencer framework: a study of factors influencing click of "Like" option by users on Facebook'. The title of the research itself introduces the dimensions of the interrelated steps. All other steps, such as stating the objective, choosing the orientation to qualitative research, and research tools and sample collection techniques, are all related to the title and are also interrelated and not independent.

Research approach

The next step to be followed is to develop approaches to the research problem. In this study, exploratory research is adopted. Since one doesn't know the real problem while undertaking research, exploratory research helps to identify and explore the different dimensions of the problem so that a better understanding of the research framework can be developed. The exploratory research procedure is unstructured and highly flexible which helps the research to delve deep into the issues and identify the problem. When the research objective is to develop an understanding of some phenomenon in great detail and depth, qualitative research can be applied. It helps to learn how a phenomenon occurs in its natural settings and thus, to understand the role of the Like option as an influencer and the factors that affect clicking the Like option on Facebook, qualitative research was adopted for the study.

There are different techniques to performing qualitative research. For this study, a phenomenological approach to research was adopted. Phenomenology represents a philosophical approach to studying human experiences based on the idea that human experience itself is inherently subjective and determined by the context in which people live. This approach is highly unstructured and provides every opportunity for gaining new insights. The qualitative method allowed for the ability to identify specific data concepts for coding and determining categories/factors and thematic patterns.

Data collection tools

The technique of conversational analysis was followed to assess the research problem. The principal goal of conversational analysis is to explicate and interpret how participants achieve everyday courses of action by orienting to the underlying structural organization of talk-in-interaction. The kinds of data analyzed should include naturally occurring data from either ordinary conversation (i.e. ordinary chatting among friends) or institutional talk (e.g. classroom talk, oral proficiency interviews, conferences etc.). The technique focuses on participants' perspectives and interpretation of behaviour, events and situations as against an outsider imposed model and scale. The conversational data was collected using a focus group interview and an in-depth interview to gain understanding of the role of Like as an influencer. The respondents were asked to share their experiences about using Facebook and reasons behind clicking on the Like option. The in-depth interviews provided an understanding of the factors that affect the clicking of the Like option on Facebook and also helped in assessing the role of Like as an influencer on the purchasing decision of a user. Coding each interview revealed certain factors such as gender, trust, brand recognition, personality traits and social tie strength, which make a Facebook user click on the Like option for a post/status update by his/her friend for a certain product/service. The interviews were analysed through pattern recognition software NVivo10® for Windows, for specific key words that were indicative of the subject's trait or behaviour.

Whereas the focus-interview focused on individual student's perceptions of the Like option as an influencer, the second set of in-depth interviews treated the interviewed representatives of Delhi Technological University (DTU) as Facebook experts and sought to extract their knowledge about gender, personality traits and social-tie strength as factors affecting the clicking of the Like option.

An integrative framework was then proposed that can be used to identify the dimensions and components of the Like option on Facebook as an influencer and describe how these dimensions can affect the purchasing behaviour of a Facebook user. The Like-Influencer framework can be used by marketers to adjust their marketing campaigns and strategies in a way that creates positive brand recall for their product/service.

Sampling tool

A sampling tool is used to gather important and useful information from the population. Purposive sampling, one of the most common sampling strategies, groups participants according to preselected criteria relevant to a particular research question.

Since the research problem was identifying both whether the Like option can be treated as a purchasing decision influencer and the pertinent factors affecting the minds of Facebook users when they click on the Like option, a purposive sampling technique was used to collect data. The participants were selected by the researchers through purposeful sampling based on availability and willingness. There were ten male and ten female students of DTU who participated in the study. Of the twenty participants, ten were in the IV year, eight in the III year and two in the II year of Engineering. The age group of the participants was 21-23, and each student was interviewed individually for 20-30 minutes. The rationale behind choosing students in this age group was based on the results of the survey done by the Pew Research Center in 2015. As per this survey, 24 per cent of youth in the age group 18–27 go online 'almost constantly', facilitated by the widespread availability of smartphones. Aided by the convenience and constant access provided by mobile devices, especially smartphones, 92 per cent of youth report going online daily – including the 24 per cent who say they go online 'almost constantly'. More than half (56 per cent) of youth – defined in this report as those between the ages of 18 and 27 – go online several times a day, and 12 per cent report once-a-day use. Just 6 per cent of youth report going online weekly, and 2 per cent go online less often than weekly.

Thus, the prime target demographic for many organizational marketing efforts, and engaging these key consumers on Facebook should be the primary motive.

The study participants were informed that an audio recording of the interview was to be made. There was an additional written recording and transcription of the audio recordings of data. In the case of two participants, Skype interviews were undertaken. Participants were advised that interview questions were asked for the purpose of research only.

A copy of the transcribed in-depth interview was sent by email to each of the respondents to review for accuracy. Every respondent was instructed to make any necessary transcription changes and send the updated transcription to the researcher by email. Updates given by the participants included spelling and grammar corrections/deletions of the text. The inaudible text in the transcript was corrected by the researcher.

Results

The population of the study included twenty students of Delhi Technological University, divided equally between male and female. Of the twenty participants, ten were in the IV year, eight in the III year and two in the II year of Engineering. Data triangulation was done to validate the data and research by cross verifying the same information. This triangulation of data strengthened the research as it increased its credibility and validity. The triangulation of data is achieved when multiple theories, materials or methods are used. Data source triangulation, methodology triangulation and theory triangulation are the most common approaches for data triangulation.

The researcher combined three methods to gather data, namely literature review, focus group interview and in-depth interview, while conducting the primary research at different times and with different participants, which helped to identify inconsistencies in data sets. The focus group interview was conducted with two groups with eight participants each. The in-depth interview was conducted with twenty students, of which eighteen were interviewed for 20–30 minutes each individually. The interview was conducted by audio recording and written recording. Audio recording allowed the researcher to go back and supplement the written notes as well as provide quotations from participants using their own voice. The recorded data was transcribed verbatim by a third party. The third party signed a confidentiality agreement to ensure the anonymity and security of the study participants and their responses. An identification code was given to each study participant, from 1 to 20, so as to ensure anonymity. The letters SP (study participant) were used to identify each participant to assist in determining participant's responses in place of using the actual name of the participant. Transcriptions provided the researcher with both visual and auditory means of comprehending the data, thus enhancing the understanding and immersion in the data. The remaining two participants were interviewed using the web-based communication device Skype. The interview was recorded by hand and then transcribed.

Qualitative data analysis software was used to organize the data. Collecting infromation through in-depth interviews results in extremely large amounts of data thus, the ability to readily code and effectively analyse data is of paramount importance. For the present study, NVivo10® data analysis software was used as it provides convenient coding and node structuring to facilitate the different coding steps in phenomenology and grounded theory. However, the software does not perform the analysis for the researcher. The organized data was carefully examined and the data analysis was conducted manually, which helped to see codes both within a given scenario and across scenarios.

The purpose of the research was to assess the role of the Like option on Facebook as an influencer and subsequently identify the factors that affect the user when he/she clicks the Like option. On the basis of emerging factors, a framework was developed to identify the Like option on Facebook as an influencer and the factors affecting its use. Due to the dynamic nature of the phenomenology approach, the interview guide evolves as the process unfolds and, as such, the researcher chose to present in the research paper the types of topics discussed with the participants rather than providing explicit interview questions. The proposed research topic was 'Does a Facebook friend clicking the Like option influence a purchasing decision?' If yes, then what are the factors that influence the decision?

Four emergent themes resulted from the focus group. First, the linkage between brand recall and a friend's endorsement was established. Second, trust for a Facebook friend on the basis of established credibility and subsequent clicking of Like was also identified. Third, brand recall and the friend's credibility lead to future purchasing intent. Fourth, female users of Facebook, as compared to male, were influenced the most in their purchasing decisions by a friend clicking Like for a product/service.

During the in-depth interview, the focus was on the mind of the Facebook user when he/she clicks on the Like option. The online relationships were established by the strength of social ties and gender differences. Weak ties are connections between individuals belonging to distant areas of the social graph, or the ones that happen to have most of their relationships in different national, linguistic, age or common experience groups. During the interview, the participants were asked to assess the strength of their own friendship ties (NVivo10® helped to compute tie strength as a function of type and frequency of user's interactions). It was found that females who have stronger ties had a significantly higher frequency of liking, commenting and messaging than males. Strong social support makes a Facebook user feel connected to friends while building trust with those friends. Since better social support leads to better relationships, it can lead to purchasing intent. Thus, those with stronger social ties have greater influence on others and greater credibility. However, the Like option was also treated as a social support measure, particularly in the case of females.

The personality traits of the Facebook user was another emerging theme that affected the clicking of the Like option. It was found that people high in extraversion, agreeableness and openness are associated with higher information disclosure. Presenting a positive, likeable self-image or attempting to define one's relationship with the recipient also emerged as another sub-theme. People high in extraversion and agreeableness had a higher intention of sharing and disseminating knowledge and thus clicked on Like, while people high in neuroticism and conscientiousness had greater concern over online privacy and refrained from sharing information and clicking the Like option. Highly self-monitoring people exhibited social appropriateness cues to receive validation from others, which may influence their 'Likes'. They were much more engaged, active and connected than the average Facebook user. However, there were categories of such personality types who click on the Like option for different reasons. These are:

'**Potential customers**' who click on the Like option for a post related to a product/service and are willing to act quickly when content catches their interest.

'**Friends**' who click on Like to support a business/brand.

'**Sweepstakers**' who click on Like to win a giveaway offered by the brand site.

'**Happy Campers**' who click on Like to interact with the brand site on a regular basis.

'**Fair-weather friends**' who Like, but equally would leave negative feedback if the brand did something they do not approve of.

'**Enthusiasts**' who click Like to show the world that they like a famous global brand with the intention of enhancing self-esteem.

'**Advocates**' who regularly interact with the brand page through clicking on Like and posting comments and feedback.

The research revealed that factors like gender, personality type and social ties have a bearing on the clicking of the Like option of Facebook. The framework proposed by researchers Mariani and Mohammed (2014), which predicts the behaviour a Facebook user may exhibit when a friend endorses a brand by clicking Like, was included in the framework proposed in the current study. Mariani and Mohammed's existing framework (as highlighted in blue in Figure 19.1) demonstrates that if a friend clicks Like for a brand within their network, attention (Goodrich 2011) will be triggered by friends within the user's Facebook network. Attention should create future recognition (Yang 2012) of a brand because a friend's recommendation is more credible (Hof 2011), which also creates trust (Ha 2004) leading to future purchase intent. Clear connections were established between the importance of trust (Ha 2004) created from clicking Like and how it leads to motivation to purchase a global brand. Taking this framework forward, brand recall was linked to trust and the credibility of a Facebook friend who endorsed a particular product/ service by clicking on Like. Gender differences also had a bearing on providing social support on Facebook. Keeping in mind the themes identified, a Like-Influencer Framework was proposed, as shown in Figure 19.1.

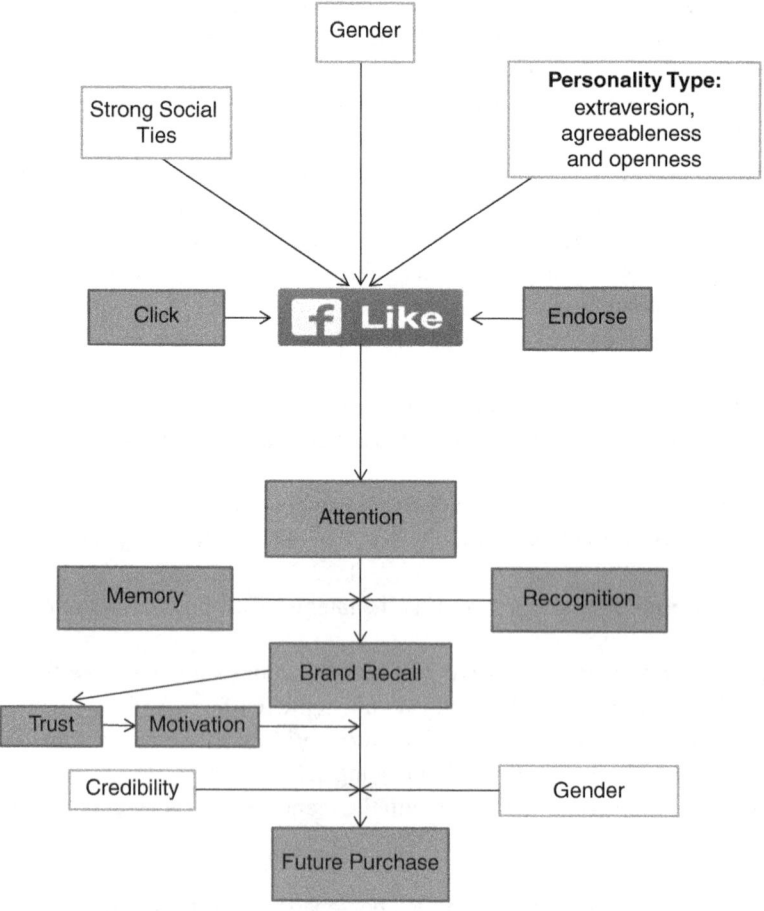

FIGURE 19.1 Like-influencer framework.

Conclusion, limitations and future implications

The study provides insights into how a friend's endorsement of a product/service through the Like option on Facebook has a linkage to/influence on the user's purchasing decision. It also revealed how factors like gender, personality type and social ties have a bearing on clicking the Like option on Facebook. Brand recall was linked to trust and credibility of a Facebook friend who endorses a particular product/service by clicking on Like. Gender differences also had a bearing on providing social support on Facebook.

The study contributes to the area of marketing, corporate communication and human resources and organizational behaviour. The Like-Influencer Framework can be used for market research and may be extended to the cultural dimension for future research.

The limitation of this study is that it only focused on students in the age group 21 to 23, that is, those who use Facebook with the most enthusiasm. Thus, this sample may not represent the whole research population and therefore, future research may be conducted with a larger population for a more generalized understanding of the proposed Like-Influencer Framework.

Appendix – I (Scenarios/Topics)

Scenario I: Your friend has recently liked a global brand and also purchased it. Would you consider purchasing it to show off your taste to other people?

Response: would like to have updates from this brand on my newsfeed/showing off would make my Facebook page look good

Scenario II: What are different situations/reasons for which you purchase a certain brand/like it?

Response: my friends like the brand/liking this brand shows off my taste to other people/received an offer for clicking on Like/my friend asked me to like the brand/I entered a competition by clicking on Like/ there was a campaign to reach a target number of likes

Scenario III: What kind of friends do you have on Facebook? What are your social ties with them?

Response: most of my Facebook friends are people I interact with every day/ are true friends, rather that acquaintances/are people I like to spend time with away from Facebook/are so close to me that it is hard to imagine life without them

Scenario IV: Extraversion/Agreeableness/Conscientiousness/Neuroticism/ Openness?

Response: is talkative, social and assertive/good natured, co-operative and trustworthy/responsible, orderly and dependable/imaginative, independent-minded and has divergent thinking

Does not worry much/not prone to anxiety/depression

Scenario V: Homophily

Response: my friends are of the same gender as I am/they are quite similar to me/think like me/behave like me/have the same social status/are culturally similar to me

Scenario VI: If my friend posts his/her opinion about a product/service, my immediate response is…

Response: I instantly click Like/I share my views/I comment as a reply to her post/I send a private message

Appendix – II (Themes/Sub-themes)

Brand recall
Friend's endorsement
Trust
Credibility
Future purchasing intent
Gender
Personality type – Extraversion, Agreeableness, Openness
Social ties – Strong
Potential customers
Friends
Sweepstakers
Happy campers
Fair-weather friends
Enthusiasts
Advocates

References

Acar, A. 2008, 'Antecedents and consequences of online social networking behavior: the case of Facebook', *Journal of Website Promotion*, 3, p. 62–83.

Amichai, Y., G. Vinitzky. 2010. 'Social network use and personality', *Computers on Human Behaviour*, 26, p. 1289–1295.

Andrade, R. 1965. 'Trait psychology and componential analysis', *American Anthropologist*, 67, p. 215–228.

Bramoulle, J., S. Currarinin, M. Jackson, P. Pin and B. Rogers. 2012. 'Homophily and long-run integration in social networks', *Journal of Economic Theory*, 147:5, p. 1754–1786.

Correa, T., A. Hinsley, H. Zuniga. 2010. 'Who interacts on the web? The intersection of users' personality and social media use', *Computers in Human Behaviour*, 26, p. 247–253.

Coulson, N. 2005. 'Receiving social support online: an analysis of a computer-mediated support group for individuals living with irritable bowel syndrome', *CyberPsychology & Behaviour*, 8:6, p. 580–584.

Denissen, J., L. Penke. 2008. 'Individual reaction norms underlying the Five Factor Model of personality: first steps towards a theory-based conceptual framework', *Journal of Research in Personality*, 42, p. 1285–1302.

Facebook. 2010. 'The value of a Liker'. Available at http://www.facebook.com/note. php?note_id=150630338305797. Accessed 16 July 2013.

Gonzales, A., J. Hancock. 2011. 'Mirror mirror on my Facebook wall: effects of exposure to Facebook on self-esteem', *CyberPsychology, Behaviour and Social Networking*, 14:1–2, p. 79–83.

Goodrich, K. 2011. 'Anarchy of effects? Exploring attention to online advertising and multiple outcomes', *Psychology and Marketing*, 28:4, p. 417–440.

Granovetter, M. 1983. 'The strength of weak ties: a network theory revisited', *Sociological Theory*, 1:1, p. 201–233.

Gruen, T, T. Osmonbekov, A. Czaplewski. 2006. 'EWOM: The impact of customer-to-customer online know-how exchange on customer value and loyalty', *Journal of Business Research*, 59:4, p. 449–456.

Ha, Y. 2004. 'Factors influencing consumer perceptions of brand trust online', *Journal of Product & Brand Management*, 13:4–5, p. 329–342.

Haque, A., A. Momen., S. Sultana and F. Yasmin. 2013. 'Effectiveness of Facebook towards online brand awareness: a study on Malaysian Facebook user perspective', *Australian Journal of Basic and Applied Sciences*, 7:2, p. 197–203.

Hof, R. 2011. 'You are the ad. Facebook has emerged from a privacy scandal to become online advertising's next great hope. Its goal: turning us all into marketers', *Technology Review*, 114:3, p. 64–69.

Hoffman, D. and M. Fodor. 2010. 'Can you measure the ROI of your social media marketing?', *MIT Sloan Management Review*, 52:1, p. 41–49.

Kotler, P. and K. Keller. 2012. *Marketing Management* (fourteenth edition). Upper Saddle River, New Jersey: Pearson Education, Inc.

Lauren, P., H. Kuo, Yu. Chiu, S. Chang. 2015. 'Social support on Facebook: the influence of tie strength and gender differences', *International Journal of Electronic Commerce Studies*, 6:1, p. 37–50. DOI:10.7903/ijecs.1391.

Leary, M., and R. Kowalski. 1990. 'Impression management: a literature review and two-component model', *Psychological Bulletin*, p. 107–134.

Malar, L., H. Krohmer, W. Hoyer, B. Nyffenegger. 2011. 'Emotional brand attachment and brand personality: the relative importance of the actual and the ideal self', *Journal of Marketing*, 75, p. 35–52.

Manago, A., M. Graham, P. Greenfield, and G. Salimkhan. 2008. 'Self-presentation and gender on MySpace', *Journal of Applied Developmental Psychology*, 29:6, p. 446–458.

Mariani, R. and D. Mohammed. 2014. 'Like a global endorsement: how clicking Like influences Facebook users' recall and future purchasing intentions', *Journal of Management Policy and Practice*, 15:4, p. 51–63.

Nelson, F., E. Riebe, and B. Sharp. 2012. 'What's not to like? Can a Facebook fan base give a brand the advertising reach it needs?', *Journal of Advertising Research*, 52:2, p. 262–269.

Newman, M. W., D. Lauterbach, S. A. Munson, P. Resnick and M. Morris. 2011. 'It's not that I don't have problems, I'm just not putting them on Facebook: challenges and opportunities in using online social networks for health', paper presented at the ACM 2011 conference on Computer Supported Cooperative Work, Hangzhou, China, March 19–23, 2011. Available at http://dx.doi.org/10.1145/1958824.1958876.

Paradise, A., and M. Sullivan. 2012. '(In)Visible threats? The Third Person Effect in perceptions of the influence of Facebook', *Cyberpsychology, Behaviour and Social Networking*, 15:1, p. 55–60.

Park, D., J. Lee and I. Han. 2007. 'The effect of on-line consumer reviews on consumer purchasing intention: the moderating role of involvement', *International Journal of Electronic Commerce*, 11:4, p. 125–148.

Pasquale, D., F. Emilio, F. Giamcomo and P. Alessandro. 2014. 'On Facebook, most ties are weak', *Communications of the ACM*, 57:11, p. 78–84.

Reevy, G. and C. Maslach. 2001. 'Use of social support: gender and personality differences', *Sex Roles*, 44:7–8, p. 437–459.

Ross, C., E. Orr, M. Sisic *et al.* 2009. 'Personality and motivations asscociated with Facebook use', *Computers in Human Behaviour*, 25, p. 578–586.

Sharma, R., H. Sharma, and P. Sharma. 2014. 'Measuring the influence and intensity of customer's sentiments in Facebook and Twitter', *GSTF Journal of Psychology (JPsych)*, 1:2. DOI:10.5176/2345-7872_1.2.19.

Shih, C. 2011. *The Facebook Era: Tapping Online Social Networks to Market, Sell and Innovate*. Boston, MA: Pearson Education.

Shweder, R. 1975. 'How relevant is an individual difference theory of personality?', *Journal of Personality*, 43, p. 455–484.

Tufekci, Z. 2008. 'Grooming, gossip, Facebook and MySpace: what can we learn about these sites from those who won't assimilate?', *Information, Communication & Society*, 11:4, p. 544–564.

Wallace, E., I. Buil, L. Chernatony and M. Hogan. 2014. 'Who "Likes" you … and why? A typology of Facebook fans from "Fan"-atics and Self-Expressives to Utilitarians and Authentics', *Journal of Advertising Research*, p. 92–109. DOI:10.2501/JAR-54-1-092-109.

Wilson, K., S. Fornasier, K. and K. White. 2010. 'Psychological predictors of young adults' use of social networking sites', *CyberPsychology, Behaviour & Social Networking*, 13, p. 173–177.

Yang, T. 2012. 'The decision behavior of Facebook users', *Journal of Computer Information Systems*, 52:3, p. 50–59.

Zhang, J., and T. Daughtery. 2009. 'Third-person effect and social networking: implications for online marketing and word-of-mouth communication', *American Journal of Business*, 24, p. 55–63.

20

MECHANISMS FOR INCENTIVIZING AND ENCOURAGING ONLINE SOCIAL INTERACTIONS – AN EXPERIMENT ANALYSING THE ROLE OF RECOMMENDATIONS AND REWARDS ON ADVERTISEMENT SHARING BEHAVIOUR

William Feitosa

Introduction

The objective of this chapter is to evaluate people's propensity to share online advertising content, verifying the role played by the incentives offered by companies for sharing, compared to a referral from a friend. In addition, we compare sharing behaviour in terms of emotions (arousal generated in different valences), perceived usefulness of content and respondent's income.

Some previous studies have focused on advertisement sharing, that is, whether the referral increases the propensity to share, or whether emotion or specifically arousal increases sharing (Botha and Reyneke 2013; Berger and Milkman 2012; Dobele *et al.* 2007), or if sharing is more common among specific groups, such as Hispanics in the US (Korgaonkar, Petrescu and Gironda 2016), generation Y (Botha and Reyneke 2013), men/women (Haryani and Motwani 2015) or college-aged users (Shu-Chuan 2011; Yang and Wang 2015), but no study has examined all variables in the same data set and compared them, as this study does. Moreover, previous studies have not studied the difference between negative and positive advertising in terms of incentive: is there moderation between valence and incentives?

Word-of-mouth (WOM) has been studied by marketing researchers and practitioners for several years (Lazarsfeld *et al.* 1948; Goldenberg, Libai and Muller 2001; Shimp 2010; Blythe 2013; Tuten and Solomon 2015). Social interactions about products, services and brands are important for companies' success. In recent years, technologies like online social networks have changed the way these interactions occur, since they organize contacts and make access to this information easier, amplifying the audience and accelerating communication. Each online social interaction allows people to share something about themselves: an idea, a file, a recommendation, an opinion. More than ever, questions like how a person can influence their contacts, or why a person engages with word-of-mouth, online or offline, which medium and which person is the most influential, are in the spotlight (Mingxue *et al.* 2011; Sweetney, Soutar and Mazzarol 2014; Berger and Milkman 2012; Berger and Iyengar 2013; Ling *et al.* 2005). It is known that online social interactions can enhance communication efforts (Godes *et al.* 2005), once they are cheaper than other alternatives to communicate. They are also considered more reliable than traditional communication (Keller and Fay 2009).

But how do companies encourage people to engage with online social interactions, spreading positive content about them and their brands? Moreover, is it possible to motivate a person to engage in this type of activity? What kind of incentive is most effective?

Psychological research has proposed that motivation can be intrinsic – internal reasons, such as interests, satisfaction, emotional status, overall health – or extrinsic – external reasons, such as approvals, rewards, concordances, reactances (Ryan and Deci 2000, p. 61). Even extrinsic motivation is somehow based on internal reasons such as beliefs, culture and attitudes, but this is formed by social interactions. It means that what motivates someone in an online social interaction can vary according to the person's profile and how this person considers these extrinsic factors. Therefore, an incentive given by a company to consumers needs to fit their profiles and take into account different kinds of motivation.

Companies have tried different methods of motivating people to spread their content (Godes *et al.* 2005). First, in order to consider intrinsic consumer motivation, extra care with regard to content creation is necessary. Here, it is important to further consider how content can be interpreted by the consumer, in order to create the right content for the right market segment, such as memes, useful content, homophilous influence consideration, i.e. by choosing the right influencers, and timing. Thus, if companies create good and attractive content, they can stimulate people to share it, increasing interest in online social interactions. If the content can improve the sharer's self-image – i.e. make it more likely for him/her to be seen as a smart and cool person, WOM motivation will grow.

Second, it is essential to consider extrinsic motivation. Among important external factors, financial rewards (monetary prizes and discounts) or non-financial (gifts, badges, contest campaigns and becoming part of a group) are both possibilities. Some anecdotal evidence indicates that the less consumer involvement with a product, the more effective are financial WOM incentives. Table 20.1 shows these practices and relates them to the motivation intended.

As a consequence, some content, i.e. videos like Volvo's 'The Epic Split Feat' with Van Damme (67,000,000 views in two months), go viral – people share them on online social networks on a large scale. On the other hand, many types of content can inspire activists or haters to create negative versions of them, asserting or showing criticism about the product or the company's practices.

TABLE 20.1 Some consumer incentive practices to increase sharing propensity

	Motivation intended	
	Intrinsic	*Extrinsic*
Objective	Give consumer internal (psychological, self-image) reasons to share	Give consumer external (sociological, financial) reasons to share
Some incentive practices	A friend tip	Offers (i.e. an online exclusive discount or sales promotion)
	Memes and good, useful, interesting, awesome, humour or emotional content	Raffles, contests (i.e. 'share a photo with the product. The best photo wins a prize'), prizes (i.e. gifts, monetary prizes or free product samples)
	A famous person recommends	Badges, milestones (i.e. a 'share a photo with the product and win an online medal' promo, normally part of a referral programme or relationship programme)
	An influential person recommends	Share to be part of a brand community or exclusive team

Source: authors.

Hypothesis

In order to create useful and attractive advertisements and increase the chances of retransmission, companies have looked at different aspects and approaches of their messages, such as the use of humour or testimonies or the offering of incentives. Some benefit programmes have tried to incentivize people to engage online and retransmit messages by giving out rewards, such as discounts, cash prizes or free product samples, among other offers, to customers who are willing to spread messages about the company – the existence of awards increases the likelihood of consumers making comments about the company and its message.

In the online environment, companies have offered special rewards in the form of avatars, badges and medals to identify those who collaborate more and motivate them to remain working, because people share more when they are reminded of how special they are, or when they achieve challenging goals (Antin and Churchill 2011; Ryu and Feick 2007).

Based on this, we can derive the following hypotheses:

Hypothesis 1: An advertisement with an incentive has a greater propensity to be shared than advertisement without incentives.

Hypothesis 2: An advertisement with an incentive has a greater perceived usefulness than an advertisement without incentives.

On the other hand, other authors indicate that the dissemination and sharing of opinions from friends prevails over seeing an advertisement. The opinion of friends would, in this context, be more useful than an advertisement (Lazarsfeld *et al.* 1948; Ling *et al.* 2005).

Some anecdotal evidence has shown that people are more likely to share online advertisements when they receive them from a sender who is known by them, in comparison to those sent by companies – social ties make advertisement more shareable (Shen *et al.* 2016). People have a greater propensity to share when they have an ethnic identification with the sender (Kongaokar, Petrescu and Gironda 2016). Further, stealth marketing videos, those in which the brand is not easily visible, are more attractive for clients than traditional ads (Wendt, Griesbaum and Kölle 2016).

As a result, we can make the following hypotheses:

> Hypothesis 3: An advertisement with a friend's recommendation has greater likelihood of being shared than an advertisement without recommendation.

> Hypothesis 4: An advertisement with a friend's recommendation has greater perceived value than an advertisement without recommendation.

Yet, some content characteristics can change the way people share the content. First, how exciting the content is has an effect (Dobele *et al.* 2007; Berger and Milkman 2012; Botha and Reyneke 2013). People tend to more frequently share that which causes emotional impact. Arousal is an attribute of emotions and it can measure how exciting an emotion is, based on, for example, the perception about how strong an emotion was. Thus, it is possible to theorize that:

> Hypothesis 5: The more people get excited about the incentive, the more likely they are to share it.

It is also usual that negative content has a deeper psychological impact on people. Negative information receives more attention and is processed slowly and deeply (Ahluwalia 2002; Baumeister *et al.* 2001; Berger and Milkman 2012). Although people want to give good news and show both a positive mood and status in order to receive approval from others and improve their image in the eyes of their peers, bad news is shown more frequently on media. For instance, alerts and rumours tend to spread quickly. This is what happens when activists do demarketing, spreading negative communication about companies (Gundlach *et al.* 2010). From this, it is possible to theorize that:

> Hypothesis 6: Positive content has a greater likelihood of being shared than negative content.

Considering the sharer profile, it is reasonable, based on ideas such as (i) Veblen's (1899) trickle-down theory, in which lower classes often imitate upper classes, or (ii) Rogers (2003) diffusion theory, in which early adopters are followed by others or, yet, (iii) Lazarsfeld *et al.* (1948) theory of influencers, in which influencers are the first to adopt a behaviour, with general people following afterwards because they want to imitate the influencers. Therefore, people can differ on sharing, based on their income.

So, it is possible to theorize that:

> Hypothesis 7: Higher income people will have a higher propensity to share, and greater perceived usefulness in sharing, when an incentive is offered.

> Hypothesis 8: Lower income people will have a higher propensity to share, and greater perceived usefulness in sharing, when a known people's tip was given.

Method

To test these hypotheses, we have conducted a three factorial experiment (control – no incentive and no recommendation advertisement, and treatment – advertisement with incentive to share and with a friend's recommendation) x 2 (positive and negative valence). The experimental design was applied among 199 undergraduate students, randomly assigned to each of the six scenarios. Data collection took place between 6 November and 17 December 2013, and students received academic credits. Therefore, convenience sampling was performed.

Check manipulation was performed: negative emotions averaged 2.36 while positive averaged 3.70, suggesting that manipulation was successful (p-value < 0.000). To check the differences between the propensity to share, perceived usefulness and arousal in different emotional valences, ANOVAs were performed for each condition, comparing the base scenario, the advertisement alone (control), with the other two – advertisement with an incentive and with a recommendation (treatment).

All the variables (propensity to share, perceived usefulness, arousal) were measured by multi-item scales present in the literature and adapted (Berger and Milkman 2012; Sweetney *et al.* 2014). All scales were 5-points Likert.

In all scenarios a video was shown to respondents, who answered a questionnaire about it. The videos were about Kit Kat, a chocolate bar from Nestlé, a Swiss confectionery maker. In the positive scenario, the ad was about babies dancing after someone eats a bar, and in the negative scenario, an ad was by Greenpeace and showed the death of orangutans caused by devastation of a rainforest in Asia, where palm oil used by Nestlé to produce Kit Kat comes from. All videos were available on YouTube, and were collected and edited. The videos were formatted to be same size, quality and duration. In the scenario with a friend's recommendation, respondents needed to think of a close and reliable friend and imagine that he/she had recommended the ad. In the advertisement with an incentive scenario, respondents were exposed to the following promotion: 'Share this video and win a Greenpeace t-shirt', in the negative scenario, and 'Share this video and win a Nestlé kit', in the positive scenario.

Data analysis

The influence of the valence was observed by the mean difference between positive and negative in each of the dependent variables. The relationship with the propensity to share was not significant (p-value = 0.66 and 0.67), so Hypothesis 6 was not confirmed.

However, for usefulness and arousal, the relationship was significant. Arousal generated by negative valence was greater than positive valence (3.36 versus 3.01, p-value = 0.019) and negative content had higher perceived usefulness than positive (3.25 versus 2.61, p-value < 0.000).

Regarding the variable format advertising, all tests of statistical significance showed a value greater than 0.05, when considered individually or together with emotional valence. However, the propensity to share is related to the other variables. The correlation between the propensity to share and usefulness is high: 0.72 (p-value < 0.000). The correlation with arousal also exists: 0.59 (p-value < 0.000). Therefore, Hypothesis 5 was supported.

Here, we can observe a positive relationship between these factors: when arousal is high, perceived usefulness and propensity to share are also high, for any valence or advertising format. Moreover, for higher arousal levels, the propensity to share had statistical significance with the valence (F = 4.782; p-value = 0.031), i.e. for those who considered the videos highly exciting (139 among 197 respondents), the propensity to share with friends was higher for positive content (3.56) than for negative content (3.24).

The same conclusion is obtained regarding perceived usefulness: for higher perceived usefulness levels, the propensity to share was statistically related to both the valence (F = 18.810; p-value < 0.001) and advertisement format (F = 5.010; p-value = 0.008). That is, for those who considered the videos useful (113 among 197 respondents), the propensity to share was higher for positive than for negative content (3.93 vs. 3.36). In this case, propensity can vary as a result of the format of the advertisement: friends' recommendations have higher levels of propensity to be shared (3.9) than recommendations with promotion (3.4) or without promotion (3.6).

Arousal level equal to or greater than 3 had higher ratings of propensity to share (3.5) than lower arousal (2.1). The content with high arousal generated higher propensities to share than the same valence and low arousal.

The content with positive valence generated higher propensity to share than that with negative valence, both with low and high perceived usefulness. On average, negative valence content had a greater perceived usefulness than positive (3.25 to 2.61, p-value < 0.000).

The gender variable showed differences in arousal variable: women had higher arousal than men: 3.36 versus 2.97 (F = 7.372, p = 0.007).

The income variable had significant relationships with the dependent variables: (i) the propensity to share (3.3, low income, high income 2.9, p = 0.014); and (ii) perceived usefulness (3.2, low income, 2.7, high income, p = 0.004). Further, Figures 20.1 and 20.2, and Tables 20.2 and 20.3, show that, among higher income respondents, usefulness is high when there is a prize for negative advertisement sharing (3.37), and the propensity to share level is high if it was a friend's recommendation, and for a positive advertisement (3.38). Therefore, Hypothesis 7 was supported. In addition, among lower income respondents, propensity to share and usefulness are high for positive advertisements, with no incentive. However, negative advertisements have a higher propensity to be

SHARE INTENTIONS (p<0,05)

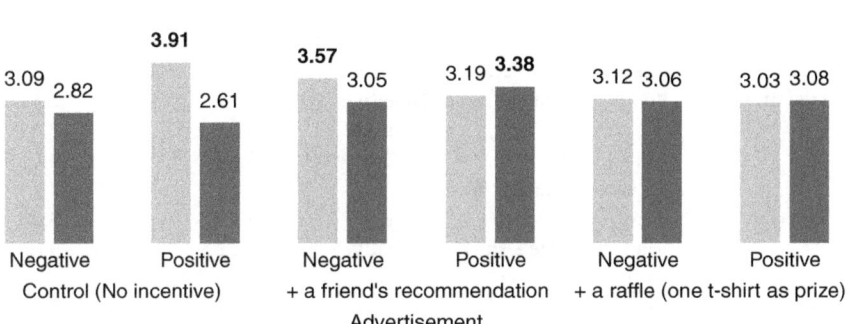

FIGURE 20.1 Share intentions.

USEFULNESS (p<0,05)

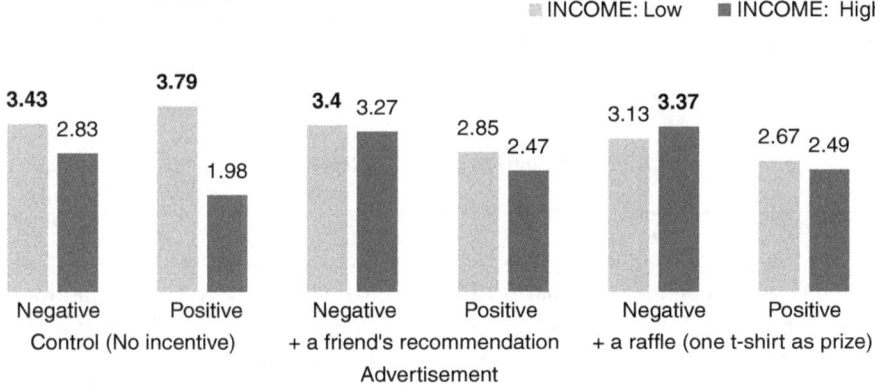

FIGURE 20.2 Usefulness.

shared and higher usefulness if they were recommended by a friend. Therefore, Hypothesis 8 was supported for negative ads.

It was observed that, among respondents with lower income, all the mentioned dependent variables have higher averages than among respondents with higher income. In other words, perhaps these higher income respondents, and the higher income population, are more critical and skeptical of advertisements, even the negative ones.

Furthermore, income was then used as a co-variable in some of the relationships between dependent and independent variables, since their means were different depending on the level of income. The first relationship considered was between the format of the advertisement and the propensity to share (p = 0.049): when income is low, the propensity to share is higher in advertisements without recommendation (3.55, against 3.37 with recommendation, and 3.01, with a reward).

TABLE 20.2 Share intentions

Share intentions		Valence	Income	
			Low	High
Advertisement	control (no incentive)	Negative	3.09	2.82
		Positive	**3.91**	2.61
	+ a friend's recommendation	Negative	**3.57**	3.05
		Positive	3.19	**3.38**
	+ a raffle (one t-shirt as prize)	Negative	3.12	3.06
		Positive	3.03	3.08

TABLE 20.3 Share intentions, part two

Perceived utility		Valence	Income	
			Low	High
Advertisement	control (no incentive)	Negative	**3.43**	2.83
		Positive	**3.79**	1.98
	+ a friend's recommendation	Negative	**3.40**	3.27
		Positive	2.85	2.47
	+ a raffle (one t-shirt as prize)	Negative	3.13	**3.37**
		Positive	2.67	2.49

Among higher income respondents, the propensity to share was greater in the friend's recommendation scenario (3.21, compared to 3.1, with a promotional incentive, and 2.7, with just advertisement). Therefore, it is possible that a promotion or a friend's recommendation has a stronger effect when the client has a higher income. It could be that this population has a different attitude, compared to a lower income population, to financial and relationship issues when they decide to share something.

The second relationship considered is that between valence and arousal ($p = 0.012$): when the valence is negative, the arousal is higher when income is high (3.49 for high income, compared to 3.28 for low income), and when the valence is positive, the arousal is higher when income is low (3.37, low income, compared to 2.78, high income). Apparently, the type of use of social networks can change depending on the income: it is possible that low-income users in social networks seek to meet new consumption opportunities, while those with high incomes seek to make better choices.

The third relationship examined is that between the format of advertising and its usefulness ($p = 0.007$); low-income respondents considered that the control scenario, with just the advertising, had greater perceived usefulness than other scenarios (3.57, versus 3.14, with a recommendation, and 2.94, with a reward). Among high-income users, on the other hand, the relationship is reversed: the highest usefulness occurs when there is a reward (2.91 against 2.87, with a recommendation, and 2.34, for the control scenario).

Finally, the fourth relationship examined is between the format of the advertisement, its valence and the propensity to share ($p = 0.033$), indicating the control scenario (no reward, no recommendation) is more likely to be shared (3.91) than other formats and valences when income is low. An advertisement with a friend's recommendation is more likely to be shared when the valence is negative. When income is high, the relationship is reversed: the higher propensity to share occurs when there is a friend's recommendation and a positive valence (3.38).

Finally, it will be discussed whether the hypotheses of this study were confirmed: Hypotheses H1 and H2 – Advertising with reward programs generate a greater propensity to share than advertising without incentives and are more useful than advertising without incentives – were rejected because there was no statistical significance in the difference of means t-test for the propensity to share or usefulness.

Hypotheses H3 and H4 – a tip from a friend makes the content more useful and increases the propensity to share – were partially rejected. For the total sample, there was no statistical significance, but when considering only those whose arousal was high (greater than or equal to 3), the propensity to share is higher than without the tip (3.55 versus 3.26, p-value = 0.05). This fact also occurs among those who consider high perceived usefulness: the propensity to share is higher than without it (3.83 versus 3.46, p-value = 0.01).

Final thoughts

The advertisement videos of negative valence were considered more useful and more exciting than the positive valence ones. The format of the advertisement (with or without promotion or recommendation) had no statistically significant relationship with any of the variables.

However, considering only those who experienced higher levels of arousal or perceived usefulness (equal to or above 3 on a Likert 5-point scale), the propensity to share was statistically significant: positive content was more likely to be shared than negative content, even if referred by friends.

The fact that the propensity to share is more intense among those who considered the content exciting or useful is consistent with the theory: the idea that it is useful or not is subjective, as is the sensitivity of an individual to the arousal.

However, the fact that the format of the advertisement has not presented interaction with the valence deserves consideration: a referral from a friend or a promotion as an incentive for sharing, regardless of whether the content is positive or negative, is also perceived by the consumer. Different people can consider the same incentive in different ways.

The moderating role of income needs to be further investigated, given that the propensity to share in low-income populations is significant for positive content, while high-income populations have a greater propensity to share when encouraged by friends or promotions. Maybe, while higher-income people seek better consumption choices, and, for this, an opinion, an offer or information about a product's origins makes a difference, among lower income people the main motivation is for starting consumption – opinions and negative information are not above consumption itself.

This study has as theoretical contribution a wider notion about incentives and their relation with online sharing. Some incentives are more effective than others, and income is a moderator. This study supports the idea that people share videos when they consider them useful, exciting and positive.

As managerial contributions, this study shows that it is necessary to consider different approaches among higher and lower income people in terms of online advertisement sharing. It is likely that higher income people are more interested in showing how discerning they are, and they expect to get something in return for ad sharing, while low income people are interested in good news, being part of a market and showing that they are part of it. On the other hand, if low income people receive negative advertisements from a friend, they will share intensively. Managers need to consider this when launching a new product or in a communication campaign.

The study findings are limited to two advertisements and two incentives used to manipulate the perceived usefulness, arousal and propensity to share. Moreover, the respondents are from Brazil and, in spite of Greenpeace and Nestlé having huge local operations, the results could vary if we chose different brands, or if data collection took place in other countries, or if a wider range of respondents than students was considered. Past attitudes towards the ads or brands used could influence results. Future studies may also investigate other types of positive and negative communications and other kinds of incentives, such as discounts or higher value gifts. Moreover, this study considered online videos alone. Further studies could compare traditional media and online media.

References

Ahluwalia, R. 2002. 'How prevalent is the negativity effect in consumer environments?' *Journal of Consumer Research*, 29 (Sept).

Antin, J. and E. Churchill. 2011. 'Badges in social media – a social psychological perspective'. *CHI 2011 Gamification Workshop Proceedings, 1–4.*.

Baumeister, R., E. Blatslavsky, C. Finkenauer and K. Vohls. 2001. 'Bad is stronger than good'. *Review of General Psychology*, 5:4, p. 323–370.

Berger, J. and R. Iyengar. 2013. 'Communication channels and word of mouth: how the medium shapes the message'. *Journal of Consumer Research*, 40 (October), p. 567–579.

Berger, J. and K. L. Milkman. 2012. 'What makes online content viral?' *Journal of Marketing Research*, XLIX (April), p. 192–205. doi:10.1509/jmr.10.0353

Blythe, J. 2013. *Consumer Behaviour* (second ed.). London: Sage.

Botha, E. and M. Reyneke. 2013. 'To share or not to share: the role of content and emotion in viral marketing', *Journal of Public Affairs*, 13:2, p. 160–171.

Dobele, A., A. Lindgreen, M. Beverland, J. Vanhamme and R. Wijk. 2007. 'Why pass on viral messages? Because they connect emotionally'. *Business Horizons*, 50:4, p. 291–304.

Godes, D., D. Mayslin, Y. Chen, S. Das, C. Dellarocas, B. Pfeiffer, B. Libai, S. Sen, M. Shi and P. Verlegh. 2005. 'The firm's management of social interactions', *Marketing Letters*, 16:3/4, p. 415–428.

Goldenberg, J., B. Libai and E. Muller. 2001. 'Talk of the network: a complex systems look at the underlying process of word-of-mouth'. *Marketing Letters*, 12:3., p. 211–223. Available at http://www.springerlink.com/index/T24301H2268N5V46.pdf.

Haryani, S. and B. Motwani. 2015. 'Gender difference in consumer perception towards online viral marketing communication', *Journal of Marketing & Business Communication*, 4:3, p. 28–37.

Gundlach, G. T., K. D. Bradford and W. L. Wilkie. 2010. 'Countermarketing and demarketing against product diversion: forensic research in the firearms industry'. *Journal of Public Policy & Marketing*, 29:1, p. 103–122.

Korgaonkar, P., M. Petrescu and J. Gironda. 2016. 'Hispanics and viral advertising', *Journal of Retailing and Consumer Service*, 32, p. 46–59.

Lazarsfeld, P. F., B. Berelson and H. Gaudet. 1948. *The People's Choice*. New York: Columbia University Press.

Ling, K., G. Beenen, P. Ludford, X. Wang, K. Chang, X. Li, D. Cosley, D. Frankowski, L. Terveen, A. M. Rashid, P. Resnick, and R. Kraut. 2005. 'Using social psychology to motivate contributions to online communities'. *Journal of Computer-Mediated Communication*, 10:4, doi:10.1111/j.1083-6101.2005.tb00273.x

Keller, E. and B. Fay. 2009. *Comparing Online and Offline Word of Mouth: Quantity, Quality, and Impact*. New Brunswick, NJ: Keller Fay Group.

Minxue H., C. Fengyan, S. L. Alex, and N. Tsang. 2011. 'Making your online voice loud: the critical role of WOM information', *European Journal of Marketing*, 45:7/8, p. 1277–1297.

Rogers, E. 2003. *Diffusion of Innovations* (fifth ed.). New York: Free Press.

Ryan, R. M. and E. L. Deci. 2000. 'Intrinsic and extrinsic motivations: classic definitions and new directions'. *Contemporary Educational Psychology*, New York, 25:1, p. 54–67.

Ryu, G. and L. Feick. 2007. 'A penny for your thoughts: referral reward programs and referral'. *Journal of Marketing*, 71, p. 84–94.

Shen, G., J. Chiou, C. Wang, H. Li. 2016. 'Effective marketing communication via social networking site: the moderating role of the social tie', *Journal of Business Research*, 69:6, p. 2265–2270.

Shimp, T. 2010. *Integrated Marketing Communications in Advertisement and Promotion* (eighth ed.). London: Cengage.

Shu-Chuan, C. 2011. 'Viral advertising in social media: participation in Facebook groups and responses among college-aged users', *Journal of Interactive Advertising*, 12:1, p. 30–43.

Sweetney, J., G. Soutar and T. Mazzarol. 2014. 'Factors enhancing word-of-mouth influence: positive and negative service-related messages', *European Journal of Marketing*, 48:1, p. 336–359.

Tuten, T. and M. Solomon. 2015. *Social Media Marketing* (second edition). London: Sage.

Veblen, T. 1899. *The Theory of the Leisure Class*. New York: Macmillan.

Wendt, L., J. Griesbaum, R. Kölle. 2016. 'Product advertising and viral stealth marketing in online videos', *Aslib Journal of Information Management*, 68:3, p. 250–264.

Yang, C. and Y. Wang. 2015. 'Social sharing of online videos: examining American consumers' video sharing attitudes, intent and behavior', *Psychology & Marketing*, 32:9, p. 907–919.

21

THE RISE OF SOCIAL MEDIA

Implications for emerging markets

Ogechi Adeola

The direct, unfiltered, brutally honest nature of much online discussion is gold dust to big companies that want to spot trends, or find out what customers really think of them.

–The Economist, March 2006

Introduction

The Internet has become a vast new universe in which firms can build shopping outposts for consumers and has also had the greatest impact on marketing communication since television (Falls and Deckers 2011). Social networking, the Internet's conversational platform, has captured users' imaginations through online experiences in which they can contribute and interact in real time. The two-way nature of social media presents a fundamental change in how businesses interact with their customers, who can now tell companies how they feel about their brands and services, and at the same time, through word-of-mouth (WOM), spread the word about their shopping experience (Akhtar 2011; Jackson 2011). The Internet has become a living thing.

The goal of social media marketing is to create content that users will share with their social networks and thereby help boost brand exposure and increase customer reach. Two notable changes in consumer behaviour have become a reality: increased engagement and networked interconnectedness. Consequently, consumers now have more power (Hennig-Thurau, Hofacker and Bloching 2013; Labrecque *et al.* 2013), actively participating in the marketplace by sharing brand and product experiences with scores of friends or other consumers via social media.

Rapid changes in the communication landscape engendered by participatory Internet use have, most markedly in the last decade, created a marketing environment in which consumers have become active participants who choose to seek, create and share information via multiple channels and devices. This is a major shift from traditional, uni-directional media to multi-directional Internet-based applications such as Web 2.0., which allow users (i.e. consumers) to become the producers and managers of communication. Due to its novelty and apparent effectiveness, social media presents huge opportunities for marketing campaigns (Miller and Lammas 2011; Thackeray *et al.* 2008).

Many businesses in emerging markets think they have met the Internet's marketing challenges. They have created a Web presence, maintained and updated their sites, and communicated with email. This 'digital disruption' in the marketplace, however, has just begun. Facebook, Twitter, YouTube and Google+ have opened their doors to the world, and the power of social media has begun to affect consumers and businesses with breathtaking speed. For example, Lazada, an e-Commerce presence in the Philippines, has over 15 million fans on Facebook. Claro Brasil has more than 6 million Twitter followers. Turkish Airlines has over 2 million followers on Google+. On YouTube, social media site PGMexicoMdo has more than 300 million viewers (Socialbakers.com 2016).

The emergence of social media networks has facilitated the development of eWOM – electronic word-of-mouth – a phenomenon receiving mounting attention from researchers, practitioners and policy makers (Boyd and Ellison 2008; Chu and Kim 2011; Ellison, Steinfield and Lampe 2007; Thelwall 2008, 2009; Pan and Crotts 2012; Valenzuela, Park and Kee 2009). Social media facilitates and shapes eWOM in the marketplace. However, the implications for emerging markets have not yet been fully examined.

Advertisers characteristically seek innovative ways to seduce their target audiences, and social media offers a new method of communication. Ultimately, advertisers in emerging markets will find it necessary to go beyond 'old school' marketing methods (i.e. television, print) to achieve their corporate marketing objectives. This is equally true in developing as well as developed economies, but there is currently little evidence in emerging markets of efforts to build a unified understanding of the opportunities social media offers to marketing communications. This study will identify the implications of social media in online marketing campaigns in emerging markets.

This chapter presents a background for social media trends, a theoretical framework of eWOM, the engagement of brand communities in this social media age, and possibilities for building on social media opportunities in emerging markets. The Kumbaya effect, a kind of excitement related to adopting social media, will draw attention to this potential pitfall, and a yin-yang approach to selecting traditional and social media will be shown to be an effective strategy.

Social media trends in emerging markets

We don't have a choice on whether we DO social media, the question is how well we do it.

–Erik Qualman, Digital Media Expert, Professor and Author

Social media has changed marketing from a monologue to a multilogue. 'Companies can now talk to customers and customers to companies, but customers can also talk to other customers, prospects, and the public in general' (Falls and Deckers 2011, p. 4). Application of this uncontrollable multilogue could initially be shocking to businesses in emerging markets, and while many play-it-safe companies, especially small businesses, are wary of the concept, smart companies are beginning to see this as an opportunity to gain insights into customer demands and expectations. Social media is not slowly creeping into the emerging markets: despite some companies shying away from it, social media has arrived in the marketplace, and it is not going away (Falls and Deckers 2011).

Emerging economies and emerging markets account for approximately 60 per cent of the world's population; a significant demographic for social media (Olenski 2013). A Pew Research Center report found that:

> [W]hile people in advanced economies still use the Internet more and own more high-tech gadgets, the rest of the emerging world is catching up. ... Roughly three-quarters or more of internet users in the Middle East (86%), Latin America (82%) and Africa (76%) say they use social networks, compared with 71% in the U.S. and 65% across six European nations.
>
> *(2016, p. 1)*

As illustrated in Figure 21.1, Internet users in emerging markets demonstrate an enthusiasm for social media use that is outpacing that of the U.S. and Europe.

As businesses in emerging markets grow in size and revenue, technology use increases, especially among populations with more education and higher incomes. In some emerging markets, including Korea, Nigeria, Ghana and China, more people are gaining access to the Internet, and they are using it more frequently (Pew Research Center 2016). Social media is a new experience in emerging markets and less saturated than in the U.S. and Europe, but as the world's fastest growing,

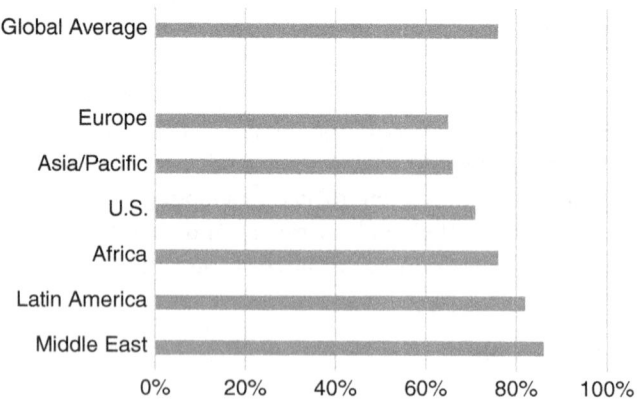

FIGURE 21.1 Social network users.

Source: Pew Research Center 2016.

content-hungry consumer base, these markets are becoming e-Commerce gold-mines (Olenski 2013).

Many businesses in emerging markets rely on high cost, traditional marketing devices such as TV and radio commercials, billboards and print ads, but only a fraction of the intended consumer demographic sees these ads or trusts them. Some businesses may open a Twitter account or Facebook page with low-priority, automated promotions. However, social media marketing needs to be more than simple announcements:

> Social media is about being social with a purpose. It means listening to what your customers are saying. Listening to what they're complaining about, and then fixing it; listening to what they're asking, and then answering it; listening to what they're happy about, and then thanking them; and listening to what they're telling their friends about, and then rewarding them when appropriate.
>
> *(Falls and Deckers 2011, p. 36)*

Consumers trust the recommendations of friends and online communities. Personal ratings and review sites offer information on products and services submitted by users who have bought and tried products or services of interest. Social media marketing may 'become more important than advertising as a trusted source of information' (Karami and Naghibi 2014, p. 13). Social media can serve as the new WOM, a less expensive platform for emerging economy businesses to implement their marketing campaigns (Yadav and Tripathi 2016).

Theoretical framework

Word-of-mouth (WOM) is 'the act of exchanging marketing information among consumers, and plays an essential role in changing consumer attitudes and behaviour towards products and services' (Chu and Kim 2011, p. 47). The influence of WOM on consumer decision making can be traced back to the 1960s (Engel, Blackwell and Kegerreis 1969) when studies found that consumers making purchasing decisions often relied on WOM from friends, family and other acquaintances, whose firsthand experiences were deemed to be more trustworthy than company-generated messages (Chu and Kim 2011; Crotts 1999; Perdue 1993). Information acquired from friends and family is construed to 'be more credible, honest, and trustworthy than that generated from marketers, since the communicators are not compensated for the referral. Advancements in the Internet and Web 2.0 technologies now allow consumers to access personally meaningful critiques not only from friends and relatives but from strangers' (Pan and Crotts 2012, p. 43).

Hennig-Thurau *et al.* defined eWOM as 'any positive or negative statement made by potential, actual, or former customers about a product or company, which is made available to a multitude of people and institutions via the Internet' (2004, p. 39). Email, blogs, virtual consumer communities, consumer review websites and forums, and social networking sites are all sources of eWOM (Dwyer, Hiltz and Passerini 2007; Hung and Li 2007; Thorson and Rodgers 2006).

Social media delivers eWOM as consumers freely create and disseminate brand-related information (Vollmer and Precourt 2008). Consumers can provide feedback to a business by liking or disliking and providing reviews, thereby passing along their views to their social connections (Interactive Advertising Bureau 2009).

Brand communities and management in the social media age

With the help of technological advancement, the concept of bounded brand communities has now transcended geography (Muniz and O'Guinn 2001), giving rise to social-media-based brand communities. Vodafone Egypt, Volkswagen de Mexico, Turkish Airlines and DHL Africa are examples of popular brands in emerging markets that have created brand communities on Facebook, Twitter, Google+ and YouTube. These communities provide member benefits, facilitate information sharing and enhance customers' favourable associations with the product, the brand and the company.

Social media communities can, via eWOM, cement relationships among customers, products, brands and marketers, and these relationships generate brand loyalty (Laroche, Habibi and Richard 2013). Other benefits are enhanced information sharing (Kaplan and Haenlein 2010; Schau, Muniz and Arnould 2009; Szmigin and Reppel 2001; Von Hippel 2005); interaction with highly committed customers (Anderson 2006); co-creation of value from close interaction with customers (Schau *et al.*); and increased brand loyalty, the first priority for all businesses (McAlexander, Schouten and Koening 2002).

In current times, traditional product-centered marketing has given way to market- and consumer-centered marketing. According to Kotler (1999, as cited in Falls and Deckers 2011, p. 14):

> Old marketing thinking is, fortunately, now giving way to newer ways of thinking. Smart marketing companies are improving their customer knowledge, customer connection technologies, and understanding of customer economics. They are inviting customers to co-design the product. They are ready to make flexible marketing offerings. They are using more targeted media and integrating their marketing communications to deliver a consistent message through every customer contact. They are utilizing more technologies such as video-conferencing, sales automation, software, Internet web pages, and Intranets and Extranets. They are reachable seven days a week, twenty-four hours a day ... In sum, they have found ways to deliver superior value to their customers.

Social media is powerful when utilized strategically (Coon 2010). It no longer takes years to build a reputation through trade shows, conferences and trade journals. Building eWOM with like-minded people through social networks can establish a solid reputation in a few months.

Jumia in Nigeria is an example of how a business used social media to expand rapidly, propagate its customer base and enhance service quality. 'Leveraging on social networks and online channels, Jumia introduced the novel idea of shopping online which was quickly and widely accepted by Nigerians, leading to them reaching the 500,000 fans landmark in less than a year' (Jumia Nigeria 2016, p. 1). Jumia began awarding 'Customer of the Month' status to its most active participants on their Facebook and Twitter pages. Now five years old, Jumia has more than 7 million Facebook fans and is the largest social network in the world.

Gaining control of the plethora of multimedia content aimed at consumers requires focused attention (Gensler *et al.* 2013). One of the far-reaching implications of social media is that 'companies have, at least partially, lost control of marketing activities. Nowhere is the loss of control more critical than in the area of branding, where the firm strives to manage consumer reactions … . [Firms in emerging markets need to accept that] the game has changed and … therefore [that they need to] co-create brand stories with active consumers, instead of continuing to do so autonomously' (Hennig-Thurau, Hofacker and Bloching 2013, p. 238).

The Indian Railways Fan Club Association is a powerful example of effective brand story co-creation with active consumers in an emerging market:

[M]embers in love with the brand upload pictures, videos, share their trip details and various other experiences. It boasts photographs of some trains and engines that were a part of the British history and had been in use during the pre-independent days … . The community has various online discussion forums which range from the history of locomotives to the ideas about naming of trains in the country. It also has various forums where the users share their knowledge, for example, about the trains and the railway station codes for various stations in the country (Banerjee and Banerjee 2015, p. 23–25).

Social media platform possibilities in emerging markets

Social media platforms include social networks, text messaging, discussion forums, photo sharing, weblogs and wikis (Harris 2009; Laroche, Habibi and Richard 2013); social media marketing, however, is mostly associated with Facebook, Twitter and YouTube. Strategic use of the hashtag can be integrated to increase brand awareness.

Facebook: Facebook is a powerhouse of marketing activity with more than 1.5 billion monthly active users (aka 'Friends'), with 50 per cent of these logging in daily. Facebook builds online communities and finds new customers for emerging markets such as Lazada in the Philippines (15 million Friends), Jumia in Nigeria (7 million Friends) and Quilmes Cerveza in Argentina (over 4 million Friends).

Twitter: Twitter is a microblogging system that has become a powerful social medium and a speedy way to circulate information. Companies can easily share information with their target audience in real time; build relationships with customers, partners and influencers; and gather market feedback. Examples of emerging market businesses connecting and building relationships with customers on Twitter are Claro Brasil in Brazil (6 million followers), Reliance Mobile in India (2 million followers) and BTS SkyTrain in Thailand (over 1 million followers).

YouTube: Businesses increase brand awareness and attract consumers with product descriptions, presentations, tutorials or 'tips and tricks' when they upload and share videos on YouTube. Examples of emerging market businesses that are increasing their brand awareness on YouTube are PGMexicoMdo from Mexico (over 300 million views), Itau from Brazil (over 200 million views) and Berniaga in Indonesia (over 90 million views).

Other social networking sites serve special interest niches. LinkedIn offers over 400 million professionals a means of effectively promoting their products and services, brand, and message, as well as maintaining a professional presence for their staff. LinkedIn company pages include information about career opportunities, branding possibilities and analytics. Google+ is an interest-based social network that supports emerging market businesses, brands and artists as they develop a public identity and share their business information. Turkish Airlines (over 2 million followers), Nokia India (over 1 million followers) and Vodafone Egypt (over 1.5 million followers) have developed a presence on Google+. Pinterest and Instagram are the two most popular photo sharing sites, largely benefitting businesses that depend on consumers' visual assessments (e.g. clothing stores, design firms, landscaping companies, restaurants and art galleries).

Some Western social networks are blocked in emerging markets, so local platforms increase the possibility of attracting regional consumers. Strong local networks include QQ in China; Hi5 in Peru; Kontakte in Russia; Orkut in Brazil and India; and Maktoob, the most popular choice all through the Arab world (Olenski 2013). Brands that invest more time in these popular local equivalents will increase eWOM, sway brand perceptions and enhance brand loyalty.

The Kumbaya effect

Many businesses in emerging markets are now using social media and have begun to generate eWOM. Being present on a social media site, however, is not just about joining the conversation, which can lead to unrealistic expectations about its ultimate value – what has been called 'the Kumbaya effect' (Falls and Deckers 2011). Kumbaya, a popular African-American campfire folk song from the 1930s, is about unity, social circles of support and building community. The Kumbaya effect happens when a company gets lost in the euphoria of social media conversations, creating eWOM and interacting with others.

Being social is about 'reaching for the lifetime value of a customer, not the end-of-month quota. It is about bringing a value system to your company that holds the customer in the highest regard' (Falls and Deckers 2011, p. 239). To be perceived as a social-minded business, a company must perceive itself as a stakeholder that brings value to its consumer community. As businesses are building online conversations and consumer-centric business models, they risk falling victim to the Kumbaya effect if they lose sight of strategies to drive business and build revenue. Successful businesses must remain both consumer-centric and business-aware.

Yin-Yang: the necessity of balance

This study does not recommend that companies in emerging markets replace traditional marketing/WOM with social media. More people are likely to see a TV commercial than a tweet. However, in contrast to traditional media, social media marketing delivers messages to a more interested audience. Marketing campaigns are well served by what Falls and Deckers (2011) termed 'yin-yang'. In Chinese philosophy, yin-yang describes how opposite forces are complementary and interdependent in the natural world, creating the balance in all things. According to Falls and Deckers, 'the full circle of social media marketing and social business recommendations has a pleasant yin-yang feeling to it' (2011, p. 246).

Conclusion

There are merits to using both traditional media (WOM) and social media (eWOM) marketing. Traditional media is an outbound marketing approach that delivers a message via television, radio or print and hopes consumers respond positively to the ads. Inbound marketing is achieved as online users see advertising pop up on social media or even in their mailbox.

Over time, consumers may choose to 'Like' a company on Facebook, follow it on Twitter or subscribe to its blog. Social media marketing actions become participatory, not interruptive; consumers are primed to consider and purchase from companies with which they have become accustomed and even trust.

Emerging market businesses will find that their competition may already have a head start in the full utilization of social networks as marketing tools. In this era of consumer-centric marketing, successful brands go beyond owning a Facebook page to engage their customers through the strategic use of social media that transforms marketing into an enjoyable, engaging and natural experience.

Twitter, Facebook and LinkedIn are actively vying for users' attention, and local platforms increase the possibility of engaging regional consumers. Brands that invest more time in these popular local equivalents hold the power to sway brand perceptions, create eWOM and enhance brand loyalty.

One strategy for avoiding the Kumbaya effect is for businesses to adopt a 'general store' concept. In the rural segments of many emerging markets, there are hubs where people regularly seek out information. This is often a general store that serves as a small community's post office, newspaper and even bank all in one place. There is community around these hubs. By building communications and information hubs around a business via social media marketing/eWOM, any business can cultivate the general store concept around its brand.

This overview of social media within the marketing realm encourages yin-yang, the value of balance. Instead of giving up on traditional channels, companies can add social media and eWOM to their marketing campaigns. A company that combines both WOM and eWOM, engages in social interaction with their audience and claims a role in the consumer conversation, has a greater chance of success.

References

Akhtar, S. 2011. 'Social media and brand loyalty'. Cited in Eren-Erdoğmuş, İ., & Ergun, S. (2017). *The Impact of Social Media on Social Movements: The Case of Anti-Consumption*. In *Online Communities as Agents of Change and Social Movements* (pp. 224–252), Hershey, PA: IGI Global.

Anderson, C. 2006. *The Long Tail: Why the Future of Business Is Selling More of Less*. New York: Hyperion.

Banerjee, S. and S. C. Banerjee. 2015. 'Brand communities: an emerging marketing tool'. *IUP Journal of Brand Management*, 12:1, p. 22.

Boyd, D. M. and N. B. Ellison. 2008. 'Social network sites: definition, history, and scholarship'. *Journal of Computer-Mediated Communication*, 13:1, p. 210–230.

Chu, S. C. and Y. Kim. 2011. 'Determinants of consumer engagement in electronic word-of-mouth (eWOM) in social networking sites'. *International Journal of Advertising*, 30:1, p. 47–75.

Coon, M. 2010. 'Social media marketing: successful case studies of businesses using Facebook and YouTube'. Masters Project, Stanford University.

Crotts, J. 1999. 'Consumer decision making and prepurchase information search'. *Consumer Behavior in Travel and Tourism*, p. 149–168.

Dwyer, C., S. Hiltz and K. Passerini. 2007. 'Trust and privacy concern within social networking sites: a comparison of Facebook and MySpace'. *AMCIS* 2007 Proceedings, p. 339.

Ellison, N. B., C. Steinfield and C. Lampe. 2007. 'The benefits of Facebook "friends": social capital and college students' use of online social network sites'. *Journal of Computer-Mediated Communication*, 12:4, p. 1143–1168.

Engel, J. F., R. D. Blackwell and R. J. Kegerreis. 1969. 'How information is used to adopt an innovation'. *Journal of Advertising Research*, 9:4, p. 3–8.

Falls, J. and E. Deckers. 2011. *No bullshit social media: the all-business, no-hype guide to social media marketing*. Indianapolis, IN: Que Publishing.

Gensler, S., F. Völckner, Y. Liu-Thompkins and C. Wiertz. 2013. 'Managing brands in the social media environment'. *Journal of Interactive Marketing*, 27:4, p. 242–256.

Harris, R. 2009. 'Social media ecosystem mapped as a wiring diagram'. Retrieved from: http://harrissocialmedia.com/2009/9/3/ Accessed 17.04.17.

Hennig-Thurau, T., K. P. Gwinner, G. Walsh and D. D. Gremler. 2004. 'Electronic word-of-mouth via consumer-opinion platforms: what motivates consumers to articulate themselves on the internet?'. *Journal of Interactive Marketing*, 18(1), p. 38–52

Hennig-Thurau, T., C. F. Hofacker, and B. Bloching. 2013. 'Marketing the pinball way: understanding how social media change the generation of value for consumers and companies'. *Journal of Interactive Marketing*, 27:4, p. 237–241.

Hung, K. H. and S. Y. Li. 2007. 'The influence of eWOM on virtual consumer communities: social capital, consumer learning, and behavioral outcomes', *Journal of Advertising Research*, 47:4, p. 485–495.

Interactive Advertising Bureau. 2009. 'IAB social advertising best practices'. Available at http://www.iab.net/media/file/Social-Advertising-Best-Practices-0509.pdf. Accessed 12 February 2010.

Jackson, N. 2011. 'Infographic: using social media to build brand loyalty'. Available at http://www.theatlantic.com/technology/archive/2011/07/infographic-using-social-media-to-build-brand-loyalty/241701/. Accessed 7 January 2012.

Jumia Nigeria. 2016. 'Social media & customer of the month'. Available at https://www.jumia.com.ng/jumia-social-customer-month/. Accessed 4 August 2016.

Kaplan, A. M. and M. Haenlein. 2010. 'Users of the world, unite! The challenges and opportunities of social media'. *Business Horizons*, 53, p. 59–68.

Karami, S. and H. S. Naghibi. 2014. 'Social media marketing (SMM) strategies for small to medium enterprises (SMEs)'. *International Journal of Sales & Marketing*, 4:4, p. 11–20.

Labrecque, L. I., J. vor dem Esche, C. Mathwick, T. P. Novak and C. F. Hofacker. 2013. 'Consumer power: evolution in the digital age'. *Journal of Interactive Marketing*, 27:4, p. 257–269.

Laroche, M., M. R. Habibi and M. O. Richard. 2013. 'To be or not to be in social media: how brand loyalty is affected by social media?' *International Journal of Information Management*, 33:1, p. 76–82.

McAlexander, J. H., W. J. Schouten and F. H. Koening. 2002. 'Building brand community'. *Journal of Marketing*, 66:1, p. 38–54.

Miller, R. and N. Lammas. 2011. 'Social media and its implications for viral marketing', *Asia Pacific Public Relations Journal*, 11:1, p. 1–9.

Muniz, M. A. and C. T. O'Guinn. 2001. 'Brand community'. *Journal of Consumer Research*, 27:4, p. 412–432.

Olenski, S. 2013. 'Social media usage up 800% for US online adults in just 8 years'. Available at http://www.forbes.com/sites/steveolenski/2013/09/06/social-media-usage-up-800-for-us-online-adults-in-just-8-years. Accessed 5 February 2015.

Pan, B. and J. C. Crotts. 2012. 'Theoretical models of social media, marketing implications, and future research directions'. *Social Media in Travel, Tourism and Hospitality*, 46, p. 73–83.

Perdue, R. R. 1993. 'External information search in marine recreational fishing'. *Leisure Sciences*, 15:3, p. 169–187.

Pew Research Center. 2016. 'Smartphone ownership and internet usage continues to climb in emerging economies'. Available at http://www.pewglobal.org/2016/02/22/smartphone-ownership-and-Internet-usage-continues-to-climb-in-emerging-economies/. Accessed 27 July 2016.

Schau, J. H., M. A. Muniz and J. E. Arnould. 2009. 'How brand community practices create value'. *Journal of Marketing*, 73:5, p. 30–51.

Socialbakers.com. 2016. 'Statistics of the top Facebook pages'. Available at https://www.socialbakers.com/statistics/facebook/pages/total/. Accessed 4 August 2016.

Szmigin, I. and A. E. Reppel. 2001. 'Internet community bonding: the case of macnews.de'. *European Journal of Marketing*, 38:5/6, p. 626–640.

Thackeray, R., B. L. Neiger, C. L. Hanson and J. F. McKenzie. 2008. 'Enhancing promotional strategies within social marketing programs: use of Web 2.0 social media'. *Health Promotion Practice*, 9:4, p. 338–343.

Thelwall, M. 2008. 'Social networks, gender, and friending: an analysis of MySpace member profiles'. *Journal of the American Society for Information Science and Technology*, 59:8, p. 1321–1330.

Thelwall, M. 2009. 'Homophily in MySpace'. *Journal of the American Society for Information Science & Technology*, 60:2, p. 219–231.

Thorson, K. S. and S. Rodgers. 2006. 'Relationships between blogs as eWOM and interactivity, perceived interactivity, and parasocial interaction'. *Journal of Interactive Advertising*, 6:2, p. 5–44.

Valenzuela, S., N. Park and K. F. Kee. 2009. 'Is there social capital in a social network site? Facebook use and college students' life satisfaction, trust, and participation'. Available at http://onlinelibrary.wiley.com/doi/10.1111/j.1083-6101.2009.01474.x/abstract. Accessed 9 October 2016.

Vollmer, C. and G. Precourt. 2008. *Always On: Advertising, Marketing, and Media in an Era of Consumer Control.* New York: McGraw-Hill.

Von Hippel, E. 2005. *Democratizing Innovation.* Boston: The MIT Press.

Yadav, V. K. and D. M. Tripathi. 2016. 'Social media marketing and effectiveness of brand communication'. *Imperial Journal of Interdisciplinary Research*, 2:7, p. 1043–1047.

22

PROFILING YOUTH ON THE BASIS OF THEIR MOTIVATIONS FOR SOCIAL MEDIA POLITICAL PARTICIPATION

Implications for political marketers

Devinder Pal Singh

Introduction

Social media have transformed the contemporaneous political landscape. Political stakeholders have been increasingly engaging social media networks to market themselves and amplify their visibility and success. Social media are popular among young people (Correa *et al.* 2010) and have emerged as a significant tool for expression, dissemination and consumption of political information among the youth. Though the global youth population has reached a notable height of 1.8 billion (UNFPA 2014), youth participation in politics is comparatively low (UNDP 2013). Political parties usually target more superior segments, where young voters are generally excluded from political discourse and activities (Bennett 2008). Young people have distinct needs and wants that can be fulfilled only with their participation in the political process (Levine 2008). The youth population has the potential to turn economies or threaten nations unless their needs are realized and protected (UNFPA 2014). The challenge is more profound for emerging economies like India, where 89 per cent of the world's youth live (UNFPA 2014). Political measures that are youth-inclusive remain crucial for global economic growth and stability.

Young people widely employ social media for political participation (Holt *et al.* 2013), so it is essential to understand the way in which the youth use social media. Particular motivations have been identified as salient factors that drive media consumption (Li 2014; You *et al.* 2013). Their importance is more noticeable in the Web 2.0 environment, where users are able to not only consume but also share information (You *et al.* 2013; Kushin and Yamamoto 2010). Understanding the motivations for political social media usage merits thoughtful consideration. Unfolding the motivations for social media political participation is the desideratum for the involvement of young people in politics. Further, it is worthwhile identifying and understanding the distinct motivation-based segments among the youth.

The extant literature has offered four principal motivations that account for social media usage. They include hedonic motivations (Xu *et al.* 2012; Baumgartner and Morris 2010; Tosun 2012), utilitarian motivations (Dumlao and Ha 2013; Ernst *et al.* 2013; Perse 1992), 'information seeking' (Park 2013; Kim and Johnson 2012) and 'expressive participation' (Park 2013). Hedonic motivations represent the sensory, fun, fantastical, entertaining, experiential and emotive aspects of an individual's experience (Babin *et al.* 1994; Hirschman and Holbrook 1982). Utilitarian motivations signify goal-oriented behaviour driven by considerations like functionality, utility, efficiency and rationality (Farrag *et al.* 2010; Babin *et al.* 1994). 'Information seeking' denotes an individual's propensity to consume information (Li 2014; Himelboim *et al.* 2012; Case 2007). 'Expressive participation' refers to the expression of political opinions and involvement in social media political discussion (Bakker and Paterson 2011; Stanyer 2005).

Though researchers have examined the motivations behind social media use in general, very few studies have attempted to explain the use of social media for political participation. Despite the importance of youth participation in social media political participation, the literature is devoid of any typology based on motivations for political participation in the context of social media. With the increasing importance of social media, it is imperative for political marketers to better understand the various youth segments. This chapter attempts to fill this gap and has two-fold objectives. First, it aims to identify key motivations that influence social media political participation. Further, it aims to categorize youth into discrete segments and develop a typology of youth based on the motivations for political participation in the context of social media. It is envisaged that the identification of discernable segments will assist political marketers in targeting each of these segments with the appropriate social media marketing mix. The understanding of each of these segments will assist political marketers to develop strategies to target young voters.

Literature review

Motivations for using social media

Motivations are the important constructs in consumer analysis (Ruggiero 2000) and are the primary influence that propels a user to choose a particular medium (Li 2014; You *et al.* 2013). The relevance of motivations is more pronounced in the social media environment, where users are able to not only consume but also generate and share content (You *et al.* 2013; Kushin and Yamamoto 2010).

Prior researchers have investigated various motivations for social media use. Trammell, Tarkowski, Hofmokl and Sapp (2006) identify 'self expression' as the main motive for using blogs. Joinson (2008) in a study on a UK sample examined the motivations behind participation in a social networking site (SNS). The author identifies seven reasons for using such a site: 'social connection', 'shared identities', 'posting photographs', 'social investigation', 'social network surfing' and 'status updating'.

Barker (2009), in a study on the US population, identifies five motives for using SNSs, namely 'communication', 'collective self-esteem', 'pastime', 'entertainment' and 'learning'. Similarly, Brandtzæg and Heim (2009), in a study on Norwegian populations, cite four reasons for SNS use: 'new relations', 'contacting friends', 'socializing' and 'information'. Park, Kee and Valenzuela (2009) found the following reasons for using an SNS: 'socializing', 'entertainment', 'self-status seeking', and 'information seeking'. Rafaeli, Hayat and Ariel (2009) examined the motivations behind contributing to Wikipedia and found that 'getting information', 'sharing information' and 'entertainment' were the main reasons.

Quan-Haase and Young (2010), in a Canadian study, found 'hedonic' gratification to be behind social media use, while a study by Dunne, Lawlor and Rowley (2010) identifies 'identity creation' and 'peer acceptance' as the main reasons for social media use. Parra-López *et al.* (2010) conclude that the main reasons for social media use are functional, psychological, hedonic and social.

Cheung, Chiu and Lee (2011) posit that 'purposive value', 'self discovery', 'interpersonal connectivity', 'social enhancement' and 'entertainment' are the main reasons that people in Hong Kong use social media. Similarly, Kim, Sohn and Choi (2011) found four motives behind SNS use: 'seeking friends', 'social support', 'entertainment', 'information' and 'convenience'. Smock, Ellison, Lampe and Wohn (2011) conclude that the gratifications derived from social media use are 'entertainment', 'expressive information sharing', 'escapism', 'companionship', 'social interaction' and 'passing time'. Likewise, Lin and Lu (2011) identify 'usefulness' and 'enjoyment' as the main reasons for social media use.

In a study in Turkey, Tosun (2012) identified the following motives for social media use: 'maintaining long distance relationships', 'entertainment', 'photo-related activities', 'organizing social activities', 'passive observations' and 'relationships'. Xu *et al.* (2012) identify hedonic and utilitarian motivations as the main drivers of SNS use. Similarly, Pöyry, Parvinen and Malmivaara (2013) identify hedonic and utilitarian motivations for SNS usage. Hassouneh and Brengman (2014) identify six motivations for social media use in the context of the virtual world: 'manipulation', 'friendship', 'achievement', 'role playing', 'escapism' and 'relationships'.

In the context of social media usage for political purpose, the prior research has identified diverse motivations. Kim and Johnson (2012) examine the following main motivations for using political blogs: 'political surveillance', 'expression and affiliation', 'convenience/information-seeking' and 'entertainment'. Park (2013) has identified four reasons for people to use Twitter in the context of political engagement: 'information seeking', 'mobilization' and 'public expression'.

Though the extant research on social media provides an array of motivations, they can largely be grouped and summarized under four categories, namely *'hedonic motivations'* (Xu *et al.* 2012; Smock *et al.* 2011; Baumgartner and

Morris 2010; Tosun 2012; Parra-López *et al.* 2010), '*utilitarian motivations*' (Dumlao and Ha 2013; Ernst *et al.* 2013; Parra-Lópezet *et al.* 2010), '*expressive participation*' (Park 2013; Smock *et al.* 2011; Trammell, Tarkowski, Hofmokl and Sapp 2006) and '*information seeking*' (Park 2013; Kim and Johnson 2012; Kim, Sohn and Choi 2011; Park, Kee and Valenzuela 2009).

Hedonic and utilitarian motivations

Utilitarian motivations refer to goal-oriented considerations like utility, function-ality, instrumentality and rationality that guide behaviour (Babin *et al.* 1994). Utilitarian behaviour is deliberate, task-related, efficient and rational (Farrag *et al.* 2010). Hedonic motivations denote 'the multi-sensory, fantasy and emotive aspects of one's experience' (Hirschman and Holbrook 1982). They involve play-fulness, fun, fantasy, escapism and entertainment (Babin *et al.* 1994; Hirschman and Holbrook 1982). The value underlying hedonic consumption is experiential and emotional in nature (Batra and Ahtola 1991; Hirschman and Holbrook 1982). Hedonic motivations are linked to pleasure, affection, leisure, escapism, fantasy, entertainment and social presence.

Literature lacks a consensus on whether people adopt social media for utilitar-ian or hedonic considerations. Xu *et al.* (2012) find that utilitarian gratifications positively predict social media usage. Dumlao and Ha (2013) argue that utilitarian and hedonic aspects of social media sites act as important motivations for their continued use. Similarly other researchers (Ernst; Pfeiffer and Rothlauf 2013; Holbert *et al.* 2007) believe that social media satiates both hedonic and utilitarian desires. Past research indicates the role of both utilitarian and hedonic motivations in social media consumption but very few studies have attempted to integrate them with the political realm.

Information seeking

'Information seeking' denotes an individual's quest for information (Case 2007). Information seeking orientation refers to the tendency in favour of specific things in the information seeking process (Li 2014). 'Information seeking' for political information motivates social media consumption (Park 2013; Tosun 2012) and fos-ters political involvement (Himelboim *et al.* 2012; Vitak *et al.* 2010). The extent of social media participation is a factor of an individual's predisposition towards polit-ical information (Macafee 2013). Social media is a convenient platform to gratify political information needs, so information search induces social media consump-tion and political participation (Zhang, Johnson, Seltzer and Bichard 2009).

Expressive participation

Expressive participation denotes participation in social media political dis-course and expression of one's political opinions (Stanyer 2005). It represents citizen journalism where amateur journalists contribute and publish on social media (Bakker and Paterson 2011). Expressive participation may include posting political messages and political endorsements, and political engagement (Gil de Zúñiga, Puig-I-Abril and Rojas 2010). It also include activities like commenting on political issues, persuading others to vote, participate or act; circulating links to political stories, and following candidates on social media (Rainie, Smith, Schlozman and Verba 2012; Kushin and Yamamoto 2010). Expressive participation has become a phenomenon of social, economic and political significance because one can now create and generate news (Lee and Ma 2012), and it augments one's status on the social network (Osatuyi 2013). Expressive participation fosters social media usage (Park 2013; Tosun 2012) and political participation (Park 2013; Conroy *et al.* 2012; Kushin and Yamamoto 2010; Gil de Zúñiga *et al.* 2010; Rojas and Puig-i-Abril 2009).

The literature review exhibits that hedonic (Xu *et al.* 2012; Baumgartner and Morris 2010; Tosun 2012), utilitarian (Dumlao and Ha 2013; Ernst *et al.* 2013; Perse 1992), information seeking (Park 2013; Kim and Johnson 2012) and expressive participation (Park 2013) are the principal motives for social media political participation. This study employs these motivations to profile youth and develop a typology in the context of social media political participation.

Empirical study

The study was conducted through a survey in a north Indian city that has the highest Internet density, according to the census report (2011). Data was collected with a self-administered questionnaire containing multiple items derived from the extant literature (Table 22.1). The study was conducted on university students following the announcement of the 2014 general elections. The timing of the study was considered appropriate as, during the election process, voters are usually exposed to electoral campaigns and they start paying attention to political events. Four hundred respondents were approached for data collection. The effective sample size consisted of 348 as only completely filled questionnaires were used for analysis.

Results

Exploratory factor analysis (EFA) employing varimax rotation was conducted to confirm the prevalence of motivations as in prior research on social media. Table 22.1 exhibits the four extracted factors along with their corresponding items and their respective loadings.

Factor scores from the four factors extracted through EFA were employed to conduct a cluster analysis to identify various youth segments based on their social-media-based political participation. Two-step clustering was done to segment the youth. In the first step, hierarchical cluster was used to decide the number of

TABLE 22.1 Factor analysis of social media motivations

Scale items	Factor loadings				Variance %	Coefficient Alpha
	Expressive participation (Kushin and Yamamoto, 2010)	Utilitarian motivations (Cotte et al. 2006)	Information seeking (Vazquez and Xu, 2009)	Hedonic motivations (Pöyry et al. 2013)		
I write blog posts on political issues.	**.641**	−.001	.125	.282	15.305	0.765
I create and post online audio, video, animation, photos or computer artwork to express political views.	**.723**	.211	.058	.145		
I share political news, video clips or others' blog posts online.	**.779**	.155	.071	.116		
I participate in online political discussions (e.g. on discussion boards and chat rooms).	**.783**	.140	.043	−.005		
Social media are a convenient source of political information.	.033	**.659**	.130	.276	14.528	0.744
Social media help me in finding the political information that I'm looking for.	.240	**.692**	.127	−.092		
The information I get via social media helps me in deciding whom to vote for.	.137	**.752**	.145	.206		
The opinions and experiences of others on social media help me in decision-making.	.143	**.728**	.134	.188		
Social media are a convenient source of political information.	.118	−.009	**.739**	.110	14.247	0.734
Social media help me in finding the political information that I'm looking for.	.098	.238	**.676**	−.014		

	Factor 1	Factor 2	Factor 3	Factor 4
The information I get via social media helps me in deciding whom to vote for.	.058	.101	**.772**	.079
The opinions and experiences of others on social media help me in decision-making.	.023	.186	**.702**	.171
I enjoy reading and sharing election information through social media.	.196	.295	.005	**.731**
It is truly a joy to use and share election information through social media.	.209	.137	.035	**.773**
Compared to other things, sharing election information through social media is truly enjoyable.	.019	.055	.221	**.786**
Election-related information can provide a fun experience.	.294	.132	.199	**.343**
			13.696	0.711

TABLE 22.2 Cluster analysis

Motivations	Cluster 1 Activists	Cluster 2 Hedonists	Cluster 3 Utilitarians	Cluster 4 Versatile	F-value	p<
Expressive Participation	.59297	.00169	−1.42656	.70057	183.368	.000*
Utilitarian Motivations	−.03404	−.74372	.34160	.80183	65.766	.000*
Information Seeking	.22541	.26380	−.05766	−.53791	13.289	.000*
Hedonic Motivations	−1.28443	.45192	−.01614	.55430	116.256	.000*
Respondents (no.)	76	118	72	82		
Respondents (%)	21.84	33.91	20.69	23.56		

* Significant at .01 level.

clusters by observing coefficients in the agglomeration schedule. The hierarchical clustering method helped in the identification of four initial seeds, which was used as input in the k-means clustering to arrive at four stable segments. The four segments can be distinguished in terms of their characteristics, which can be interpreted as below (Table 22.2):

Activists (Cluster 1): This cluster consisted of respondents who scored the second highest on expressive participation. This group comprises 21.84 per cent of the sample and is also motivated by 'information seeking'. Hedonic and utilitarian aspects of social media political participation do not impact this segment. The group seems to have a penchant for information seeking that could have been employed for 'expressive participation'. The cluster is more discernable by information seeking, and generation of political information on social media. Citizen journalism of this segment is exhibited through social media political postings, endorsements, comments and persuasion. This group can be labelled as 'activists' as they are motivated both by the generation and consumption of political content on the social media network.

Hedonists (Cluster 2): The second segment comprises 33.91 per cent of the sample. As evident from Table 22.2 this group scored quite highly on hedonic motivations. This group is motivated less by 'expressive participation', and least by utilitarian motivations. This cluster scored highly on 'information seeking'. It can be deduced that the group seeks information for hedonic purposes. Hence, this group has been labelled as 'hedonists'.

Utilitarians (Cluster 3): This group comprises 20.69 per cent of the sample. 'Expressive participation', 'information seeking' and hedonic motivations do not motivate this segment. The group scores the highest on utilitarian motivations exhibiting that the group members use political information to make political decisions. Being least motivated by information seeking and expressive participation, this cluster appears to be more goal-oriented and focused on political outcomes, so this group was labelled as 'utilitarian'.

The Versatile (Cluster 4): The fourth cluster comprises 23.56 per cent of the sample. This group scores the highest on 'expressive participation', 'utilitarian motivations' and 'hedonic motivations'. 'Information seeking' least motivates this group. This indicates that this group is multifaceted as it is motivated both by hedonic and utilitarian factors, along with expressive participation. This segment could be generating political information that is both goal focused and entertainment oriented. The group can be aptly labelled as 'versatile'.

The ANOVA results exhibit that the four clusters differ considerably on the four motivations, consisting of 'expressive participation' (F = 183.369, P < .01), 'utilitarian motivations' (F = 65.77, P < .01), 'information seeking' (F = 13.29, P < .01), and 'hedonic motivations' (F = 116.26, P < .01).

Table 22.3 exhibits the demographic characteristics of the three clusters. As is evident from the table, the three clusters are not significantly different from each other on the various demographic variables.

The four clusters are comprised mostly of males, primarily of single youngsters between 20 and 30 years of age, mostly of postgraduates and graduates, and high-income respondents.

Discussion

This research offers one of the foremost systematic studies on social-media-based political participation of youth. The study has succeeded to the extent of identifying the evolving youth segments based on motivations for social media political participation. The findings have profound implications for political marketers.

The results demonstrate that the largest group, namely 'hedonists', is more motivated by hedonic considerations. 'Information seeking' also stimulates this group, indicating that the segment indulges in 'information seeking' to gratify their hedonistic needs. Since hedonists relish humour and entertainment content, political marketers can target this cluster with the delivery of fun, humour, entertainment and enjoyable matter on social media. Satire and jokes can go viral instantaneously and become a meaningful part of politico-social discourse. This may augment political involvement and engender a positive stance towards a political brand.

The 'versatile' is the next largest group motivated by 'utilitarian motivations', 'information seeking' and 'hedonic motivations'. The versatile youth are highly utilitarian and hedonistic in approach. They are highly motivated by 'expressive participation'. This suggests that this segment is politically involved in social media through 'expressive participation'. Group members derive utilitarian value from social media political participation for achieving the desired political goals. Political marketers can orchestrate social media campaigns to provide this versatile group with a platform to instantly produce, express, share and consume the

TABLE 22.3 Demographic characteristics

Demographic variables Percentage within segment		Cluster 1 Activists	Cluster 2 Hedonists	Cluster 3 Utilitarians	Cluster 4 Versatile	χ^2 value	$p<$
Gender	Male	59.2%	59.3%	58.3%	65.9%	4.616	.594
	Female	40.8%	40.7%	41.7%	34.1%		
Marital Status	Married	5.3%	11%	1.4%	3.7%	11.34	.078
	Single	94.7%	87.3%	98.6%	95.1%		
	Divorced	0%	1.7%	0%	1.2%		
Age	Below 20	15.8%	11.0%	16.7%	17.1%	9.72	.837
	20–30	78.9%	78.8%	80.6%	78.0%		
	30–40	5.3%	7.6%	2.8%	3.7%		
	40–50	0%	2.6%	0.7%	1.2%		
Education	Graduation (10+2)	23.7%	15.3%	25%	25.6%	12.47	.409
	Bachelor	31.6%	40.7%	38.9%	45.1%		
	Post Graduate	36.8%	39%	31.9%	25.6%		
	Professional	6.6%	5.1%	4.2%	3.7%		
	Others	1.3%	0%	0%	0%		
Monthly Income (Indian Rupees)	Below 15,000	14.3%	13%	6.8%	7.6%	2.54	.303
	15,000–30,000	16.3%	17.4%	14.8%	8.4%		
	30001–45,000	16.3%	20.7%	17%	24.4%		
	45,001–60, 000	10.2%	6.5%	9.1%	11.8%		
	60,001–75,000	16.3%	13%	23.9%	11.8%		
	Above 75,000	26.5%	29.3%	28.4%	36%		

content. It can assist marketers to convert 'tweets' and 'Likes' into votes. The platforms could provide the seed for future brand communities of political parties and candidates.

This group also derives pleasure through indulgence in the creation and dissemination of humourous content. This cluster can be targeted through jokes, parody and comic videos. Marketers can involve 'hedonist' and the 'versatile' groups by delivering fun and entertaining consumption experiences on social media platforms to obtain a positive political response.

'Activists' are motivated both by 'expressive participation' and 'information seeking'. They could be employing political information extracted from social media to form opinions and express themselves. Expressive participation is cost effective, so it is an important tool of political participation (Gil de Zúñiga *et al.* 2010). Marketers should foster pleasant conversations and stimuli so that consumers are encouraged to surf the Internet and spend more time on the social media. This could lead to the genesis of positive word-of-mouth for political parties.

High-quality, participant-generated content could nurture the growth of an exciting social media environment, which could make a positive contribution to the image of political parties. Political marketers could initiate 'expressive participation' by providing stimulating content. Online discussions and content ought to be monitored for the creation of social networks that could surface as brand communities for political parties. These communities of interest can be targeted for positioning of political brands. Content generated through 'expressive participation' could serve as a feedback mechanism and can be used for tactical planning.

The utilitarian group is motivated only by utilitarian motivation. This group can employ information generated by political networks for making decisions and forming opinions about political players. The websites of political parties do not encourage political participation, as they do not provide information in the manner that effectively informs their cause and philosophy (Karandhikar 2012). This segment has to be targeted with quality information substantiated with data, facts and figures. The group needs to be convinced of the particular political ideology and viewpoint. This cluster in information perusal is also exposed to the social media content generated through expressive participation. 'Expressive participation' content could influence utilitarians and ultimately influence voting decisions. Therefore, it is advisable that political marketers channelize social media discussions in a manner that is in consonance with their political objectives.

The involvement of political parties in social media discourse can gratify the information seeking goals of the youth with adequate credible information. It is essential that political marketers employ the philosophy and positive work of the parties as unique selling propositions. This will assist in the construction of positive perception and attitude towards political brands. Political stakeholders need to be social media savvy, so that they continuously detect, collect and analyse relevant political information to produce cordial social networks for the achievement of objectives.

Conclusion

Contemporary youth are deeply immersed in social media. Profiling youth on the basis of their motivations for social media political participation would help political marketers to target the identified segments. The knowledge of the evolving segments can be efficaciously employed for the achievement of objectives and can foster political participation. Political participation would generate trust in the political system and amplify social capital. Increased political participation has positive implications for the future of democracy. It is anticipated that this study can be gainfully employed for electoral advantage.

References

Babin, B. J., W. R. Darden and M. Griffin. 1994. 'Work and/or fun: measuring hedonic and utilitarian shopping value', *Journal of Consumer Research*, 20, p. 644–656.

Bakker, T. and C. Paterson. 2011. 'The new frontiers of journalism: citizen participation in the United Kingdom and the Netherlands'. In K. Brants and K. Voltmer (eds.), *Political Communication in Postmodern Democracy: Challenging the Primacy of Politics*. London: Palgrave Macmillan, p. 183–199.

Barker, V. 2009. 'Older adolescents' motivations for social network site use: the influence of gender, group, identity, and collective self-esteem'. *Cyberpsychology & Behavior*, 12(2), p. 209–213.

Batra, R. and O. T. Ahtola. 1991. 'Measuring the hedonic and utilitarian sources of consumer attitudes', *Marketing Letters*, 2(2), p. 159–170.

Baumgartner, J. C., and J. S. Morris. 2010. 'My face tube politics: social networking web sites and political engagement of young adults', *Social Science Computer Review*, 28(1), p. 24–44.

Bennett, W. L. 2008. 'Changing citizenship in the digital age'. In W. L. Bennett (ed.), *Civic Life Online: Learning How Digital Media Can Engage Youth*. Cambridge, MA: The MIT Press, p. 1–24

Brandtzæg, P. B., and J. Heim. 2009. 'Why people use social networking sites'. In A. A. Ozok and P. Zaphiris (eds.), *Online Communities*. Springer-Verlag Berlin Heidelberg, p. 143–152.

Case, D. O. 2007. *Looking for Information: A Survey of Research on Information Seeking, Needs and Behavior*. London: UK Academic Press.

Cheung, C. M. K., P.-Y. Chiu and M. K. O. Lee. 2011. 'Online social networks: why do students use Facebook?', *Computers in Human Behavior*, 27, p. 1337–1343.

Conroy, M., J. T. Feezell and M. Guerrero. 2012. 'Facebook and political engagement: a study of online political group membership and offline political engagement'. *Computers in Human Behavior*, 28, p. 1535–1546.

Correa, T., A. W. Hinsley and H. Gil de Zúñiga. 2010. 'Who interacts on the Web?: the intersection of users' personality and social media use', *Computers in Human Behavior*, 26, p. 247–253.

Cotte, J., T. G. Chowdhury, S. Ratneshwar and L. M. Ricci. 2006. 'Pleasure or utility? time planning style and Web usage behaviors', *Journal of Interactive Marketing*, 20(1), p. 45–57.

Dumlao, J. A. A., and S. H. Ha. 2013. 'Motivational and social capital factors influencing the success of social network sites: Twitter case'. Available at http://aisel.aisnet.org/pacis2013/2.

Dunne, Á., M.-A. Lawlor and J. Rowley. 2010. 'Young people's use of online social networking sites: a uses and gratifications perspective', *Journal of Research in Interactive Marketing*, 4(1), p. 46–58.

Ernst, C.-P. H., J. Pfeiffer and F. Rothlauf. 2013. 'Hedonic and utilitarian motivations of social network site adoption'. Available at http://wi.bwl.uni-mainz.de/publikationen/ernst-WP-01-2013.pdf.

Farrag, D. A., I. M. E. Sayed and R. W. Belk. 2010. 'Mall shopping motives and activities: a multi method approach', *Journal of International Consumer Marketing*, 22, p. 95–115.

Gil de Zúñiga, H., A. Veenstra, E. Vraga and D. Shah. 2010. 'Digital democracy: reimagining pathways to political participation', *Journal of Information Technology & Politics*, 7, p. 36–31.

Hassouneh, D. and M. Brengman. 2014. 'A motivation-based typology of social virtual world users', *Computers in Human Behavior*, 33, p. 330–338.

Himelboim, I., R. W. Lariscy, S. F. Tinkham and K. D. Sweetser. 2012. 'Social media and online political communication: the role of interpersonal informational trust and openness', *Journal of Broadcasting & Electronic Media*, 56(1), p. 92–115.

Hirschman, E. C. and M. B. Holbrook. 1982. 'Hedonic consumption: emerging concepts, methods and propositions', *Journal of Marketing*, 46(3), p. 92–101.

Holbert, R. L., J. L. Lambe, A. D. Dudo and K. A. Carlton. 2007. 'Primacy effects of the daily show and national TV news viewing: young viewers, political gratifications, and internal political self-efficacy', *Journal of Broadcasting & Electronic Media*, 51(1), p. 20–38.

Holt, K., A. Shehata, J. Strömbäck and E. Ljungberg. 2013. 'Age and the effects of news media attention and social media use on political interest and participation: do social media function as leveller?', *European Journal of Communication*, 28, p. 19–34.

Joinson, A. N. 2008. '"Looking at", "Looking up" or "Keeping up with" people? Motives and Uses of Facebook'. Available at http://digitalintelligencetoday.com/downloads/Joinson_Facebook.pdf.

Kim, D. and T. J. Johnson. 2012. 'Political blog readers: predictors of motivations for accessing political blogs', *Telematics and Informatics*, 29, p. 99–109.

Kim, Y., D. Sohn and S. M. Choi. 2011. 'Cultural difference in motivations for using social network sites: a comparative study of American and Korean college students'. *Computers in Human Behavior*, 27, p. 365–372.

Kushin, M. J. and M. Yamamoto. 2010. 'Did social media really matter? College students' use of online media and political decision making in the 2008 elections', *Mass Communication and Society*, 13, p. 608–630.

Lee, C. S. and L. Ma. 2012. 'News sharing in social media: the effect of gratifications and prior experience', *Computers in Human Behavior*, 28, p. 331–339.

Li, X. 2014. 'Perceived channel efficiency and motivation and orientation of information seeking as predictors of media dependency', *Telematics and Informatics*, 31, p. 628–639.

Lin, K.-Y. and H.-P. Lu, 2011. 'Why people use social networking sites: an empirical study integrating network externalities and motivation theory', *Computers in Human Behavior*, 27, p. 1152–1161.

Levine, P. 2008. 'A public voice for youth: the audience problem in digital media and civic education'. In W. L. Bennett (ed.), *Civic Life Online: Learning How Digital Media Can Engage Youth*. Cambridge; London: The MIT Press, p. 119–139.

Macafee, T. 2013. 'Some of the things are not like the others: examining motivations and political predispositions among political Facebook activity', *Computers in Human Behavior*, 29, p. 266–277.

Osatuyi, B. 2013. 'Information sharing on social media sites', *Computers in Human Behavior*, 29, p. 2622–2631.

Parra-Lopez, E., J. Bulchand-Gidumal, D. Gutierrez-Tano and R. Diaz-Armas. 2010. 'Intentions to use social media in organizing and taking vacation trips', *Computers in Human Behavior*, 27(2), p. 640–654.

Park, C. S. 2013. 'Does Twitter motivate involvement in politics? Tweeting, opinion leadership, and political engagement', *Computers in Human Behavior*, 29, p. 1641–1648.

Park, N., K. F. Kee and S. Valenzuela. 2009. 'Being immersed in social networking environment: Facebook groups, uses and gratifications, and social outcomes'. *CyberPscyhology & Behavior*, 12(6), p. 729–732.

Perse, E. M. 1992. 'Predicting attention to local television news: need for cognition and motives for viewing', *Communication Reports*, 5(1), p. 40–49.

Pöyry, E., P. Parvinen and T. Malmivaara. 2013. 'Can we get from liking to buying? Behavioral differences in hedonic and utilitarian Facebook usage', *Electronic Commerce Research and Applications*, 12, p. 224–235.

Quan-Haase, A. and A. L. Young. 2010. 'Uses and gratifications of social media: a comparison of Facebook and instant messaging', *Bulletin of Science, Technology & Society*, 30(5), p. 350–361.

Rafaeli, S., T. Hayat and Y. Ariel. 2009. 'Knowledge building and motivations in Wikipedia: participation as "Ba"'. In F. J. Ricardo (ed.), *Cyberculture and New Media*. New York: Rodopi, p. 52–69.

Rainie, L., A. Smith, K. L. Schlozman, H. Brady and S. Verba. 2012. 'Social media and political engagement'. Retrieved from http://www.pewinternet.org/2012/10/19/additional-analysis-2/.

Rojas, H., and E. Puig-i-Abril. 2009. 'Mobilizers mobilized: information, expression, mobilization and participation in the digital age', *Journal of Computer-Mediated Communication*, 14(4), p. 902–927.

Ruggiero, T. E. 2000. 'Uses and gratifications theory in the 21st century', *Mass Communication & Society*, 3(1), p. 3–37.

Smock, A. D., N. B. Ellison, C. Lampe and D. Y. Wohn. 2011. 'Facebook as a toolkit: a uses and gratifications approach to unbundling feature use', *Computers in Human Behavior*, 27, p. 2322–2329.

Stanyer, J. 2005. 'The British public and political attitude expression: the emergence of a self-expressive political culture?', *Contemporary Politics*, 11, p. 19–32.

Tosun, L. P. 2012. 'Motives for Facebook use and expressing "true self" on the Internet', *Computers in Human Behavior*, 28, p. 1510–1517.

Trammell, K. D., A. Tarkowski, J. Hofmokl and A. M. Sapp. 2006. 'Examining Polish bloggers through content analysis', *Journal of Computer-Mediated Communication*, 11(3), p. 702–723.

UNFPA. 2014. 'The power of 1.8 billion'. Available at http://www.unfpa.org/sites/ default/ files/pub-pdf/EN-SWOP14-Report_FINAL-web.pdf.

UNDP. 2013. 'Enhancing youth political participation throughout the electoral cycle'. Retrieved from http://www.undp.org/content/undp/en/home/librarypage/democratic-governance/ electoral_systemsandprocesses/enhancing-youth-political-participation-throughout-the-electoral.html.

Vazquez, D. and X. Xu. 2009. 'Investigating linkages between online purchase behavior variables'. *International Journal of Retail & Distribution Management*, 37(5), p. 408–419.

Vitak, J., P. Zube, A. Smock, C. T. Carr, N. Ellison and C. Lampe. 2010. 'It's complicated: Facebook users' political participation in the 2008 election', *Cyberpsychology*, 14(3), p. 107–114.

Xu, C., S. Ryan, V. Prybutok and C. Wen. 2012. 'It is not for fun: an examination of social network site usage', *Information & Management*, 49, p. 210–217.

You, K. H., S. A. Lee, J. K. Lee and H. Kang. 2013. 'Why read online news? The structural relationships among motivators, behaviors, and consumption in South Korea', *Information, Communication & Society*, 16(10), p. 1574–1595.

Zhang, W., T. J. Johnson, T. Seltzer and S. L. Bichard. 2009. 'The revolution will be networked: the influence of social networking sites on political attitudes and behaviour', *Social Science Computer Review*, 28(1), p. 75–92.

23

PRIVACY AND INFORMATION TRADING ON SOCIAL MEDIA APPLICATIONS

Sandhya Narayanan and Richa Agrawal

Social media – a data-rich commerce platform

Internet users had for a long time been passive expenders of web content. They read it, they watched it and they used it to buy products and services. But with the arrival of Web 2.0, consumers started using social networking platforms for creating, modifying, sharing and discussing content, and now, with the advent of social media apps, all such conversations and discussions have moved on to mobile devices – smartphones and tablets that have fundamentally different display, handling and interaction methods when compared to desktop computers (Kourouthanassis *et al.* 2012). Easy use, handling and accessibility of mobile apps has facilitated an almost 24/7 connection and interaction for users through social media apps. As consumers around the globe spend more time on social media apps, it is inevitable that some of their posts and comments are about their shopping activities, experiences, likes and dislikes. Such discussions on social media enable companies to learn about their consumers' preferences, views and interests. This, along with the fact that mobile apps are capable of sensing and recording critical information pertaining to users such as location, content, context and so on, means mobile apps are not only providing easy access to customer's vital information but also offering businesses an opportunity to get to know and understand their customers and use this knowledge when formulating market segmentation, targeting and communication strategies. Given that social media platforms also allow companies to engage their target customers in one-to-one communication, social media are spaces where consumer-oriented companies are strategizing to operate.

Much of the attraction of the social media options lies, however, in their ability to capture and make available the much desired consumer data. The enormous amounts of first-hand consumer data available through social media are something that businesses want to capitalize on. Such capitalization on consumers' personal data may be seen as an intrusion into personal space and a serious threat to consumer privacy. In this chapter, we explore social media apps and information sharing over such apps from the consumer's/user's perspective.

Apps – a convenient social media platform

Smart phones and apps have literally put social media into consumers' pockets. The innovative features and functionalities offered by social media through the 'app' avatar has users adopting it at a rapid pace. Social media apps are making it possible for users to broadcast their updates live with a swipe, tap or flick of their fingers. Apps have empowered users to broadcast their updates in a variety of formats such as text, photo, audio, video, GIF (graphical interchange format) and so on. Much of the content uploaded on social media is event-based and allows users to share time, location and other details making their updates more real and relevant. On the whole, social media apps are making it convenient for the user to communicate their updates in an effective manner.

Social media apps also simplify the user's day-to-day tasks by remembering their preferences, login details, authorization credentials and so on, on the go (which the user would have had to painstakingly remember before the advent of such apps), resulting in a hassle-free experience. More importantly, social media apps provide cross-app integration, that is, they allow users to interact with multiple apps at the same time enabling them to share their content seamlessly across various social networking platforms. For example, a user can publish content on Facebook and can share the same content to his Twitter account with a click on the app. Further, a user's mobile phone does not contain social media apps alone but also a variety of other apps including e-Commerce apps, news apps and so on. Social media apps work in tandem with e-Commerce apps housed on the mobile device and also maintain a record of users' shopping habits. Based on these recorded shopping habits, social media apps then notify users about the best deals, discounts and other promotions available. Social media apps also learn about users' media habits from their past Internet searches and other sources, and suggest new products that a user might like. In short, social media apps assist users in their shopping pursuits.

Convenience – consumer information storage

When performing their ubiquitous functions, social media apps, and for that matter many other apps, seek the user's permission to access a variety of data from their smartphones. Social media apps, for example, seek access to the user's camera, location, SMS, notifications, touch-ID and so on. Typically, permissions requested by apps are crucial to enable them to perform their basic services and functions. Social media apps, for example, may require access to a user's location to enable the user to broadcast their whereabouts to their friends and followers on social media. Interestingly, once the app is granted permission to access data, the app may not use the data for the intended purpose but store all such data for later use. Such a repository of data may then be used by businesses for various promotional, customer targeting and other marketing activities. Social media apps that access a user's location may, for example, use location data to send location-based promotional offers to the users on behalf of third parties.

It may be noted that permissions sought by the app while being downloaded are *not on demand* i.e. the user cannot grant partial permissions regarding the data requested by the app. In order to be able to use the app, the user has to, by default, grant permission to all the requests made by the app. Thus, the user has no control over individual permissions. Although operating systems like the iOS limit data access by third party apps, this is not the case with Android, a widely-used operating system. Although these permissions are required for the working of the app, by accepting the terms and conditions and granting the requested permissions when downloading apps, consumers invariably give developers the right to access/harvest their vital personal and private information.

A free networking platform – how?

Most social media apps are available to users free of charge, that is, users do not have to pay any fee for downloading and using social media apps. Though the networking platform is available for free, it must be noted that social media apps access, capture, store and use customers' personal and private information. While this intrudes on or infringes customer privacy, customers (who have no real choice in the matter except perhaps to not download the app) allow the apps to access their personal information. In fact, the successful functioning of a mobile app or service depends greatly on how relevant, time-specific and granular or accurate the captured information by the app really is. Mobile users who are keen on enjoying the personalized services and benefits that apps can offer, ignore the threat to their privacy and willingly divulge their personal information. Posting 'selfies' on various social networking sites for example, not only reveals an individual's personal interests but also leaves digital footprints, allowing marketers to analyse consumer profiles. However, since posting selfies allows users to represent themselves better in the virtual world, they seem not to worry too much about the loss of privacy. It seems that consumers do not worry greatly about divulging their personal information in exchange for the benefits provided by social media apps. Personal data, it seems, has become a commodity that consumers are willing to trade in order to gain access to, or derive benefits from, these apps (Beldad *et al.* 2011).

Data commoditization and information sharing

As is evident from the preceding discussion, users are happy to trade their personal data in order to enjoy the benefits provided by an app. As per the 'privacy calculus theory' in information privacy literature, information disclosure is a trade-off between benefits and costs. Privacy calculus theory states that consumer predisposition towards disclosing personal information is influenced by a number of competing factors and that consumers conduct a risk-benefit analysis before divulging any personal information (Li 2012). As per the privacy calculus theory, consumers are likely to disclose personal information via mobile devices if their perceived benefits in return for doing so are high. In the case of social media apps, where the aim is to provide personalized services to the user, the success of the app or service depends heavily on the collection and analysis of detailed personal information. Thus, in receiving personalized services, consumers face the risk of having their personal information (e.g. location, shopping preference, medical history and social networks) compromised due to the lack of security and control across servers and/or client sites. It is therefore quite likely that customers will share with, or divulge information to, social media apps, only when the expected benefits (both tangible and intangible) clearly outweigh the risks of such a transaction.

Information boundary theory (IBT), which is based on Petronio's communication management theory, postulates that people create an information boundary around themselves and regulate their information silo by framing their own rules of 'boundary opening' and 'boundary closure'. According to this theory, people disclose (open the boundary) or withhold (close the boundary) information to fortify their benefits or mitigate their losses (Staton *et al.* 2003). The theory explains that people disclose information, that is open the information boundary, when the disclosure of information gives them some benefit or alleviates some risk. Similarly, people withhold information, that is, close the information boundary for some gain or to mitigate losses.

It may be prudent to mention here that consumers do not attach the same degree of significance or criticality to all of their personal information. While they may consider some information to be vital, crucial and extremely confidential, they may also consider some other personal information to be unimportant or even trivial. Since the value attached by consumers to their personal information is different, that is, the relative value attached to one kind of information is different from the value attached to another kind of information, consumers may be expected to act differently when trading different personal information. Consumers may be expected to be more willing and open while exchanging the information they consider to be trivial to gain app-based benefits, than when exchanging or trading information they consider crucial and highly confidential.

The study

To understand how consumers share their different personal data over social media apps, twenty smartphone users were contacted and interviewed over a period of two months. The sample comprised both men and women aged between 20 and 40 years. All the respondents were well-educated, having completed at least their undergraduate degree, and could converse in English very well.

Conversations with the respondents revealed that there are simple and complex mental models that govern the sharing of personal information. The simple models operate at two extreme ends of the information sharing continuum (Figure 23.1).

At one end of the continuum, that is Part B (Figure 23.1), consumers are open to freely sharing their personal information, for example, information pertaining to their name, demography, interests and so on. Since most of this information is required for creating a profile on social media, consumers see such information as either non-premium or as 'already out there' and hence do not mind giving or sharing this information. No control is therefore exercised by consumers, who tend to disclose such information willingly and voluntarily. Voluntary disclosure of information is perhaps driven by the consumers' need to regulate their image in the eyes of others by arranging what they get to see or know about them (Wang *et al.* 2016). We refer to all such information as freely available information since there is no expectation of any tangible benefit(s) in return, at the time of sharing such information. The mental model governing the sharing of all information at this end is thus relatively simple – everything can be shared without much worry or analysis. Either there is no boundary regulating the sharing/exchange of information, that is the boundary is non-existent, or if it does exist then it is completely permeable.

In opposition to this, information at the other extreme end of the continuum, i.e. Part A, is something that consumers are not open or willing to trading at all. Information at this end pertains to the information that consumers don't want the 'world to know'. Such information is considered too personal or private to be divulged. For example, one of our respondents (F, 28 years) said, '…. my phone contains very personal photos and I do not want anyone to see'; another respondent (M, 25 years]) said, "… I don't want to share my location details with anyone'; another respondent (M, 22 years) said, "I obviously have concerns over … reading my text messages'. Consumers are afraid of sharing such information due to its sensitive nature. Very strict control is maintained as far as the sharing of such information is concerned. When apps try to access such personal and private information, consumers feel that their personal space is being encroached upon and refrain from availing of any of the potential benefits, despite the assurances of data safety and security offered by businesses. The mental model governing the exchange or sharing of such critical information is pretty simple – no information can be shared or traded, no matter what the benefit or assurance given is. The boundary here that holds back all information is solid and non-permeable in nature, preventing the information from being leaked or exchanged.

It is between these two extreme ends of the information exchange continuum that complex mental models governing the sharing of personal information operate (see Part C in Figure 23.1). All information in Part C is open to trade or exchange by the individual for some benefit or gain in return. Information in Part C ranges from less freely tradable to more easily tradable, depending on the value attached by the customer to the respective information. Information that is less valuable (information closer to Part B) is freely traded in exchange for benefits.

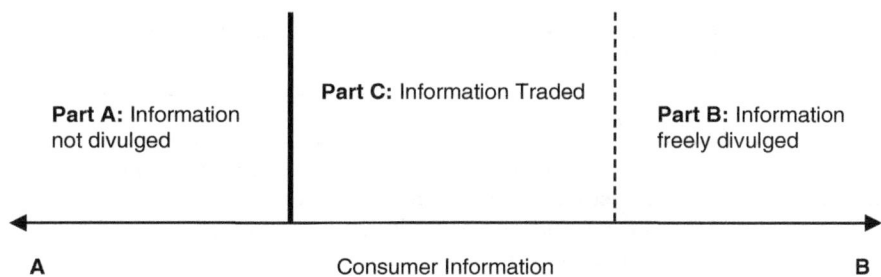

FIGURE 23.1 Information sharing continuum.

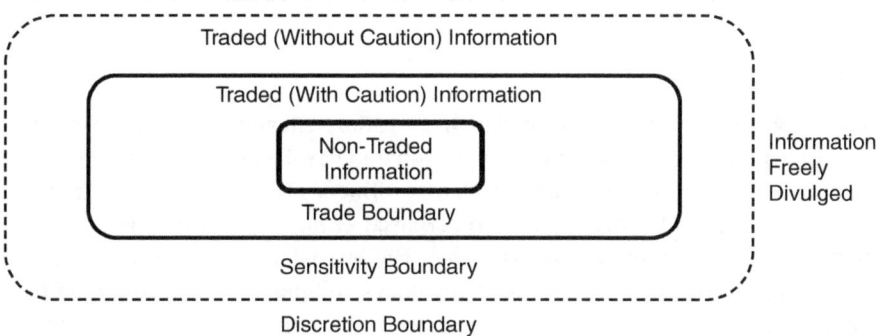

FIGURE 23.2 Customer's mental model of data organisation.

For instance, one of our respondents said, 'I like playing games on my mobile phone ... as long as I can play games without paying, why not share my personal information?'. On the other hand, some other information may be shared/traded by consumers only after getting some kind of non-disclosure assurance from the app (this would be information closer to Part A). One of the respondents said, "We provide our data (to apps) ... If the app company is sharing personal information or device identifiers with third parties, their privacy policy should identify those third parties and they must provide information to them about how users can contact those parties'.

Evidently, consumer information trading is subject to careful evaluation of the benefits received in exchange for the information given. Consumers usually conduct a risk benefit analysis of the motivational factors that allow or inhibit information disclosure (Awad *et al.* 2006). Boundaries governing the sharing of information in this zone therefore show varying degrees of data permeability and mobility. It would help businesses to understand what factors influence the permeability of the boundaries and the mobility or exchange of data in this zone. The extant review of the relevant literature, and reading and re-reading of the transcripts, helped us in identifying seven constructs that determine the permeability and mobility of data across boundaries in this zone. These constructs are: personality, perceived risk, benefits, culture, trust, concern for privacy and situation.

TABLE 23.1 Constructs influencing the permeability of information exchange/trade boundary

Constructs	Explanation
Personality	Introverts and extroverts handle and share data differently
Perceived risk	The plausible negative outcome of information trade
Trust	Is the information traded with a trustworthy app?
Benefits	The benefits reaped from using the app
Culture	People from open and closed cultures trade information differently
Concern for privacy	Inherent in consumers – high, medium, low
Situation	Is there a need to trade information?

Personality

Personality traits of the users impact their readiness/tendency to disclose personal information and thereby the information trade/exchange boundaries (Bansal *et al.* 2010). Moreover, personality traits also influence the level of criticality that a person attaches to his/her information (Bansal *et al.* 2010). Thus, people with different personality traits will tend to have different mental organizations of data. In addition, personality traits are an individual's rudimentary disposition across various behaviours and may thus be expected to have a say in information trading behaviours, as well (Bansal *et al.* 2010). Personality or trait theories suggest that personality traits, for example extraversion, agreeableness, conscientiousness and neuroticism, have an impact on the privacy perception and behaviour of an individual (Li 2012). In our interviews we found some respondents did not have any concerns about sharing personal information – 'I really do not have any issues with sharing my information with apps' (F, 23 years) – while a select few were reluctant to share their information. They felt such information sharing was an infringement on their personal space. One participant said, 'I don't like to share my information … with anyone' (M, 25).

Perceived risk

Risk is one such element that prevents an individual from sharing his/her personal information. Personal data disclosure may have many risks associated with it. As per the available literature, the four major risks associated with data sharing are: the collection of private information; unauthorized secondary use of the private information; improper access of private information; and erroneous storage of personal information (Junglas *et al.* 2008). Almost all participants spoke of perceived risk during the interviews. One of the respondents said, 'The primary concern is about the consequences of sharing the data. With the development in science and technology, there is an increase in cyber crime and my concern is the information I give should not fall into wrong hands and should not be misused' (F, 20 years). Another respondent said, ' … Worried about my personal data falling into the hands of anti-social elements who may put them to illegal use which could harm mine or my family's safety' (M, 39). In addition to these statements, we also gathered that the possibility of an individual's personal information being hacked and made available is seen as a major potential risk by users. Moreover, since improper data storage systems can lead to unwarranted data leaks, consumers carefully consider all these factors before trading their personal information.

Trust

Though consumers may be willing to trade information, they tend to share personal information only when they are comfortable with the party seeking it. Clearly, a consumer's willingness to disclose or trade their information is directly proportional to the amount of trust they place in the app to which they are disseminating the information (Norberg *et al.* 2007). Though consumers have innate tendencies to trade or not trade personal information, consumers respond positively to data requests from trustworthy companies (Taylor *et al.*, 2015). Many of the respondents in our study explicitly mentioned that they would be willing to share relevant information with those mobile apps that they felt were trustworthy. The sharing of information would be more likely if the app was also considered trustworthy within their peer group. Almost all the respondents said that they refrained from downloading and sharing information from 'unknown' apps, owing to the sheer lack of trust.

Benefits

Trading/sharing of personal information occurs only because consumers have something to gain from the apps. Thus, consumers part with their personal information in exchange for something that has some value (Norberg *et al.* 2007). Users may trade or exchange personal information for benefits like better service, discounts and so on. Monetary benefits, such as attractive initial discounts, may be provided by apps to gain access to more personal and private information. Benefits offered by apps in exchange can be both monetary and non-monetary, and tangible or intangible, and include discounts, incentives, convenience or improved services from the app.

Concern for privacy

Westin, in his 1996 study, created the general privacy concern index that classified people into three groups on the basis of the levels of privacy concern they represented. The three groups are: *privacy fundamentalists*, *privacy pragmatics* and *privacy unconcerned* (Kumaraguru *et al.* 2005a). The Fundamentalists are those who generally harbour a distrust of the entities that ask for their personal information and are concerned about the use of information beyond the looked-for transactions. They believe in having stringent laws and regulations that protect privacy and have remedial measures for privacy violation. Pragmatics operate in a practical manner and assess the benefits of the apps and the intrusiveness the information disclosure would bring. They are also logical about the parties seeking information and don't believe in them easily and want the entities to make efforts to, or invest in, earning their trust. The unconcerned, on the other hand, do not attach importance to privacy rules and laws and have good faith in the entities seeking their information (Kumaraguru *et al.* 2005a).

When trading information with apps, fundamentalists would generally choose privacy controls over app-based benefits; for example, one of our respondents (M, 26 years) said this: '… I like to keep my data secure and protected … the apps should allow me to disable sharing'. Pragmatics on the other hand would evaluate and decide how much personal information to trade for the benefits available; as one of our respondents (M, 27 years) put it, 'I don't prefer using mobile apps, because apps can track me from my mobile … I use apps when there are promotions and then later I delete the app, simple, isn't it?' The Unconcerned, however, are usually more open to trading their data for benefits; for instance, one respondent (F, 24 years) said, 'Honestly, I don't really care about privacy … I just want to use the apps (social media) and have fun.'

Culture

Hofstede's model is one of the most widely accepted models that addresses cultural differences in terms of five major dimensions: power distance (PDI); individualism (IDV); masculinity (MAS); uncertainty avoidance (UAI); and long-term orientation (LTO). When it comes to new and uncertain behaviours like exchanging information with the apps, individualism and uncertainty avoidance play a critical role (Krasnova *et al.* 2012). Since culture and values are deeply rooted in an individual and beliefs and traditions are genetically ingrained, in a way culture prompts a user to respond to a situation in a certain manner, heuristically.

A consumer thus coming from a culture that is high on individualism and low on uncertainty avoidance will be less willing to trade data than a consumer from a high uncertainty, avoidance culture.

Indians, hailing from a collectivist culture, i.e. a culture low on individualism, in general are easily able to entrust their personal information to others (Kumaraguru *et al.* 2005b). In our interviews, we found that the respondents did not have any qualms about sharing their data; they were primarily concerned about the misuse of the data. For example, one interviewee (M, 25 years) said, 'Ya, I use apps just like my friends … my data is out there and I have no clear idea about it (privacy). I like to believe that they won't misuse it.' This is quite different from individuals from American culture who are not comfortable sharing their personal information at all (Kumaraguru *et al.*, 2005b).

Situation

The response of an individual or a consumer is highly dependent on the situation in which the data transaction is taking place. The behaviour of a consumer, especially the trade-offs the consumer is willing to make, is highly situation specific (Metzger 2007). For example, a consumer in general is resistant to sharing their location information. But in an emergency situation, a consumer might consider sharing their location data with the apps to get some timely help. When a consumer's situation requires certain conveniences that an app can offer them, they will be willing to share their personal information in exchange for that convenience; however, they might not have done so if their situation were less demanding. Thus, the information trading behaviour of an individual can vary greatly from situation to situation.

The permeability of the information exchange/trade boundary is greatly determined by the interaction of all the above-mentioned constructs. It may be noted that the enquiry made in the present study is preliminary in nature and is aimed at starting a conversation or discussion rather than providing conclusive thoughts on the zones and models of information sharing and the factors influencing the permeability and flexibility of the information exchange/trade boundary. Yet the initial enquiry as made by us in the present study, concerning the nature of information trading or sharing, reveals that the extent of information sharing is not characteristic of a particular business/app but of the consumer and the factors that influence his/her privacy concerns. Thus, while competing apps offering similar benefits and having comparable trustworthiness may expect to get similar amounts of personal information from users, they may in reality not succeed as individuals' perceptions of risk and benefits may vary. In order to capture more data from users, app providers should not only need keep in mind the permeability of their target segment's data boundary but they also need to build a trustworthy image and provide assurances of safety and data security.

Conclusion

App-based social media networks have become increasingly indispensable in today's world and modern-day individuals can hardly do without them. It is clear that social media mobile apps are beneficial because, with the help of these apps, the ease of doing business has improved. Social media apps are not merely used for virtual networking, but are becoming a formidable commerce platform armed with data. However, there are certain fundamental concerns relating to the use of apps, which pertain to the use and handling of collected information. To use apps freely, the apps need to collect information from the user. Over time, as users share personal information on apps, app companies gain control of this information and users lose any say in how the information should be used and shared. App companies may even sell users' personal data to third parties for financial gains. Moreover, since the app companies hoard large amounts of consumer data, there is always a chance of data being leaked or hacked. Given the risk involved in sharing personal data while using apps, users may resort to falsification of personal data (Keith et al. 2013). At other times, consumers may portray an indifferent attitude towards data sharing as they see others around them sharing personal information on apps without much concern.

To have a mutually beneficial data exchange, social media app companies and marketers should strive to bring transparency into their data exchange practices. They must outline clearly the amount of data capture that is implied in using the app and the intended use of this data. They must also explain the consequences of data sharing, so that users can make an informed decision. The privacy policy must also reassure their users that their data will be safeguarded. In addition, we feel it would help to have a standard rule or policy on information trading exchange and sharing. It would perhaps pay to have a system that rates the apps on the basis of their data collection, storage and handling practices. Such a rating could be done by an authorized central agency or institution recognized by the government to restore faith and trust in the apps, and make consumers feel more confident when dealing with apps.

References

Awad, N. F. and M. S. Krishnan. 2006. 'The personalization privacy paradox: an empirical evaluation of information transparency and the willingness to be profiled online for personalization'. *MIS Quarterly*, p. 13–28.

Bansal, G. and D. Gefen. 2010. 'The impact of personal dispositions on information sensitivity, privacy concern and trust in disclosing health information online'. *Decision Support Systems*, 49:2, p. 138–150.

Beldad, A., M. de Jong, and M. Steehouder. 2011. 'A comprehensive theoretical framework for personal information-related behaviors on the internet'. *The Information Society*, 27:4, p. 220–232.

Junglas, I. A., N. A. Johnson and C. Spitzmüller. 2008. 'Personality traits and concern for privacy: an empirical study in the context of location-based services'. *European Journal of Information Systems*, 17:4, p. 387–402.

Keith, M. J., S. C. Thompson, J. Hale, P. B. Lowry and C. Greer. 2013. 'Information disclosure on mobile devices: re-examining privacy calculus with actual user behavior'. *International Journal of Human-Computer Studies*, 71:12, p. 1163–1173.

Krasnova, H., N. F. Veltri and O. Günther. 2012. 'Self-disclosure and privacy calculus on social networking sites: the role of culture'. *Business & Information Systems Engineering*, 4:3, p. 127–135.

Kourouthanassis, P. E. and G. M. Giaglis. 2012. 'Introduction to the special issue mobile commerce: the past, present, and future of mobile commerce research'. *International Journal of Electronic Commerce*, 16:4, p. 5–18.

Kumaraguru, P. and L. F. Cranor. 2005a. 'Privacy indexes: a survey of Westin's studies'. ISRI Technical Report.

Kumaraguru, P. and L. F. Cranor. 2005b. 'Privacy in India: attitudes and awareness'. In *International Workshop on Privacy Enhancing Technologies*. Berlin: Springer, p. 243–258.

Li, Y. 2012. 'Empirical studies on online information privacy concerns: literature review and an integrative framework'. *Communications of the Association for Information Systems*, 28:1, p. 453–496.

Metzger, M. J. 2007. 'Communication privacy management in electronic commerce'. *Journal of Computer-Mediated Communication*, 12:2, p. 335–361.

Norberg, P. A., D. R. Horne and D. A. Horne. 2007. 'The privacy paradox: personal information disclosure intentions versus behaviors'. *Journal of Consumer Affairs*, 41:1, p. 100–126.

Stanton, J. M. and K. R. Stam. 2002. 'Information technology, privacy, and power within organizations: a view from boundary theory and social exchange perspectives'. *Surveillance & Society*, 1:2, p. 152–190.

Taylor, J. F., J. Ferguson and P. S. Ellen. 2015. 'From trait to state: understanding privacy concerns'. *Journal of Consumer Marketing*, 32:2, p. 99–112.

Wang, T., T. D. Duong and C. C. Chen. 2016. 'Intention to disclose personal information via mobile applications: a privacy calculus perspective'. *International Journal of Information Management*, 36:4, p. 531–542.

INDEX

advertising equivalency (AEV) value 127
affective message appeals 106–7
Alcatel 93
Al-Dhuhli I. 15
Alexander, M. 135
ALS Ice Bucket Challenge 217
Altman, I. 78
Ang, L. 36
Announcement tweets 7
Apple 93
Application Programming Interface (API) 209
apps: companies 317; convenience of 309
Ariel, Y. 295
Attention–Interest–Desire–Action (AIDA) model 121–2

B2B, social media marketing for 46–59; benefits and challenges of marketing adoption 47–8; buyer decision journey, stages of 51–4; perception of risk 47; performance measurement 54–5; return on investment 55–7; strategy development and tactical implementation 50–1; Technology Acceptance Model 48–50; Theory of Planned Behaviour 48; Theory of Reasoned Action 48; Unified Theory of Acceptance and Use of Technology 48
Baldus, B. J. 134
Bali, S. 37–8
Barker, V. 295
Beatty, S. 134

Belanger, C. H. 37–8
Belk, R. 65
Berelson, B. 274
Berry, L. L. 36
blogs 117
Blu 93
Bochnak, R. 26
brand advocates 157
brand communities and management 35, 286–7
branding see human brands, social media stakeholder co-creation of celebrities as
brands and advertisements, attitudes towards 206–16; anonymized comments 213; challenges 210; consent 212–13; content identification 208; data access 212; data analysis 209–10; data extraction 208–9; data ownership 211–12; demography 210–11; ethics 213; media selection 208; monthly active users 211; results 210; social media and brand communication 206–8; social networking sites 207; user-generated qualitative data 208
brands on Twitter 189
Brandtzag, P. B. 295
Braun, V. 209
Braynov, S. B. 251
Breidbach, C. F. 136
Brengman, M. 295
Brock, W. 163, 166–8
Brodie, R. 136
Brodie, R. J. 134

Brown, B. P. 47
Brown, S. P. 106
Buckner, H. T. 79
Buhalis, D. 137
Burke, S. J.

Calantone, R. 134
Calder, B. J. 134
Castronovo, C. 86
celebrities as human brands *see* human
    brands, social media stakeholder
    co-creation of celebrities as
celebrity identity, stakeholders of 66
Cellebrite 92–3
Chen, Y. F. 163
Chervany, N. L. 229
Cheung, C. M. K. 295
Chiu, P.-Y. 295
Chouk, I. 248
Christodoulides, G. 134
Citizen Relationship Management (CRM)
    by the Government of India through
    social media channels 1–19; account
    types 9; analysis 6–14; Announcement
    tweets 7; framework 17; government
    programme development 4; Help tweets
    7; implications 14; Interaction tweets 7;
    literature review 3–6; methodology 6;
    Recognition tweets 7; relevance of study
    2–3; risks of social media 5; social
    media, CRM and 2
Clarke, V. 38, 209
cMOOCs (connectivist MOOCs) 21
co-creation, social media in 62–3
Collective Mind Theory 233
Colley, R. 123
communication response hierarchy models
    120–2
communicative engagement 37
community building services 118
conceptual model development *see* en-
    gagement interface, consumer engage-
    ment/return on
Conduit, J. 103, 122
consideration set 151
consumer-business relationships
    (C2BR) 247
consumer decision-making, influence
    of social media on 149–61; brand
    advocates 157; consideration set 151;
    customer engagement circle 153; elec-
    tronic word-of-mouth 154; engagement
    circle approach 152–7; evaluation stage
    155; full online customer journey 153;

information search 154; purchase funnel
    151; purchase stages 152; traditional
    funnel approach 151–2
consumer information storage 309–10
consumer information trading 313
consumer-to-business (C2B)
    interactions 246
consumer-to-consumer (C2C)
    interactions 246
consuming behaviour 104–5
contributing behaviour 104
Convery, I. 210, 212–13
cost benefit analysis 127
Cox, D. 210, 212–13
creating behaviour 104
creepiness *see* online personalized
    communications, consumer's
    perspective of
Crotts, J. C. 77–8
Culnan, M. J. 175
culture, dimensions of 316
customer engagement circle 153
Cvijikj, I. P. 112
cybersecurity 92–3

Dabrowski, D. 134
DAGMAR approach 123
Dalela, V. 134
data: extraction 208–9; ownership 211–12;
    triangulation of 263; visualization
    202–4
Deckers, E. 289
DHL Africa 286
Dimoka, A. 155
distributive engagement 37
Dolan, R. 103, 122
Dolbec, P. Y. 65
Dorsey, J. 84
Dove 235
Drolet, A. 105
Dumlao, J. A. A. 296
Dunne, A. 295
Durlauf, S. N. 163, 166–8

Egan, J. 36
Ekland-Olson, S. 76
Electronic Frontier Foundation (EFF) 94
electronic word-of-mouth (eWOM)
    154, 258
engagement and return on engagement
    117–31; advertising equivalency value
    127; Attention–Interest–Desire–Action
    model 121–2; benefits of social media
    118–19; communication for engagement

119–20; communication response hierarchy models 120–2; cost benefit analysis 127; DAGMAR approach for setting social media objectives 123; effective social media strategy 119–20; engaging the customer 123–4; gauging conversations 128–9; hierarchy of effects model 122; information-processing model 122; innovation adoption model 122; metrics 125–8
engagement interface, consumer engagement/return on 132–48; conceptual model 138–9; consumer engagement 134–5; consumer engagement/social media interface 135–6; engagement platforms 136; interactive consumer experience 134; managerial implications 142–3; return on social media engagement 136–7; ROI, definition of 137; social media investments made by consumers 138; social media's direct monetizing capabilities, increasing range of 136; theoretical implications 139–42
engagement, rational and affective appeals facilitating 102–16; affective message appeals 106–7; blogs 117; characterizing consumers' online brand related behaviour 104–5; community building services 118; creating behaviour 104; findings 109–12; implications 112–13; literature review 103–4; rational message appeals 105–6; research design 107–8; social bookmarking services 117; social geolocation and meeting services 118; social media sharing services 117; social networking services 117; social news services 118; social usage types 104; strategic delivery of online content 113; strategically enhancing online engagement behaviour 105–7
ethics 213
eWOM, relationships cemented via 286
exploratory factor analysis (EFA) 297
expressive participation 296
Eysenbach, G. 212

Facebook 6, 83, 91, 185, 212, 286; *see also* Like-influencer framework
Fahy, J. 103, 122
Falco, T. 15
Falls, J. 289
Faulds, D. J. 207

Faust, K. 79
FirCry.com 234
Fischer, E. 15, 65
Fodor, M. 138, 223
Foursquare 28
Frewer, L. J. 36
full online customer journey 153

Gaudet, H. 274
gauging conversations 128–9
Giddens, A. 60, 67
Glass, N. 84
Glynn, M. S. 134
Goh, K.-Y. 155
Goodman, S. 122
Goodrich, K. 259
Goodwin, C. 175
Google 93
Google Chromebooks 95
Google Plus 84, 286
government: programme development 4; regulations 99
Granovetter, G. 154
Granovetter, M. 258
Gremler, D. D. 157
Grönroos, C. 34
Gwinner, K. P. 157

Ha, S. H. 296
Habibi, M. 35
Haenlein, M. 26, 76, 132, 206–7, 235
Halinen, A. 36
Hansen, D. 23
hardware encryption 93–5
Harker, M. J. 34, 36
Hassouneh, D. 295
Hayat, T. 295
Heath, R. L. 37
hedonic motivations 295
Heim, J. 295
Help tweets 7
Hemsley-Brown, J. V. 34
Heng, C.-S. 155
Hennig-Thurau, T. 157
hierarchy of effects model 122
higher education institutions and universities, digital transformation of 20–30; challenges threatening higher education, overcoming of 23–6; connectivist MOOCs 21; digital transformation of media 26–8; enhancing prestige and market share 21–2; entrepreneurial mindset 22–3; key challenges 21–3; SWOT analysis

21; synchronous small online course 21; *see also* universities' social media marketing, integrating community and relationship building into (case study)
Hof, R. 259
Hoffman, D. L. 138, 223
Hoffman, E. 25
Hofmokl, J. 294
Hofstede, G. H. 237
Hollebeek, L. 136
Hollebeek, L. D. 134, 185
Homer, P. M. 106
Hong Kong, reasons for using social media in 295
Huang, J. H. 163
Huang, L. 86
Hubert, M. 237
human brands, social media stakeholder co-creation of celebrities as 60–74; actor-network theory 60; archival netnographic research 65; celebrity identity, stakeholders of 66; co-creation, social media in 62–3; findings 66; legitimization 68; negotiation and social construction 67–70; parasocialization 69; projection of influence 69–70; reflexivity 67; research inquiry 63–5; S-D Logic 61–2; structuration theory 60

Ilic, A. 134
incentivizing and encouraging online social interactions, mechanisms for 271–81; data analysis 275–9; hypotheses 273–5; method 275; motivation 272; negative information 274; perceived usefulness 276; share intentions 276; word-of-mouth 271
information-processing model 122
information seeking 154, 296–7
Inman, J. J. 106
innovation adoption model 122
Instagram 91, 185
Interaction tweets 7
interactive consumer experience 134
intrusion *see* online personalized communications, consumer's perspective of
Ioanăs, E. 15
Ioannides, Y. M. 167
ISIS terrorists 93
Ismael, S. 15

Jaakkola, E. 135
Johnson, T. J. 295

Joinson, A. N. 294
Juric, B. 134

Kaplan, A. 21, 26–7
Kaplan, A. M. 76, 132, 206–7, 235
Karakiza, M. 15
Kee, K. F. 295
Kenning, P. 237
key performance indicators (KPIs) 54, 191
Khan, G. F. 5, 15
Kik 91
Kim, D. 295
Kim, D. J. 251
KLM 190
Kozinets, R. V. 65
Kumbaya effect 288–9

Laroche, M. 35
Latour, B. 60
Lau-Gesk, L. 105
Lavidge, R. J. 122
Lawlor, M.-A. 295
Lazarsfeld, P. F. 274
LeBoeuf, K. 211
Lee, M. 28
Lee, M. K. O. 295
Lee, S. K. 5, 15
legitimization 68
Lehtinen, U. 34
Leitch, S. 37
Lewis, E. 151
LG 93
Like-influencer framework 258–70; eWOM marketing. 258; focus group, emergent themes of 264; future implications 267; gender differences 266; interpersonal relationships 258; literature review 259–61; personality types 265; qualitative data analysis software 264; Qualitative research 261; research methodology 261–3; results 263–6; scenarios 267–8; 'Strength of Weak Ties' 258; Third Party Effect 260; triangulation of data 263
Lin, H.-F. 237
Lin, K.-Y. 295
Lin, Z. 155
LinkedIn 81–3, 185
Logan, A. 62
Longden, B. 37–8
Lu, H.-P. 295
Lusch, R. F. 62

McGuire, W. J. 122
Mcknight, D. H. 229

McLoughlin, C. 28
McLuhan, M. 79
Macnamara, J. 36
macro theories 79–80
Malita, L. 207
Malmivaara, T. 295
Malthouse, E. C. 112, 134, 136
Mamalakis, E. 137
Mangold, W. G. 207
Mariani, R. 266
marketer-generated (MGC) social media communication 150
Marsh, R. 36
means-end equation 36
measurement and monitoring 184–205; audit 187–9; brands on Twitter 189; build KPIs 191, 193–4; comparative analysis 196–7; data visualization 202–4; importance of 185–6; influence and engagement 192–3; objectives 189–91; performance metrics 191–2; quantifying of targets 194–5; raising revenues 193; reach 191–2; sentiment visualization 199–201; social media landscape 184–5; Social Monitoring and Measurement process 186–91
media impressions 126
Media Theory (McLuhan) 79
Men, L. R. 207
Michahelles, F. 112
Microsoft 93
micro theories 78–9
Milberg, S. J. 213
Milne, G. R. 47
Mims, C. 163
'mobile' generation 81
mobile technologies *see* smartphones (social media apps and), secrecy, safety and security of
Mogaji, E. 211
Mohammed, D. 266
Moller, K. 36
Monnot, J. 251
monthly active users (MAUs) 211
MOOC *see* higher education institutions and universities, digital transformation of
Moon, K. K. 207
Moorman, M. 112
Morgan, R. 134
Motion, J. 37
Mukhaini, E. A. 15
Muntinga, D. G. 112

NCapture 209
negative information 274
Nestlé 275
net generation 36
'netizens' revolution 81
network based choice formation 162–71; birth or death of a state 168; consumer interaction within a community 163–5; dynamic social interactions, choices formed under 168; forms of network formation 166–8; incentivizing 169; path network 167; set of choice options 165–6; signalling 169; star network 167; validating existing models 169; what firms should do 168–70; why consumers join online communities 163
network-based relationship marketing 36
Neuendorf, K. A. 107
Ngai, E. W. 207
number spoofing 95
NVivo 209

Oakes, P. J. 79
Obama, Barack 91
old marketing thinking 286
online distance learning courses, categories of 27
online personalized communications, consumer's perspective of 172–83; context 181; creepy matters 179; data unknowingly provided 172; firm activities 173; limitation and control 175–6; mitigating perceptions of creepiness 179–81; non-intrusion and seclusion 174–5; perceived creepiness, privacy and 174–6; transparency and control 180; trust 181; what is creepy 176–9
online social networks (OSNs) 260
ooVoo 91
Open University 27
Oplatka, I. 34

paid reach 192
Palu-ay, L. 34
Pan, B. 77–8
parasocialization 69
Park, N. 295
Parra-Lopez, E. 295
Parvinen, P. 295
Pavlou, P. A. 251
PDCA (Plan-Do-Check-Act) quality control approach 253
pedagogical content developers, students evolving into 28

perceived risk 314–15
personalized marketing 90
Pinterest 91, 185
Planned Behaviour, Theory of 48
political participation, profiling youth on
    basis of their motivations for 293–307;
    empirical study 297; expressive partici-
    pation 296; hedonic motivations 295;
    information seeking 296–7; literature
    review 294–7; reasons for using social
    media in 295; results 297–301; utilitar-
    ian motivations 296
Pongsakornrungsilp, S. 61
Pöyry, E. 295
privacy: definition of 175; perceived
    creepiness and 174–6; security versus 91
privacy and information trading 308–19;
    apps, convenience of 309; benefits
    315; concern for privacy 315–16;
    consumer information storage 309–10;
    consumer information trading 313;
    culture, dimensions of 316; data
    commoditization and information
    sharing 310–11; data rich commerce
    platform, social media as 308–9; free
    networking platform 310; perceived
    risk 314–15; personality 314; situation
    316–17; study 311–17; trust 315
pseudo theories 80
psychological risk 5
Pucciarelli, F. 21
purchase funnel 151
purchase stages 152–7

Qualls, W. 249
Quan-Haase, A. 295

Rafaeli, S. 295
Ramirez, G. B. 34
Rao, H. R. 251
rational message appeals 105–6
Rautio, A. 137
Reasoned Action, Theory of 48, 237
Recognition tweets 7
reflexivity 67
relationship marketing 34–5
return on engagement *see* engagement and
    return on engagement
return on investment (ROI) 125, 137, 223
return on social media engagement
    (ROSME) 133, 137
Reuber, A. R. 15
Richard, M. 35
Riedl, R. 237

rise of social media (implications
    for emerging markets) 282–92;
    balance 289; brand communities and
    management 286–7; emerging markets,
    social media platform possibilities in
    287–8; emerging markets, social media
    trends in 283–5; eWOM, relationships
    cemented via 286; Kumbaya effect
    288–9; old marketing thinking 286;
    theoretical framework 285–6
risks of social media 5
Rogers, E. 274
Rogers, E. M. 48, 122
Rossmann, D. 35
Rowe, G. 36
Rowley, J. 295
Rumour Transmission, Theory of 79

Sahlin, D. 117
Samsung 93
Sankaranarayanan, R. 35
Sapp, A. M. 294
Schachner, L. 137
Schaedel, U. 134
Schelling, F. W. J. 167
Schivinski, B. 134
Schroeder, J. E. 61
S-D Logic 62
Secure Electronic Transactions (SET) 250
Secure Socket Layer (SSL) 250
self-service technologies (SSTs) 246
sentiment visualization 199–201
Shannon, C. E. 120
Shenton, A. K. 210
Sheppard, B. H. 247
Sherman, D. M. 247
Shneiderman, B. 23
Siamagka, N. T. 49–50
Skiera, B. 112
Skype 91
smartphones (social media apps and),
    secrecy, safety and security of 90–101;
    Cellebrite 92–3; cybersecurity 92–3;
    examples 90; hardware encryption
    93–5; law enforcement criminal data
    acquisition process work 92; number
    spoofing 95; rational messages 105;
    social engineering hacking 95–6; social
    media policy 95–6; trust 98
Smit, E. G. 112
Smith, H. J. 213
Smith, M. A. 23
SMOC *see* higher education institutions
    and universities, digital transformation of

Snapchat 91, 185
Snow, D. A. 76
social bookmarking services 117
social capital 234
social commerce (s-Commerce) 230
social currency, investing in *see* social recruitment
social engineering hacking 95–6
Social Exchange Theory 232
social geolocation and meeting services 118
Social Identity Theory 79, 232
Social Media Return on Investment (SMROI) 125
social media sharing services 117
Social Monitoring and Measurement (SMM) 186; *see also* measurement and monitoring
social networking services 117
social networking sites (SNS) 35, 207, 294
social news services 118
social recruitment 75–89; advantages 85; challenges 85; macro theories 79–80; McLuhan's Media Theory 79; micro theories 78–9; need for 80–1; overflow 77; pseudo theories 80; Social Identity Theory 79; social media networks, power of 76–7; Social Networking Theory 79; theoretical framework 77–80; Theory of Rumour Transmission 79; tools 81–5; trends 81; understanding social media 76
Song, Y. I. 251
spectatorship 36
SPOC *see* higher education institutions and universities, digital transformation of
Sridhar, S. 163
Srinivasan, R. 163
SSOC *see* higher education institutions and universities, digital transformation of
star network 167
STARTSocial networks 41
Statista.com 162
Steiner, G. A. 122
Stoica, I. 15
Stoke, R. 222
Stone, B. 84
strategizing social media presence 217–26; categories of social media 235; cultural dimension, theory on 237; listening to online reactions 222; popularity of social media 217–18; possibilities 225; return on investment 223; social media landscape in 2016 218; strategizing

social media presence 218–25; theory in practice 221
'Strength of Weak Ties' 258
Sultan, F. 249
Swani, K. 47
Swar, B. 5, 15
SWOT analysis (higher education) 21

Tao, S. S. 207
Tapscott, D. 36
Target, personal data collected by 173
Tarkowski, A. 294
Technology Acceptance Model (TAM) 48
Telegram 91
Theory of Planned Behaviour (TPB) 48
Theory of Reasoned Action (TRA) 48, 237
Third Party Effect (TPE) 260
Till, J. E. 212
Tosun, L. P. 295
trading *see* privacy and information trading
Trammell, K. D. 294
trust: levels of 229; perceived creepiness and 181; test of 98
trust in social media marketing 227–45; antecedents of trust 229–31; categories of social media 235; Collective Mind Theory 233; cultural dimension, theory on 237; homophily among individuals 234; implications for businesses 237; importance of trust 228–9; personal characteristics 236–7; security breaches 236; social capital 234; social commerce 230; Social Exchange Theory 232; Social Identity Theory 232; social media design characteristics 235–6; store characteristics 231–2; structural characteristics of social media 232–5; transaction complexity 228; trust, levels of 229; Trust Transference Theory 235
trust relationships in social networks 246–57; challenges in operationalizing communication strategies 253–4; communication strategies 251–3; consumer-to-business relationships on the web 247–51; consumer-related variables 250; foundation of trust 247–8; perceived site quality 249–50; physical absence of the other party 248–9; Plan-Do-Check-Act quality control approach 253; potential findings 254; risk and increased vulnerability 249; security and privacy 250; self-service technologies 246; virtual environment, risk in 251
Trust Transference Theory 235

Tsai, W. S. 207
Tumblr 91
Turkey, motives for social media use in 295
Turkish Airlines 286
Turner, J. C. 79
Twitter 6, 84, 185, 211, 286

Unified Theory of Acceptance and Use of
    Technology (UTAUT) 48
universities' social media marketing,
    integrating community and relationship
    building into (case study) 31–45; 'brand
    communities' 35; communicative
    engagement 37; content production
    39–40; controversy 32; debate on
    marketing universities 32–4; distributive
    engagement 37; emerging tactics of
    community building, emerging tactics
    of 40–1; empowerment 42; how social
    media can help 35–7; lack of strategies
    38–9; means-end equation 36; methods
    37–8; net generation 36; network-based
    relationship marketing 36; purpose of
    relationship marketing and community
    building 34–5; relationship marketing,
    definition of 34; relinquished control
    36; RELMIX framework 34; research
    validity 38; spectatorship 36; user-
    generated content 37
Urban, G. L. 249
user-generated content (UGC) 37, 150
user-generated qualitative data 208
utilitarian motivations 296

Valenzuela, S. 295
Vargo, S. L. 62

Vent 91
Vine 91
viral reach 192
virtual environment, risk in 251
virtual game worlds 207
Vivek, S. D. 134
Vodafone Egypt 286
Volkswagen de Mexico 286
Voorhees, C. 134

Walsh, G. 157
Wasserman, S. 79
Weaver, W. 120
Web 2.0 76
Wege, E. 12
Westin, A. 175
WhatsApp 91
Williams, E. 84
Williams, K. B. 93
Williams, P. 105
word-of-mouth (WOM) 271, 285

Xu, C. 296

YikYak 91
Young, A. L. 295
Young, S. W. H. 35
YouTube 84, 91, 275, 286

Zerfass, A. 36
Zhang, J. 260
Zhang, M. 112
Zimmer, M. 210, 212
Zimmerman J. 117
Zuckerberg, M. 28, 83
Zurcher, L. A. Jr 76